D1594304

The Idea of the Garden in the Renaissance

The Idea of the Garden in the Renaissance

Terry Comito

Rutgers University Press
New Brunswick, New Jersey

Publication of this book was partially supported by a grant from the American Council of Learned Societies to the Rutgers University Press in recognition of its contribution to humanistic scholarship. The funds were provided by the Andrew W. Mellon Foundation and are to be applied to the publication of first and second books by scholars in the humanities.

LIBRARY OF CONGRESS CATALOGING IN PUBLICATION DATA

Comito, Terry, 1935–
The idea of the garden in the Renaissance.

Bibliography: p.
Includes index.

1. Gardens—Symbolic aspects. 2. Gardens, Renaissance. 3. Gardens, Medieval. 4. Renaissance.
I. Title
SB470.7.C65 712'.01 77-12798
ISBN 0-8135-0841-X

To My Mother and Father

Contents

List of Plates

Preface

In the chapters that follow I trace some traditional themes that have been associated with actual gardens in the Renaissance and earlier, as well as with gardens used as settings for, or as images in, literary, religious, or philosophical works. What emerges most insistently from all this diversity of matter is a sense of the garden as the scene of those privileged moments when the self takes possession of the world, a sense of that interpenetration of self and world which is given its historically most definitive statement in the story of Eden. The association of gardens with Eden is of course a commonplace that scarcely needs remarking, but it is with the mechanism or the inner life of this association that I have tried to concern myself. In particular, this essay has taken shape under the conviction that the significance of medieval and Renaissance gardens, the attitudes to which they give form, may be discovered not only in the fixed symbolic systems, literary or theological, into which gardens have been incorporated, but also and perhaps more fundamentally, in the sorts of activity considered appropriate for gardens. I argue that what is shared by monks, poets, philosophers, lovers—even, we shall see, constructors of artificial perspective—is a nostalgia for Paradise. Gardens set aside for poetry or contemplation or love all participate in a glamour appropriate to sacred places; and conversely, activities so apparently distinct as poetry or contemplation or love take on, through their association with gardens, the aspect of a single quest, a turning outward to the world, a search for an equilibrium in which mind and thing constitute one another in a creative blossoming like that of the first Garden. Something like this is what I have in mind when I speak of the "idea" of the garden in the Renaissance.

I suppose the question we first need to pose is quite simply, why gardens? One source of their perennial appeal must surely be the peculiar way their forms make visible an area in which art and life, mind and nature, finally intersect. Our usual terminology, our way of talking about art and nature as exhaustive and mutually exclusive, implies some permanent rift between the ambitious conceivings of culture and the world in which it exists and which it may either deface or correct but never truly possess:

> Nature we draw to Art, which then forsakes
> To be herselfe, when she with Art combines.[1]

But gardens are places in which men come home again, in which they realize, as Polixines argues in *The Winter's Tale* and as manuals of practical instruction again and again proclaim, that "art itself is nature." The lesson of such didactic horticulturists is the comforting one that the mind's fabrications need not obscure what is real but may in fact reveal or clarify the contours of its actual situation. We may thus discover in gardens models of the way in which the mind conceives its relation to the world external to itself; but gardens are more than models, for the stuff of which they are contrived is the living substance of nature. They become arenas in which the externality of the world is at least temporarily overcome, a truce proclaimed in the continual battle between the shows of things and the desires of the mind. The medieval enclosed garden, Versailles, the English garden: each of these is clearly enough a place in which a peculiar sensibility comes to recognize its true dimensions. They are not so much collections of objects—rocks and stones and trees—as thought itself made visible and even tangible. This is why it has been possible to treat the very forms taken by gardens in the tradition with which I am concerned as paradigmatic of all the mind's attempts, through poetry, philosophy, or love, to find itself mirrored in the world of things.

It is this emphasis, I think, that distinguishes *The Idea of the Garden in the Renaissance* from some other recent books. Since this essay was begun, several writers, from whom I have tried belatedly to profit, have dealt with medieval or Renaissance gardens in literary terms, in terms of the history of ideas, or with the vocabulary of something like a Jungian psychology.[2] I have wanted to consider the uses, practical or imaginative, to which gardens are put in relation to the ways in which these gardens organize space. The vehicle of the idea I try to delineate is therefore not primarily literary or intellectual nor is it a universal psychological mechanism. It is, rather, the actual configuration of gardens, so far as this configuration, within the period with which I am concerned, embodies a particular way of experiencing space and of estimating its human possibilities. I am interested in gardens, in other words, as expressions of a tradition of sensibility, of a characteristic imaginative style, even, if I may be forgiven a ponderous notion, of a special way of being in the world. And I have asked myself how far we may understand garden images when they occur in religious, literary, or philosophical works as articulating, in terms of these particular disciplines, what is given immediately in perception of such fundamental intuitions.

The Renaissance garden is of course the culmination or fulfillment of traditions whose sources must be traced in classical and medieval gardens. In delineating these traditions, I have not focused chiefly on their chronological development, although I have tried along the way to suggest some possible lines of demarcation. My major concern has been to identify the components of what I take to be a coherent sensibility. The allusion in Chapter One to Weber's concept of ideal types may seem pretentious—surely I would claim no comparable methodological rigor—but it does serve to indicate that I am attempting, not to be clairvoyant about the feelings of actual gardeners, but to construct a model, to evoke a "spirit," in a sense not impossibly remote from Weber's, of Renaissance gardens. Any such attempt must necessarily be selective, and all I can claim in my defense is that I have usually tried to forgo the sort of generalization that resonates through this preface and to cling as closely as I can to the specificity of the phenomena I consider.

I should like to offer special thanks to the Research Council of Rutgers University for a summer grant, to Professors James Wilhelm of Rutgers and Seth Benardete of New York University for advice on translations (my own, unless otherwise noted), and to my typist Annette Liberson. To other friends and colleagues I have incurred many debts for advice and encouragement, much more than I could begin to specify here: Morton Bloomfield, Maurice Charney, Rosalie Colie, Harry Levin, Bridget Gellert Lyons, Robert Lyons, Fred Main, Elliot Rubinstein, Thomas Van Laan.

JUNE 1976

I

Charles in Naples

An Introduction to Renaissance Gardens

CHARLES VIII OF FRANCE went to Naples in 1495 as a conqueror, not a tourist, but he was not on this account any less assiduously a student of new sights. "You would not believe the beautiful gardens I have in this city," he writes home, "for, upon my word, it seems that only Adam and Eve are lacking to make it a terrestrial paradise, it is so lovely, and so full of all good and singular things."[1] Now the king's topos is licensed by an abundance of classical and scriptural precedents, and a purely philological pedantry would be quick to recognize in *paradise* the Persian word for a pleasure park. People in gardens, for one reason or another, have often found themselves thinking of man's first home. But we need to attend more closely to the particular tone in which Charles gives voice to this familiar assertion.

The role the French king imagines for himself in his new realm is quite different, for example, from the life John Evelyn proposes for the "Paradisean and Hortulan saints" he hopes to gather around him in seventeenth-century England. If for him gardens "signifie . . . *rem sacram et divinam,*" it is because "persons of antient simplicity" can find refuge in such places while "brutish and ambitious persons seeke themselves in the ruines of our miserable . . . country."[2] Charles's gardens, though, are no stoic retreat, but the furthest point of his adventure out into the world, discoveries exceeding all belief; and because what he discovers is the nature of his own possession, he cannot remain an indifferent or merely curious spectator. In the seventeenth century, men talk a little complacently of being "Inhabitant[s] of Paradise and Heaven upon Earth,"[3] as if from their royalist fastness they needed only to shepherd jealously the prerogatives of "antient simplicity," abstemiously plucking "the first roses of spring, and apples of autumn."[4] But Charles is quite overwhelmed by the beauty and singularity of a world he confronts as if for the first time, one that throws into question the resources of mind or imagination on which he had hitherto depended. "The charming language of master Alain Chartier, the subtlety of master Jean de Meun, and the hand of Fouquet would not know how to speak, to write, or to paint" the delights of the "maison de plaisance" his party has encountered.[5] Charles's only royalty, like Adam's, is precisely an openness to all this newness and variety that eye has not seen nor ear heard: a dawning awareness that these things are his and the surmise that he can in time make himself at home among them.

In this chapter I assemble some data that may help us begin to understand Charles's remark in an inward way, as a moment of sensibility. I have assumed that such moments are, in their particularity, not susceptible to univocal classification, but can be grasped only by analogy to other such moments. Accordingly, I propose to bring together a number of phenomena—images in art or literature, occurrences in the physical world—that cluster around Charles's Neapolitan trip, in the hope that, without losing the specificity that still clings to them, they will yield up their inwardness, and from their juxtaposition something like an ideal type will emerge. Such a type would be useful not only for some future sociology of Renaissance gardens—these essays claim to be nothing of the sort—but also for assessing the resonances of the gardens and garden images with which so much of the literature of the period is preoccupied. I would hope to find in Charles's remarks about the gardens of Naples, in other words, a point of departure of the sort Auerbach has described: an "easily comprehensible set of phenomena whose interpretation is a radiation out from them and which orders and interprets a greater region than they themselves occupy."[6]

1

It is not surprising that Charles should no longer think so much of his castle at Amboise as he used to.[7] For more northern races, the Kingdom of Naples had always been a place of wonders, a "pleasure garden amidst a waste of thorns" as Frederick II called it.[8] Earlier travelers than Charles had begun to spread abroad stories of the sorcerer Virgil and his magic garden, stories that seem to epitomize all the exotic possibilities the South offered their awakening senses. These tales center around the talismanic potency of images and speak of a garden walled around by air from all the enmity or impurity of the elements.[9] The poet's enchantment and the gardener's are united in a common enterprise (one to which Jacopo Sannazaro and Giovanni Pontano were again laying claim): the miraculous transformation of the world into a privileged sanctuary, a blossoming garden. In such a place, it is natural for rulers to dream of an absolutism less abstract than merely political power: the dream of an Adamic sovereignty over the world. Long before Charles, Arab poets had sung of Sicilian gardens that offer all the joys of a "terrestrial paradise" to the Norman lords whose heritage the French king was claiming, men who like their Saracen predecessors "aspire to glory" in the midst of great parks and pleasure grounds.[10] Dante's contemporary, Pietro de Crescenzi, dedicates his treatise on agriculture—it becomes the canonical account of gardens for the later Middle Ages—to Charles II of Naples, whom he promises not merely delight but "renovation" (*rinnovare*).[11] The claim Pietro makes for his subject is the testimony it offers that in certain earthly matters, at least, great men may fully realize their wills; a similar sense of the Southern landscape's responsiveness to human need may have contributed a century and a half later to Manetti's proclamation, at the behest of Alfonso I of Naples, of the particular dignity of man as the shaper and creator of his own world.[12] Alfonso and his successor Ferrante, in any case, rebuilt the great park Robert of Anjou had constructed for the Castel Nuovo; and around the time of Charles's conquest, Pontano was still claiming that villa gardens were a necessary adjunct of the "splendid man."[13]

For Charles and his contemporaries, furthermore, such splendor would exist not in a daydream of Celtic faerie (of the sort Roger of Artois, for example, brought home to his pleasure gardens at Hesdin in the thirteenth century),[14] but in the world of politics and history. As Brunetto Latini had insisted nearly three centuries before, at a time when strife-torn "Fiorenza" no longer "flowered and brought forth fruit," the meadows, trees, and arbors in which men delight are possible only when states have "joy and delight without war and without quarrel."[15] More recently, in the 1470s, Francesco Bandini had contrasted the discord of Florentine politics with the *giocondità* of Naples, a joy that embraces at once the *humanità* and *magnificentia* of Ferrante's reign, the cultivation of his court, and the splendor of his gardens, with their heavenly air ("un fresco di paradiso") and their variety of fruit such as (Bandini says) the elect enjoy in the earthly paradise.[16]

Now the gardens of which Charles was no doubt speaking, those of Alfonso's Poggio Reale, embody just such a peculiarly political harmony and splendor. Alfonso's whole building program, in the first place, seems to have been designed to enlist his dynasty in the legendary tradition of the perpetual renewal of Naples (Neopolis), and to proclaim for his father Ferrante, whose bastardy was potentially troublesome, a tangible magnificence in which, both at home and abroad, his true legitimacy might be recognized.[17] Furthermore, the Poggio Reale itself had been built shortly before Charles's arrival as an outcome of Lorenzo de' Medici's visit in 1480 to negotiate a peace between Naples and Florence. Later historians like Guicciardini took the incident to exemplify the skill and greatness of spirit by which Lorenzo had established a golden age, an era when all Italy was "cultivated no less in the mountainous and sterile places than in the fertile regions and plains."[18] This is more than a metaphor, though perhaps less than an empirical fact. Lorenzo's own policy, after all, seems to have relied at least as much on this sort of rhetoric of reviving time and flourishing peace as upon any sophisticated dialectics of power.[19] The golden age in which Florence reposed beneath the shade of its blessed laurel[20] may have been a myth quite outside the realities of political power, but it became the medium in which power was transacted, and contemporary observers agree upon its efficacy.[21] Lorenzo's mission to Naples was attended by his usual pomp and displays of magnanimity; and where might the harmonies he so famously evoked out of discord[22] be heard more clearly than in the gardens on Mount Vomero?—gardens in which, while Alfonso was still in the field near Siena, Lorenzo and Ippolita Maria Sforza renewed their old acquaintance and dynastic sympathies. Some weeks later, the peace concluded, she wrote him, hoping that he "often think[s] of our garden, which is now most beautiful and in full bloom."[23] And shortly thereafter, Lorenzo dispatched his own architect, Giuliano da Majano, to Naples in order to perpetuate this concord: by building for Alfonso the villa that Serilo would single out as a work that modern genius could set against all the wonders of antiquity. Naples, Serlio explains, is above all other cities in Italy called *gentile,* not only for the nobility of its lords, but above all on account of its villas and gardens. And the Poggio Reale, pre-eminent among all these pleasant places, is taken to embody not only the canons of classical taste (Serlio tidies its rectangular forms into square ones) but also the happiness of Italy in her era of peace and unity. "The loveliest gardens with diverse compartments, orchards with fruit of every sort in the greatest abundance": all this and much more serves only to reinforce his lament, "O Italy, how has your delight, for our discords, been extinguished!"[24]

Of course we can scarcely suppose that Charles would have felt all this as poignantly as his Italian victims. Still, he could hardly have been unaware of the aura of Lorenzo's greatness; and the striking new forms of Alfonso's villa embody this greatness in an unexampled way, one that suggests how political magnificence might be linked to the traditional dream of the South of which I have already spoken. Serlio's book shows a plan markedly similar to Lorenzo's own Poggio a Cajano (*shown in Plate 1*), and it has sometimes been supposed that Lorenzo himself constructed the model for his former enemy's pleasure house.[25] What distinguishes both villas from their predecessors, in any case, is the force of an idea: not only material splendor, but a new sense of the possibilities inherent in cultivated existence. Alberti would have said that it is Nature's own harmonies we experience in the careful symmetry of the two plans, a rigor that anticipates the Platonizing geometry of Palladio in the next century.[26] Even more important is the "change from closed to open planning, so that the building is freed from encircling walls and turns outward to the landscape rather than inward toward a court."[27] The medieval French castle with its four corner towers is turned inside out by Lorenzo's architects, opened to light and air, perforated by windows and loggias, brought into relation with the gardens that surround it and the prospect lying beyond. The buildings are no longer fortresses of the sort Alberti objected to as "altogether inconsistent with the peaceable Aspect of a well-governed City or Commonwealth."[28] Rather, they are above all (as Serlio recognized)[29] places for looking at the countryside, points from which the eye may range abroad over prospects of "known Hills and Mountains," the "pleasant Landskips, flowery Meads, open Champains, shady Groves, or limped Brooks" in which it delights.[30] No wonder then that both villas should lay claim to the mythological potency of the landscape itself. Poliziano and Lorenzo dedicate Poggio a Cajano to the deity of the place, Ambra, the nymph who turns herself to stone; and the Poggio Reale is celebrated by Pontano as the scene of the nuptials of Parthenope, Naples' legendary founder, and the river Sebeto.[31] In the frieze of the Florentine villa's facade—itself derived from ancient temple architecture—at least one critic has seen not only a commemoration of the greatness of the Medici, but also, measuring and in some sense constituting this greatness, a "sort of religious celebration of the rhythms of nature."[32]

For if *dominus* (lord) is to be inferred from *domus* (home)[33] his dignity in such places as these will be measured not by the rigor with which he repulses the world's assaults, but precisely by the magnanimous openness to the world by which, with a generous spirit, "con animo grande,"[34] he makes its riches his own. We may take as paradigmatic the way in which artists entrusted with the decoration of villas at about this time were abandoning military exploits and, instead, cutting through solid walls with illusionistic landscapes, or, like Botticelli, turning to poetic evocations of the countryside's mysterious potencies.[35] In the frescoes of the Palazzo Schifanoia in Ferrara, the illuminators' vision of the cycle of the months, with its sense of an ideal accord between man and nature, becomes the scene in which the life of the Estensi court is actually played out, and the measure—so humanist advisors were soon to be urging—of its true *magnificentia.*[36] Ercole d'Este had spent his childhood in Naples, the companion of Prince Ferrante, and the mere names of the now vanished pleasure houses he embellished memorialize ambitions that finally receive distinctive architectural expression in the villas of Lorenzo and Alfonso: Belriguardo, Belfiore, Il Paradiso.

Certainly what strikes visitors to both Poggio a Cajano and Poggio Reale is a sense of their inclusiveness, of mastery achieved over immense richness. A poetic chronicle of Charles's expedition describes the flowers at Poggio Reale, "full of sweetness" and in blossom all year long, fruit trees (with exotic dates and oranges: Serlio too remarked on their copiousness), grottoes, a deer park, "ymaiges anticques" of alabaster or marble, and finally, animating the whole, a great fountain "that is so full of living waters, so overflowing, that it might supply and bathe all Naples and plentifully slake the thirst of all its animals."[37] The fountains admired by the French visitors did in fact, through the recently restored Acqua Bolla, supply the water by which all Naples, her publicists claimed, was being renewed. Parthenope herself, Pontano writes, bathes at Poggio Reale, and Alfonso's aqueducts become water gods, plunging from mountain heights to celebrate her nuptials: "they descend, O sister, grove and deep river tumble to the marriage couch; a thousand caves pour forth their deities."[38] Poggio a Cajano too was notable for its water works; and Poliziano joined in the chorus of praise for the aqueduct by which Lorenzo "with that magnificence which characterizes all his undertakings"[39] diverted to his own use the waters of the Ambra:

> Go on, Lorenzo, thou the muse's pride,
> Pierce the hard rock and scoop the mountain's side;
> The distant streams shall hear thy potent call,
> And the proud arch receive them as they fall.
> Thence o'er thy fields the genial waters lead,
> That with luxuriant verdure crown the mead.[40]

He gathers peacocks for his garden from Sicily, and in 1487 receives from the Sultan of Babylon a gift of parrots, apes, a famous giraffe, and other exotic fauna.[41] Serlio mentions at Poggio Reale, too, "places for various birds, both great and small." This collectors' passion corresponds to the pleasure which travelers like King Charles take in listing breathlessly the sheer variety of their discoveries, and it issues eventually in undertakings like Lorenzo's botanical garden at the Villa Careggi.

Thirty years later, the Sultan's gift was commemorated, and explicated, by Leo X's program for the Great Hall at Poggio a Cajano.[42] Andrea del Sarto renders the cages of parrots and apes as a *Tribute to Caesar;* opposite is Franciabigio's *Triumph of Cicero;* and on the lunette at one end of the hall Pontormo's *Vertumnus and Pomona* assimilates all this classicizing pomp to the actualities of the Tuscan countryside: a pastoral world that "invites our access into it," a critic said recently, with "an illusion of the quality, almost breathable, of country air."[43] The achievement of classical greatness, both political and intellectual, is felt as a conquest and transformation of space, of the natural world.

It must have been possibilities like these that ripened for Charles in Naples and gave substance to his exclamation of delight. The infatuation we detect in his letter is not directed toward mere personal luxury. He has, rather, discovered his proper role, and it is one to which Cola di Rienzo and, in his very different way, Frederick II had also pretended, and for which Dante had imagined another Earthly Paradise: the "nest" of human powers where man discovers in the mastery of his own nature the type or promise of eternal benediction.[44] Only Adam and Eve are lacking to make Naples just such a place, and now Charles marches ceremoniously through its streets to assume the crown of his lost empire. Illiterate and dwarfish though the French king may have been, even the tough-minded Philippe de Commynes sees something miraculous in his progress through Italy: hailed in millennial terms by Savonarola, celebrated as at once a new Augustus and a new Charlemagne, crowned King of Jerusalem, and dreaming of a crusade that would make Constantinople his as well.[45] The people hail him as Emperor,[46] and Charles carries with him not only his scepter, but also the imperial orb with which, less than a year before, Alfonso II was coronated: a "round golden apple" ("pomme d'or ronde": in Germany it was called a *Reichsapfel*) plucked in the gardens of Naples. The orb had been associated with Charlemagne, but it was a dignity French kings did not ordinarily assume, except (after Charles) in laying claim to the Kingdom of Naples, where the symbol had a flourishing tradition.[47] Its history, in fact, compacts a number of the elements we have been distinguishing in Charles's adventure. The golden sphere is at once the sign of the rebirth of the Roman imperium under a Christian kosmokrator and the sacred apple Mary presents her child—a new Eve and a new Adam repairing the injuries inflicted by our first parents.[48]

When Charles returned to France, he took with him an entourage of Italian artists and craftsmen, including the gardener Pasella da Mercigliano, to embellish his own castle at Amboise.[49] Since Michelet, historians have cited the expedition as the beginning of the Renaissance in France, the decisive turning toward a "culture méridionale et antique."[50] The new gardens at Amboise do more than merely exemplify this turn. It may have seemed to dazzled courtiers that what Charles "brought into the heart of France from the depths of Italy was nothing more or less than the whole of Italian art"; but as a recent historian has noted, it was particularly the splendor of the landscape and of the life lived under its auspices that struck the French invaders.[51] Charles brought back painters and tentmakers too—87,000 pounds of treasure, an observer says, that would take twenty pages to describe[52]—but it was the garden that provided the image by which he conceived his action and by which we may try to define its inner meaning.

2

To claim all this—the foreign policy of the Medici and the French Renaissance—as explication of Charles's presumably casual remark is no doubt to strain credibility. I am trying to show the way images and events come together and illuminate one another, even where clearly there is no parity of historical importance. Two more items connected with the Neapolitan adventure, a poem and a painting, complete the present constellation by suggesting another prototype for Charles's "terrestrial paradise"—the gardens of Hesperides.

King Charles had already been greeted in Vienna (in 1490) as a new

Hercules and presented with golden apples for his labors in restoring order to the garden of France.[53] We should not attach too much significance, I suppose, to the fact that Charles's orb looked to a French observer in Naples like a "pomme d'or ronde," although Hans Eworth's famous painting at Hampton Court suggests how easily this popular usage could take on its mythological connotations: the Queen, having won the judgment of Paris, is awarded the orb of empire rather than Strife's sinister apple.[54] In any case, the peculiar glamour of the citrus for which Naples was renowned might well force the city's military heroes into Herculean postures. The Normans, it was said, were lured in the eleventh century to drive the Saracens out of the southern kingdom with a promise of great citrus groves.[55] And among the spoils of Charles's expedition were cuttings for an orangery at Amboise, branches of which were presented annually to French kings for years thereafter. (Alfonso, on the other hand, was reputed to have fled Naples with seeds and cuttings from his garden.)[56] It is not surprising, then, though it may be mildly ironic, that Pontano should celebrate Francesco Gonzaga's victory over Charles (at Fornovo) by dedicating to him his poem *De hortis Hesperidum:*

> But you, O Prince in whom the house of Gonzaga and all Mantua rejoices, do not I pray you absent yourself from our singing, now that arms and grave labors are done . . . nor scorn the gardener's toil, adornment and storied reward of Herculean might.[57]

The myths of garden and golden age may tend in Pontano's hands to be reduced to idyll or sentiment, but what is extended to his northern patron is more than the placid joys of villa life he had so often sung and set over against the exigencies of war or public affairs.[58] Like the *Georgics* on which it is modeled, *De hortis Hesperidum* is a celebration of "human industry," of the *ingenium* that will not rest content (Pontano says) until it raises itself to the very summit of Olympus.[59] Venus herself brought citrus trees to Italy so that the descendants of Aeneas might restore (*renovare*) their ancient brightness;[60] the gardener's apparently humble craft sustains from age to age the goddess' sacred tree, sprung from Adonis as an everlasting monument to the eternity of love and beauty (1.526–80). Accordingly, like Marvell in "Upon Appleton House," Pontano is able to recognize the cosmic hero beneath the playfully pastoral trappings of the topiary gardener, whose skill summons the formless mass into shapes of beauty ("informemque gregem ad speciosa vocato"):

> Let one climb into a high tower or battlement, another stretch into a bow and discharge its arrows, let another fortify the trenches or engird the walls, another summon the rout to arms and call the ranks to battle. . . . So has skill [*ars*], time, natural strength, and perennially watchful nurture transformed that grove, that even now, in the leaves and branches of the garden, you see new shapes distinguish themselves, like diverse weavings of woolen threads in a great canopy. (1.512–25)

Pontano's language in this passage is continually allusive: to the traditional theology of creation, to the Renaissance concern with the area of man's own creativity—the unending debate over the relative claims of chance, time, and virtue.[61] Taking form as it does under the auspices of such notions, the garden is not just the hero's resting place, but an adjunct of his splendor: the golden world he brings into being by pressing time into the service of his art and his innate capacities.

However sensuous they may appear, therefore, the groves of the Hesperides should not be confused with the deceptive garden Voluptas offers Hercules at the crossroads: their fruit is not the temptation, but (as Pontano says) the ornament and reward of virtue.[62] But they are different in important respects from the Paradise imagined by a more traditional piety. God created man outside the garden, theologians had often argued, precisely in order to demonstrate that its felicity (like all human virtue) is only a gift.[63] Some aspects of Hercules' story remained during the Middle Ages intractable to Christian interpretation, and in particular the implication that (as Joachim Du Bellay later wrote) "Hercule se feit Dieu par la seule vertu."[64] The hero is conscious of such *vertu* above all in moments when he chooses his own path; the energies of will—prodigies like Tamburlaine or Coriolanus will serve as limiting cases—claim freedom from external determination and give allegiance only to the laws of their own development. Even at best, however, the deification that proceeds entirely from the natural cannot pass beyond it. As Lactantius objected, the story of the choice at the crossroads makes no vertical separation between good and evil, so that the arena of morality is bounded by the "apex of human glory" to which Petrarch was tempted: "the sweet felicity of an earthly crown."[65]

Something of the same tendency may inform another work dedicated to Francesco. Since the victory at Fornovo was in fact in question and the Venetian allies were dissatisfied, the performance of the Italian troops was celebrated with a certain deliberate grandeur. Medals were struck and Mantegna's *Madonna della Vittoria,* a year later, was pompously installed in a new chapel in gratitude for blessings received.[66] The Virgin of course had traditionally been painted with the fruits of virtue as well as the flowers of faith,[67] but the citrus bower to which Francesco is ushered may well remind us of the Hesperides, so thoroughly has the hero's act of supplication been transformed into a memorial of his victories. A critic has observed that the altarpiece adapts the medieval theme of the Madonna of Mercy to the exigencies of Renaissance patronage.[68] One way in which the new emphasis is suggested is by the presence of the Christ child; if, as has been observed, this makes for a piety more immediately human,[69] the very centrality of God immanent in the flesh makes the Virgin's role more passive, closer to that of any earthly regent. No longer the gigantic presence of earlier treatments of the motif, she inclines forward with a very personal gesture of benediction, while Francesco himself, resplendent in his armor, is led into her presence by figures representative of his own physical and spiritual prowess.[70] Engraved beneath the throne is Eden at the moment of the Fall; above it, surrounding it, filling the picture, is the great bower of citrus and choiring birds, Paradise regained.[71] And this goal or reward of Francesco's striving does not, like the rose hedges of medieval enclosed gardens, present an impassive or lush symbolic façade, but opens out (like the Renaissance garden itself) onto infinite space.[72]

The nature of the aspiration implicit in the scene may be suggested by two other bowers that seem to have been connected with Mantegna's design and to share with it a new sense of the availability of space, illusionistically rendered beyond the fruit and flowers of garden trellises. These are not painted scenes but actual places. Francesco's wife Isabella d'Este (who was originally to have kneeled beside her husband before the Madonna's arbor)[73] was at about this time fitting out, first in the Castello and then overlooking her garden in the Corte Vecchio, the "lovely grotto" already celebrated by Boiardo,[74] a retreat for which Mantegna was commissioned to paint two garden scenes, one of sensuous delight and the other of flourishing virtue. And a few years later, Correggio borrowed from Mantegna's altarpiece the trellises with which, for the Abbess Gioanna di Piacenza, he decorated the ceilings of the Camera di San Paolo in Parma.[75] Both apartments have carefully planned humanistic programs to rationalize the sensuous luxury of their appointments and so suggest to us the sort of response that luxury was intended to elicit. What we find in both cases is an adaptation of Mantegna's flourishing arbor to the needs of secular majesty: an adaptation which seems to insist, as does the Hesperides story itself, that the terrestrial paradise is something virtue achieves and that it is achieved within the limits of natural experience.

The later Middle Ages, remembering that *humilitas* (humility) comes from *humus* (earth), had already brought the Virgin down from her distant heavenly throne and seated her on the ground to suckle mankind's redeemer "with hir swete mylk."[76] The garden in which she often found herself in such representations would no longer be a mere attribute, but would seem like an actual place—made fruitful by this "aqueduct" of the waters of life[77]—not so different iconographically from the haunts of more earthly goddesses like Ceres or Flora. The remarkable thing about a devotional manual like Henry Hawkins' *Partheneia sacra*—a much later work (1633), but one we may nevertheless take to represent the final development of the motif of the Virgin in a garden—is the degree to which it calls up and depends upon an actual feeling for nature. When Hawkins speaks of Mary as the "Paradice of flowers" or the "Nurse that suckles al things with her milke," we have to do not with conventional emblems, but with an active attempt to seize upon the nature of deity as it is revealed in its works.[78]

The next step is for cultivated ladies like Isabella or Gioanna, ladies in whom classical learning flourished as much as Christian pieties, actually to construct similar bowers in which to install themselves. The measure of their victory, perhaps after all more substantial than Francesco's, is the personal space they manage to set aside for wit and elegance over against the perplexities of Mantuan politics or the resentment of the citizens of Parma, who had been seeking to enforce on Gioanna the rules of strict claustration.[79] The spirit of these places, "so green and beautiful that [they] might be Paradise itself,"[80] is suggested by the reconciled opposites of Mantegna's paintings, the grotto of sensuous pleasures purified by an energetic Minerva, or, more succinctly, by one of the mottoes at San Paolo: "All Is Accessible to Virtue."[81] Cardinal Briçonnet was careful to specify that what was found in Charles's Neapolitan "paradise" was "every sort of *worldly* pleasure."[82] But to an enthusiastic courtier, such distinctions are difficult to draw: Isabella's Grotta (embodying a taste she might well have learned in Naples, and surely sustained by her continuing association with Neapolitan humanists) is so "divine" a spot as to "give light and glory to hell itself."[83] Recent iconographers have not agreed upon the precise nature of the armistice between reason and sensuality Isabella's decorative program was to have contrived; but all see in the splendor of her apartment a new claim to mastery over the external world and the experience of the senses.[84] In its punning scheme, the good fortune attendant upon triumphant virtue ("virtue duce, comite fortuna") becomes indistinguishable from an honest Comus; and although the Abbess Gioanna reigns over her bower as a new Diana, both she and Isabella make room for Priapus, god of those ancient gardens to which the ladies' wit and learning have given them entry.[85] Perhaps the most characteristic of the Abbess' mottoes is one that neatly locates the common ground of literary nostalgia and philosophic daring, the sensuous life of Virgil's humble shepherds and the Hermetic aspiration by whose light Pico and others were proclaiming man's essential dignity: "All Things Are Full of Jove."[86]

Throughout the sixteenth century, the changing forms of the gardens themselves reflect the growing absolutism of their owners' claims upon the world, a greater and greater domination of the natural terrain by what Wölfflin calls a "tectonic Spirit."[87] And in both gardens for which elaborately worked out symbolic programs have survived, the Villa d'Este at Tivoli and Duke Cosimo de' Medici's Castello, it is the figure of Hercules that humanist advisors seize upon to explicate the nature and implications of this new mastery. The paths and fountains of the Villa d'Este are articulated by the story of Hercules' choice at the crossroads and dedicated to "honest pleasure," whose golden apples, an inscription claims, have been rescued from the sleepless dragon.[88] At Castello, Hercules subdues Antaeus, offspring of Earth and Water, in the midst of an enclosed garden bounded by the four seasons (now harmoniously related) and lined with the virtues of the Medici together with the social benefits that flow from them.[89] Both places, in other words, celebrate the victory that frees the energies of nature for man's honest delectation; and both, very concretely, not in idea only, extend the bounty won by their patron to the actual countryside over which he rules and which becomes thereby another Hesperides.

The cult of Hercules had in fact been particularly important at Hadrian's Villa, so that Cardinal Ippolite, in glorifying his family's legendary ancestor, could also claim to be restoring his subjects to the care of their ancient protector:[90] in the gardens of the Villa d'Este, a walk of a hundred fountains links the Fountain of Tivoli with a display of the glories of classic Rome, silhouetted against a prospect over the city walls. But we may want to draw a different moral, one consonant with traditional objections to the Hercules legend, from Vasari's account of the difficulties encountered at Castello. The great jet of water Hercules forces from the mouth of Antaeus was to have passed through an elaborate series of fountains and made the garden the "richest, the most magnificent, and the most ornate" in Europe. The project, however, was never completed. And Vasari complains that the sculptor Tribolo, to whom it had been entrusted, abandoned his true calling and ruined his reputation in fruitlessly attempting to divert rivers from their natural courses.

3

Edmund Spenser seems to have had in mind a similar overreaching of natural boundaries when (in *Mother Hubberds Tale*) he attacked niggardly lords who lift up "loftie towres" to threaten the sky, while "auncient houses," holdings of men of real pedigree, fall into disrepair and ruin.[91] The most famous of these towers and the most influential on other English buildings were at Theobalds, in whose gardens and courtyards, designed for the queen's entertainment, Burghley was trying to naturalize for the first time on English soil the splendor of Italian villa life. And the model to which he and his architects turned seems to have been Serlio's plan for the Poggio Reale.[92] We may accept Spenser's hint that such buildings were significant on grounds other than the purely aesthetic: the Poggio Reale came to Burghley with an appeal not wholly explained by its conformity to canons of taste. Like Cardinal Briçonnet and the other men around Charles VIII (like the Medici, indeed), Burghley was a "new man." For such men—and this is what makes Herculean striving a possible figure for the assiduousness of a William Cecil—culture is precisely the cultivation or fabrication of an identity, a stand taken in the *humanitas* constituted outside the realm of social or historical circumstance—though for a man like Burghley, society and history may be its goal. This is of course a commonplace of Renaissance studies: to build greatly (*magnum facere*) is first of all to construct one's own magnificence.[93] And as Lawrence Stone's monumental study has shown, nowhere was such construction more urgent, construction of buildings and also of a less tangible but equally serviceable magnificence, than in the England of Elizabeth.[94]

Burghley's passion for genealogy has subjected him to a certain amount of derision, but the "flimsy fantasies of his hired ancestor-manufacturers"[95] found in his ambitious building program an expression substantial enough to constitute a new reality, even if they did not accurately record an old one. Burghley House was renovated for the seat of his new barony and elaborately adorned with the newly "discovered" coats of arms; and at Theobalds the Lord Treasurer planned no less than a "conspectus of the universe, the nations, of England and her governors, considered as a setting for England's queen."[96] The presence chamber looked out on one side upon a great fountain court, inspired by Serlio's plan, and, on the other, upon gardens so extensive, according to an early visitor, that "one might walk two miles . . . before he came to the end"[97] at a huge moat which enclosed the whole estate. The chamber itself was a kind of grotto, with water streaming out of a rock, the Zodiac with sun and moon on the ceiling, and, on the walls, six trees, "all complete and natural," hung with birds' nests and the heraldic shields of England's nobility. When the steward of the house opened the window, which looked out upon the beautiful pleasure garden, a visitor recounts, "birds flew into the hall, perched themselves upon the trees, and began to sing."[98] Everywhere, the regal pretensions of Theobalds are embodied in its transformations of the natural world, a perfected cosmos that seems to encapsulate and to make available all the greatness of history. There was a summerhouse where wanderers in the gardens might repose next to marble figures of the twelve Caesars; and the portico that linked the gardens with the fountain court—Burghley perhaps remembered Alberti's advice—was "well painted with Kinges and Queenes of England and the pedigree of old Lord Burley and divers other antient families."[99]

In practice, Elizabeth's visits seem to have been very mixed blessings indeed; but it is partly because places like Theobalds (or Holdenby or Wollaton)[100] were erected for her progresses through her realm that their glamour was not just that of stone and glass. Burghley's establishment was exalted by the very awesomeness of the standard by which it had to measure itself—if never quite live up to. The "prodigy houses" were part of a fantastic landscape, a pastoral world which blossomed under the radiance of a royal sun and came to incarnate something of its reflected greatness:

> Now th'ayre is sweeter than sweet balme,
> Now Satyres daunce about the Palme:
> Now earth, with verdure newly dight,
> Gives perfect signes of her delight.
> O beauteous Queene of second Troy,
> Accept of our unfained joy.[101]

The houses, and above all the gardens, were settings where festive courtiers found themselves in bowers whose blossoms (like the knots and mazes Peele describes at Theobalds in 1591) had all become royal virtues: Graces made flesh in pansies, twelve Virtues in roses, and the Muses in "nine several flowers, being of sundry natures, yet all sweet, all sovereign."[102] On the one hand, such pageantry again exemplified the fabricating powers of humanist rhetoric, this time in the service of the whole state; pastoral poetry and the spirit of cultivated recreation were called upon to hedge the queen in a divinity that in earlier ages might have been hers on more somber authority. But at the same time, her very presence made civility flourish in a wilderness,[103] and lords might count themselves magnificent

> that could so highli cast order for such a Jupiter, & all hiz Gods besid, that none with hiz influens, good property, or present, wear wanting: but all weis redy at hand, in such order and aboundans, for the honoring and delight of so high a Prins, oour most gracious Queen & souerain.[104]

The lord in question in this passage is Burghley's great rival, the Earl of Leicester; and Robert Laneham's description of Kenilworth may be taken as an almost canonical account not only of the pleasures of gardens, but also of the way in which these pleasures, in their regal abundance and harmony, become an amplitude of mind. Gascoigne's pageantry for the queen's visit to Kenilworth had celebrated her power to charm the wild man and make the wilderness blossom in perpetual spring:

> The windes resound your worth,
>   the rockes record your name:
> These hils, these dales, these woods, these waves,
>   these fields pronounce your fame.[105]

It is in effect as a pronouncement of royalty that Laneham, too, praises these gardens. Kenilworth is a place in which the mind reassumes its absolute dominion over a world from which all savagery has been purged, and in which (as in the gardens of Naples) it finds proclaimed the measure of its own proper dignity or true nobility:

> then, the woods, the waters . . . the deer, the peepl . . . the frute trees, the plants, the earbs, the floourz, the chaunge in coolers, the Burds flyttering, the Foountaine streaming, the Fysh swymming: all in such delectable varietee, order, dignitee: whearby at one moment, in one place, at hande, without trauell, to haue to full fruition of so many Gods blessinges, to entyer delight unto al sencez (if al can take) at ones: for Etymon of the woord woorthy to

> bee calld Paradys: and though not so goodly az Paradis, for want of the fayr Rivers, yet better a great deel by the lak of so unhappy a tree. Argument most certein of a right nobl minde, that in this soort coold haue thus all contriued.[106]

4

Nicholas Bacon's estate was only a few miles from Theobalds, and it is pleasant to suppose that Francis Bacon, when later he wrote to explain how men of his own age might emulate the first Gardener, would remember the "gardens, fountains, and walks" on which (according to a contemporary biographer) his uncle Cecil lavished his personal attention.[107] To the account of Burghley's estates, we must add some notice of his practical involvement in horticultural concerns, since much the same impulse seems to lie behind both interests. Cecil had been associated in Protector Somerset's household with William Turner, the "father of English botany," with whom he later corresponded; among his own wards was "my cousin Zouch," Baron of Harringworth, a botanical amateur and patron of Matthias de l'Obel, whose *Stirpium adversaria nova* (1570) was dedicated to Elizabeth.[108] And finally, the gardens at Theobalds and also those of Cecil House in the Strand were under the care of John Gerard, author of the famous *Herball,* which he dedicated to his employer.[109]

The gardens of a great lord, Gerard explains in the dedicatory letter, are places where "a man doth behold a flourishing shew of sommer beauties in the middest of winters force."[110] He goes on to make clear that in compiling the herbal he is merely preserving and making more widely available the work he has been pursuing for Burghley at Theobalds. What the book offers is perpetual spring, all "dame Natures store" in a little room (B2^{v}); and at the same time—another garden book dedicated to Burghley develops this figure[111]—its unassuming beauties are a foretaste of the heavenly gardens reserved for the greatness of its patron. Even the greatest, Gerard observes, have not scorned so humble a tribute. To dedicate the gardener's labors to a noble lord is simply to render back to him the blossoming that is at once the benefit conferred by his influence and the sensible measure of his greatness. This is particularly clear in a dedication to Elizabeth:

> Blessed is the task, and worthy to bear thy name, O mighty Elizabeth, by whose moderation alone joyous Peace and her Olive so flourish in England that the British people may walk at random in the sunlight and gather in safety fragrant blossoms.[112]

Millennial gardens of this sort have of course always flourished in the rhetorician's art. What is important for our purposes about Elizabethan garden books is their claim, simply as part of their practical intention, to extend such royalty to ordinary men and to make such places their everyday habitation.

As one might expect, to be sure, the authors of practical gardening manuals generally moralize their topic, for a predominantly middle-class audience, in terms that recall the sterner passages of the *Georgics* rather than the exhilaration of the Fourth Eclogue.[113] The admonition that "there will ever be something to doe"[114] is an appropriate one for the sensibility—we may call it "puritan"—for whom the lessons of agriculture will inevitably be those of the story of the Fall:

> Such is the condition of all earthly things, whereby a man receiveth profit or pleasure, that they degenerate presently without good ordering. Man himselfe left to himselfe growes from his heavenly and spirituall generation and becommeth beastly, yea devillish to his owne kind, unlesse he be regenerate. No marvell then if Trees make their shootes, and put their spraies disorderly.[115]

In such handbooks of the Good Husband's regimen, the chapter on the ornaments of gardens is at best an island of whim and sensibility, a momentary release from the "works of [one's] lawful calling" and the iron laws of the seasons' labors.[116] And even here of course the haven is reached only through "the straits of painfull toyle";[117] there are always weeds to be rooted out, trees to be "reformed" by "good government,"[118] walls to be held rigidly against a world of invaders. The tone of these exhortations is remarkably like that of the anonymous monk of Clairvaux whose weedy field reminded him of Solomon's warning against the "bastard slips" of the ungodly;[119] or like those statesmen in Shakespeare whose gardens grow only usurping sprays and caterpillars of the commonwealth.[120] Yet even so rigid and emblematic a use of nature, appropriate to sermons or to drama still in the thrall of rhetoric, postulates an Eden to be restored, although at the price of unremitting vigilance. Quite automatically, the gardener takes as the background of his labors the place of "authority, Majesty, and abundance," and remembers the time when "the whole earth was . . . a Tempe."[121]

Even in these handbooks, moreover, there is a different sort of perception, one that always threatens to escape from the categories designed to press it into the service of exhortation or warning. The sense of the inexhaustible fertility of "the mother, and nurse of everie living thing"[122] may be dressed up in Neoplatonic or Hermetic guise, but first of all it is an immediate intuition of men whose practice allows them not only to see with their eyes "but also feele with [their] handes in the secrete workes of nature";[123] men for whom growing things are the hairs of earth's body or for whom the sap of trees (in which man recognizes the analogue of his own blood) is milk drawn from the teats of mother earth.[124] To an authority on fertilizer, nature may be the "bad and barren earth,"[125] but more commonly it is precisely with earth's untutored fruitfulness that the gardener must contend. In circumstances like these, the Fall's curse may seem less a degeneration of nature than man's alienation from a still unimpaired bounty, an alienation imposed by his own need to labor for profit. Would you find fault with nature, Ambrose demands, because not all men are good?[126]

To botanists, however, there are no "weeds" among the "severall Tribes and Kindreds of Natures beauty,"[127] and the great princes (like Burghley or Elizabeth) to whom they dedicate their labors are required only to contemplate the wealth of "the plentifull Treasury of Nature"[128] opened up before them, not to toil in its production. A writer on the country farm may greet the "courteous reader" with precepts of "paynefull toyle and laborious husbandrie"; but to his aristocratic patron the dedication speaks only of the fruitfulness of "this great mother of the world": the divine Pandora from whose never-drying breasts "millions of streams" feed both young and old, a largesse by which princes may measure their own "power, magnificence, and renowne."[129] Another writer makes the same distinction in dedicating his tract both to those "plain clouted shooes" who will find it a means for greater profit in their "manuall workes" and to the rarer sort who will find pleasure in "provok[ing] Nature to play, and to shew some of her pleasing varieties."[130]

If the practical handbooks reveal the influence of the *Georgics,* the herbals seem frequently to acknowledge their debt to a quite different tradition, one which appears to have reached them by way of the encyclopedias of the twelfth and thirteenth centuries: the tradition of hexaemeral meditations on the integrity of creation in its first days. The Renaissance popularity of Basil and Ambrose and the rest is well known; and a compendium like Trevisa's version of Bartholmaeus Anglicus' *Liber de proprietatibus rerum* (one of the first "herbals" printed in English) suggests how difficult it might become to distinguish scientific from meditative impulses.[131] In any case, what seems constantly to be implied by the prefatory matter of the new botanical works is a special election conferred upon their aristocratic readers, a new freedom based on the power they effortlessly wield over the world. "Although Adam lost the place for his transgression," writes John Parkinson in his *Paradisi in sole* (*Paradisus terrestris, or a Garden of All Sorts of Pleasant Flowers*), "yet he lost not the naturall knowledge, nor use of them." And it is clear that knowledge and use will soon restore the sort of place we have already seen Gerard promising Burghley; a park in the sun, the title assures us, will become a paradise. What art repairs is not the recalcitrance of matter itself (withered branches or gnarled roots), but simply ignorance, forgetfulness of the possibilities the world continues to offer. Many great men—and we may suppose that Charles VIII was of their number—have hitherto "not known either what to choose, or what to desire."[132]

Just how seriously Parkinson intended to address the imaginations of such men is suggested by the woodcut of the terrestrial paradise on the title page of his book. No mere emblem, this realm impregnated by winds and illuminated by a divine sun is a place—the whole world's garden[133]—where merely human figures are overwhelmed by the exuberant yet symmetrical vitality of the living things spread out for their "pleasures and necessities." We may remember that it was precisely within the tradition of Renaissance herbals that artists first developed techniques capable of seizing all this visual wealth and making it available to the mind or imagination.[134] For our present purposes, what is most notable about the title pages of sixteenth- and seventeenth-century garden books, about the face these books present to the world, is the way in which traditional images or allegories are transformed in this context and adapted to a vision of quite new possibilities.

The dry and flourishing trees of Christian myth or iconography, for example, seem very different when their promise of perpetual resuscitation is encountered in an actual garden, rather than in some visionary pilgrimage back to Eden or forward to the heavenly paradise.[135] The frontispiece of Emanuel Sweert's *Florilegium* (Frankfort, 1612) may serve to illustrate this motif, as well as a number of other commonplaces we shall assemble, by way of summary, from a fairly wide range of space and time. The *hortus conclusus* of monk or mystic is again and again discovered to flourish in every man's country estate. Such gardens may still be dedicated to the hope that "God providing, all things will flower,"[136] but they are walled no longer by an ascetic discipline, and in fact are bounded only by the limits of the four continents whose rarities enrich them.[137] The bare-breasted goddesses of the garden books (Ceres, Flora, Diana of Ephesus) keep the visible attribute of the Virgin's charity, the universal nurse from whose proffered breast all men are nourished.[138] And the petals with which their realms are impregnated from above may remind us of the divine emanation, sometimes in a garden, by which the Annunciation had been imagined ("Water with heav'nly showers her wombe unsown," a poet prays, "And drop downe cloudes of flow'rs").[139] But the fecundity unlocked by Ceres' key is a purely natural one; and if like the Virgin she is attended by sun and moon, it is not to witness her elevation above all temporality but precisely to claim for her the seasons' particular beneficence.[140] The Word that hovers over her garden is immanent in the whole world, and its incarnation is presided over, time after time, by figures representative of human art. Sweert's fountain of Minerva—"bountiful Minerva" she is called in another garden setting, "instructing men in all the arts"[141]—finds its parallel elsewhere in Adam with his hoe and Solomon with his book,[142] or in Hercules entering the garden whose promise, like the promise of Naples to King Charles, is "potentia subjecta nobis."[143] (*See Plates 2–12.*)

II

Sacred Space and the Image of Paradise

The Cloister Garden

THE FORM OF THE MEDIEVAL GARDEN, so far as we can reconstruct it, is remarkably fixed: an open area within a mass, generally organized around a center. This is the form of the monk's cloister and of the secular courtyard, and, when gardens move outside the castle, an enclosing wall maintains the old disposition. Even Renaissance gardens keep the same design motifs, although disposing them differently in space, until they are superseded by the picturesque or English garden of the eighteenth century.

Now when we speak of the forms of a garden, we are talking about ways of organizing space. Gardening is the art of environment, and we should expect to find in a garden some evidence of its planner's sense of how he is related to the world. What I want to suggest now is that the association of gardens and paradise may depend on the sort of places gardens in the Middle Ages and Renaissance actually were; and that the third term linking gardens and paradise is a certain conception of space or perhaps a certain way of experiencing space.

1

> Let [man] look upon that resplendent luminary set like an everlasting lamp to lighten the universe; let him remember that the earth is but a speck in comparison with the vast circuit which this star describes; and let him then consider with amazement that this circuit is itself no wider than a pinpoint beside that which is embraced by the stars that roll in the firmament. *But if our sight stops here, let imagination pass beyond.*[1]

It is not just the metaphysical shudder that makes Pascal here so conveniently represent for us the modern feeling about space. More important is the unspoken assumption that lies behind this awe and agitation. Pascal's figure seems to owe something to Lucretius' cosmic traveler, hurling his spear from the putative limits of the world.[2] Here, though, the figure no longer functions merely as a counter in a logical demonstration, but comes to define the very structure of a new sensibility. Space is to be experienced as distance, an imagined extension where parallel lines, far beyond the convergence of man's feeble eyebeams, will never meet. "By virtue of space I am comprehended and engulfed in the universe as a mere point."[3] And this is true not only because of man's limitations, but first of all because the physical universe itself has been pre-empted by a Euclidean system of homogeneous points, "an immeasurable blank field on which the mind [can] describe all the perfect figures of geometry, but which [has] no inherent shape of its own."[4]

It may require an effort of our own imaginations to conceive how radical a shift of sensibility this represents. For Aristotle, space had been "not a distance, but something surrounding, or containing, a limit."[5] Against those who would situate things, and indeed the whole cosmos, in mere vacancy, Aristotelian (and Scholastic) physics insist that the place of anything is "the innermost motionless boundary of what contains."[6] What is crucial is not the technical argument, but the imaginative choice that precedes all argument. Because the paradigm for his cosmological imagining is "something like a vessel" (*Physics,* 209b27, 211b1)—a winesack, a pitcher, a ship on a river—Aristotle is able to answer the proponents of the void as if they were claiming an empty *place,* which he has no trouble in showing to be a contradiction in terms.[7] The "room" in which an object extends itself is not a neutral blankness on which it is inscribed, but the concrete, particular place by which it is encompassed;[8] and what we should now call space is not an emptiness in which we are lost, but simply the aggregate of all those places in which we find ourselves, the "place universal," the most inclusive of the nested spheres of Ptolemaic astronomy.[9]

The choice of a basic term from which all other terms in a system are derived is important because it represents the sort of initial commitment to the imagination a thinker has made. The emptiness of atomist physics, for example, is postulated to leave "room" for an entirely random movement. The inane of Lucretius represents a world in which questions of logistics—the rain of matter that endlessly replenishes the effect of decay, the chance coherence of infinite worlds—replace the ethical or theological ones of his rivals: he is above all concerned with ridding the universe of a center, literal or metaphorical (*De rerum natura,* 1.1052–82). Aristotle's system, on the other hand, is concerned not with distances but with situations, and it is intended to answer such questions as where one is or where one is going. This essentially dramatic intelligibility of motion demands a stable universe fixed around a real center, bounded by an actual limit. In our own experience, Aristotle explains, distinctions of direction may seem relative to our particular position, but "in nature each is distinct, taken apart by itself."[10] What this means in human terms is that not only the celestial spheres but any space is essentially definable; which is to say both that it has a boundary, an objective form, and that it is intelligible to the human mind. All space is in this sense cosmic: not indeterminate but of itself constituting an order, not merely existent but constructed like a temple[11]—an image that Cicero shares with Christian exegetes concerned with insisting that there was no where as well as no when before the original creative act.[12] The imagined coherence of space implies, indeed, a whole cosmology. It is a renewed sense of the commodiousness of the *locus universitatis* that gives rise, in the spatializing imagination of the twelfth century, to dreams of the Lady Natura, by whose power all things are enclosed and assigned their proper places,[13] and by whose skill the world is articulated so intricately that we are reminded, in the wheels and diagrams of the encyclopedists, of the knots and parterres of a formal garden.[14]

The order involved in this conception of space, furthermore, is qualitative as well as dimensional. Above and below "do not differ merely in relative position," Aristotle says, "but also as possessing distinct potencies" (*Physics*, 208b22) so that the earth moves to the center, fire to the circumference, each element seeking its "natural place." The very idea of place, after all, implies some relation of suitability between container and the thing contained. We speak of something being "in its place," and as even Copernicus remarked, "nothing is so contrary to the order of the universe . . . as for a thing to be out of its place [*locum suum*]."[15] The word *topos* itself has etymologically a concretely scenic sense, a place in which something occurs;[16] a sense that is preserved in the Aristotelian categories, where place is one attribute of objects, and especially in the topical rhetorics where this purely logical relation becomes a sympathetic bond, exploitable for persuasion.[17] When a rhetorical lover strives to persuade his lady that the pleasant spot in which they find themselves is a place peculiarly fit for love and pleasure, the *locus amoenus* becoming (as Petronius argued) *dignus amore locus,*[18] it may sound to us like merely an opportunistic sort of pathetic fallacy. But Aristotle had in mind something quite different. All striving is toward a fullness of being discovered in the universe, not projected onto it. Almost in spite of himself, Aristotle falls into speaking as if objects and places define one another mutually.

> The movement of each body to its own place is motion toward its own form. . . . whenever air comes into being out of water, light out of heavy, it goes to the upper place. It is forthwith light: becoming is at an end, and in that place it has being.[19]

The parabolic or mythological sense of his remarks is here very close to the surface. What must concern us is the sense of the distinct potencies of places and, in particular, what these potencies imply about the relation between man and the cosmos.

As a recent commentator has observed, the notion of natural places seems to have been a vestige of an earlier way of thinking.[20] What was new in Aristotle's physical thought was the determination to isolate the essential nature of being from questions of locality or of origin, distinguishing matter from space and both space and matter from the principle of genesis. The study of nature was to be dissociated from the various cosmogonies that had hitherto been its vehicle, so that the philosopher could devote himself to principles rather than beginnings.[21] Yet (inevitable as the distinctions may seem today) these notions were all merged in the physics of Aristotle's predecessors; and although he was concerned with making corrections, he was working within the context they had established, and he accepted from them the imaginative paradigms that gave structure to his own thought. To illustrate his notion of place, for example, Aristotle cites Hesiod's chaos,[22] no mere location but the "seat" and mother of gods; and like countless later commentators, he wrestles with the mysterious "receptacle" of the *Timaeus*. Plato's conception resists rational formulation so stubbornly precisely because it is (as Plato himself is the first to point out) an irreducibly mythical notion, neither matter nor space, but matrix: mother, nurse, womb of all becoming.[23] The notion of space as a container also places Aristotle in the tradition of Anaximander, who long before had observed that "worlds are born of infinite space that contains them all"; his *apeiron* is no formless void, but, infinite only in its inexhaustible potency, constitutes a sphere that "encompasses" and "governs" all things.[24] Plato preserves the image, while altering the content, in his world soul "wrapped round the body of the world," which itself must be spherical to "embrace" and "comprehend . . . all the figures there are."[25]

In all these cases, the nature of a being is defined in terms of its origin, the seed from which it grows, and neither of these can be considered apart from its particular environment, its place or "seat" in the universe.[26] Aristotle's predecessors, in other words, had not yet divorced their curiosity about natural essences from a more primitive responsiveness to the power by which such essences are manifested at particular moments and in concrete places. The "undifferentiated, unreflecting" mythological consciousness, Ernst Cassirer has written, "refuses to draw a distinction which is not inherent in the immediate content of experience."[27] Since the immediacy of its intuitions does not dissociate idea from image, it will prefer to the abstractions of logic or mathematics the terms of narrative: space and time, place and coming to birth. It is necessarily, therefore, involved with thought of a magical or theological sort. "All things are full of gods" when man's discovery of power in the external world and in his own nature is conceived not as an act of measuring or charting, but as a dramatic encounter.[28] The question is of what posture the knowing mind assumes before the world. "Whereas scientific thought takes an attitude of inquiry and doubt towards the 'object', . . . myth . . . 'has' the object only insofar as it is overpowered by it . . . is simply possessed by it."[29] Men bring themselves into contact with the forces that govern their world only by an openness to the world, only by submitting themselves to particular moments of experience. It is this sense of the external world as the living scene of man's knowing and experiencing, not merely the inert material on which he operates, that is preserved in the notion of natural places. Mircea Eliade has said that the fundamental religious intuition is just such a "feeling of solidarity with the surrounding microcosm": a heightened response to the potency of "all that surrounds man, the whole 'place'," which comes to be figured as "the cosmos—repository of a wealth of sacred forces."[30] And when Cicero considers the animation of the world, from whose womb all things are brought forth, he still can feel that the embracing air somehow sees, hears, and speaks *with* man: "Nobiscum videt nobiscum audit nobiscum sonat."[31] In Aristotle's cosmology, as even more openly in the *Timaeus* or the Milesian speculations, this mythical element remains latent, ready to emerge again in stories of the world egg, laid by the sun, or of the navel of the world, the cosmic uterus from which all beings spring to birth.[32]

What is important, however, is not so much a particular myth as a fundamental modality of mythological thought, or rather of those experiences of the sacred that precede the formulation of myth:

> We characterize the distance between the potent and the relatively powerless as the relationship between the sacred and profane, or secular. The "sacred" is what has been placed within boundaries, the exceptional (Latin, *sanctus*); its powerfulness creates for it a place of its own.[33]

It is only because space is taken to be in its nature (as it is in immediate experience) heterogeneous that the sacred may be distinguished from the profane; the shade and solemnity of certain groves may "demonstrate" the presence of gods, Seneca says, and men "erect altars where great streams burst forth from hidden sources."[34] And the essential basis of this fundamental intuition of sacred space is the experience of boundary or limit that separates it from the amorphous profane: a temple, Varro says, is "a place whose limits are defined."[35] In being selected or specified—the sacred precincts of city, temple, or home are not so much constructed by man as discovered, sought out by mysterious skill—a mere locality becomes a position: not a point arbitrarily inscribed on a neutral expanse, but *some* place, a real center around which a world, a cosmos, may be oriented.[36] Seen in this perspective, Aristotle's insistence on the cosmic nature of space, its essential definability by center and circumference, may be taken as a rationalization and generalization of what is meant by the sacred. Man has a place in the universe, and his destiny depends on occupying it, taking his stand in it; religion's chief imperative (*relegere:* to pay attention)[37] is that man take cognizance of where he is. Behind the cosmologists' doctrine of natural places we can discern the lineaments of the old *moirai* or destinies, an expression of the sense that man's fate depends not on any temporal economy but on the compartmentalization of space, the division of the cosmos into zones governed by particular potencies.[38]

A second way in which the idea of natural places is in touch with the primitive experience of space has to do—I have already suggested as much—with how man encounters these potencies. Our own habits tend to assign the experience of feeling to an autonomous subjectivity and to consign what is left over to the objects of the world. But when the primitive mind is overwhelmed by those intensities of fear or exaltation we have been calling the sacred, it can find in its experience no suggestion that what has occurred has only an inner reality. In the immediacy of such experience, "the undifferentiated intuition of 'existence' as such," no interior distance is left in which subject and object, image and thing, can be distinguished.[39] The mind is not distinct from the contents of its perception, nor objects from the emotional or motor responses they evoke. In such privileged moments, moments in which man finds himself involved with power, mind and world are not opposites set over against each other, but a single intensity marking itself off from the relative formlessness of the quotidian. Sacred place and awakened self are identical: the seat of a potency which is at once pneuma and psyche, the "ground" of cosmic being and of man's own self as well.[40] What is involved is a reciprocal relationship between man and scene that is not merely an operation of one fixed entity on another, but a mutual coming to birth. Or, in the words of a modern psychologist, man seeks to "make a world in which to find a place to discover a self."[41]

2

For man, the Christian tradition has always assumed that the paradigmatic place is Eden.[42] Writer after writer, particularly those associated with the traditions of monastic thought, conceive the whole economy of salvation in terms of man's return to this *locus voluptatis* (Genesis 2:10)—not merely a pleasant spot (the wording of the Vulgate invites conflation with the rhetorician's *locus amoenus*) but pleasure's own place, the place where man can achieve that fruition which constitutes true pleasure.[43] In a fallen world his life is a Babylonian captivity, an unending exile in an alien land, *regio dissimilitudinis;* Eden is man's true homeland, the seat of his being.[44] What is preserved here is of course the old tradition of thinking of man's life as a pilgrimage towards "the country of the soul,"[45] but particularly in Augustinian thought this theme gets an important new emphasis. Plotinus (from whom Augustine has been supposed to have received the motif) and, even more emphatically, the pagan gnostics use the notion of the soul's homeland to define the total alienation of spiritual life from the created universe—a mere prison of the soul and realm of darkness.[46] Augustine, on the other hand, defines man's journey in terms that do not distinguish it from other cosmic processes, but on the contrary assimilate it to the very order the gnostics were concerned to escape:

> By reason of its weight the body strives towards its own place [*locum suum*]. . . . Fire tends upwards; a stone downward. They are impelled by their own weights; they seek their own places . . . Not put in proper order, they are without rest; when they are set in due order, they are at rest. My love is my weight! I am borne about by it, wheresoever I am borne. By your gift we are enkindled, and we are borne upwards.[47]

Drawing on the scriptural notion (Wisdom 11:21) that creation is ordered by "measure, number, and weight,"[48] Augustine revivifies the mythic content of Aristotle's doctrine of natural places, and in doing so leaves open the possibility (despite hesitations and contradictions) that supernatural goals are to be pursued in this world. If physics is taken as in some sense the key to eschatology, then all space is at least potentially Edenic. Man is at home in a universe that affords all things the places ("locis suis") in which they may achieve fruition.[49]

The cosmic structure of Eden, indeed, is well established in dogma and tradition. "Since even in Paradise itself, the tree of knowledge was placed in the middle of the Garden," Sir Thomas Browne writes, "whatever was the ambient figure, there wanted not a centre and [given the four rivers of scripture] rule of decussation."[50] Browne's flamboyant geometrizing in *The Garden of Cyrus* is merely a variant of a long-lived preoccupation among Christian thinkers with tetrads, a tradition that associates with Eden the figure in which Pythagoras, who is supposed to have formulated the very notion of cosmos, saw the paradigm of all reality: the loving concord of opposites that binds together the universe.[51] The very fixity of the iconography of Paradise (visual and literary) should warn us that we have to do with an archetype. The four rivers springing from a center are not a topological curiosity, but, read in terms of this Pythagorean tradition, the axis of the world; and Browne is prodigal in illustrating their avatars. His remark about Eden comes in the context of his discussion of the "groves and sacred Plantations of Antiquity," where he wonders if these holy places revealed the same attention to the "aspect, manner, form, and order in Architectonicall relations" as did the buildings themselves. His interest, in other words, is in the organization of space that makes it sacred. And in fact, as Cassirer has pointed out, the sacred significance of four is most fundamentally connected with an intuition of the coherence of space, ordered by the cardinal directions; so that "anything which shows an actual four-fold organization . . . seems attached, as though by inner magical ties, to certain parts of space."[52] Christian thinkers adapted the cosmic X of the *Timaeus* in order to explain how the Cross might "bound down the mobility of the world" and "shape the shapeless"; and the four points of this veritable Tree of Life, by which the whole universe was granted a "rule of decussation," were associated with the rivers of Paradise from whose intersection it originally sprang.[53] The rivers do not so much stand for as in some sense really include—embody in spatial form—the four seasons, the four elements, the four humors, and even the four virtues and the four gospels: all the co-ordinates of man's physical and spiritual cosmos. Definitively embodying these world harmonies, Eden is "the real music, the original and model of all other";[54] and Adam, so long as he ruled in Paradise, was a "citizen of the world," taking the cosmos as his motherland and fulfilling the promise of his name, in which theologians found symbolized the four directions and so the inner reality of the whole world.[55]

But even apart from this sort of speculation, Paradise was habitually imagined in terms that reinforce its sacredness. It is space set aside, difficult of access over rough seas or narrow mountainous paths, but (like all taboo ground) strangely easy to come by, a goal "seeking will not find."[56] This is perfectly obvious; but in dwelling on the ring of fire that keeps man out we are apt to forget the extent to which this sense of enclosure is not the accidental result of the Fall, but part of Eden's essential nature. As Milton knew, it is the fallen world that is a "fenceless" one; and the wall of Eden, for generations of thinkers and contemplatives, is "the safety which makes all tranquil . . . the peace which unites all together."[57] In Philo, for example, the function of the four rivers, like that of the virtues they suggest, is in bounding, encircling;[58] the wall of the Enclosed Garden of the Canticles, with which Paradise is conflated, is a guarantee of integrity, virtue's barrier against the wild boar of the world.[59] Again and again, Eden is imagined in early Christian thought or literature in terms that suggest the Midrashic conception of a "secret place."[60] ("The subject of Paradise should not . . . be treated lightly," Ambrose cautions. Men must not be eager to "disclose that which leads to danger by its very revelation.")[61] It is God's "secret region,"[62] *hortus Dei* set off by a wall of trees,[63] a "happy retreat,"[64] a "place apart,"[65] "the chosen place."[66] That man, rather than wandering at large over the earth, should have such a special place reserved for him is for a fourth-century writer a demonstration of God's special providence; centuries later Dante's dreamer discovers in the Earthly Paradise "the place chosen to be the nest of human nature."[67] Even the literalizing Raleigh betrays some suggestion of the old feeling. Eden is established "in the very navel of this our world . . . that from thence, as from a centre, the universal might be filled with people and planted."[68]

The theological imagination is of course as subject as any other to failure or evasion.[69] The notion of Eden may be adulterated to a mere nostalgia for bucolic or sensual simplifications or it may be bureaucratized into a rigid allegory, made a mere name for abstractions. Nevertheless, even allegory assumes some proportion between vehicle and tenor. Even where disapproval of physical space as it now exists is most keen, the notion of a return to Eden—where "All the Creatures were Divine Flowers in this Garden, animated with a Divine Life, cloth'd with a Divine Beauty"[70]—will continue at least to imply some possible adjustment in the relation of man to the physical world, no mere flight to a wholly spiritual realm. And if the dream of Eden can be used to justify a longing to escape from the world, it can also embody aspirations toward the discovery of a world, toward a repose that comes rather with fullness than with absence of being:

> Adam was expelled, after his sin, into this world, which is called the desert place. Now Paradise is not in the desert but on the earth. Similarly, what the Lord promised the faithful in the Evangelist is not desert, but the Earth—which is that of the living.[71]

As Father Daniélou observes, the Paradise Origen imagines here—and it represents, he says, the basic conviction of patristic thinking—is at once a revelation of the divine and man's "natural place," both *terra beata,* the blessed land, and *terra vera,* the true one. Origen may draw upon Socrates' myth of the "true earth" (*Phaedo,* 109b–111c), but he emphatically rejects any suggestion that he is concerned with what "the Greeks call 'ideas' " or with "any unsubstantial region of thought." The language of Scripture sets before his imagination a realm that represents not an undoing of creation but on the contrary the fulfillment of its original promise. Paradise is the place where the earth, "contained and enclosed . . . surrounded and confined" by the true heaven, becomes the "safe and most sure abode" of "the end and perfection of all things."[72]

Milton has Michael say of Eden that:

> God attributes to place
> No sanctitie, if none be thither brought
> By Men who there frequent, or therein dwell.[73]

But this reversal of the usual relation between agent and scene[74] is an innovation of the thinker that can scarcely be followed by the poet, who is able to indicate the sanctity of his protagonists only as their participation in the pastoral innocence and vitality of the scene.[75] This extreme of antisacramentalism may be intended only to comfort our first parents, but it cuts the poetic ground out from under Milton, or would if actually implemented, because it denies the relevance of his imagery. I mention it here only to suggest the way in which a tradition of sensibility can impose its own logic on doctrine. Even the Protestant Du Bartas is willing to consider the Tree of Life a "sacrament" through which Adam and Eve are able to participate in the sanctity of the Earthly Paradise:

> For, as the ayre of those fresh dales and hils
> Preserved him from Epidemick ills,
> This fruit . . .
> Had barr'd the passage of twice-childish age,
> And ever-more excluded all the rage
> Of painful griefs . . .[76]

The same intuition of a potency communicating itself to human behavior through the place itself is implicit in the tradition, which Du Bartas cites, that God created man outside the garden so he would recognize that his powers in Eden were only conditional.[77] And it is suggested by the nature of the task assigned Adam and Eve during their sojourn in the garden. We are not surprised to find that Milton's Eden requires the vigilance of constant pruning and restraint, but God himself is the gardener in Du Bartas:

> He plants, he proins, he pares, he trimmeth round
> Th'ever green beauties of a fruitfull ground.[78]

Human labors do not create the "allies, beds, and borders," the "art-less Bridges," the fashionable maze and topiary satyrs (537–70); rather, they unfold into action the order and harmony already implicit in the scene. The nightingale's natural song predictably outdoes Arion, Orpheus, Linus, and Amphion (130–31): to this form-conferring music the labors of Adam and Eve are "like the guise of cuning Dauncers" (325–26), or else

> . . . the Sun's calm course, who pain-lesse ay
> About the Welkin posteth night and day. (340–41)

As Augustine had observed long before, the agriculture of our first parents was not labor but *exhilaratio voluntatis,* the will's joyful participation in divine creativity; and where, he asked, "can reason speak more intimately with nature than when setting out seeds, planting slips, or trimming shrubs?"[79]

The characteristic endeavor of the imagination, when it is seriously engaged with Eden, seems to be in intuiting an interpenetration of man and scene. Two passages from widely separated places and times, seventeenth-century England and fourth-century Syria, may be taken to suggest the persistence of this challenge and the consistency of the terms with which it is met:

> You never Enjoy the World aright, till the Sea it self floweth in your Veins, till you are Clothed with the Heavens, and Crowned with the Stars: and Perceiv your self to be the Sole Heir of the whole World.[80]

> If you choose to climb to the summit of a tree, its branches spread out in layers beneath your feet and invite you to lie down in the midst of its bosom, in the chamber of its branches, whose floor is all scattered with flowers. Who has ever seen the feast at the heart of the tree, with fruits of every savor

> within reach of the hands? The dew permits you to cleanse them and the leaves to wipe them dry. Above the head are clouds of fruits and beneath the feet a carpet of flowers. You will be anointed with its sap, you will breath its perfume.[81]

Traherne's attempt to clothe himself with the cosmos; Ephraem's longing to place himself at the very center of the nourishing source; the desire of poets like Peter Damian in the eleventh century or Henry Vaughan in the seventeenth to blossom along with the paradisiac landscape: these impulses represent the quality of experience that underlies and validates treating Eden as a metaphor for the virtuous soul. The sense of interpenetration may be formulated in a number of ways: as the harmonic correspondence of microcosm and macrocosm,[82] as the reading of a Neoplatonic Book of Creatures,[83] or in popular myths of fountains of youth or magical balms.[84] Yet the distance between these formulations is not so great as it may seem; they refer us to similar experiences. However narrowly pharmaceutical we may find (for example) Du Bartas' magic tree (superior to modern simples it "salveth all sores, sans pain, delay, or cost"), the image of balm may serve in a writer like Ephraem to give objective form to an otherwise indefinable sense of the life-giving potencies of the whole milieu of Eden.[85] And what we mean by seeing God in nature can only be experiencing the sensible milieu as value, as proportionate to the human mind and revelatory of human possibilities—unless of course we are merely arguing from design in the eighteenth-century manner, but in this case God is a hypothesis, not an object of apprehension. "We cannot fully know ourselves," says Ambrose, "without first knowing the nature of all living creatures."[86] Traherne's great theme is that Edenic man is the possessor of the whole world;[87] we must understand this possession not as the exercise of power over the world, but as participation in it, possession by it. Dante's Earthly Paradise is not merely the place set aside for man but the "nest" that fosters him; it is the "holy ground full of every seed," and what flowers here most notably is "the human root" (*Purgatorio,* 28.118–19, 142).

The repertory of images by which many generations were to imagine Paradise was codified and also given its theological underpinnings by the hexaemera and biblical epics of the fourth and fifth centuries, works which were again immensely popular in the Renaissance.[88] Commentators have noticed the formulaic rigidity that grew up in this tradition. But for our purposes what is significant is that the most fundamental of these images or metaphors all seem to suggest, in different ways, that in Eden man discovered rather than brought those influences which were important and that what he discovered was a reality which defined his own being.

> Earth has welcomed you with its own plants, water with its fish, air with its birds; the continent in its turn is ready to offer you its rich treasures.[89]

Again and again we are told that God or nature "is not content with a single gift";[90] the key words again and again are *dare, porrigere, munerare,* to give, grant, reward—imagery of largesse, outpouring.[91] These images may be rationalized to explain the creation in terms of the Platonic idea of God's "self-transcending fecundity"[92] (Claudius Marius Victor explains that God gives us the gift of creation because he is too rich to need it)[93] or to enforce something like the Augustinian distinction between using and enjoying (man possesses the world legitimately so far as he merely uses what is given in trust)[94] or simply to urge gratitude for benefits received. But prior to any of these didactic uses, this sort of language has an expressive function. To see the garden as a gift is to associate it with the inconceivable act of Creation itself. What is thereby dramatized is a sense of awe and wonder before the totally gratuitous that blossoms suddenly into form, a fullness of being that comes from without—infinite riches discovered in a single place.[95] It is something of the same feeling, perhaps, that lies behind the distinction Pliny draws between Tellus, the goddess of the field, and Pomona, the deity of the garden. All that men possess from Tellus, Pomona says, they have earned by toil, but "my gifts are perfect before they leave me . . . and proffer themselves unasked."[96] The experience of the sacred is perennially one of being surprised by joy; and the special capacity of these images of giving is to renew our sense of the nature of such encounters: the *mysterium fascinans,* a philosopher of religion has written, "at its highest point of stress . . . becomes the 'overabounding,' 'exuberant'."[97]

The real gift of course is neither pleasure nor profit, but life itself.[98] This substantiality of man's involvement in what is given may be suggested merely by the energy with which its prodigality is catalogued, so that the emphasis is thrown on the process of giving rather than on specific gifts. Or another image may be used at once to make explicit man's participation in the scene and to suggest the dogmatic or liturgical relevance of that participation—to postulate, in fact, a whole ecology of salvation. As Traherne says, man will not be heir to the world until he makes it his garment (*Centuries,* 1.29–30). In Paradise, the cosmos is man's crown, jewel, ornament, the mark of his honor or dignity;[99] and it becomes, in anticipation of the heavenly Paradise to be regained, dowry or earnest money of the soul's (or the Church's) final union with the divine.[100] The place set apart for the "nest" of human nature was granted, Dante says, "for earnest of eternal peace"; according to Avitus, Paradise is given "pro thalamo," as the marriage chamber not merely of human love but of the greater union already prefigured.[101] The connection between Eden's vivifying fertility and the notion of a divine marriage is of course not accidental. The pervasiveness in the hexaemera and biblical epics of the language of classical pastoral—Proba's *Cento* was not the last poem to hope to offer its readers "Virgil changed for the better"—may well remind us of earlier celebrations of the marriage of Heaven and Earth.[102] Poets would readily find theological justification for the notion that the two realms mingled in Eden;[103] and Avitus' *jungere* (to couple) gives this meeting a sexual connotation, as does Du Bartas' description of the "all clasping heav'ns" in a realm where "Heav'n had not thundered on our heads as yet,/Nor giv'n the Earth her sad Divorce's Writ."[104]

Or the gifts of Eden may be laid out before man like a great banquet.[105] For Plato the heavenly feast is that absolute possession of reality which wisdom achieves only by flying far above the world.[106] But in Eden man's communion is with the whole of creation in all its immediacy, a sacramental participation that is renewed in the ritual meal of the Church or in the illumination of mystics who anticipate the refreshment promised the blessed in the heavenly Paradise, reclining "at table in the kingdom of God."[107] And when this nourishment is imagined most intensely the fruitfulness of Paradise becomes *ubertas,* the plenty of an unfailing breast.[108] Plato's nurse of all being is thus resanctified in a figure that assigns to the fecundity of the first garden the nurturing charity later manifested in the Mother of God and Mother Church. As Philo writes:

> The earth also, as we all know, is a mother, for which reason the earliest men thought fit to call her . . . "All-Mother" and "Fruit-Bearer" and "Pandora" or "Give-all" . . . and [nature bestowed upon her] by way of breasts, streams of rivers and springs.[109]

3

All Christians may live their lives in hope of finding a way to Paradise, but it is only the monk who goes to a special place to pursue this goal. A twelfth-century writer is not eccentric when he divides all creation into five regions: the world, purgatory, hell, heaven, and the *paradisus claustralis.*[110] The notion that the cloistered life is a "provisional paradise" is the very basis of monastic culture.[111] The monastery is a harbor away from the tempest of the profane world, the soul's true homeland; above all, it is *paradisus claustri, hortus Christi,* a "corner of Paradise" reserved even in this world of profane space, a foretaste of the eternal Sabbath by which all profane time is contained and transcended.[112] And it is important to recall that the monastic orders were founded precisely out of the need to find some place in the world, some incarnation, for those ambitions the desert fathers had been able to deal with only by flight and negation. The whole pressure of Western monasticism (as Gerhart Ladner especially has shown) is to extend a merely personal and interior reformation into the social world, to realize the city of God here below.[113] Paradisiac joy is to be achieved not merely in flashes of contemplation in which the created world is rendered invisible. It is, rather, the savor of the whole ordination of monastic life,[114] an order which, intimately mingling inner and outer disciplines, can no more be distinguished from particular persons and places than monastic thought can be severed from devotional voice and concrete image.[115]

The monks inherited not only many of their buildings but also much of their vocabulary from the late Latin villa cult in which the Roman feeling for *terra mater* enjoyed a last efflorescence and transmutation.[116] Even Jerome's rather ascetic monastery in Bethlehem was celebrated in Virgilian terms as the "little villa of Christ," although the "lovely vision" its busy gardeners were promised is the austere one of the *Georgics*.[117] Augustine, in particular, went to school with Plato and Cicero as well as with the desert fathers in order to learn the nature of the monastic ideal. His whole life was punctuated by a series of rural retreats in which he sought to "gather the fruits of a bountiful leisure," *otium liberale* in which the mind may be "cultivated" to receive a "divine planting."[118] At Cassiciacum, where he hoped to find in philosophy a harbor from the tempest of this life,[119] he discovered in the gardens and baths of Verecundus' villa at once a reminder of the philosophers' *gymnasia*[120] and a suitable place ("aptus locus") for defining his own vision of the blessed life (*De beata vita,* 1.6); and when finally he established an actual monastery, it was in the *hortus* (villa garden?) of Bishop Valerius:[121] we may suppose that all these stages of the itinerary of Augustine's soul retain some memory of its starting point, the garden of Milan in which he first turned toward God.

Monasteries continue to be academies, *gymnasia* of the divine philosophy;[122] and the pastoral leisure of the classical tradition comes to define the monk's perpetual Sabbath—no longer an escape from life's real concerns or even a refuge in simplicity from the uncertainties of fortune but an active confrontation of the greater reality, *negotiosum otium,* a busy leisure.[123] What remains of the classical ideal is exemplified in Bernard's remark that more is learned "under the shade of trees" than is taught in all the schools; the implication, as Gilson points out, is that the natural scene, with which the monk is permanently in contact, has been "integrated even into the mystical life itself."[124] Basil was as responsive as Seneca to the numinous quality of woods, gorges, and waterfalls; and in his hermitage, an "island . . . cut off from all the world," he finds the "key" to a redolence of earth and air surpassing the fabulous "paradise" of Homer's Calypso.[125] Monasteries have names like *Mons angelorum* (Mountain of Angels) or *Vallis paradisi* (Valley of Paradise), the Benedictines finding spiritual aspiration on actual mountains, the Cistercians discovering humility in actual valleys.[126] If it is true that monastic writers are rarely interested in the merely picturesque, it is also frequently very difficult, when the paradise topos is applied in praise of a specific place, to distinguish allegory from literal description—as in William of Malmsbury's panegyric to Thorney Abbey:

> In the middle of wild swampland where the trees are intertwined in an inextricable thicket, there is a plain with very green vegetation which attracts the eye by reason of its fertility; no obstacle impedes the walker. Not a particle of the soil is left to lie fallow; here the earth bears fruit trees, there grapevines cover the ground or are held on high trellises. In this place cultivation rivals nature; what the latter has forgotten the former brings forth. . . . Truly this isle is the home of chastity, the dwelling place of probity, the school of those who love Divine Wisdom. In short, this is an image of Paradise; it makes one think already of heaven.[127]

The roses and lilies of the monk's garden of delights slide easily enough into symbol, of course, and it is not easy to sense much response to an actual scene in the sort of abstract moralizing we may typify by Honorius' *De claustro:*

> The fountain in this *locus voluptatis* is the baptismal font of the monastery. The Tree of Life is in Paradise, the body of our Lord in the monastery. Trees of various fruits are the various books of sacred Scripture.[128]

Nevertheless, even such instances may have been experienced more inwardly than we suppose. Honorius' didacticism may take on a somewhat different vibration, for example, when we notice that the response "O radix Jesse" was frequently entrusted to the gardener of the monastery.[129]

The phrase *paradisus claustralis* itself punningly confuses the physical cloisters with the whole monastic regimen. The cloister garden is pre-eminently the monastic place, and this is true not only because it is the means of communicating between the different buildings of the establishment nor even because it is the center of the monk's daily course of study (the symbol of contemplation, Durandus calls it; but also where the carrels are).[130] The crucial intuition is suggested in the eleventh century by Hildebert of Lavardin:

> The house displays a four-square shape. The court is adorned by four porticoes, which—enclosed by three buildings that the body's use demands and

> by a fourth that is the house of God—give both movement and rest to the monks, and life itself, so that here the sheep are contained as within a fold. The first of these buildings stores food and drink, with which the adjacent building refreshes them. The third building attends to limbs grown weary from the day's labor; the fourth resounds perpetually with the praises of God.[131]

If the three sides of the court are given over to the uses of the body, the fourth is *domus Domini,* the former busy with quotidian labor, the latter resonant with unremitting praises. It is in this intermediate position that the monks discover an image of their own place in the scheme of salvation. Historians have conjectured that the cloister develops architecturally from the pillared atrium of the basilica, the "paradise" in which holy water was dispensed, sanctuary afforded, and the poor fed.[132] It functions, in any case, in the same way: as the anteroom of the house of God, the porch of Solomon's Temple,[133] with water for purification, and flowers (actual roses and lilies, not just symbolic virtues) destined for the altar.[134] As such, the cloister becomes the type of Adam's Paradise—itself the promise and anteroom of the Heavenly Kingdom—and, indeed, the epitome of all natural beauty of place, which is to the purified, a commentator says, a trumpet blast summoning them to the darkness of the inner tabernacle.[135] Here we are tested, wrote Hugh de Fouillory in his *De claustro animae,* so that there we may be refreshed:[136] the cloister embodies the whole discipline of the monk's life, a discipline in which the lineaments of his reward are already typologically present.

In the seventeenth century, John Theodore De Bry, who also illustrated Fludd's Hermetic and Pythagorean account of the creation, was still recommending a fantastic elaboration of the form of the monastery garden—a square enclosure divided into four smaller squares by intersecting paths, often with a fountain, well, or tree at their intersection—to anyone who wanted to taste the joys of heaven while still on earth.[137] De Bry provides his readers, to be sure, with a design for knots whose permutations of the square are quite beyond the imagination of monastic gardeners, and the claim he makes for the efficacy of his design may seem exaggerated. But his remarks do suggest with great clarity that it is not only the function of the cloister garden that associates it with Paradise but its form as well, the form it transmits to secular gardens and to the gardens of the Renaissance. De Bry's readers might have been reminded of the rivers of Eden, which the Vulgate pictures flowing from a fountain and to which tradition had given the form of a cross, as well as of the "foursquare" city of Revelations (21:16), where Eden is anagogically fulfilled.[138] We shall concern ourselves, however, more with the structural than with the representational qualities of the cloister, less with contrived symbolism than with the penumbra of connotation taken on by certain forms and felt to be somehow intrinsic to them.[139]

We have already indicated that it is for their cosmic suggestiveness that the four rivers are seized upon so enthusiastically. First Augustine and Boethius and then the school of Chartres keep alive the tradition that finds in number the essential constituent of all form; and for this tradition the square, expressing as it does the proportion of equality, is of special importance.[140] *Aequalitas* is "integrity of being," that equilibrium attained by whatsoever has fully realized its nature: the cloister, Hugh says, should be a perfect square, like the atrium of Ezekiel's temple, in order to express the measure and equanimity of the monastic life and to anticipate the perfection of the divine.[141] At Cluny, artists multiplied the "quaternities" in which they had been taught to discover an "intuition of the Godhead";[142] and when four seasons or four elements are arranged around Christ as their ruler, the cosmic diagram that appears is the quincunx of Eden or of the cloister. All this argues not programmatic allegory (although such allegories did exist) but a quality of sensibility. Builders, aware that there is no art without knowledge, adjust the practical formulas of their skill in order to participate in cosmic reality. Romanesque architects seem already to have been concerned with "musical" proportions; and later a Villard de Honnecourt or a Matthew Roriczer prided himself on the ability to generate all proportions from the square and the equilateral triangle inscribed in it: in Milan in 1400 builders found their inspiration for a quincuncial ordination of towers in the fact that "the Lord God is seated in Paradise in the center of the throne, and around the throne are the four Evangelists."[143]

Since it is from Vitruvius that medieval architects learned their veneration for the technical prowess the square unlocks,[144] it may be significant that the Abbey of St. Gall is the source both of the earliest surviving plans for a monastery (c. 822) and of the manuscript of Vitruvius that Poggio found there in 1416.[145] The plan, in any case, seems to be the first modern instance of construction planned *ad quadratum,* church, cloister, and all the monastic buildings being laid out as multiples of the square choir (40 x 40) in which the monks approach the high altar.[146] Even before such discriminations are made, however, what strikes one about the plan's devotion to the rectilinear is its diagrammatic quality, its (perhaps deceptive) air of being as much geometrical fantasy as actual blueprint.[147] Or more precisely, it seems to be, as the artist's own language suggests, an act of exemplification (*exemplata*), almost indeed a Platonic archetype of a monastery, drawn up in Charlemagne's own circle for what became the most important intellectual and artistic center of the empire.[148] (*See Plate 13.*)

The relationships between the various buildings are not highly developed, so that to an observer from almost any point within the complex they would "not form an organic whole" (as a modern writer has complained). But from this lack of "striving after external effect," it does not follow that the scheme is "utilitarian rather than aesthetic."[149] The intention of the design is not to present a vista for guests, but to articulate and give boundary to the life that goes on within, just as the councils from which the plan originated were concerned with ordering and regularizing the whole monastic regimen.[150] Although the actual site seems to have been triangular, everything in the plan is confined rigidly with a rectangle of "pure and ideal regularity":[151] the huge barns to the west of the main complex look rather as if they were simply filling out the form. The individual units, moreover, are almost obsessively symmetrical; and again and again they are organized around central squares, whose precise functions in many cases have baffled interpretation as much as they must have taxed the ingenuity of the original architect—if indeed he was primarily concerned with imagining their uses. The diagram itself fails to acknowledge the diversity of functions, so engrossed is it in the identity of form. Early interpreters of the plan often found it difficult to decide if a given square referred to a small building inside an open court, or a small opening in the ceiling of a large room.[152] Greater philological sophistication seems to have deciphered some of these puzzles, but the visual effect of the plan remains the same. It is almost as if the difference between a body and a hole were secondary, like the differences between square tables and square ponds and square parterres—merely specified after the fact. What does seem important is the visible manifestation of the shape of the underlying module and the rhythmical repetition of this shape.

Of such a plan, the cloister garden must be the center, literally and symbolically. Monastic writers like Hildebert seem characteristically to orient themselves in space by supposing that their buildings radiate outward from the cloister.[153] Here, the form that organizes the nave at St. Gall into nestlike enclosures and is obscurely incarnated in stables and fireplaces achieves at last a pure architectural expression. The paradise of the cloister is a square space and nothing else, a space, like the atrium Ezekiel saw in the heavenly Temple, one hundred units long and broad, inscribed in the center of the whole.[154] And it is precisely here, as we have seen, that monastic life assumes its characteristic form, halfway between this world and the next. The connection between the *aequalitas* of the cloister and of the monks' life, as indeed Charlemagne's reformers must have assumed, is not just metaphorical. The architecture of the place imposes itself on the human activity that comes within its precincts.[155] Processions to and from the church proceed regularly along the galleries, and the square can be crossed only on the paths that mark its axes—unlike the Roman atrium that permits random wandering as do those places in the monastery where merely quotidian concerns are to be pursued. Even to read the explanatory notations on the diagram of the cloister, one must revolve the parchment around its center: *"quattuor/semitae/per transversum/claustri"* (four paths for crossing the cloister).

At this point I should like to set side by side some terms that were not necessarily linked in monastic thought but whose juxtaposition might help to suggest the way in which dogma and feeling converge on the forms of the cloister. This may be a somewhat arbitrary procedure but I hope it is a useful one. First let us consider that, if monastic life is an attempt to return to Paradise, it is in this simply an extension or translation into history of what is achieved in the timeless moment of baptism,[156] which from the earliest times was also thought of as a re-entry into Eden.[157] Now this baptismal return is a double action. It is first the death of the old Adam, through a participation in Christ's sacrifice; and it is secondly a rebirth in "water and in spirit."[158] Accordingly, the paradisiac nature of the monastic life may be said to have two aspects, at once *paradisus claustri* and *paradisus delicii,*[159] at once a death to the world—claustration involves separation, confinement, ascesis—and a flourishing in the joys of a reborn nature.

Before it is applied to the square courtyard of the abbey, the word *claustra* itself suggests the notion of confinement, whether by a physical wall or by a rigid order of discipline; the very vagueness of the word's application (it was used also by topographers to indicate natural amphitheaters and enclosed valleys, like Petrarch's Vaucluse) suggests that the different sorts of enclosure are not clearly distinguished.[160] It is evident, then, that what we have been talking about so far, what we have been responding to in the diagram of St. Gall, is this sense of cosmic enclosure and ordination that the cloister has in common with Paradise:

> The solitude [*secretum*] of the cloister truly exhibits an image of heaven. Just as the virtuous are segregated there from the sinners, so in the cloister the professors of a religious life are sequestered from the worldly.[161]

Space is given form by number that encloses and limits it; submitting to this order, men participate in its form. Hildebert's account of the four sides of the cloister is continuous with his celebration of the lifegiving rigor of monastic rule. "Nothing is confused, where everything is done in order," and this is made visible in the central garden where the monks are nourished like sheep in a fold ("velut in caulis contineantur oves"),[162] or like Dante in the "nest" of his being. The whole notion is illustrated nicely by an early seventeenth-century engraving that contrasts the original Eden, grown wild and overrun with satyrs and Death, with the garden of Christ, its bed like that of the cloister, rigidly quadrangular and still displaying the compasses with which God originally shaped and enclosed all things by measure, number, and weight.[163]

But it is a garden with a center as well as a limit. Or to put the matter somewhat more precisely, the cloister itself is not merely what contains, but the place toward which everything converges or from which everything streams, a garden of delights as well as a garden enclosed. Seen in these terms, as the source of the quality that permeates the whole, the cloister's relation to the rest of the abbey is reminiscent of the disposition of Eastern monasteries, particularly those of Mt. Athos: fortresses walled against the outside world, without much internal plan, but finding a center in their basilica (at the Great Lavra, surrounded by square porticoes and alleys of cypress) or, as in an engraving of Rossikon, by what looks like the tholos with which medieval illuminators indicated the Fountain of Life.[164] And as the cloister is the center of the monastery, so its own center, at St. Gall, is another square, traversed again by two axes—leafy ornaments, like stylized foliage—whose juncture is marked by a circle; a similar design is repeated in the twin cloisters of the hospital and the novitiate. Readers of the plan have not always agreed whether the "savina" designed by the circle is a tree, a font of holy water, or an arrangement for watering the garden.[165]

Trees and fountains, of course, are both centers of Eden, and both were subject to a variety of allegorical interpretations.[166] The Tree of Life is the cosmic tree whose branches support the world, realized for all eternity in the cross, approximated by every good man who, planted in Paradise, flourishes beside the waters. The Fountain of Life, *fons et origo bonorum,* flows again from the womb of Mary or from the side of Christ or every day from the baptismal fonts of the Church. The "paradises" of the basilicas would naturally capitalize on this sort of symbolism, since their "copious streams of flowing water" were used for purification before entering the sanctuary;[167] pine-cone fountains of the sort associated in Byzantine royal liturgy with the Tree of Life are represented in the West by the famous Pigna in the atrium of Old St. Peter's, and by the cone at Charlemagne's Aachen, which sent its water in four directions through tubes identified as Phison, Gehon, Euphrates, and Tygris.[168] We hear occasionally of symbolic cloister fountains,[169] and we are told that the trees of the cloister are virtues or that its fountain stands for baptism.[170] In the center of the grove of the monk's cemetery, inscribed within a perfect square, the designer of St. Gall erected a cross, the true Tree of Life "in qua perpetuae poma salutis olent."[171] But underlying such particular symbolisms, giving them point and human application, is the more immediate sense of the tree or the fountain as quite literally the embodiment of all the forces latent in the space of the garden, their source or epitome. Whether it is applied to the original creation, to the Church, or to Mary, what the image of the Fountain of Life suggests is the germination of a fruitful seed, the stirrings of a womb divinely impregnated.[172] The doctrinal usages all point back to some intuition of cosmic fecundity, of Creation as a miracle concretely apprehended in water or vegetation; and of this intuition the garden of the cloister—where the soul, according to an eighth-century writer, is "girt about with bubbling waters"[173]—is not merely a sign, but a direct presentation.

This sense of a center and a limit, a way of experiencing space prior to any specific interpretation, seems to be implicit in the medieval artist's shorthand for gardens, a fence enclosing a tree or a fountain.[174] One feels its operation in a sketch of a Carthusian monastery, where every cell has its private garden for meditation and every garden its single centrally placed tree;[175] or in the illumination for the *Roman de la Rose* —whose deity had usurped the title of *fons et origo bonorum*[176]—in which the human figures are insignificant beside the presence, dominating and vaguely priapic, of a great spherical fountain set in a round pool.[177] It is this sense of space as both formed and potent, and therefore as the place of man's own coming to birth, which seems to have been passed on, along with the forms that incarnate it, by the monastery garden.

III

Gardens of Poetry and Philosophy

THE SPACE OF MEDIEVAL AND RENAISSANCE GARDENS, even when the diagram of the monastic cloister is not precisely reproduced, is endlessly reticulated and preoccupied with symmetries. So too, even without any theological program, these gardens are felt to be not neutral or decorative backgrounds, but places whose potencies are communicated to, and realized in, human action of specific kinds.

One tradition that enforces this sense is a purely linguistic one. As we have seen, the concept of place evolves etymologically from the notation of places in which certain sorts of activity occur. The word *locus* itself preserves this way of thinking: not only (a) a place, but also (b) an opportunity, an occasion, and therefore (c) a situation, state, or condition. The word that begins by pointing to where ends by specifying what. This range of meanings, whereby a subject is defined by its position, is passed on to the rhetorical tradition, which from the very beginning concerns itself with place. This concern is directed especially to the second sense of the word, the one in which actor and scene are held in a nice suspension. The scene may in encomiastic rhetoric be praised for its own sake, but in judicial rhetoric the argument from place considers the scene as establishing the likelihood of deeds to be approved or condemned.[1] Medieval poetics adopts this usage, applying the lawyer's energy in deduction to the structure of dramatic action, so that describing a place is the means of defining its function as an "opportunity" for the behavior with which the poem deals.[2] The scenic art is the art of motivation.

The three sorts of activity that traditionally and repeatedly find their proper place in gardens are poetry, philosophy, and love.[3] It is Plato who provides notable early gardens (or at least *loci amoeni*) for all three: the garden of the Muses in *Ion*, the philosopher's nymph-haunted plane tree in *Phaedrus*, and Love's garden of Plenty and Poverty in the *Symposium*. By Plutarch's time, the garden setting (Plutarch does not clearly distinguish the plane tree by the Ilissus from Eros' garden, and both are the property of poets) seemed a distinctly Platonic topos, and, indeed, something of a literary affectation.[4] Nevertheless, for Plato, and for any more or less Platonic scheme of thought, it does make sense to speak of poetry, wisdom, and love as man's attempt to possess an external world. The metaphor of possession is of course explicit in Plato's account of love; and all three activities are presented as varieties of divine madness, ecstatic "possession" in which the soul eludes the ordinary limits of the self in order to discover the self's true nourishment, exchanging the "food of illusion" for the banquet of the gods, and returning once again to its proper abode. All three, that is, are concerned with contrasts between profane space and that "place" of Being where the self may flourish.[5]

Both these traditions, the rhetorical and the philosophic, assume that thought takes place in the world, not merely within a space of its own creating, and that this engagement is essential to thought's very nature. In the Renaissance, matters that we might treat more abstractly, discussions of poetry, or of love, or courtesy, are habitually framed by an elaborate composition of place; and the place is usually a garden, a villa, a *locus amoenus*. Even tales are not turned loose to sound only in the reader's mind, but are retained within the matrix of the place and time of their telling. No doubt actual gardens would often provide a convenient retreat for such intellectual recreations, and Professor T. F. Crane has catalogued a number of instances in his *Italian Social Customs of the Sixteeneth Century* (New Haven, 1920). The question that must concern us is why the bond between an activity and its place is felt to be so intimate and what this implies about gardens and also about storytelling or philosophizing: our own standards of relevance, after all, would tend to reject as digressive the question of where the poet or philosopher may be imagined to speak. At least once, the question of the relevance of place is made explicit. The physician Girolamo Fracastoro begins his dialogue on poetry, *Naugerius* (1555), with the description of a pretty retreat near Verona, and goes on immediately to wonder whether "poets and philosophers are determined [*efficiantur*] by their nature or by some art or by their surroundings [*loco*]."[6] Navagero, looking all about him, bursts into song, "as if touched by the Muses," while della Torre stares silently into space. The discussions of poetry and intellection are initiated in order to determine why the "influence" of the *locus amoenus,* with its fountain, greensward, and singing birds, "makes one a poet and the other a philosopher." The distinction will depend, as della Torre says, not merely on the nature of each, but also on "how the impulses are produced which stimulate our minds": imagination and perception are both conceived, in the debate that follows, as being in dialogue with the world. "This very air . . . that we breath," says della Torre, "must be inhabited by diverse spirits, which dwell especially in these solitudes, woods, and fountains, where the poets say the gods themselves are present. These spirits go in and out of our bodies, and different ones affect us in different ways" (p. 51).

I am not interested here so much in Fracastoro's theories as in his assumption that the conventional composition of place does not merely decorate the dialogue, but represents a necessary dimension of the thought itself, a necessity, we shall see, suggested by more purely literary means in other dialogues. The possibility he raises—and this was implicit in my sketchy remarks about Plato's gardens—is that the rhetorician's habitual way of talking about gardens of poetry, philosophy, or love may coincide with some more fundamental intuition of the mind's encounter with the world; that behind the topoi we may discover a more primitive sense of the sacred potency of space. The rest of this chapter, in any case, will devote itself not to the history of a literary motif, but to some actual gardens, places that were especially important for establishing fashion and that seem to center in themselves the sort of mythic consciousness we have been discussing.

1

Unlike their prototypes in French romance, Boccaccio's literary gardens seem to claim the authority not of dream or of a dreamlike other world, but of actual places, the landscape of Fiesole or the already flourishing gardens of Angevin Naples. The constant play of autobiographical suggestion has the effect of placing romantic fantasy within the boundaries of the everyday world, as if goddesses and elusive nymphs were simply the furthest extension, in the sensibility of the poet, of what the natural scene itself might offer: as if, indeed, the paradise of Venus might be discovered in the gardens of the Castel Nuovo, or as if, just outside plague-devastated Florence, Poggio Gherardo or Villa Palmieri might shelter a party of youths and maidens "not meant for death." A good deal of harmless antiquarianism has been expended on seeking out specific sites.[7] More important for our purposes is the general sense, to which this commemorative habit testifies, of a connection between the poet's vision and the particular place in the world he occupies. And in the frame story of the *Decameron* this reflexive awareness receives an objective form. The gardens through which the party makes its way constitute the grove of Boccaccio's own Muse, brought down, as he implies, from the lofty Parnassus of his censorious critics, but not on that account any less divine.[8]

Certainly the tales, as he himself claims, are expressions of a particular time and a particular place, to whose decorum, quite different from that of a school or a church, they conform. They are not accidentally but essentially tales told in "gardens and places of recreation [*luogo di sollazzo*]."[9] And the Enclosed Garden of the third day (entered on the Sabbath, after Friday's devotions and Saturday's purification), like the Valle delle Donne of the seventh (reached by a narrow path, "via assai stretta" [6. conclusion. 19]), is not merely a convenient location, but a place in which re-creation is ritually achieved, in which solace is discovered. Like the tapestries in which their spirit is preserved, these gardens are striking in the density of the life they enclose: carpeted with "at least a thousand varieties of flowers," alive with "at least a hundred varieties of charming animals" that only gradually, so much is there to see, become visible to the inquiring eye (3. introduction. 8, 13). The space itself is redolent with scents, "odorifera e dilettevoli ombra" (3. introduction. 6); the air resonant, reverberating with music in which human voices join.[10] No part of such gardens, in short, is "sanza festa," (without celebration [*Filocolo,* 4.72]); and this palpable quality is one the youths and maidens discover they can inhabit.

Allegorical gardens of Rhetoric or Learning—in the tradition of Martianus Capella, whose epic described their nuptials—often had promised such *copia* to those learned enough to take possession of them; in the *Metamorphosis Goliae,* for example, Apollo's grove seems the *locus universitatis* itself, a place full of the images of all things in cosmic harmony.[11] Boccaccio's young men and women seem to discover in Fiesole actual gardens that extend a similar promise to all who surrender to their charms. This is already prefigured at Naples in *Filocolo,* where the whole machinery of the Questions of Love is introduced as a way of articulating ("con pue ordine") the sweetness of the moment when Fiametta's party sits beside a crystalline fountain and "quivi di diverse cose, chi mirando l'acqua chi cogliendo fiori, incominciarono a parlare": here, some gazing into the water, others gathering flowers, they began to speak of many things (4.17). The language of lovers and poets, unlike that of the clerk or philosopher, takes form in this moment of release, this moment, we may say, of sensibility, when the mind drifts in crystalline depths or wanders among the flowers. But it does take form. In the *Decameron,* the sensuous variety of an earthly paradise is complemented by the rigor of the Valle delle Donne, whose perfect circle, drawn as if with a compass, is laid out by Nature herself, and ordered as a theater for "innocent delight"—the clarity of its waters reveals the nakedness of the seven swimmers—as though it had come from the hands of expert gardeners (6. conclusion. 10, 20-21, 24). It is not surprising, in such surroundings, that the storytellers' topics should all celebrate resolutions and restorations won through experience itself, where wit collaborates with accident to shape fortune to its demands. Whether we choose to emphasize about the tales the artfulness of their form or the naturalism of their content, they represent the party's attempt to appropriate the order and abundance offered by the gardens themselves.[12]

In a world from which divine and human law seem to have fled (Introduction. 23; 6. conclusion. 9), it is only in such places as these that the soul can recover its own poise between *licenza* and *ordine, festa* and *ragione*. Boccaccio's language suggests that the honest delight of the poet, for all its humility, represents not a loss but a recovery of self, quite literally a re-creation. To the shipwrecked Filocolo, the gardens of Naples, discovered close upon the ashes of Virgil, offer a kind of resurrection (4.10, 4.14); the *Decameron* moves more deliberately from stony wilderness paths (Introduction. 4) to paradisiac rewards. The company of youths and maidens does not flee the world so much as seek out, under more open skies (Introduction. 66), a place which is not merely a decorous backdrop for human action, but a part of its essential definition. The world revealed by the gardens is in effect a mirror, like the one of which Emelia somewhat cryptically sings at the end of the first day, in which the self discovers its "own beauty . . . which overjoys the mind." For the more censorious mood of the *Genealogy,* Narcissus' pool seems no more than the dangerous temptation of worldly pleasures, although even here Boccaccio concedes a short-lived splendor to the youth's blossoming; he is undone, after all, just by the perception of his own wealth, rendered needy by the plenty ("la molta copia") he discovers in himself.[13] But in the *Decameron,* as in the *Filocolo,* the reflection of all this plenty makes the world shine with an unaccustomed light: a sunbeam glancing off the fountain clothes Fiametta with a starlike radiance, and "besides the splendour it brought to her face, it did so lighten the place as among the fresh shade it yielded a marvelous lustre to the whole company."[14] It is with this lustre, "di nuova luce," that the poet also hopes to shine.

The poet's retirement to woods and mountains is rather testily defended by Boccaccio in the *Genealogy* (14.11); but the insistent anaphora of the *locus amoenus* he evokes ("ibi . . . ibi . . . ibi . . .") does build up, even with the most conventional means, a sense of place, some place, with "distinct potencies," not merely an evasion of the intrigues and disappointments of cities or courts. As Boccaccio observes, though, it is his older friend Petrarch who most definitively "reinstated Apollo in his ancient sanctuary."[15] His assessment receives an oddly literal confirmation at the sixteenth-century villa of San Vigilio, whose Garden of Apollo, complete with the god's shrine, is irrigated by a bust of Petrarch: water pouring through his eyes sustains what an inscription describes as "a strong tall laurel, the most beautiful on the whole shore."[16] The example of Petrarch's life, nevertheless, may remind us that such devices—no Renaissance garden is without its Parnassus mount or garden of the Muses—had for their paradigm a concern more serious than exterior decoration. The poet's own references to the gardens he plants to be a "seat of the Muses"[17] suggest, if only by their frequency and vehemence, some pressure of actual experience. Plato had cited the myth of the Muses' garden in *Ion* to demonstrate that the poet's song carried him into realms unknown to his daily self. Petrarch, in going from Avignon to Vaucluse, feels as if "nothing is the same": "alter hominum, alter aquarum, alter terrarum habitus."[18] And this *spatium dissimilis* is defined in terms that suggest the sort of intuition of the sacred we have been considering. His "transalpine Helicon . . . where the Sorgue gushes forth," with its gardens "sacred" to Apollo and Bacchus,

> is a place below the cliff and surrounded by water, confined indeed but very stimulating, where even an inert mind may rise to lofty thoughts.
>
> (locus est alta sub rupe ac mediis in undis, angustus quidem sed plenus stimulis ardentibus, quibus piger licet animus in altissimas curas possit assurgere.)[19]

Quite untranslatably, Petrarch's Latin suggests the sense of nesting in the midst of mountains and water, in a *locus plenus* where the mind rises to the altitude of the scene itself. And it is perhaps not coincidental that the place should also suggest the convergence of the two demands, "angustus . . . sed plenus," that must govern the poet's special care: the language, balanced between concision and copiousness, by which he must try to possess that elevation the scene appears to offer.[20] In such places as Vaucluse, the cultivation of the mind and of the soil—Petrarch is fond of elaborating the Ciceronian pun on *cultus*[21]—seem curiously to be identified. We shall have to examine more carefully the language in which this is implicit.

But we may begin by reminding ourselves of the really extraordinary degree to which Petrarch was able to link together with a horticultural image all the different threads of his thought and feeling, and the way in which even the external events of his life seemed to conspire to make this inevitable. "I was born in Arezzo. In a back street, Garden Lane, was the seed cast, and there sprang that arid flower, that insipid fruit that was I."[22] Later, what binds together his love and his Muse is not only their accidental coincidence in Laura/laurel. It is, more profoundly, the sense of growth, blossoming, coming to fruition, which is the way both love and poetry are experienced; and this flourishing of the self—like spring, a "renewing" of the "first time"[23]—is ultimately not distinguished from the *re*-flourishing of classical culture. Love's metamorphosis of Petrarch into a laurel in *Rime* 23 prefigures the moment when, crowned with laurel for his coronation on Capitoline Hill, he will renew rites that flourished (*floruerunt*) in antiqiuty.[24] Scipio, "'ancient flower of virtue and of arms," and Laura, "new flower of honesty and of beauty," cast an equal light, and the poet claims both for his own.[25] "Laurea cognomen tribuit michi, laurea famam,/Laurea divitias";[26] in his own gardens, indeed, he sets out the laurel with all the solemnity due a sacred tree.[27]

We should not take too literally, I suppose, the accusation in the *Secretum* that Petrarch is acting like a pagan priest;[28] more is involved, though, than metaphor. Petrarch is throughout his life a practical gardener—he refers to "my little gardens, planted with these hands"[29]—pursuing his hobby on a small or large scale wherever he goes and recording his progress on the margins of his Palladius. When he transforms the vines and olives of Vaucluse into a contest of Bacchus and Minerva,[30] we may suppose that he is responding not only to classical usage, but also to his own experience of the fertility of the place. But the guide to all his labors is Virgil, who figures on his bookplate as the author of the *Eclogues* and *Georgics,* writing under a laurel tree; and the garden of Apollo at Vaucluse reminds Petrarch of the garden island of *De legibus,* where Cicero pursued his labors open to all the influences of trees, birds, and rippling waters.[31] As much as his literary endeavors, in other words, Petrarch's gardening is a matter of *imitatio*. The aim of both, after all, is to make things grow, to bring them to birth, and at times their relation seems almost a kind of sympathetic magic. "As a gardener devotes himself to plants and trees, so do I to words and to songs."[32] The mind's field, "arvum ingenii," is discovered to germinate best in the open air by a "murmuring stream . . . grateful to the Muses";[33] and again and again Petrarch testifies to the power with which the spirit of such places, the "ingenium loci," speaks to his own imagination: "suasere," "suggessit," "hortata est."[34] Wandering in the hills near Vaucluse he is inspired to celebrate Scipio, that *fiore antico* who first had woven laurel into the garland with which Petrarch himself was to be crowned; later, it is a woodland scene in Italy that awakens the poet from his torpor—"struck all at once by the beauty of the place"—and sends him back to his labors with an ardor he finds amazing.[35] His first eclogues too, Petrarch says, were composed with incredible speed, so powerfully was the poet "persuaded" by "the quality of the place [*loci habitus*] and the retirement of the woods" (*Familiares,* 10.4.11). Vaucluse becomes in these works the very grove of the Muses, where, as on Capitoline Hill, they dance about the sacred laurel; and, more pedantically, its echoing spring suggests the community of the learned who greet the poet upon his descent from the heights.[36] Nor, Petrarch claims, did the bourgeoning summer speak less tellingly of Cola di Rienzo, the shepherd king who would restore the ancient homestead of his mother Rome, "mighty queen of the woodlands" (*Bucolicum carmen,* 5.38). Indeed, Petrarch says that "almost all my little works were either completed or begun or conceived" in Vaucluse;[37] and we cannot, any more than the poet, consider this an accident.

The myth of the soul's true country seems to have haunted Petrarch and appeared a key to his own restless wandering. "Conceived in exile and born in exile," he habitually translates his hopes and fears into spatial terms, images of wilderness and paradise, of sinking or soaring.[38] Stephen Gilman has seen in the *De remediis* an oscillation between a sense of space as a "circumstance of value" on one hand, and as "indifferent and dimensional" on the other.[39] Once the observation has been made, its relevance to much else in Petrarch immediately becomes obvious. The poet in the *Rime* wanders through landscapes drained of value, revelatory only of absences ("O poggi, o valli, o fiumi, o selve, o campi/ testimon de la mia grave vita"):[40] through dry or savage woods, rough ways, dark valleys and deserted caves, storm-tossed seas.[41] But (like Dante) what he is always trying to return to is "my own nest, where I was nourished so sweetly":[42] "dolce loco," "beato loco,"[43] space set aside and overflowing with value, the place of the lovely lady on the green grass.[44] Now it is possible to argue that Petrarch simply projects his emotions onto the landscape, indulges in a sentimental rather than a naive view of nature; but if we remain within the world of the poems themselves, we find that the implication is just the opposite. Whatever her status in real life, Laura here very frequently serves merely to embody the vitality of the paradisiac place; and her "footsteps" which the poet is concerned to track through a world that can only imperfectly retain their impress are a secularization of the *vestigia Dei* by which the divine immanence is revealed.[45] The poet's situation is no different from that of all sons of Adam who, exiled from their proper seat, must content themselves with but the "utmost skirts of glory" and only "farr off his steps adore."[46] Laura is the *object* of Petrarch's concern only so far as she eludes his grasp. Experienced, she is not only *lauro* but also *l'aura, l'aere, l'aurora*—breeze, air, dawn—the whole vivifying milieu of the natural paradise.[47] These puns, it should be noticed in passing, are not a game but a way of making discoveries: word and reality lose their hard, merely public outlines at the same time, and the scene becomes a possession of the self.

Petrarch has occasion enough in his own life to feel the power of place. "Quid non mutatio loci potest?" What may not be done by change of place? he asks; translated, the very nature of fruit or flowers, or of men, will alter.[48] This is, as Petrarch says, his obsessive theme.[49] It is of course most often in the gardens of Vaucluse that he finds his own "harbor of solitude," a retreat from the empty sea of fortune; and the nature of this safety is suggested to him by the very name of the place, *clausa vallis,* a vale enclosed:

> and nature meant it to be [so] called, for she has hidden it among the encompassing hills away from every road and every common intrusion, and has not permitted it to be seen by any save those that dwell in it.[50]

Petrarch may moralize this sense of enclosure to suggest a Horatian or even monastic sobriety,[51] or he may describe it in terms that suggest the very womb of the earthly paradise;[52] but, in any case, it is with the sense of the encompassing itself that he appears preoccupied, as in the verse which attempts to enclose his whole life in the valley: "Valle locus Clausa . . . Valle puer Clausa . . . Valle vir in Clausa."[53] Vaucluse is hollowed out around the source of the river Sorgue, a place of "mingled horror and pleasure" to Petrarch;[54] and he is quick to notice the implications of the river's name: "surgit sorgia," the Sorgue surges.[55] The water issues from a grotto at the base of a natural amphitheater, its walls of rock terraced on three sides and rising to a height of 350 feet.[56] The spectacle reminds Petrarch of Seneca's observation that "we erect altars at places where great streams burst suddenly from hidden sources":

> Such altars . . . I have long thought of erecting, if opportunity should favor my wishes, there in my little garden which lies in the shadow of the cliffs and overhangs the stream.[57]

Petrarch builds his garden here for the Muses' seat in order to appropriate not just the power of growing things but (what embraces and includes this power) the numinous quality of the whole place: space experienced as cosmic, defined and instinct with potentialities, *locus plenus,* as we have already observed him calling it.

He keeps returning to Vaucluse as to a single fixed point in all his peregrinations: "I remember it," Petrarch says half a century later, "as if it were today." It is the spot he seized upon even as a boy as "just right for me," *locus aptissimus,* where he is free to follow his own nature.[58] Or perhaps we should say, discover his own nature, for with the world slipping away all about him—"so we are whirled by destiny's wheel"—the most difficult task is precisely the one Petrarch has set for himself, "to know myself as I am, to become what I wish to be."[59] What he finds in his enclosed valley is in effect his natural place—at once "patria," "Helicon," and "Rome and Athens": home, inspiration, golden age; fatherland, poetry, liberal culture.[60] The three terms, I am suggesting, are approximations of a single intuition. The strangeness and newness of Vaucluse (like that of Dante's Earthly Paradise, or of the perpetual

Sabbath of his brother's cloister) is of a place beyond profane time and space, but the source of their reality. Petrarch's sense of his home is one of a gathering in of all things "from all places and every age, in this narrow valley."[61] His garden of the Muses is finally a *locus humanitatis,* where, participating again in his own nature (the "informing light" of *Rime,* 7), man may finally blossom into laurel.

Although it may play a similar role, the spring of the Sorgue is qualitatively different from the fountain of the monastery garden; and although the honorific image for space continues to be a nook or nest, Petrarch is not oblivious to the temptations of distance. One way in which he looks toward the Renaissance is his willingness to commit to the Edenic paradigm many of the unruly energies of the profane world. The ascent of Mount Ventoux is not an idle holiday, but an attempt to translate the feats of spiritual mountain climbers—he uses the image again as the basis of his coronation oration—into the physical world.[62] It does not appear to have been a successful attempt, ending as it does with the two heights rigidly distinguished—"nothing is admirable besides the mind; compared to its greatness nothing is great."[63] The initial stupefying moment of liberation gives way to an experience in which the prospect is seen as no more than the interval that separates, the measure (as in *Rime,* 129) of all his woe:

> At first I stood there almost benumbed, overwhelmed by a gale such as I had never felt before and by the unusually open and wide view [*spectaculo liberiore*]. Athos and Olympus grew less incredible. . . . From there I turned my eyes in the direction of Italy. . . . The Alps . . . looked as if they were quite near me, though they are far, far away [*cum tamen magno distent intervallo*]. I was longing I must confess, for Italian air. . . . An incredibly strong desire seized me to see my friend and my native land. . . . Then another thought took possession of my mind, leading it from the contemplation of space to that of time, and I said to myself: "This day marks the completion of the tenth year since you gave up the studies of your boyhood. . . . O immutable Wisdom! How many and how great were the changes you have had to undergo in your moral habits since then." I will not speak of what is still left undone, for I am not yet in port that I might think in security of the storms I have had to endure.[64]

Space translates itself into time, both expressions of mutation, of loss and unfulfillment; and if the attrition involved is not quite a meaningless one (it is still the scene of moral struggle), it is nevertheless in the realm of storm and tempest, with no port in sight.[65]

The distractions of the mind when it is brought out from human habitation and confronted only with the sky is recognized also in the *Life of Solitude:* the distractions of "a view which stretches out in all directions [*prospectu vago*]" and of "too open a sky."[66] Quintilian, whom Petrarch is answering, seems to be thinking of the dangers of too much variety, but it soon becomes clear that the "freedom" Petrarch himself must come to terms with is, as on Mount Ventoux, not a lateral but a vertical one, "the freedom of the extended prospect." In the solitude of Vaucluse, however, a new equilibrium seems to have become possible. Untrammeled perspectives here are finally made compatible with a sense of cosmic enclosure, and actual physical space is assimilated to the purely interior distances of contemplatives and poets:

> they raise themselves aloft on the wings of their genius, for they must needs be carried away with more than human rapture if they would speak with more than human power. This, I have observed, is without doubt achieved most effectively and happily in free and open places. Wherefore I have often looked upon a mountain song as if it were a frolicking goat, the gayest and choicest in the whole flock, and being reminded of its origin by its native grace, I have said to myself, "Thou hast tasted of the grass of the Alps, thou comest from above."[67]

The intuition is not peculiar to Petrarch. As throughout the *Life of Solitude,* he is building on the traditions of monastic thought, and he here establishes his claim on what has been an important exception to the usual medieval distaste for mountains as the "warts and wens" of a fallen nature.[68] Peter the Venerable, for example, recognizes, as Petrarch did, the dangers to the solitary of windows open to the world, but defended the possibility that presumably lay behind his own order's choice of mountainous sites: "The sky opened generously to his spirit," a recent commentator has written, "he penetrated it by contemplation, he received from it grace and light."[69] Peter's friend John of Salisbury recorded a similar sensation, discovering himself on the "mount of Jove; on the one hand looking up to the heaven of the mountain; on the other shuddering at the hell of the valleys; feeling myself so much nearer to heaven that I was more sure that my prayer would be heard."[70] Petrarch, however, does not merely use these physical immensities to obliterate the self in anticipation of a Pentecostal re-creation from above. The songs that come to him from on high are (as we have suggested) precisely the means by which his potential humanity is finally to be articulated: what is involved, therefore, is no mere vertigo, but the aesthetic possession of physical space.

Such moments of poise may be difficult to sustain. Even at Vaucluse, Petrarch knew from experience the recalcitrance of the physical, and in a series of mock-heroic verse epistles he tells of the reluctance with which the nymphs of the place yielded up their rights to the more human mystery of the Muses.[71] But he did win from them a corner for his garden of Bacchus, and in such victories, as we shall see later with more particularity, the Renaissance garden discovers its peculiar aspirations.

2

During the Renaissance, philosophers as distinct in other respects as Savonarola and the studious nobles of *Love's Labors Lost* assume as a matter of course that the mind's banquet is best conducted in some variety of Socrates' original *locus amoenus* by the Illissus, the "Platonicall garden or orchard, otherwise called an Academe."[72] In the rest of this chapter I want to suggest that what such garden philosophers have in common is not merely a habitual way of framing their speculations but certain assumptions about the nature of thought, about the way the thinking mind engages the world. It is a question not so much of a series of doctrines as of a tradition of sensibility, one which, like the poet's, seeks to discover in an often delusive and mutable world the clarity and efficacy of sacred space. The mechanism of this sensibility has been well described by Tacitus: the mind withdraws, he says, "into a pure and innocent place," and in that "holy seat" comes to fruition.[73]

Certainly, at the very beginning of the tradition, the famous glade of the *Phaedrus,* with its plane tree, grass, and running water, is more than a cool spot in which to lie down. The place to which Socrates allows himself to be led (he has always been, he remarks, a kind of stranger in his own land) is the haunt of nymphs and only a short distance from the site of Boreas' rape of the mortal Oreithyia, whose sons, like Socrates' ideal lover in the dialogue, discovered that they "could soar into the sky."[74] The implications of the scene did not escape Plato's commentators. The Alexandrian Hermias (whom Ficino later translated) explains that the nymphs are goddesses who preside over palingenesis, and Boreas figures as the principle of generation in Porphyry's account of the Cave of Nymphs.[75] The nearby sanctuary of Agra, modern archeologists inform us, was in fact where initiates were prepared in the Lesser Mysteries for the revelations of Eleusis.[76] In the dialogue itself, however, the function of the place seems more strictly dramatic. Socrates does not draw any moral from the proximity of Agra, and he is scornful of the "superficial erudition" that would reduce myth to rational formulas (229e). The river in the noonday heat, the glade with its figures and images, the tree with its gift-bearing cicadas: all these are not mere emblems, but presences evoked with great care in all their phenomenal reality.[77]

At first, Socrates had supposed that "trees and countryside have no desire to teach me anything" (230d). Confronted with the unsuspected realities of the place, however, his language becomes uncharacteristically "dithyrambic" (238c–d), and gradually a sense awakens in him that his ideas have come to him from "some other source, flowing in through my ears, filling me like a pitcher."[78] Socrates is not being merely playful. A doctor friend had told Phaedrus that country walks are more refreshing than those beneath colonnades, and from its opening lines the concern of the dialogue is in getting "outside the walls" (227a). This will prove good advice for the mind's health too. Its first test is the scene's assault on the limits of Socrates' own urban rationalism—he professes at first to hope that the "threat" of the place's deity can be averted (238d)—and the conversation goes on to posit the necessity of eluding other walls as well: the body in which the soul is imprisoned like an oyster in a shell (250c); the dead language of Lysias' conventional rhetoric, an art of mere arrangement (236a), whose written words lie inert on the page, like the forced blooms of an Adonis garden, rather than fructifying the soul with the mysterious potency of the living voice (276a–277a). The unity of the dialogue is in precisely this impulse to open the self to those influences from without by which its own hidden or forgotten potentialities may be nurtured. True love and true rhetoric are at one in helping to set the soul beside its habitual self, to startle it with unsuspected possibilities:

> Once [the lover] has received the emanation of beauty through his eyes, he grows warm, and through the perspiration that ensues, he irrigates the sprouting of his wing. When he is quite warm, the outer layers of the seedling unfurl—parts which by reason of their close-drawn rigidity had for a long time prevented anything from blossoming. (251b)

It is this blossoming that is the gift of the cicadas; prophets of the Muses (262d), they bring the wakeful mind into participation with the "noblest song of them all," a harmony that embraces "the heavens and all the story of gods and men."[79] "Do you go now," Socrates concludes, "and tell Lysias that we two went down the stream where is the holy place of the nymphs, and there listened to words which charged us to deliver a message" (278b). The noontime hush and brilliance of the glade near Agra has, after all, been a sort of initiation for Socrates and Phaedrus, at least a "memorandum" of the "pure light of final revelation" in which, not yet fallen from the true place of Being, the soul had gazed upon the mystery of its own nature—the *telete* (mystery) in which the soul's own *telos* (end) is discovered:[80]

> This is clearly the reason why it is right for only the philosopher's mind to have wings; for he remains always, so far as he can, through memory in the field of precisely those entities in whose presence, as though he were a god, he is himself divine. And if a man makes right use of such entities as memoranda, always being perfectly initiated into perfect mysteries [*teleous aei teletas teloumenos*], he alone becomes truly perfected [*teleos ontōs monos gignetai*]. (249c)

As Socrates' punning indicates,[81] the language of mysteries is appropriate to the experience by the Ilissus just because it posits an identity between spectacle and spectator, and suggests that in the moment of revelation man becomes one with the holy scene, becomes transparent, in the act of vision, to the divine ground of his own being. If the philosopher is somewhat ironic in his relation to the nymphs of Ilissus, as he is indeed toward the "poetical" words they inspire (257a)—toward all words, finally—his irony does not constitute rejection. On the contrary, it exemplifies, over against the worldly wisdom of Lysias, that foolishness, that openness of the self, which the dialogue celebrates as a divine madness.

Later tradition represented Plato himself as the singer of enchanted groves, "a sweet-voiced speaker, musical in prose as the cicada who, perched on the trees of Hecademus, pours forth a strain as delicate as a lily."[82] Just how seriously the Academy, in which Plato is supposed to have dedicated a shrine to the Muses,[83] was intended to institutionalize the situation of the *Phaedrus* is tantalizingly unclear. Archeological evidence seems to suggest that the groves of Academus, near the spot at Colonus where the aged Oedipus had been entrusted to the care of choiring Muses,[84] was not a public park or recreation ground, but a holy place comparable to Eleusis: a gateway to the underworld, reached by a tomb-lined sacred way and adjacent to shrines of chthonian deities.[85] The Academy itself seems to have been incorporated legally as a society of the Muses, which might indicate some analogy between the site of the Academy and its intentions. We should remember that the Muses preside not only over the poet's flights but, as astral deities, embodiments of cosmic harmony, over the sage's own attempt to return to the soul's homeland: they become psychopomps in an initiation that is for the philosopher a virtual apotheosis.[86] Such motifs, to be sure, are developed more insistently in Plotinus and in the theurgy of his successors. But as we have seen, Plato had begun the use of the language of the mysteries; and if in the later Academy he was himself worshipped under the patronage of the Muses, the cue for this heroization would seem to have come from the words he assigns Socrates in the *Phaedo*. Recognizing that philosophy is the "true music," he enlists himself in the service of Apollo so that, at his death, he might sing with swanlike prophecy of "the real sky and the real light and the real earth."[87]

All this suggests why a tradition of thought should have become so firmly associated with a tradition of place, a sacred place whose beauty lies not merely in the gardener's skill, but in what a modern archeologist describes as "the radiance of a purifying harmony."[88] Even the peripatetics, it now appears, strolled not in the portico of the Lyceum, but in the sacred groves—*péripatoi*—that were its setting.[89] And the revival of academies coincides, not fortuitously, with the revival of gardening in Cicero's Rome, Ficino's Italy, and again in seventeenth-century England: just so long, in fact, as learned societies were able to imagine that their concern was not with mere data or abstraction, but with the cultivation of the soul, its participation in those harmonies entrusted by Plato to the Muses, and perpetually to be rediscovered in what Lipsius called "the ceremonies and communion of true gardens."[90]

The nature of this communion may be suggested by a remark Cicero attributes to his friend Marcus Piso. They find themselves alone in the Academy, and the proximity of Plato's garden "not only recalls his memory but seems to bring the actual man before [their] eyes . . . such powers of suggestion does the place possess."[91] Cicero's own assiduous cultivation of Hellenic fashions in gardening, his grottoes and statuary, his "Academy" and "Lyceum" at Tusculum, the statue of Hermathena which seems to turn the whole *gymnasium* in which it is placed into "a work of art offered to the goddess": all these seem to have been designed to participate in the efficacy of just such a power.[92] It is not mere coincidence that the garden in *De oratore,* where Cicero seeks to recreate the highest reaches of thought in the best days of the republic, should remind ("admonuit") the learned Scaevola of Socrates' plane tree and river (1.7.28). For all Cicero's enthusiasm for the sacred landscape of the Greeks,[93] however, we must admit that it is less the nymphs themselves who are here evoked than the philosopher they inspired (much as a poet in the eighteenth century could imitate nature by imitating Homer). Scaevola remarks that the spot was eminent less for tree and river than for the dialogue itself; and we may feel that something has decidedly been lost when Crassus points out that whereas Socrates had to sit on the grass, his own garden is well provided with cushions and seats (1.7. 28–29).

But only this domestication of Hellenic culture makes it accessible. Just as Cicero's dialogues (and the *De oratore* in particular) seek to assimilate the philosopher's wisdom to the eloquence of public life, so his gardens, quite literally, make a place in Rome for Greek thought.[94] Crassus himself speaks for the traditional Roman feeling that intellection is a mere impertinence; but as Catulus points out, it is precisely his garden that renders their discussion appropriate, even for a man whose ultimate commitment is to action:

> And, although you are justified in deeming those people tactless who take no heed of seasons, places, or persons, yet do you really think this scene ill-fitting, where this very colonnade, in which we are now walking, this exercise-ground, and these benches placed at so many points, in some degree awaken memories of the gymnastic schools and the discussions of the Greeks? Or can it be the season that is ill-chosen, occurring as it does during a holiday [*in tanto otio*] of a length such as we seldom enjoy and find especially welcome at the present time?[95]

Any alternative to public action continues to be considered a holiday, a form of *otium* or leisure. Socrates' "choir" of philosophers claimed not even to know the way to the market place, so devoted were they to the pursuit of their own natures; but Crassus' real business is preserving the toppling structure of the state: he has come to the villa only for the "recruiting of his energies."[96] Yet in this milieu, temporarily removed from the turbulence of Rome and surrounded by reminders of Greek thought and culture, even the statesman can find in leisure something other than the mere boyishness or inaction Crassus professes to want (2.6.22,24). Decorum of place, indeed, like the exigencies of time, demands that his *otium* be not laziness or idleness but what Cicero calls "otium cum dignitate": the moment of repose when thought is freed to speak with itself,[97] when the mind recovers that private equilibrium which is not the opposite but rather the necessary substrate of public efficacy.[98]

Cicero's holy places are constructed rather than discovered, but the end they serve is not mere antiquarianism, the claims of memory alone, but transformation as well. It is necessary, says Piso in *De finibus* (5.2.6), "to imitate your heroes as well as to know about them"; and having proposed to imitate Socrates beneath his plane tree (1.7.28), Crassus and his friends are surprised, perhaps a little embarrassed, to discover that they have been disputing "as in the schools, and very much in the Greek mode" (2.3.13). It is this sort of efficacy that makes serious Cicero's sense of the Academy's rebirth in his own paideia; a seriousness he passes on to Petrarch and to Ficino and his circle, and which keeps him, as an amateur of gardens, from mere fancy dress and stage setting.

Remarking the *vis admonitionis* of places, the power by which they "speak" to us, Piso goes on to say that it is "no wonder the scientific training of the memory is based upon locality" (*De finibus,* 5.1.2). The remark is worth noting because it suggests that the decorum linking thought and place may be functional as well as traditional. As formulated in the handbooks, to be sure, the orator's mnemonics involved a purely artificial construction of spatial diagrams in which the ideas of a speech, reduced to a series of images, were ranged like letters on a tablet, or, more tellingly, like objects organized in space by a painter of perspectives.[99] But the system seems to have involved not merely an association of ideas (an anchor reminds Quintilian's student of nautical matters, a weapon of military ones), but also an elaborate composition of place, almost in some accounts a hallucination; the *Rhetorica ad Herennium* advises that places should be relatively unfrequented, neither too shadowy nor too bright, and that they should be arranged one after another at a distance of about thirty feet.[100] The essential point is the one Quintilian makes when he remarks that the art of memory is born of our experience of actual places, is discovered, in fact, in our sense that locality impresses upon the mind the very "seat" of our thought and action (11.2.17). We are not surprised, accordingly, to find a Renaissance memory expert conflating with the *Ad Herennium*'s advice on *loci* Petrarch's praise of solitude, and claiming for his own tradition the poet's inquiry into the possibilities, as the special place of study or meditation, of meadows, streams, and pleasant fields.[101] Throughout their history, in fact, there is a leakage into ostensibly technical memory systems of animistic or magical ideas about the potency of images and of what Albert the Great calls "solemn and rare places," a quest for those "luoghi eterni" in which the mind will be liberated from its earthly prison: a sort of culmination is represented by Bruno's grandiose scheme to seize the inner power of the universe by ranging talismanic images of all things in their proper cosmic places.[102] We may in fact see in these developments a kind of reversion to the mythical content of the original system. What seems to lie behind these curious and elaborate schemes, classical as well as Renaissance, is a faith in the inherent connections between thought and things, mind and the physical world, and, further, a faith that we may "keep hold of as it were by an act of sight things that we can scarcely embrace by an act of thought."[103] For Cicero, as in a very different sense for Bruno, the image is the "shadow of the idea," and its place or seat in the world is the means by which the idea may be grasped.

It seems to have been from the places (topoi) of memory systems that Aristotle borrowed his term to describe the repertory of key notions from which, on any given occasion, an orator derives his arguments, the "topics" of invention.[104] The later history of the two sorts of places, mnemonic and rhetorical, suggests that their verbal identity was not fortuitous. Systems of memory and invention tend to merge in the Renaissance—Lull and Ramus are particularly significant in this respect—because they have in common certain habits of thought. If the mental world is conceived as a spatial structure, a network of compartments or places, and if this network is ultimately not to be distinguished from the underlying structure of the cosmos, then to understand any given matter is to remember its position, to see its natural place in the order of things. Place becomes the very principle of order, and as a Renaissance authority writes, the order of places is a double one: "seats" of argument in which the structure of thought is discovered and "seats" of images by which the mind retains its discoveries.[105]

Cicero's way of talking about the topics underlines their incipiently spatial character[106] and at the same time suggests that they function in a manner analogous to certain specific places in the real world: we may, in fact, begin to see yet another reason why thought's place should be a garden. For Cicero, *inventio* is not so much invention as discovery, and the art of topics tells "where to search and the locality of what you are anxious to find" (*De oratore,* 2.35.150). The topics are "seats" of the argument ("sedes et quasi domicilia omnium argumentorum"), "hiding places" in which the orator's themes must be "sought out" or "dug up."[107] But they are not mere classificatory pigeonholes; on the contrary, they are above all productive, generating innumerable applications from a few principles: a "source" from which "a general flood bursts forth," matters that of their own power (*vis*) give birth (*parient*) to the orator's words.[108] In the *Orator,* Cicero explains that the places were devised by Aristotle not for subtle analysis but to provide his students with "copiam rhetorum" (14.46), a rhetorical abundance, which like nature's own—Cicero is here urging the necessity of judgment as well as invention—must be used with discretion:

> just as fruitful and fertile fields produce not only crops but harmful weeds, so sometimes from these categories arguments are derived which are inconsequential, immaterial, or useless. (15.48)

The topics, then, are on the one hand conceived of in terms of the powers of natural places, and the metaphor that comes readily to mind is the fertility of field or garden; on the other hand, certain real places, like Cicero's Academy, are attributed the same efficacy (*vis admonitionis*) that the student is instructed to discover in the *loci* of rhetorical technique. There would seem to be a myth implicit in this way of speaking. An idea flourishes from its place, the "sedes argumentorum," like a Hesiodic god from its material seat, and the two cannot finally be separated. The idea is indeed the spiritual power discovered in the visual image or rather in the act of perception itself, in the initial concrete encounter with the world. This is, in any case, what I take to be the real seriousness behind Cicero's gardens and behind the often elaborate composition of place in his dialogues: a feeling that intellectual action cannot be divorced from its cosmic scene and that, if the first is to be communicated, the second must somehow be reconstituted. Such is, indeed, a possible interpretation of Plato's own insistence on the primacy of the spoken word; there is in living thought, beyond any conceptual abstraction, some residue of intuition, of vision, and this is what one means by being inspired by the deities of a place. Such deities, perhaps, admonish us from the Queen's gardens at Asolo, where Bembo's friends strive in their debate to give love "a certain form, in order that he might be more completely known" ("those very laurel trees which listen to us would still provide the evidence if they could speak");[109] or from the landscape, "verie plentifull and full of fruites," through which Castiglione takes us to hear how the nature of a true courtier, "a good seede in a fruitfull soyle," may properly be cultivated.[110] They are clearly present in many of the Ciceronian dialogues on which the Renaissance exercises were modelled.

Cicero speaks, for example, of the authority he is able to give his *De senectute* by having it spoken by Cato.[111] The authority in question is one of the imagination—"in reading my own work on Old Age I am at times so affected that I imagine Cato is the speaker and not myself"[112]—and it is the authority not only of a person but also of a place. Underlying the conceptual content of the dialogue is Cato's praise of husbandry, a panegyric that goes beyond the actual Cato's rather narrowly utilitarian arguments to an enthusiastic apprehension of the *vis* and *natura* of the soil itself:

> For these pleasures have an account in the bank of Mother Earth who never protests a draft, but always returns the principal with interest added. . . . And yet what I enjoy is not the fruit alone, but I also enjoy the soil itself, its nature and its power. (15.51)

Logically, this does no more than illustrate one pleasure left old age when the pleasures of the senses have departed; dramatically, though, it gives point to everything Cato has to say. It provides the imagery by which the imagination seizes (where the mind perhaps might not) his demand for self-dependence, for a life devoted to the "cultivation" of virtues that will yield their "fruits" in old age (3.9, 6.20, 19.71), for the acceptance of death as nature's gift of ripeness to be garnered in its proper season (10.33, 19.69, 19.71).

The broadest extension of this sense of natural potency is in the *De legibus,* where the *vis naturae* is seen as the universal basis of law (1.6.19); and it is here too—we may recall Petrarch's special fondness for the book—that the peculiar relation between philosophic discourse and the *vis admonitionis* of place is most clearly exemplified. Cicero's invocation of nature is generally an incursion into mythology rather than a precise philosophic definition, an approach not to an order abstractly apprehended but to a more fluidly sensed power, mind, or will,[113] something "like a tree or an animal."[114] The figure we are concerned with in

De legibus is less the ruler of the cosmic city than an avatar of Mother Earth, "fountain of laws" (1.5.16) and source of all goods, pouring them forth for man's use as a gift of her fruitfulness:

> For this reason, Nature has lavishly yielded such a wealth of things [*tantum rerum ubertatem*] adapted to man's convenience and use that what she produces [*gignuntur*] seems intended as a gift to us and not brought forth by chance.[115]

"Ye immortal gods," exclaims Cicero's companion, "how far back you go to find the origins of justice" (1.10.28): which is, one supposes, why an inquiry into law may best take place "among the stately poplars" at Arpinum. Cicero recalls (1.5.15–16) that Plato had discussed ideal laws and the institutions of states while walking to a grotto sacred to Zeus, the very source of his subject matter. Similarly, moving from the merely popular and conventional definition of law to its true "fountainhead" in nature (1.6.19–20) is for Cicero a movement identical with the trip from the city and its babble of false opinion to the blessed *otium* of the country life, to the direct apprehension of the natural scene:

> Do you grant us . . . that all Nature is governed? Surely I will grant it, if you insist upon it, for the singing of the birds about us and the babbling of the streams relieve me from all fear that I may be overheard by any of my comrades in the School. (1.6.21)

Cicero's villa at Arpinum, as Atticus observes, is no "luxurious country-palace" with marble walks and paneled ceilings; the pleasures of the place include no artificial "Nile" or "Euripus" but an actual river, the Fibrenus with its island garden that Petrarch remembered at Vaucluse and which now reminds Cicero's guest that:

> just as you, a moment ago, in your discussion of law and justice, traced everything back to Nature, in the same way Nature is absolutely supreme in things that men seek for the recreation and delight of the soul. (2.1.1–2)

The return to nature is ethically as well as intellectually important because it is a return to one's origins and therefore to one's proper dignity, virtue being nothing other than "nature perfected and developed to its highest point" (1.8.25). The special potency of Cicero's grove and island garden is not only the sense of release and clarification they provide, but also the sense of homecoming; a homecoming which is at once cultural—the forms are those of the Greek palaestra, *Phaedrus* is again invoked (2.3.6)—and personal, the spot being bound to Cicero not only by intellectual considerations, but "in my mind and heart" (2.1.3). "This is really my own fatherland," he exclaims, "for we are descended from a very ancient family [*stirpe antiquissima*] of this district; here are our ancestral sacred rites and the origin of our race" (2.1.3). The villa at Arpinum does not symbolize but actually presents what Cicero means by Nature: the sense of the place as the "cradle" of his being, as sacred Mother ("genuit," "procrearit"), his parent by birth as Rome is by adoption, "one by nature, the other by civilization."[116] Just this special vibration, the peculiar quality of a birthplace, is in fact cited by Mircea Eliade to illustrate the survival of the primitive sense of sacred space; "we are moved, I know not how," Cicero says, "by the place itself" where such traces cluster.[117] This mysterious effectiveness of places represents in Cicero's dialogues the margin of intuition that makes his gardens in more than a conventional sense the seat of his disputations and keeps his constant appeal to Platonic inspiration from being merely fanciful.

Such homecomings are of course a primary experience for men in the Renaissance. Burckhardt's formula for the double object of their discovery, man and nature, culture and milieu, is neatly illustrated in the often quoted account of Mantegna's trip to the Lago di Garda.[118] The painter and his humanist friends decipher classical inscriptions amid "wooded gardens so like paradise they might have sprung up as an abode of the most charming of the Muses"; and crowning themselves with the laurel they find growing in these enchanted isles, they play at resurrecting the emperors of Rome. A half century later, the convivial philosophers of Erasmus' "The Godly Feast" also constitute themselves a choir of Muses in order to enter a place whose bounty reminds them of the Fortunate Isles.[119] Presided over equally by Christ, Cicero, and Saint Socrates,

Eusebius' garden is at once a "little nest" in which the self is restored to its proper kingship and a place in which nature "is not silent but talks to [man] all the time" and spreads out before him its "green feast."[120]

It is perhaps in the gardens and groves that Cosimo de' Medici presents to the young Ficino for the *academia platonica rediviva* that the Renaissance makes its most concerted attempt to lay claim to the peculiar experience of such places. A sense of discovery and transformation that may remind us of Mantegna's adventure is suggested in a poem by Ficino's friend, Ugolino Verino. A vision transports him to a paradise garden where Cosimo is his guide and then to the garden's inmost grove, where the ancient sages still walk and Plato comes forth to embrace him as a friend and to praise the new spirit in Florence.[121] Ficino himself writes to Cardinal Bessarion of that spirit in solemnly prophetic tones: "the time has come [*venerunt, iam venerunt secula illa*] when Plato may rejoice in his divine spirit, and we his family give exceeding great thanks."[122] A historian has remarked that for his family, summoned up, as Ficino claims, "out of darkness into the light,"[123] the systematization of ideas was perhaps less important than the "evocation and reproduction in practical life of the forms and exterior rites of the ancient Academy."[124] "I had two parents," Ficino says, "one gave me birth, but by the other [Cosimo] I was reborn . . . and consecrated to the divine Plato."[125] By such remarks as these we may gauge the seriousness behind the classical nicknames and roleplaying or the famous commemorative re-enactments of Socrates' symposium (the nine participants "rounded out" the number of the Muses); furthermore we may venture to guess what aura invested the gardens of Careggi, where Ficino, burning a sanctuary lamp before a copy of Lorenzo's bust of Plato, was supposed to have reinstituted the Academy's worship of its apotheosized founder.[126]

If this story is (as has been supposed) only a malicious rumor, a little myth of Ficino's own invention may help to define the nature of the sanctity which undoubtedly did invest the Academy, both the one that had passed away and the one that was coming to birth. In the preface to his translation of Plato, Ficino explains what happened to divine Philosophy, offspring of Jupiter and Minerva, once she departed from the confines of the Academy gardens. Plato her priest had suitably reverenced ("excoluit") and adorned her with sweet perfumes and a thousand flowers; but

> whenever she wanders out of the gardens of the Academy, not only does she always lose her perfumes and her flowers, but often she falls into the hands of thieves; and, stripped of the insignia of her priesthood and of her dignity, she roams about aimlessly, nude and profaned. (*Opera*, p. 1129)

Now, however, Ficino goes on to explain, since she has returned "to the walls and gardens of the Academy, she resumes her ancient loveliness, and reposes joyfully here in her native land." Ficino has been praising Plato for uniting the sentences of philosophers with the flowers of oratory and the fables of poetry, but it is with the origin and nature of thought that he is ultimately concerned, not merely its expression. Just as the Ciceronian project of classical revival seems in Ficino's thought to have been clarified and deepened by its contact with Christian eschatology and notions of personal rebirth,[127] so has Cicero's ideal of culture, of wisdom united with eloquence, become a virtual theology, *pia philosophia,* as Ficino calls it. *Humanitas,* he writes Lorenzo's young cousin, is of no earthly origin but a heaven-born nymph, "above all others beloved by god"; she is Venus herself, in fact, whose "immense gift" to those who will love her is nothing less than "the very heavens."[128] The Academy is the place where these nuptials are to be celebrated. Plato's eloquence is for Ficino no human skill but the prophet's divine frenzy; and his wisdom, now reborn at Careggi, is less a series of precepts than a divine mystery by which the soul of the initiate is to be purged and turned again toward its heavenly homeland. What Ficino objects to in the peripatetics is their divorce of philosophy from the soul's experience: the true blossoming and aroma of thought is after all its engagement of the whole man. It is not so much the potential atheism of their ideas that makes the peripatetics spoilers as it is their desacralization of thought itself.[129]

The effects of this attitude on Ficino's own philosophizing have often been studied; André Chastel in particular has remarked on the almost talismanic potency that image and fable seem to have for him and on the way in which he tends in approaching the arcana of his system to substitute poetic frenzy for dialectic.[130] What concerns us here is the way in which this experiential context of thought, without which it is naked of savor and sanctity, finds its type in the gardens of Careggi, where (the preface goes on to say) young men learn the laws of morality "in the midst of play" and poets sing beneath the laurels. We should be mistaken, I think, to dissolve the poetic immediacy of the flowers and scents with which Philosophy is garbed into mere symbols of moral efficacy. For Ficino, as for Plato or Cicero, the thinker and the seer are not distinct; and ideas abstracted from vision, from the immediate experience of the philosopher rapt beyond himself, no longer retain their living wholeness. The words that issue from Careggi, on the other hand, are "living words" because the gardens of Careggi, like those of Tusculum or Colonus, are Philosophy's proper place, the homeland where, after long alienation, thought may come to rest and assume again its true nature.[131]

If the holiness of true thought makes it appropriate for Ficino to speak of his circle as a choir of Muses, the "little Academy of Phoebus" is equally dedicated to Pan. Our aim, Ficino says, is "to offer up daily to the Muses all the goods of the country life, and to lead the Muses, in their turn, as often as possible from the bustle of the city [*ab urbanis negotiis*] to the fields of Ceres and the hills of Bacchus."[132] Lorenzo, for example, tells of being led, in search of true felicity, from the bitter tempests of civil life to the "amena valle" of Careggi, "loco . . . lieto ed adorna," where amid sweet scents and green grass he encounters Marsilio himself, playing his lyre like a newborn Orpheus.[133] The thinkers of Ficino's circle, in fact, find it as inevitable to press natural energies into the service of intellectual ones as the poets (they are often the same men) to convert them to imaginative vision.[134] This is a matter not simply of the *imitatio Platonis,* but of a sensibility inherited from two traditions in which, I have been trying to suggest, the spirit of the original Academy is transmitted and transformed: the classical tradition of pastoral retirement, with its flight from *negotium,* and the monastic tradition of contemplation, with its search for the soul's homeland.[135] Petrarch had already begun to fuse the tradition of the monastery garden with that of Cicero's Academy; and the band of disciples Petrarch's friend, the Augustinian friar Luigi Marsili, gathered about him at the convent of Santo Spirito, provides at once a model for later humanistic academies and a direct link, both personal and ideological, with Ficino's own group.[136] Villa and cloister both are implicated in Ficino's inscription for the wall of his garden; and both are transformed in the new vision of philosophy's proper place he discovers at Careggi:

> A bono in bonum omnia diriguntur. Laetus in praesens. Neque censum existimes, neque appetas dignitatem; fuge excessum, fuge negotia, laetus in praesens.[137]
>
> (All things are directed from the good to the good. Rejoicing in the present you must not prize wealth or desire dignity. Flee excess, flee affairs, rejoicing in the present.)

Ficino's refrain seems to have been borrowed from Horace's "Otium divos rogat" (*Odes,* 2.16), an earlier warning against the distractions of *negotia,* and a notable defense of *otium* against traditional Roman arguments of the sort Cicero too had been compelled to deal with.[138] But as we shall see, the Latin poet's Epicurean ideal, really a form of ataraxia, is given significantly new content in the Academy.

> laetus in praesens animus quod ultra est
> oderit curare et amara lento
> temperet risu. nihil est ab omni
> parte beatum. (25–28)
>
> (Let the soul be joyful in the present, let it disdain to be anxious for what the future has in store, and temper bitterness with a smile serene. Nothing is happy altogether.)

"Laetus in praesens" might well have for Horace, as for Ficino, the weight of a precise philosophical distinction. *Laetitia,* in Cicero's exposition of Stoic and Epicurean thought, is distinguished from *libido* by its attachment to a present rather than an anticipated good and from *gaudium,* the Stoic's purely mental joy, in being still rooted, though a gladness of the mind, in a pleasing movement of sensation.[139] At the same time, *laetus* bridges the gap between philosophic thought and pastoral celebration, between the movements of man's soul and the energies of the natural world, just as Horace's ode itself attempts to do. The smiling fields or happy glades of eighteenth-century English verse may strike us as pathetic fallacy; but *laetus,* especially in Lucretius, from whom Horace adapted many of the ode's Epicurean topics,[140] refers us rather to an objective flourishing and harmony in which man, at privileged moments, may hope to participate. A faith in some such possibility would seem to animate the tribute Lorenzo de' Medici pays to Bacchus, the Virgilian *dator laetitiae* (*Aeneid,* 1.734) who presides in the streets of Florence over the amorous *otium* of nymphs and satyrs:

> ogni tristo pensier caschi:
> facciam festa tuttavia.
> Chi vuol esser lieto, sia:
> di doman non c'è certezza.[141]

(Banish every sad thought; let us keep perpetual holiday. Who wishes to be glad, let him be: of tomorrow, there is no certainty.)

Seen in the context of these lines, whose similarity to Ficino's inscription has often been noted, the garden at Careggi sounds like a privileged place, reserved from the rest of space just as the festive moment of carnival escapes the iron laws of time ("festa tuttavia"). We may be reminded of later Italian pleasure gardens whose walls proclaim them realms set apart and dedicated to the freedom of a new golden age:

> Whoever thou art, now be a free man, and fear not the fetters of the law. . . . In this golden age that promises security to all men, the master of the house will have no iron laws.[142]

If the triumph of Bacchus is to Lorenzo's lighter moods simply a call to seize the day and the flowers thereof, for Pico the same deity presides over a mystery that will lead man through "the visible signs of nature" to the intoxicating fullness of "God's house."[143] What the two Florentines have in common, however different their tones, is an expansiveness quite distinct from the spirit of Horace's careful husbandman at his modest table (2.16.14). The *laetitia* of the Roman poet's poor fields is embraced precisely because it is minimal and does not commit one greatly to fear or desire, a necessary prudence in a world where "nothing is happy altogether." At Careggi, however, all things "a bono in bonum . . .

diriguntur." "The divine beauty shines through everything and is loved in everything," Ficino explains in the *De amore,* so that the whole created world is drawn constantly back toward that Goodness from which it is derived. Love is a circle, flowing "a bono in bonum," and the symbol of this *circuitus spiritualis* is the dance of the three Graces: Splendor, the brightness of truth and virtue; Viriditas, the beauty of form and color; and, uniting the other two in perpetual harmony, Laetitia, "that pure, salutary, and perpetual delight which we feel in music."[144] For this sort of "mystical hedonism," there can be no absolute gulf between the true pleasure in which the meditative life discovers its fruition—"love seeks no other end than pleasure," Ficino writes[145]—and the sensual delights that merely, but usefully, shadow it. Just because the created world, as Pico says, is a sign, the pleasure we take in it operates upon our souls in the same way as does the sweetness of rhetoric: *voluptas* is the "true bait of the spirit," summoning it to precisely those "insolent" joys against which Horace warns.[146]

We are now in a better position to understand the playfulness of the poets and young musicians in the garden of Ficino's Academy. It will be useful, I think, to consider the whole passage, not as a proposal for inter-disciplinary studies, but as an anatomy of the living wholeness of the Academy's philosophy—of the relation between spiritual intuition and the experience, as image or as music, of the physical world:[147]

> Here young men, joyously and easily, understand the precepts of morality in the midst of joking and the art of disputation in the midst of play. Here mature men abundantly learn the discipline of public and of private affairs. Here old men, in place of this mortal life, will await an eternal one. In the gardens of the Academy, poets will hear Apollo sing beneath the laurels. In the vestibule of the Academy, orators will watch Mercury declaiming. Under the portico and in the court, lawyers and chiefs of state will listen to Jove in person consecrating the laws, formulating usage, guiding empires. In the inner sanctuary, finally, philosophers will recognize Saturn himself, contemplating celestial mysteries. And the priests and guardians of sacred things will find in every place arms with which they vigorously may defend piety against the impious.[148]

These young poets singing in the realm of flowers and perfumes are playing, indeed, but just such games (Ficino explains earlier in the preface) as Plato himself proved more serious than all the abstract gravity of the Stoics—"platonici ludi atque ioci." The same mythology, with its recognition of the limits of discursive reason, recurs in Ficino's little treatise, *De sole:*

> The Muses do not argue with Apollo: they sing. Mercury himself . . . even while treating of grave questions with Saturn and Jove, jests with Apollo. However, he does not play merely for amusement, but sports divinely. Would that we too could play thus![149]

Even Mercury, the inventor of disputation, abandons the rigor of dialectic when he turns to the god who presides over the music of the natural world; he finds no contradiction between his playful surrender to the Muses and his pursuit of the gravest mysteries. Like Ficino, perhaps, he knows "how much more easily the sight of Beauty inspires love than words can do."[150] The gardens of the Academy exist precisely in order to make room for the divine playfulness ("in the mode of Apollo and as it were poetical") to which the true philosopher aspires, the play of the imagination in creation's various light. Like the monastic thinkers we considered in the last chapter, Ficino has discovered that it is the beauty of the garden itself that "summons"[151] man to the secrets of the inmost sanctuary.

This paradisiac immanence of value explains why Ficino's garden may press into the forms of carnival or Saturnalia, of which we have already spoken, a Christian yearning for the freedom of the era *ante legem.* P. O. Kristeller has argued that the Academy in its organization adapts the forms of lay religious guilds of the sort with which Marsili had been associated.[152] Certainly the jocose philosophers of Careggi discover in their moment of holiday, a moment of flight from care and of surrender to present joy, an analogue to the monk's or contemplative's perpetual Sabbath. For Horace, the present is a desperate holding action against fortune, against a future whose only certainty is that all joy will fall at last into a single cadence with death:[153]

> Aequam memento rebus in arduis
> servare mentem, non secus in bonis
> ab insolenti temperatam
> laetitia, moriture Delli

(Remember, when life's path is steep, to keep an even mind, and likewise, in prosperity, a spirit restrained from overweening joy, Dellius, seeing thou art doomed to die.)

At Careggi, however, the future is already possessed in a present that transcends all the privations of time:

> We must live today; he who lives tomorrow never lives. If you want to live today, live in God [*si vis hodie vivere, vive Deo*] in whom yesterday and tomorrow are nothing other than today.[154]

Elsewhere Ficino stresses man's restless dissatisfaction with any single place—he alone is a wanderer in a world where all other things rest in their natural places—and his inability to find contentment in any present moment.[155] But in speaking of Careggi, where Philosophy discovers at last her proper place, his tone is quite different. "Vive hodie," "vivendum est autem hodie," "vivat hodie ac letus in presens":[156] such phrases keep recurring in Ficino's letters, and become a kind of gloss for the exhortation on the wall of the Academy. "Hodie" (today) is not a mere segment of endless change; it is *some* time, *kairos* pregnant with a future that scripture and liturgy insist has already been accomplished: "hodie Christus natus est," "hodie mecum eris in paradiso."[157] The message of the Academy echoes not only the angels' tidings to the shepherds, but also Christ's last message of comfort, a promise that became the very basis of Christian hopes for paradise in the present life, and of the typological imagination that discovers in the visible things of creation tokens of a present mystery. The prophecies of Virgil are fulfilled by the good news of Scripture, and the language of both find their way into Ficino's jubilant proclamations. "Redeunt hodie": this day are come again sacred mysteries that flourished in the Saturnian reign.[158] And the nature of these mysteries is perhaps suggested by the oracle, with its echoes of the Lord's Prayer and its astrological lore, at once parody and parable, Ficino claims to have received on Mount Vecchio from the spirit of Cosimo de' Medici himself. The conjunction of the planets, the spirit announces, has brought into harmony for the immortals the gifts of Apollo and of Pan, and now, in the celebrations of the Academy, this double music must sound for man as well: "This is our will, Marsilius, that even as it is in heaven today, so also should it be on earth."[159]

In order to understand the sense in which this dream might be a program for Careggi, and perhaps also to gauge the distance that separates its gardens from those of the cloister, we need finally to consider the possibilities that would be revealed to Ficino in his tentative, yet deeply felt, approaches to astrology and magic.[160] The Venus-*Humanitas* Ficino tells young Lorenzo Pierfrancesco he must claim for his own spouse is no abstract educational ideal, but a "nymph of excellent comeliness": the embodiment of that cosmic beauty and harmony—"O beautiful spectacle!"—by which he can measure his own possible nobility.[161] Such a deity will lure men not only to the study, but also "through gardens and verdant meadows"; and in fact the goddess of the Academy's paideia is not finally distinct from the *alma Venus* of whom Ficino speaks in his magical or astronomical works, the planetary force that stirs, through air and odors, the vital spirits of scholars otherwise grown musty (*Opera,* p. 520). Ficino himself lived perpetually in the shade of a saturnian melancholy, and there is reason to suppose that the potency he hoped to discover in the gardens and fields of Careggi was of this specifically occult variety; that the spiritual illumination pursued by the Academy was intricately involved with, and perhaps in the last analysis not wholly distinguishable from, an enhancement of natural vitality.

The *Libri de Vita* are written "among the flowers in the domain of Careggi":[162] green is Venus' special color,[163] Ficino says, and in a chapter devoted to the "conversation of old men under the sign of Venus in green fields," he explains that to pluck the flowers of fields and gardens is to receive through pleasure the gift of life itself (*Opera,* p. 520). Materials for his study of the astrological potencies of plants would be near at hand in Lorenzo's famous botanical gardens at Careggi, where Botticelli has been supposed to have gathered the flora for his *Primavera*[164]—itself (critics have argued recently) a sort of talisman designed to secure for Lorenzo Pierfrancesco at Castello precisely those Venerean influences Ficino was seeking at Careggi.[165] This rather tenuous link is less important than our understanding that actual flowers, the crocus, lily, violet, and rose sacred to Venus, function in the same way as Botticelli's putatively talismanic images. The blooms at Careggi are neither mere signs of a wholly spiritual reality nor sources of a purely physical pleasure or relief. The principle, rather, is of a consonance between physical and spiritual and between man and the forces of his cosmos. The harmony of images, of air and odors and sounds, is the means by which the human *spiritus* may be prepared—tuned, really—to receive the astral influences of the *spiritus mundanus,* and so to participate in the harmonies by which all things are constituted in their perfection.[166]

The magician's sense of the potencies waiting in nature to be liberated had traditionally seized upon the imagery of the garden (*arbor philosophica, rosa philosophorum*) as its most telling symbol.[167] Ramon Lull, in particular, found in trees and herbs a type of the divine potency by which the natural world might serve as a ladder to the spiritual;[168] and Paracelsus' thought, which has been traced to the synthesis of the *Libri de vita,* is permeated with imagery of blossoming, of the flourishing of seeds divinely impregnated, of a flowery new creation.[169] Gardening and alchemy continued to be associated in actual practice. Jacques Gohory, a friend of de Baïf, wrote an alchemical interpretation of Colonna's garden romance, the *Hypnerotomachia,* and conducted a "lyceum" in an elaborately laid out apothecary's garden.[170] The Englishman Hugh Platt interpolates into practical advice about fertilizers and pest control (for "vulgar wits" and "country Coridons") esoteric instructions for a "philosophicall garden" in which "heavenlie influences" alone will issue in a "strange and admirable" flourishing.[171] Ficino himself found in the garden not just an example but the very archetype of the magician's proper concerns. If God himself is a heavenly farmer, the magus too cultivates the cosmos precisely as the farmer or gardener cultivates the soil.[172] In Pico's words, "as the farmer weds his elms to vines, even so does the magus wed earth to heaven."[173]

In any case, what is important is that the Hermetic apprehension of deity in all things is in the Renaissance not merely, as it seems often to have been for medieval magicians, a technical or operative concept. It is, rather, a way of seeing and experiencing the natural world. As the studies of Walker and Yates have shown, the magic of Ficino is largely a subjective operation, less concerned with altering the objective ordinance of things than with utilizing and transforming, in the operator himself, the *vis imaginativa* that is man's link with the cosmos.[174] It is through the vehemence of his imagination, writes Ficino's disciple, Francesco da Diacceto, that the magus becomes pregnant with the "kindred powers of the heavens."[175] And if images or harmonies may be manipulated for demonic power—Ficino is never unaware of the danger of such imputations—they become for the sage objects of an angelic contemplation: he is concerned not with "spirits separated from all matter" but with the powers of the natural world, not with the evocation of alien intelligences but with an ecstatic transformation of his own.[176] For Ficino and for his sixteenth-century successors, revealingly, the occult potencies of music, words, or images are not clearly distinguished from the power of their beauty, from the sort of charm or fascination that remind us of Orpheus, whose story is supposed to have adorned Ficino's own lyre.[177] The magician's art enfranchises the imagination and makes the affective life, the sensibility, the arena in which he confronts the cosmic powers, the instrument by which (as Ficino boasts) the true priest of the Muses "measures and grasps the whole world."[178] All this may suggest why a sense of magic potency finds suitable expression in the revival of the god-haunted landscape of antique pastoral. Pico's citation of the Virgilian marriage of heaven and earth suggests, indeed, that Florentine magic was above all a way of taking seriously just the motif by which the poets of twelfth-century Platonism and of courtly love had already celebrated their sense of cosmic harmony and plenitude.[179] The ancient poets, quite simply, were discovered to have been telling the truth. If Lorenzo's botanical garden was a source of Ficino's medical speculations, it was also—and by that token, one is tempted to infer—the haunt of gods, where Bembo (another assiduous amateur of gardens) was invited by a poet friend to wander among the pale olives sacred to Minerva, the myrtles of Venus, the oak trees of Jove. Every flower and every tree that grows anywhere in the world, he claims, makes of Careggi a place that realizes and surpasses all the myths of Hesperides, Alcinoüs, and Semiramis.[180]

For what is striking is the spontaneity with which on even the most casual occasions Ficino's rustic retreat is imagined in terms of the recovery of sacred space. I am suggesting that this way of speaking is not merely literary or nostalgic but records a sense of actual discovery and lays claim to what has been revealed. In the name of the place itself is uncovered the seat of the Graces, *charitum ager,*[181] and so—we may remember the similar discovery by Spenser's Callidore on Mount Acidale—the purest source of all reality. The dance of the Graces comes to symbolize all the triads whose weaving makes the universe of Florentine Platonism.[182] But however arcane the symbolism may become, we should remember that the three sisters are first of all flower-crowned goddesses of the earth's fertility, attendants of Venus whose very names would seem to refer their potencies to the landscape around Careggi: Splendor, Viriditas, Laetitia.[183] Like Petrarch responding to a comparable potency at Vaucluse, Ficino on Mount Vecchio invokes Apollo's inspiration for his Orphic songs.[184] The oracle we have already mentioned, the promise of the reconciliation of heaven and earth in the program of the Academy, gathers force from the punning that finds in Cosimo's pronouncement the voice of a cosmic Pan, the spirit of the landscape perceived as a harmonious unity, as well as of the patron who has given Ficino his own corner to cultivate. At Careggi, this spirit promises, soil and soul will be cultivated together, the flute of Pan will sound with the lyre of Apollo, and the marriage of agriculture and letters will joyously be consummated.[185]

This feeling for the sacredness of particular places, of gardens, fields, and woods, seems to embrace both homecomings implicit in that venerable pun, *in principio:* the resuscitation of a Golden Age ("in the beginning"), and the discovery of the order by which the knot of nature is secured ("in principle"). The circumstances of such returns may be suggested by a conversation that will remind us, too, of Mantegna's excursion on the Lago di Garda—or of Charles's in Naples. Near the villa traditionally associated with the *Decameron,* Ficino and Pico are discussing the salubriousness of the site—they seem to have in mind Alberti's prescriptions in the *Della famiglia*[186]—when the villa of Leonardo Bruni suddenly materializes before them. "Do we not have before us now, as in a dream, the forms we were just so earnestly imagining and hoping for?" Pico asks. "Or have we perhaps by the power of imagination alone created that form which our minds devised?"[187] To conceive the imagination's work as a dream that comes true is to make of the imagination the agency of rapture, of revelation. We may recall the voyages of other architectural visionaries of the time: Colonna, who discovers the true classical art only by winning his way to the Isle of Cythera; Filarete, for whom the paradigm and source of architectural measure is the perfection of Adam's own beauty, and who is led (like the heroes of romance) by two stags to a holy man's hilltop *locus amoenus,* the future site of his utopian Sforzinda.[188] In all these instances, the journey to a fantastic landscape becomes, paradoxically, the discovery of the real world, the recovery of one's own significant past; one's natural place, in fact. What is revealed to Pico and Ficino is the right and natural rule of building, "recta & Physica aedificandi ratio," a harmony at once aesthetic and medical, providing pleasure for the eye and salubrious air for the body. And like the earlier adventurers, they express their sense of the perfection of their discovery with the veneration due a sacred place, which they proceed, only half playfully, to fit out with holy woods and oracular presences: "Happy man," says Pico, "who has the chance when he sets aside public business to dwell in a holy shrine; a shrine, I say, for it is placed in the midst of sacred groves and surrounded by twenty temples of the gods." The physical and the spiritual are one, mediated by a sense of the past recovered, of the idea recalled and brought down to earth in the images that shadow it. And the sacred order that materializes is above all one by which the human mind takes its own measure, through which it arrives at its own proper proportion. The philosophers conclude that only a sage could have built in such a manner: *dominus* is inferred from *domus,* the greatness of the man from the propitiousness of the place.

IV

Guillaume de Lorris and the Garden of Love

SERVIUS' IDENTIFICATION of *amoenus* and *amorem*, a lovely place and a place for loving,[1] would seem to have codified a tradition that was more than literary, one that drew on an early Roman feeling for the special potency of garden gods and found new, more glamorous forms of expression in Hellenistic culture.[2] Priapus, Flora, Pomona, and even Venus herself are protectors of Roman gardens; a traveler in late antiquity tells of seeing the Knidian Aphrodite, in the midst of a lushly planted grove whose very breezes were "fraught with love," rise nude and seductively smiling from her bath, like a heroine of romance.[3] But perhaps the best exemplification of the requirements of Servius' *locus amoenus* is Calypso's grotto: a place wholly given over to love and therefore (in the commentator's second punning etymology) "quasi amunia, hoc est sine fructu" (without utility, that is, without fruit). Ruskin cites the fertility of King Alcinoüs' garden—it had become proverbial in Latin verse—as evidence of a strictly utilitarian attitude toward nature.[4] But here, in Calypso's place of love, the emphasis falls on the gratuitous lushness of fountain and flowery meadow, grove and proffered grapes. And the power of the place is not in the rigor of its geometry—as in Alcinoüs' garden, or in Cyrus's imperial grove, moralized by Xenophon and again by Browne—but in the song of the goddess that seems to animate the whole. It is a place (like later realms of Venus) discovered not where the journey returns to its starting point and restores the hero to a familiar order, but where his adventure penetrates furthest from the quotidian.

This suggests a fundamental distinction. In sacred places man discovers a special bond with the world. But if the royal garden celebrates man's power in this encounter, the enhancement and perfection of his being, in gardens of love the imagination concedes the helplessness of its rapture and the strangeness of its discovery. ("What does the intellect seek if not to transform all things into itself," Ficino asks, "and what does the will strive to do if not to transform itself into all things?")[5] Like the fairy pleasances of Celtic tradition,[6] such spots are not just conveniences for lovers but incitements to love, centers of a sometimes dangerous power. Petronius has been credited with introducing the *locus amoenus* into the repertory of ancient rhetoricians, and the garden he celebrates as fit for love ("dignus amore locus") is precisely the spot where a latter-day Circe hopes to persuade the jaded Encolpius, "ambushed in the grass," to feel "the strange insensible power of some god, drawing us together."[7] Calypso's wiles are paradigmatic for such enchantresses, but even without their mediation, the charm of the place itself often serves to melt away all the determinations of prudence or fixed intention. We may think of the gardens of Greek romance where Love himself dwells, or of the garden of *La Celestina,* under whose influence even the prudish maid Lucretia begins to "melt like snow beneath the sun" and run mad with pleasure.[8]

Juvenal complained that modern "improvements" had robbed gardens of their numinous quality, of that "certain sense of sanctity" Pliny said was always attached to garden spots.[9] But Roman amateurs (as we have seen in the case of Cicero) were still eager to claim the glamour of the sacred places in art and literature for their own more domestic constructions. The garden of love is a recurrent horticultural motif, from Hadrian's Villa with its Vale of Tempe and Temple of Venus, to the sixteenth-century Villa Doria (called "il paradiso"), whose gardens serve as a background for Jan Massys' "Cytherean Venus."[10] In the Middle Ages, the atmosphere of the erotic romance survives especially in the Eastern gardens that impressed visiting Western dignitaries like Otto I's ambassador, Bishop Liudprand,[11] and convinced the common soldiers of Marco Polo that they were being tempted by the houris of a pagan paradise.[12] It was not the sober example of Cicero or Pliny that inspired great pleasure gardens like the famous thirteenth-century park at Hesdin, but the gardens of Longus or Achilles Tatius, fantastically elaborated with fountains, pools, and automata, golden trees and choiring birds. Just this influence, in fact, was what suggested to the West the possibilities of fantasy inherent in the senses and so—especially from the twelfth century onwards and especially as it was diffused from Sicily and Naples—defined what came to be meant by the "pleasure garden," the place of "sweet repose."[13] Like Charlemagne before him, the Lord of Love in the *Roman de la Rose* has had his trees fetched from the land of the Saracens.[14] And if the queen's garden at Asolo seems to Bembo a suitable spot for discourses on love, it is partly because it reproduces—with its cross pergolas, pleached alleys, and lush vines, its emphasis on running water and the play of shadow and sunlight—the garden in which Clitophon discovered the adumbration of Leucippe's face or the grottoes and gardens in which Daphnis and Chloë discovered Eros himself.[15]

Bembo's friends, however, are anxious to understand love as well as to feel its power. Like previous artists or philosophers, they want to give love "a certain form, in order that he might be more completely known"; and realizing that their subject "can never be conceived by ear alone, however long we speak of it," they turn instinctively to the unspoken language of the queen's garden. "Those very laurel trees which listen to us would still provide the evidence if they could speak."[16] It is perhaps this dialogue between self and world, a dialogue characteristic of love's garden, that we find most difficult to understand in a literal way. Like the *Phaedrus,* Bembo's treatise is predicated on going outdoors: "let sleep lie behind the curtains of our beds [while we] go into the garden." "How wrong of us not to have come here all these days," the courtiers exclaim, as they prepare to yield themselves to the invitation of running water and attentive shadows.[17] If we are accustomed to think of feelings as subjective, as in some sense "inside," love's peculiar openness to the world will elude us. We will too quickly resolve into allegory or hyperbole a lover's hope for intimations of paradise and thereby miss the full import of those realms of Venus to which medieval and Renaissance poets are again and again conducting us. If gardens and other lovely spots seem to speak of love, it is because such places are themselves the very language by which love manifests its nature to human understanding.[18] Love and gardens are linked, in other words, by traditions of thought as well as of myth; and the two traditions interpenetrate, support, and transform one another.

The Middle Ages did not need the example of the *Phaedrus* to think of love as the soul's encounter with the world, its quest for its homeland.[19] When Renaissance theorists recovered the Platonic text, they were able to fit it into a well-established pattern, one that treated the affections in terms of cosmic adventuring, and held as it were in solution the myth that stirred in the breezes at Asolo or Hesdin and received paradigmatic expression in the *Roman de la Rose*. As I have already suggested, both Augustine and Aquinas take as their model in discussing the nature and power of love the Aristotelian movement of all things to their proper places. What we call emotion is motion toward a goal, and the goal is the actuation of what is only potential in the striving lover.[20] Cavalcanti inspired an exegetical stir by submitting his passion to scholastic categories of potency and act,[21] but his innovation lay in making abstract and intellectual what was already mimed in the behavior of his predecessors: in their insatiable searching of the world to discover their own fulfillment. Dante admires the dialectical rigor of the new style, but he is not tempted in his own imagination to divorce power from place.[22] The Earthly Paradise (*loco proprio*) in which his dreamer discovers "the functioning of his own powers"[23] merely formalizes the aspiration of the troubadours before him—their attempt to seize through the "joy" of desire that "enhancement of physical and spiritual vigor"[24] they find all about them in the wakening landscape of a new season.

> Can l'erba fresch'e.lh folha par,
> E la flors boton'el verjan,
> E.l rossinhols autet e clar
> Leva sa votz, e mou so chan,

> Joi ai de lui, e joi ai de la flor,
> E joi de me e de midons major;
> Daus totas partz sui de joi claus e sens,
> Mas sel es jois que totz autres jois vens.[25]

(When the fresh grass and the leaf appears, and the flower blossoms on the bough, and the nightingale raises high and clear its voice and pours out its song, joy I have for it, and joy for the flower, and joy for myself and for my lady yet more: on all sides I am bound and circled by joy, but that is joy which all other joys overwhelms.)

Characteristically, such lovers find themselves, like Bernart de Ventadorn, enclosed with joy: not merely happy, but en-joying, be-joyed with joy—*jauzens jauzitz.*[26] The word *joi* itself—one has only to read over the texts assembled by Father Denomy—takes on an almost incantatory power; and its transformations, especially the way it slides from active to passive participle, reinforce the sense of an ecstatic merging of subject and object, by which the poet at once awakens to the world and comes again into his own identity. "Since the air is thus refreshed, it's fitting that my person be refreshed [*renovel*]," writes Peire d'Auvergne, "so that there flower and burst forth that which within me is stirring."[27] Joy itself "blossoms";[28] and the recovered clarity of the landscape, "when the fountain's stream runs clear as it used to do,"[29] becomes an illumination of the poet's sensibility, a freshness identical with the "refinement" of the song by which he attempts to approximate the birds' own Latin.[30]

Such awakenings, as I have suggested, occur under the auspices of an Eros that takes its model from physics, all other levels of love being derived from the natural love of the elements. Although value is certainly not excluded from an analysis of potency and act, persons may be accommodated with some difficulty.[31] The problem has chiefly been raised—and we have touched upon it—in considering the monk's devotions, but the same definitions hold good for secular lovers as well. The only object of earth's desire as it plunges toward the center of the cosmos is the image of its own actuation in that place.[32] Similarly, courtly (and Platonic) lovers tend to become no more than places for each other's development: "as in a mirror, in his lover he beholds himself and does not know it."[33] The egoism involved in these infatuations—from l'Amant with his single-minded devotion to his own stratagems and sensations, to

Othello, whom moralistic critics like to accuse of being less concerned with Desdemona than with his own sense of the world[34]—is a measure at once of the difficulty and of the seriousness of the attempt. When the lover is successful in his venture (we have seen as much in Petrarch's case) the person with whom he is most inextricably engaged is simply the whole cosmos.[35] For mystic and troubadour alike, "everything in nature is changed," and "the whole earth [becomes] like a single garden of love."[36] These successes define the nature of the courtly garden: in his helpless rapture the lover is returned to himself, and the mysterious potency of space comes to seem a voice that speaks to the soul's own aspirations. To find themselves in a place of love is often, for lovers in this tradition, to give a wholly literal sense to their being *in* love with each other, for their passion is precisely this homecoming, this journey from impoverishment to possession.

The journey and its fruition will of course be imagined in a variety of modes, but the relation between lady and landscape, between emotion and place, seems to be an essential one, even where the values in which the lover seeks to participate transcend the merely natural joy of the troubadours.[37] Dante's growth in and towards the beauty he perceives through Beatrice, for example, is a spiraling apprehension of the whole world as the mirror of God, of all things as leaves in "the garden of the eternal gardener" (*Paradiso,* 26.64–65); when Beatrice reappears in the Earthly Paradise, a critic has written, her pageant "seems to break out of the forest, out of the air and the trees, as if the forest on all sides gave up its secret."[38] And in Renaissance discussions, even those Platonic lovers most scornful of the senses tend to imagine their transcendence in terms of some readjustment between man and his cosmic scene. The actualization of the possible intellect—by which man is admitted to that "new life" which is nothing other than his own essential nature—becomes a divine marriage with the spirit (Angel, Sophia, Anima Mundi), who, like the poet's lady, contains within herself "li fiori e la verdura/e ciò che luce od è bello a vedere."[39] Leone Ebreo is able to summon the awe and excitement of "the new navigation," of unknown worlds beyond familiar horizons, in order to define the moment when, in a single act of vision, the lover is united ("felice coppulatione") with all the variety of the created world.[40] Or the sensuous appeal of traditional pastoral may be pressed into the service of an ideal realm—*Phaedo's* "truth earth" again—whose greenness differs from that of our world only in being unfading. Cardinal Bembo learns from a hermit on his mountaintop (as Plato did from Diotima) that true love must leave behind "this filthy ball of earth."[41] But the terms by which he defines desire's resting place suggest nothing so much as the wonder and rapt speculation with which his friend Giorgione, a man who also (according to Vasari) took "unceasing delight in the joys of love," was discovering the hills and fields around Asolo.[42] Consider a man who has lived all his life beneath the sea, Bembo says:

> But were he to rise into our region and see the vivid greenery of fields and woods and hills; the variety of creatures, some born to feed us and some to aid us; the cities, temples, houses standing here; the many arts and ways of life; the purity of the air; the brilliance of the sun which by scattering its light through heaven, makes the day and kindles the stars with which the darkness of the night is splendid; and all the other so various and endless beauties of the world,—he would understand how mistaken he had been and would not wish his old life back at any price.[43]

The distance between Bembo and the *Roman de la Rose* is of course thoroughly visible in the distance between the Arcadian landscapes of Giorgione and Gothic miniatures of Deduit's garden.[44] In the next chapter I shall try to suggest some ways of thinking about the differences between them. Here, I want to suggest that too much is lost if we consider the garden of any lover in this tradition merely a scenic expression of the way he feels—too much of the poetic effect and too much of the real import of that effect. Just the opposite would be closer to the truth. His passion is a striving to realize, in his own nature, the reality he discovers. We shall be thinking about Deduit's garden as an enactment of this striving—even for the Renaissance Guillaume's poem remains paradigmatic, "inimitable en description"[45]—and so as a nexus of those impulses we have been associating with gardens of love. I shall be interested, in the rest of this chapter, not so much in the strictly literary themes of the *Roman de la Rose,* in the conscious designs it has on its readers, as in the phenomenology of the imagination at work in it, and in how that imagination is related to configurations of thought and feeling in the culture of which it is an expression. I shall be using, in addition to Guillaume's text, the English version which is usually attributed at least in part to Chaucer and which is, like any good translation, an interpretation and re-creation of whatever is most alive in its original.

1

What Guillaume's protagonist stumbles into is a real place, and, like the hero of any earlier romance or indeed like King Charles in Naples, he must be initiated into its possibilities gradually, even though in the end what he discovers will be himself. It has been argued that the "details of the garden . . . have nothing to do with any conceivable geographical location," but exist only insofar as they refer us to abstractions about the protagonist's state of mind.[46] But this to short-circuit the process of discovery the poem is concerned both to narrate and to exemplify: the husk is the *way* to any sentence we may discover, just as it is only in the garden that the lover comes to perceive the true nature of his goal. Later, looking back on his "twenty yer of age,/Whan that Love taketh his cariage/Of yonge folk,"[47] he can of course see the analogy between the season and his own youth; in small and great worlds both, it is a "tyme of love and jolite" (52). But the human joy is only a potentiality, and the analogy with the season therefore only possible, until the adventure has been confronted.

Surely, then, it is better to say (as Charles Williams has remarked of Beatrice) that the garden is "an exterior fact and not . . . an interior desire . . . sight and not invention."[48] Like the *Vita Nuova,* the *Roman de la Rose* is the dictation of Love himself,[49] not the poet's own ambitious fantasy. This is why Guillaume is able to call up for his hero's adventure all the peculiar glamour of the romances, the summons to new possibilities, the penetration of secret places.[50] The lover's search for and discovery of the "wiket small" (528) that admits him to the garden belongs to this tradition, as does the little path on his right hand ("a destre") that leads him to Sir Mirth.[51] We may find something of ritual, too, in the lustrations of hands and face (*Romaunt,* 96, 125) that mark his progress toward the pool of Narcissus.

But for our sense that what we are watching is an initiation, it is the rhythm of the narration itself that is most important: its constant pressing toward actualization. The lover advances in well-marked stages toward the center of a garden enclosed in a perfect square, guided by bird song sweet enough to gladden the whole world (*Romaunt,* 498), toward the fountain that is the sum of all fountains ("De la fontaine c'est la fins" [1528]), the inexhaustible source of the green that lies all around it, no more to die in winter "than may the see be drye" (1566). He moves from enclosure to enclosure through this "leu riche" (480) (a "yerd" [492], Chaucer says, a lodge or inn), until he catches sight of the "roser chargid full of rosis,/That with an hegge aboute enclos is" (1651–52). The poem itself imitates his centric progress, spiraling from the May morning to the dream of the morning to the garden itself, and marking the stages of his entry into the garden by the ecphrases or exempla (the wall, Idleness, Love's courtiers, Narcissus) that interrupt and formalize the chronological account of his expanding awareness.[52] And as we proceed toward this center, we proceed toward the pure source of what has been adumbrated from the very beginning: "So riche a yerd was never noon/Of briddes song, and braunches grene" (492–93). The odd effect of *déjà vu* with which we are launched from the actual May morning to the dream of the same morning does not mark the transition from reality to fantasy, even though "Many men sayn that in sweveninges/ Ther nys but fables and lesynges" (1–2). On the contrary, we are moving from the mere potentiality of the lover's present moment into the actuality that is to be, an actuality that comes into existence for this particular man when he seizes upon what is potential in his momentary experience and makes it his own dream.[53] The bird chorus swells progressively into angelic concord, and in the garments of the God of Love, decorated with all the splendors of creation, the "hewes ful dyvers" of earth's quaint robe find their full realization.[54] The lover's journey to the fountain source has been thought to reflect that of Phillis and Flora in the medieval Latin

Altercatio, and it is indeed very like their progression through meadow and forest to the Paradise of Love, and thence, in the center of that, to the *locus occultus* where the cult of the god flourishes most greenly.[55]

The reference to a *locus occultus* is relevant to more than the plot of Guillaume's poem. The description of a season ("chronographia") is concerned traditionally less with mere appearances than with the evocation of powers. Matthew of Vendôme's example makes clear the degree to which this figure of speech is allied to personification, the goddess incipient in the abstraction, manifesting herself in the rule she imposes on her domain:

> The seasons of the year are four: spring grows warm, summer simmers [*aestas aestuat*], autumn brings the vine, winter chills.
>
> Rosy spring runs riot with delicate flowers, and labors to paint Rhea with more flowery foliage. Summer, the friend of the sun, grows hot and, overflowing with heat, exerts herself to live up to her name. Vine-dresser autumn, cupbearer of Bacchus, toasts the delights of the grape, replenishes the barn with his harvest. Winter shivers in her ragged garb, stepmother of the flowers, bitter companion for a playful heart.[56]

It is into such a domain, alive with a deity's powers, that Guillaume's narrator awakens; the "new season" in which he finds himself is not, as has sometimes been assumed, merely a time of sensuous lushness. The emphasis, rather, is on growth, renewal, change of estate; and the sensuous qualities of the scene tend to be transmuted into adjuncts of these energies—clarity, light, or (especially in Chaucer's version) the sweetness and tenderness appropriate to the newborn.

> In tyme of love and jolite,
> That al thing *gynneth waxen* gay,
> For ther is neither busk nor hay
> In May, that it nyl shrouded ben,
> And it with *newe* leves wren.
> These wodes eek *recoveren* grene,
> That drie in wynter ben to sene;
> And the erthe *wexith* proud withalle,
> For swote dewes that on it falle,
> And the pore estat forget
> In which that wynter had it set. (52–62, italics mine)

Goliard poets and the troubadours had already adapted the renewal imagery of hymns and sequences, of hexaemera and manuals of allegory, to a secular awakening in a natural springtime, a "new time," when "the fountain's stream runs clear as it used to do."[57] If the spring opening in the courtly lyric sometimes became formulaic, its association here with the lover and his paradise of love is crucial. Love's garden is the place in which all the stirring possibilities of the time are actualized.

One such actualization is in the description of the garden itself. Nouns take the place of verbs, and the earlier "unspoken energy" and expectation are replaced by the hyperbole with which the plenitude of an achieved creation is catalogued, by an enthusiastic speaking of names.[58] But even more important for our purposes is the destiny the lover finds for himself, his participation in this creation. What the renewal imagery means for Guillaume's hero is that he will not be merely a baffled tourist in his earthly paradise: a change of place involves a change of mind, and what he seeks is not merely a diversion, but, as is the case with Dante—or with Charles in Naples—a way of life, a new life. "Whoso myghte so wel fare,/For better lyf durst hym not care" (1323–24). The splendor of the newly proud earth inspires the lover to adorn himself, and the stages by which he moves toward the center of the garden are stages in which he discovers unsuspected possibilities of his own nature:

And never saugh I, er that day
The watir that so wel lyked me;
And wondir glad was I to se
That lusty place and that ryver (120–23)

For sich solas, sich joie, and play
I trowe that nevere man ne say,
As was in that place delytous. (487–89)

And certis, whan I herde her song,
And saw the grene place among,
In herte I wex so wondir gay
That I was never erst, er that day,
So jolyf, nor so wel bigoo,
Ne merye in herte, as I was thoo. (689–94)

At every point, what is seen or heard is not mere data, but an extension of the lover's capacity for response; bird song and green bough chime in a single sensation of blossoming that is not distinguishable from the waxing emotion of his own heart:

> Alone I wente in my *plaiyng,*
> The smale foules song *harknyng,*
> That peyned hem, ful many peyre,
> To synge on bowes blosmed feyre. (105–108, italics mine)
>
> Qui de chanter mout *s'angoissoient,*
> Por les vergiers qui *florissoient.* (101–102, italics mine)

The lover's gaiety, like the joy of the troubadours, is no mere subjective mood but an objective concord in which he comes gradually to share: he is "be-joyed" by the scene as he penetrates its embrace:

> Mout estoit bele l'acordance
> De lor piteus chant a oïr;
> Toz li monz s'en doit esjoïr.
> Je endroit moi m'en esjoï
> Si durement, quant je i'oï (484–88)
>
> Ful blisful was the accordaunce
> Of swete and pitous song thei made,
> For all this world it owghte glade.
> And I mysilf so mery ferde,
> Whan I her blisful songes herde (496–500)

His adventure begins with the obscure call of the time and the obscure reflection in a river of the "medewe softe, swote and grene" (128). His early investigations of the garden are a kind of play (under the aegis of Idleness) because they represent a release from quotidian purposefulness and yet discover their own ritual manner of coherence; and it is this sense of a coherence lying beyond the range of conscious intention that makes them dreamlike as well: like the portress of Deduit's gate, who has no other care than to adorn herself, Guillaume's hero is making himself ready, although he does not know for what. It is only at the center of the garden, at the pool beneath the pine, that the call is finally answered and he *becomes* l'Amant.[59] And this occurs only when the entire place, with its thirty-five varieties of trees, its innumerable species of birds and flowers, passes into and becomes the form of his own reflection.

The pool itself marks the simultaneity of two discoveries: of the world and of the lady. The sun's bright beams, refracted by the water, make visible in the two crystals at the bottom of the pool all the garden's various light, just as the reflecting mind—where all that's made "does straight its own resemblance find"—catches the prismatic image of God's pure light shining in the mirror of creation:

> For whanne the sonne, cler in sighte,
> Cast in that well his bemys brighte,
> . . . .
> Thanne taketh the cristall stoon, ywis,
> Agayn the sonne an hundrid hewis,
> Blew, yelow, and red, that fresh and newe is.
> Yitt hath the merveilous cristall
> Such strengthe that the place overall,
> Bothe flour, and tree, and leves grene,
> And all the yerd in it is seene. (1573–82)

Platonists and mystics were used to scrutinizing the *speculum mundi* for some rays of that divine light in which they might recognize their own true nature;[60] Physis herself, in Bernard Sylvester's epic, *De mundi universitate,* first sees the approach of the divine Urania reflected in the fountain of matter.[61] But l'Amant is less concerned with the white radiance of eternity than with the dance of hues and images; and the discovery by which he is enamored is just that all this freshness and variety comes alive and can be grasped in his own "speculation":

> For ther is noon so litel thyng
> So hid, ne closid with shittyng,
> That it ne is sene, as though it were
> Peyntid in the cristall there. (1597–1600)

The marvel of the pool, in which (like Narcissus) l'Amant seems for the first time to recognize his true visage, is this revelation of the world as a resource of his own consciousness. But at the same time the stones also suggest the eyes of the beloved—twin mirrors of Narcissus in which Bernart de Ventadorn had already told of losing himself.[62] There is no necessary contradiction between these two associations. Unlike Marvell, Guillaume's hero is not alone in his paradise; the amorous red and white are no distraction but become the very means by which "the happy Garden-state" is to be comprehended. What the crystals most fascinatingly reveal is a rose bower, all enclosed with a hedge; a bower which is the epitome and innermost nest of the whole garden. The lady's eyes are to her lover's gaze an image—in the words of an earlier poet, "mundi rosa," "cunctis speculum"[63]—by which all the potencies of the garden may be focused and internalized and so become his goal, that which he must try to possess. Seen in the lady's eyes, the world appears under the aspect of desire:[64]

> For whoso loketh in that mirrour,
> Ther may nothyng ben his socour
> That he ne shall there sen somthyng
> That shal hym lede into lovyng. (1605–1608)

To be sure, the story of Narcissus with which the fountain is adorned, like the hunter Cupid who pursues the lover, suggests that love's course is not easy and that its snares may be deadly. L'Amant is himself fearfully hesitant on the brink of a "perilous" dedication to so elusive an ideal. The sweetness of love is always bitter, as Guillaume's goliard predecessors well knew,[65] and even the bird song of Deduit's garden has been "pitous" as well as sweet.[66] But the Narcissus story could also be made an argument in favor of love; it is, after all, chiefly proud ladies who must, according to Guillaume, take the tale to heart.[67] In any case, it is not the warning of Narcissus' fate that seems most fundamental to literary uses of the myth, but the promise of his goal.[68] The pool of Narcissus becomes the very *Fontaine d'Amors* (1597), the "welle" of *all* lovers, first and most importantly because, like the monk's book of creatures or like the eyes of the beloved in *Phaedrus,* what it yields to the lover's gaze is an image of himself[69]—or rather, of that self which is to be, when Love's nature unfolds itself within the lover's own experience.

The stages of his progress correspond well enough to the account in

Andreas Capellanus of the genesis of love: sight, immoderate thought, suffering (*passio*).[70] We should have to specify more firmly than the chaplain does, however, that the lover's passion *is* precisely his subjection to all that he sees, his "suffering" of—or toward—what is objectively given. Desire is a circular movement, Aquinas says, because it is the similarity of lover and beloved that moves the former, and as he moves toward his goal the likeness increases.[71] This circular interchange of object and subject is well illustrated in Dante's account, where perceived beauty is "unfolded" in the mind and then is "refolded" as the mind inclines toward its new discovery: and "that refolding is love."[72] The point to be understood is that what is seen does not merely cause what is felt but is in a sense identical with it. The conception of experience that is implied here is at the opposite pole from the notion of an autonomous subjectivity seeking in the outside world emblems of its own conduct. Love, rather, is the mode in which the will and affections participate in the cosmic scene where, literally, they find themselves.

I should perhaps make clear that in saying this I am interested less in the putative psychology of the hero than in the structure or the action of the poem itself, the phenomenology of its imagination. Moralists were quick to see and condemn the dangers inherent in turning outward to find the self; and some critics have supposed that Guillaume was intent mainly on offering his hero as an example of curiosity, the vice of the man who "begins to look around," and to "extend" the soul, rather than "attending" to its true needs.[73] I have already alluded to a poem that anticipates the images of Deduit's garden and at the same time throws into clear relief the moral risks involved. A follower of Golias, a generation or two before Guillaume, had celebrated his love as a dreamlike devotion to the rose of the world ("mundi rosa"), and he had, like Guillaume, found in his rose lady the "flower of flowers" and the "mirror of all things" ("cunctis speculum"). The sacrilege involved here (if this is how we are to judge the lover's audacity)[74] has to do with more than a consciously impudent appropriation of the Virgin's epithets. As Genius made clear to a suitably repentant lover in Jean de Meun's continuation of the *Roman,* the only true mirror is God's own mind, the carbuncle of the Trinity that is the source of its own light. The pool of Narcissus, like any earthly mirror, is a dark and turbid one, and speculation on its images is at best deceptive—Nature had earlier warned the lover about this fault in mirrors—and often enough a culpable idolatry.[75] The goliard poet had himself wondered if the pursuit of the flower of this world was not a desperate venture:

dubito, quod semina
in arena sero;
mundi florem diligens
ecce iam despero. (st. 3)

(I hesitate, for I am sowing seeds in sand. Loving the flower of the world, behold, already I despair.)

And the fate, a few years later, of Fair Rosamond might seem to confirm his foreboding:[76]

Hic jacit in tumba, Rosa mundi, non Rosa munda.
Non redolet, sed olet, quae redolere solet.

(Here lieth in tombe the rose of the world, nought a clene rose. It smelleth nought swete but it stinketh, that was wont to smelle ful swete.)

Reason, then, has ground enough for her denunciation, although she remains, it should be noted, but one voice within the dream and not its narrator.[77] The dreamer himself is disposed to recognize quite different claims. And if (as a critic has written) the garden of the *Roman* "haunts the literature of the succeeding centuries,"[78] it is because Reason's voice could not, for subsequent generations either, dispel the glamour of those claims. I am suggesting that the praise or blame we may attach to the lover is finally of less importance than the nature of his dream, the dimension of his imagination, of which the poem itself is an irreducible datum. The form by which earthly love is known in the *Roman* is not a sensual sty nor a trackless waste of the sort Comus inhabits, but a garden of all delights; a garden which claims, furthermore—although Raison and l'Ami both speak, in different ways, for the exigencies of a world inhospitable to such a dream—not only the joys of paradise, but also its order and civility. The existence or nonexistence of the witty disparagement some critics have detected is really of secondary importance if the poem enacts precisely those excesses which are theoretically disparaged: the intuition of a fulfillment achieved through embracing the world. For it is by precisely such an embrace that the poem itself achieves its own properly poetic fruition, by quite literally making sense of the world, by finding a human value in the images of the natural landscape. This is why I think it more useful to apply Capellanus' three terms to the psychology of the poem's composition than to use them in polemic against its hero. Those terms—*visio, cogitatio, passio*—correspond to the dialectic of the poetic *locus* itself: a place, an opportunity, a situation.

The three senses of *locus* become in the *Roman* the very structure of a vision that mediates between a human condition and its external setting. The garden is first of all a place seen, and in such cases the poet's skill ("enargia") is in placing the scene before his readers as if they actually were there. So far, then, we share the experience of the lover; nor is the poem's repeated insistence on his delight in the spectacle merely self-congratulatory.

> Than myght I not withholde me
> That I ne wente inne for to see
> Sir Myrthe; for my desiryng
> Was hym to seen, over alle thyng . . .
> That sighte was to me ful dere. (723–28)

The "poem as 'vision'," as Professor Gunn remarks, "calls into being the poem as 'action'."[79] Medieval writers, particularly those in the tradition of Augustine, knew that beauty is not mere spectacle but God's rhetoric in the book of creation, a call to the movement of the heart;[80] and in their own way, as we have seen, the troubadours had been responsive to such summons. The lover's "desiryng" is simply the inwardness of his seeing, the mode of his involvement with the world; and its repetition marks the incremental claims his vision makes on his behavior. A rhetorician would describe the situation by saying that the stir of potencies with which the poem begins is an *argumentum a tempore* ("The tyme is than so saverous./Hard is the hert that loveth nought/In May, whan all this mirth is wrought" [84–86]); and the garden argues in the same way.

It is not a neutral scene, but a place considered, as Matthew of Vendôme prescribes, as a probable opportunity, an occasion. Again, we share the lover's mode of vision, for to see the landscape as an opportunity is precisely to see it as an invitation to our own imaginations; an opportunity, the etymology of the word suggests, is something that opens out toward what is not yet realized, a passage. Like Phillis and Flora in their earlier journey to Love's paradise, Guillaume's hero has been able to recognize "dominus ex domo,"[81] the power in the place; and we too are called upon to seek out in the poet's places a power by which we will be humanly involved: to find the spirit in the letter, the idea in the image. No more than the lover, that is, do we in reading the poem experience the garden as merely spatial. It is space alive with potential meanings, a picture that speaks, a place that becomes, quite literally, the *domicilium argumentorum* for the whole poem. And its message is realized for us in the lover himself, not only in what he does, but in what he becomes.

His love occurs as a transposition into new terms of what already is implicit in the scene. The technique of the *descriptio* tends always to freeze the garden to a static essence, rescuing its contents from the momentary flux of perception and rendering them permanent to the mind's eye in the order of the literary paradigm itself. The lover's passion—and this as we shall see in the next chapter is what makes Guillaume's garden look forward, however tentatively, to the Renaissance garden—again "unfolds" this essence into a concrete human existence, a world of becoming, of striving toward a goal: renders it as a potentiality, as *pathos*.[82] It is at this point that we can best understand the function of the personfications the lover encounters:

> Tho myghtist thou karoles sen,
> And folk daunce and mery ben,
> And made many a fair tournyng
> Upon the grene gras springyng. (759–62)

The essential perception that Chaucer's rhymes here nicely isolate is of the moment when—the narrow gate entered, the right path taken—the bird song and springing grass reveal themselves as a dance into which the human protagonist can enter. Another such moment is rendered more fully and consciously in *The Legend of Good Women,* when the dreamer is called upon to see the God of Love coming with "wynges sprede" over the awakening countryside (Text G, 142–43), and to discover in the god's green-and-white clad consort a more proper object for the devotion he had inchoately been offering the daisies—eyes of day, vessels of light—which embroidered the "smale, softe, swote gras."

The allegorical relationship between man and scene is less a technique than a subject matter, a project of the imagination achieved in the poem itself as the images of the natural world gradually reveal their human relevance. Like the God of Love, who is clothed in flowers and covered with birds, the company the lover meets is essentially *of* the garden, yet they transpose its values into another mode, that of human behavior. Not only Pleasure and Youth and Beauty ("clere as the mone lyght . . . tendre as dew of flour" [1010–13]), but also the more strictly courtly figures must be understood first in these terms, as ways of impersonating (not always successful ways, Reason will insist) the peculiar qualities of the scene:

> About the brinkes of these welles,
> And by the stremes overal elles,
> Sprang up the grass, as thicke yset
> And softe as any veluët,
> On which men myght his lemman leye,
> As on a fetherbed, to pleye;
> For the erthe was ful softe and swete.
> Through moisture of the welle wete
> Sprong up the sote grene gras
> As fayre, as thicke, as myster was.
> But moche amended it the place,
> That th'erthe was of such a grace
> That it of floures hath plente,
> That bothe in somer and wynter be.
> There sprang the vyolet al newe,
> And fressh pervynke, riche of hewe,
> And floures yelowe, white, and rede;
> Such plente grew there never in mede.
> Full gay was al the ground, and queynt,
> And poudred, as men had it peynt,
> With many a fressh and sondri flour,
> To casten up ful good savour. (1417–38)

The gaiety and quaintness of courtly play on velvet cushions is inextricably bound to the natural landscape, whose bounty suggests some grace beyond the merely human. Largesse and Franchise cannot be understood apart from the plenitude of these streams and wells or from the sweet fecundity of the earth; nor Idleness (concerned only with adorning herself "noblement" [574]) apart from this grass at once tender and luxuriant, new-sprung and perpetual.

This is why it seems to me perverse to explain the reveling in Deduit's garden as "standing for" the life of the court. The life to which the lover's emotion admits him has for us no reality, no content, apart from our apprehension of the garden. The pool of Narcissus in fact marks a stage in the reader's own progress. Here we come to recognize that the lover's place no longer tells us merely where he is, nor does it merely offer him an opportunity. It now defines his whole situation, all the possibilities open to him *as* l'Amant. Guillaume's poem is related to Aquinas' (or Andreas') theories of love not by any anxiety for dogmatic clarity of definition, but by the primacy each accords man's cosmic scene. The self finds its limits in the natural scene, so that definition (in the radical sense) is a merging of subject and object; but on the basis of a profound realism that derives the first term from the second, "lover" from the sacred spot of Love itself.[83]

2

The poise of Guillaume's garden between subject and object may be illuminated by comparison with some of its prototypes among earlier gardens of love. Specifically, I shall want to show how it mediates between the escapist subjectivity of the Latin elegiac tradition and the rhetorical impersonality of the epithalamium, and to suggest that this shift in the literary imagination is related to the association, reinforced by Christian dreams of Paradise, between love and the doctrine of natural places. The courtly poet's paradise of love is neither an evasive daydream nor a topos to argue the grandeur of a patron; it is a place in which the self is found.

The notion of Love's domain seems to have become a commonplace in the tradition of the epithalamium, and critics have traced a direct line of influence from Claudian's tribute to Honorius and Maria at the end of the fourth century to the *Altercatio Phyllidis et Florae* (c. 1150), in which the proximate source of Deduit's garden has sometimes been found.[84] The differences between the late classical and the medieval poem are striking. Like the Venus of his epithalamium, Claudian is concerned with offering his imperial couple the whole world as dowry.[85] He begins, accordingly, with the goddess in her realm, and then brings her to earth as an expression of the lovers' triumph. This movement of the poem, which seems merely to infer the nature and value of Maria from the glittering metallic paradise which descends upon her, is paradigmatic of the poet's whole strategy: subjective qualities, whether of love or of virtue, are apprehended only in the magnitude of the tribute they compel. In Honorius' introductory monologue, the lover's usual impatience takes the odd form of boasting about the greatness of the rank (emperor and son of an emperor) he is about to offer up (31–35); and the intensity of his affection is appropriately measured by the family jewels he brings his bride (10–12), whose value is in turn defined by her superiority to what she is adorned with. The progress of Venus is an accumulation of gifts: we see her collecting the splendor of Neptune's court to adorn the bride ("these ornaments of Maria's, these our gifts" [173]) and instructing Hymen to "heap up there [on the nuptial couch] all the gathered wealth of the family" (215–218). The final tribute is of course the epithalamium itself, an ornament, a construction of glittering places offered up to the real Honorius and Maria, whose subjective selves remain outside the poem and are only suggested by the poet's anxiety that his powers are insufficient to the occasion: "our song must be such as now befits the singing" (312–13).

In "Phillis and Flora"—and this is what makes it the ancestor of the *Roman de la Rose*—we begin on earth and proceed toward paradise. We begin, furthermore, with specific human existences, the questing girls, so that the paradise of Cupid is apprehended by us as something seen, as a vision, a goal moved toward through subjective space, rather than the direct presentation of the rhetorician. The poem does not merely gesture towards the dimension of real existence, in other words, but incorporates it, however sketchily, into its actual structure.[86] In Claudian, only Venus, stupefied at the sight of Maria (241), can be allowed any amazement; we have to do with the poet's hyperbolical compliment, not a real subjectivity. But in the medieval poem, the sense of delighted or awestruck discovery is integral and may remind us of the newness of the troubadour's springtime or even of Rudolf Otto's definition of what is involved in perceiving the sacred. The key words in the girls' progress are *invenire* (to discover), *repente* (suddenly), *mirabilis* (wonderful). The place is discovered, not merely entered into, and the protagonists are overwhelmed by the miracle of new things:

> Capiuntur subito corda puellarum
> In tanto miraculo rerum novellarum. (st. 67)

Such wonder is the prototype of l'Amant's own subjective form of hyperbole (I never saw . . . I never felt), which is similarly a mode that assimilates the place to his own sensibilities, defines it in terms of his own inner space.

Claudian orders the details of Venus' realm in a purely topographical way, but the scheme the medieval poets had at their disposal, notably set forth by Matthew of Vendôme, has already altered the emphasis so as to define the garden as something experienced. It is not a collection of splendid or valuable objects, but a place full of all delights, which are defined as well as merely classified by the gratification they offer each of the five senses:[87]

> The birds please with their voices, the wood with its shade, the breeze in due season, the spring with its drink, the stream with its murmuring, with its bloom the soil. . . . Water delights the touch, viands the taste, the bird befriends the ear, loveliness the eye, a sweet scent the nose.

The influence of this paradigm is evident in both the *Altercatio* and the *Roman de la Rose*,[88] especially in Guillaume's reiterated insistence on the symmetry of the seen and the heard, which between them exhaust the phenomena of the May morning and of the garden itself.[89] But the rhetorician's concern with a purely analytic virtuosity gives way, in the poets, to a concern for mimesis. The distinction is evident in the difference between description of places in Guillaume's poem and his description of persons. The latter clearly exist only in the "now" of the poem's telling, and marshal their evidence systematically, as if less to describe than to persuade us of the beauty of the figures involved.[90] Guillaume frequently makes us aware of this interruption of the narrated time, most notably at line 585, where the action abruptly resumes after the description of Idleness. In describing places, however, the poet maintains the convention of rendering the actual form of the lover's experience "then"; he cannot, of course, "telle you all at ones" (710–12), but the "ordre," he adopts is of the stages in his dawning awareness. The form of thought which in Matthew tends always to withdraw from the spatial and temporal and move toward a hermetic play of mere concepts, here is integrated in some degree with the narrative and so left open to the experiencing self that the emphasis on the senses actually implies. As a result, even a set piece like Guillaume's tree catalogue has a certain mimetic value. The emphasis on plenitude and completeness in both poems becomes, more than just a way of demonstrating the garden's logical exhaustiveness, an expression of the wonder and enthusiasm of the protagonist's discovery, his delighted apprehension of "whatsoever man's mind can comprehend" (*Altercatio,* st. 61).

This difference of approach means that the place itself is different. Claudian's paradise interprets all the traditional figures as expressions of wealth and power. Venus' bower glows greenly because it is made of emeralds, uniting not art and nature, but art and costliness (85–93); and the golden hedge surrounding the realm is the "price" Mulciber paid for love (56–59). Spring is perpetual because frost and wind are afraid to approach (52–53); songbirds are tolerated only *sub judice diva* ("they must quit who cannot pass the test" [64]); and Cupid's customary power over mighty gods and kings becomes a form of snobbery that relegates lesser breeds (*plebes*) to an attendant crowd of *putti* (77). In such a context, it is natural that the bride herself can be apprehended only as "interest," as what is "owed" the venturesomeness of the emperor's devotion (36–37). But in the *Altercatio,* and after it, in the *Roman de la Rose,* all this heaped wealth becomes value accessible to the self.

One of the things in Love's kingdom that strikes the heroines of the *Altercatio* is a chorus of dancing maidens, "the bodies of each, the bodies of stars" (st. 67). What is involved here is not a pretty compliment, but the assimilation of the girls' trip through the spring-time woods to the soul's journey to its proper place. In the *Timaeus,* Plato says that the demiurge originally planted human souls in the stars so they could become acquainted with the nature of the universe and so be impelled, during their later confinement in merely fleshly bodies, to live with a purity that would enable them eventually to return to their "consort star[s]."[91] Thus, in Macrobius, Scipio is urged to recall that his true home is in the sky and that a man can know his own nature only "if he will look back to his first beginning and origin and 'not search for himself elsewhere'."[92] The place in which the self is to be found, in other words, is precisely the place where the body of each is the body of a star; and at least since Martianus Capella, for whom Hymen became a goddess of cosmic harmonies, learned poets had concerned themselves with imagining the scenery of the soul's ascent to the star assigned as its proper place.[93] It is on some such expedition that Phillis and Flora have set out. They had been searching for the truth about their love—their quest is the result of their altercation—and here in the *locus occultus* of Love himself they find it.

We are not surprised, therefore, to discover that the bird song, which in Claudian demonstrates the imperial power, is here an embodiment of just that order which the stars describe in their movement and to which the exiled soul must try to return:[94]

> Quidquid potest hominum comprehendi mente,
> Totum ibi virgines audiunt repente,
> Vocum differentie sunt illic inventae,
> Sonat diatesseron, sonat dyapente.
> Sonat et mirabili plaudunt armonia
> Timpanum, psalterium, lira, simphonia;
> Sonant ibi phiale voce valde pia,
> Et buxus multiplici cantum promit via.
> Sonant omnes avium lingue voce plena:
> Vox auditur merule dulcis et amena,
> Coridalus, graculus atque philomena,
> Que non cessat conqueri de transacta pena.

(All pleasurs studie can invent,
The dames eares instantly present:
Voyces in all sorts different,
The foure parts, and the diapent.
To tunes that from those voyces flie,
With admireable harmonie:
The tymbrell, harpe, and psalterie,
Rejoyce in rapting symphonie.
There did the vials voyce abounde,
In musicke angel-like profounde:
There did the phife dispredden rounde
His songe in many a variant sounde.)

Another goliard poet (in the *Metamorphosis Goliae*) had already elaborated from Martianus Capella the image of a *locus amoenus* embodying all the harmonies of the cosmos, and he makes quite clear that the intervals which delight Phillis and Flora—"sonat diatesseron, sonat dyapente"—are precisely those which order the planets in their celestial music: "that diversity of harmonizing prefigures the sevenfold order of the planets."[95] But the journey of Phillis and Flora, even though Flora's saddle is adorned with the heavenly nuptials of Mercury,[96] has been no vertical flight to a supercelestial realm, the only place in Martianus or Macrobius where such harmonies may truly be heard. Their progress has been toward the center of their own awakened feelings, like that of Guillaume's hero or of the knights in Andreas Capellanus, seeking out through concentric gardens Love's very source (1.6, Dialogue 5). And here, in the *locus occultus* of the god himself, language borrowed from Martianus and his followers merges with the tradition of secular epithalamia in order to assign the "superum carmen" of Apollo's grove[97] to living voices celebrating a human love. In the sweet fullness ("omnes . . . plena," "dulcis . . . amena") of the birds' natural song,[98] the girls are startled by a symphony of all voices and all tones:[99] an Edenic concert in which the viol (*phiala*) of medieval musicians, the classical lyre and flute, the cadenced praises of David's psaltery and timbrels,[100] all chime together and resonate—if we are to take seriously the implications of "voce pia," as the poem's Elizabethan translator does—with the hymning of the angelic choir.[101] The poet assembles all this lore in order to suggest, as does the *Metamorphosis Goliae,* the exhaustiveness of the *nexus musicus* (*Metamorphosis,* 60) by which the world is bound. But in the *Altercatio,* no longer perceived in the allegorical guise of Golias' poem ("totum sub involucro [wrappings], totum sub figura" [44]), this consonance seems to be granted the practical music of man and nature, a music presided over not by Jove, Juno, and Pallas, but by Cupid and his rowdy cohorts.

Such musical intuitions, as Leo Spitzer has remarked, are peculiarly able to weld together "the objective (factual) and the subjective (psychological) into one harmonious unity."[102] The *symphonia* by which the girls are greeted is a value as objective as the emeralds and gold in Claudian. As Boethius explains, harmony is *ratio,* proportion, not merely a pleasure in the ear: indeed, as that which binds together all things—Apollo's grove is the *locus universitatis,* the poet writes, where "the whole wood resonates in proportion" (*Metamorphosis,* 49, 20)—it constitutes the objective.[103] But the *Altercatio* reminds us that this totality is one to be "comprehended" by the mind: not just understood, but included, since the "soul carries with it into the body a memory of the music which it knew in the sky,"[104] and what it remembers is its own true proportions. In its astral body, the soul incorporated the rational motion that constitutes its beatitude;[105] nor can Phillis and Flora remain indifferent to the music they now discover:

> Virgines introeunt modico timore
> Et eundo propius crescunt in amore.
> Sonant queque volucres propio rumore,
> Accenduntur animi vario clamore. (st. 65)
>
> (The virgins something entered here,
> And sprinckled with a little feare,
> Their harts before that helde Love deare,
> In Cupids flames encreased were.
> And while each winged forester
> Their proper rumors did prefer,
> Each virgins minde made waight on her
> Applauses apt and singuler.)

The soul's response is participation in what it apprehends, *proprio rumore* kindling *vario clamore* ("applauses apt and singuler"): what follows, as

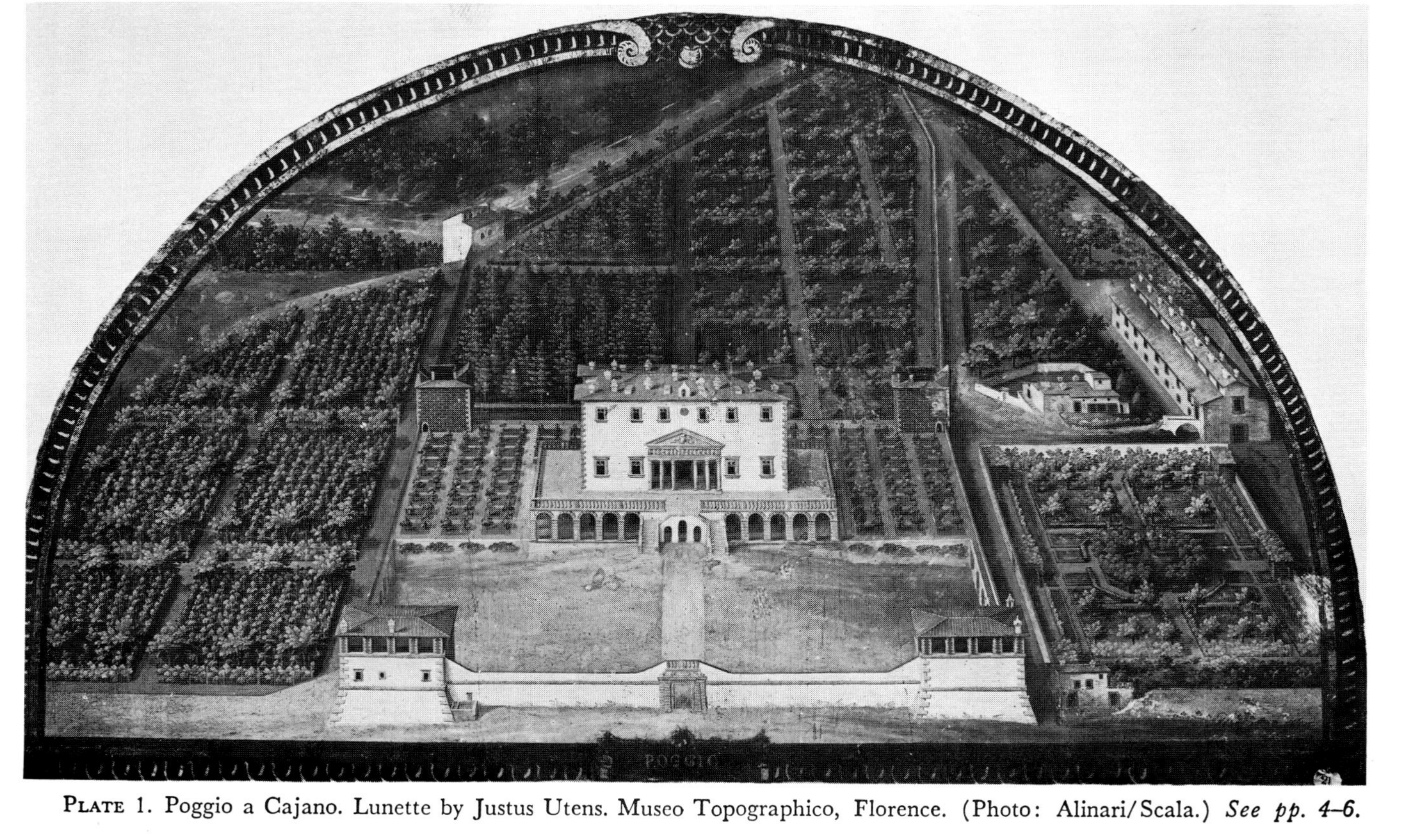

PLATE 1. Poggio a Cajano. Lunette by Justus Utens. Museo Topographico, Florence. (Photo: Alinari/Scala.) *See pp. 4–6.*

PLATE 2. John Parkinson, *Paradisi in Sole* (London, 1629). Reproduced by permission of the Arents Collections, The New York Public Library, Astor, Lenox and Tilden Foundations. *See pp. 22–24.*

PLATE 3. In the embrace of an angel reminiscent of Diana of Ephesus, Nature (Ceres with the instruments of human industry) and Grace repair the Fall. Adam Pleyer, *Abentheur des Natürlichen und Künstlichen Sachen* (Frankfort, 1656). From the collection of the Arnold Arboretum, reproduced by permission of the Houghton Library, Harvard University. *See pp. 22–24.*

ET VIR PRVDENS NON ABHORREBIT DOMINVS MEDICAMENTA E TERRA

Neuw Kreuterbuch/

Mit schönen / künstlichen vnd leblichen Figuren vnnd Conterfeyten / aller Gewächß der Kreuter / Wurtzeln / Blumen / Frücht / Getreyd / Gewürtz / der Bäume / Stauden vnd Hecken / so in Teutschen vnd Welschen Landen / auch deren so im Gelobten Landt auff dem Berg Synai / inn Hispanien / Ost vnnd West Indien / oder in der neuwen Welt wachsen / vnd zu vnser Zeit gepflantzt werden / mit eygentlicher Beschreibung derselben / auch deren Vnderscheidt / Krafft vnd Wirckung / sampt jhren rechten Namen in mancherley Sprachen / darinn auff 3000. Gewächß beschrieben vnd angezeigt werden / dergleichen vormals in keiner Sprach nie ans Liecht oder in Druck kommen.

Darinn viel vnd mancherley heylsamer Artzeney / vor allerley innerlichen vnd eusserlichen Kranckheiten vnnd Gebrechen / beyde der Menschen vnd deß Viehes / beschrieben werden / sampt jhrem nützlichen Gebrauch: Als da seindt Tränck / Säfft / Syrupen / Conseruen / gedistillierte Wasser / Latwergen / Puluer / künstliche Extracten / gemeine vnd gedistillierte Oele / Confect / Saltz / Salben / Wundtsalben / Pflaster vnd dergleichen: Darinnen auch vber tausendt Experimenten / vnd heimliche Künst angezeigt werden / die in keiner Sprach in Schrifften gefunden werden.

Allen Artzten / Apoteckern / Wundtärtzten / Marställern / Huffschmidten / Roßtäuschern / Gärtnern / Hofmeyern / Köchen / Weinkellern / Hebammen / Haußvättern / Haußmüttern / vnd allen andern Liebhabern der Artzeney vnd guter Künst dienstlich vnd nützlich: Auß langwiriger vnd gewisser erfahrung / vnserm geliebten Vatterlandt zu Ehren / mit sonderm Fleiß treuwlich beschrieben / Durch

Iacobum Theodorum Tabernæmontanum, der Artzeney Doctorem, vnd Churfürstlicher Pfaltz bestellten Medicum zu Neuwhausen.

Mit Röm. Key. May. Frey. auff zehen Jar nicht nachzudrucken / begnadet.

Franckfurt am Mayn / 1588.

ERVNT FRVCTVS EIVS IN CIBVM ET FOLIA EIVS AD MEDICINAM

PLATE 4. Eden and the modern garden. Jacob Theodorus ("Tabernaemontanus"), *Neuw Kreuterbuch* (Frankfort, 1588). Reproduced by permission of The Research Libraries, New York Botanical Garden. *See pp. 22–24.*

PLATE 5. Emanuel Sweert, *Florilegium* (Frankfort, 1612). Reproduced by permission of The Research Libraries, New York Botanical Garden. *See pp. 22–24.*

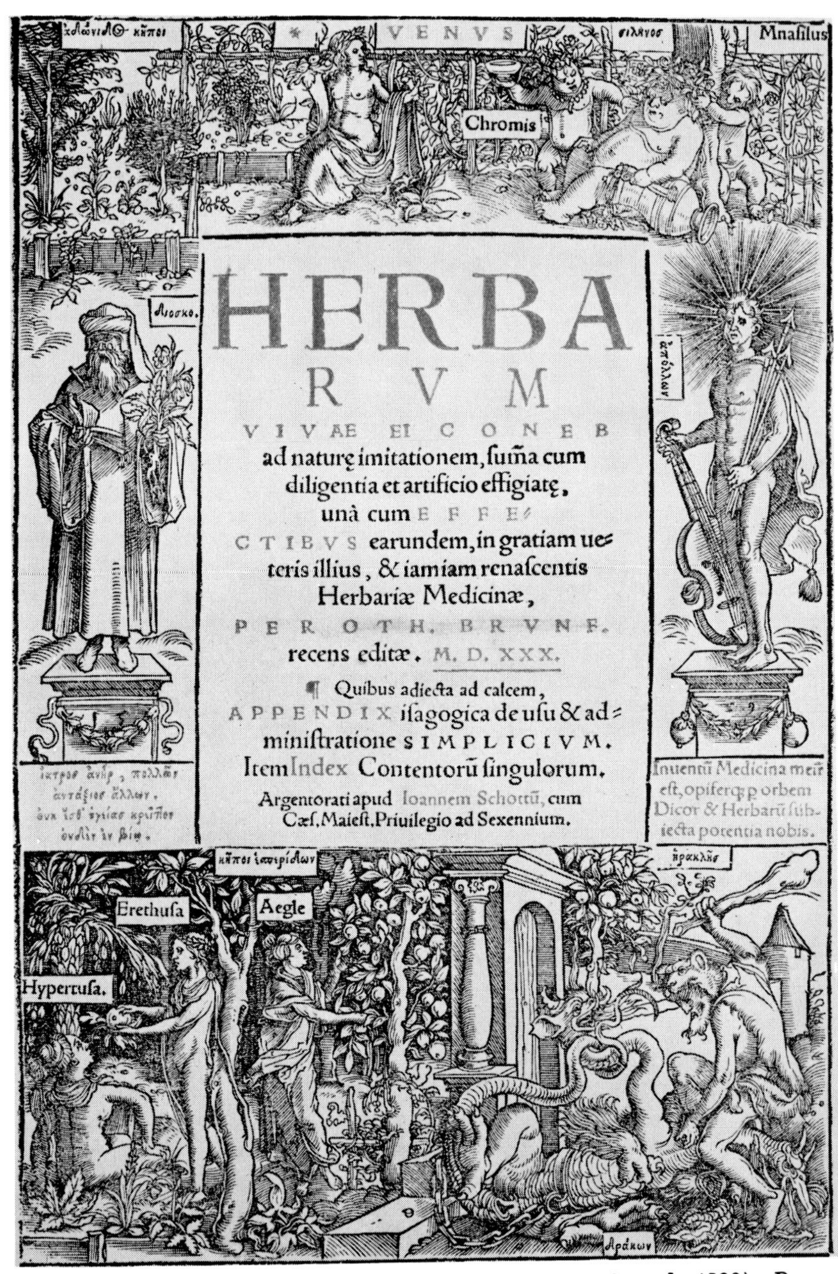

HERBA
RVM
VIVAE EICONES
ad naturę imitationem, sum̃a cum
diligentia et artificio effigiatę,
unà cum EFFE-
CTIBVS earundem, in gratiam ue-
teris illius, & iamiam renascentis
Herbariæ Medicinæ,
PER OTH. BRVNF.
recens editæ. M. D. XXX.
¶ Quibus adiecta ad calcem,
APPENDIX isagogica de usu & ad-
ministratione SIMPLICIVM.
Item Index Contentorũ singulorum.
Argentorati apud Ioannem Schottũ, cum
Cæs. Maiest. Priuilegio ad Sexennium.

Plate 6. Otto Brunfels, *Herbarum* (Argentoratum [Strasbourg], 1530). Reproduced by permission of The Metropolitan Museum of Art, Gift of Mortimer L. Schiff, 1918. *See pp. 22–24.*

PLATE 7. Dry and flourishing branches. Jan Sadeler, the Elder, *Spring*. Reproduced by permission of The Metropolitan Museum of Art, Harris Brisbane Dick Fund, 1953. *See pp. 22–24*.

PLATE 8. The four continents. John Parkinson, *Theatrum Botanicum* (London, 1640). Reproduced by permission of the Houghton Library, Harvard University. *See pp. 22–24 and 199, n. 137.*

Kreutterbuch
Deß Hochgelehrten vnnd weitberühmten Herrn D. Petri Andreæ Matthioli, Jetzt widerumb mit viel schönen neuwen Figuren / auch nützlichen Artzneyen / vnd andern guten stücken / auß sonderm fleiß gemehret / vnd verfertigt
Durch
Ioachimum Camerarium, der löblichen Reichsstatt Nürmberg Medicum. D.
Sampt dreyen wolgeordneten nützlichen Registern / der Kreutter Lateinische vnd Deutsche Namen / vnd dann die Artzeneyen / darzu dieselbigen zu gebrauchen / innhaltendt.
Mit besonderem Röm. Kays. Maiest. Priuilegio, in keinerley Format nachzudrucken.
Gedruckt zu Franckfort am Mayn /
M. D. LXXXVI.

PLATE 9. The garden restored. Pietro Andrea Mattioli, *Kreutterbuch* (Frankfort, 1586). Reproduced by permission of The Research Libraries, New York Botanical Garden. *See pp. 22–24 and 198–99, n. 136.*

PLATE 10. The garden and the four elements. Johann Coler, *Oeconomia Ruralis et Domestica* (Frankfort, 1672). From the collection of the Arnold Arboretum, reproduced by permission of the Houghton Library, Harvard University. *See pp. 22–24 and 198–99, n. 136.*

PLATE 11. Impregnation with flowers. Henri Causé, *De Koninglycke Hovenier* (Amsterdam, 1676). From the collection of the Arnold Arboretum, reproduced by permission of the Houghton Library, Harvard University. *See pp. 22–24.*

PLATE 12. Ceres with her key. Abraham Munting, *Waare Oeffnung der Planten* (Amsterdam, 1672). From the collection of the Arnold Arboretum, reproduced by permission of the Houghton Library, Harvard University. *See pp. 22–24.*

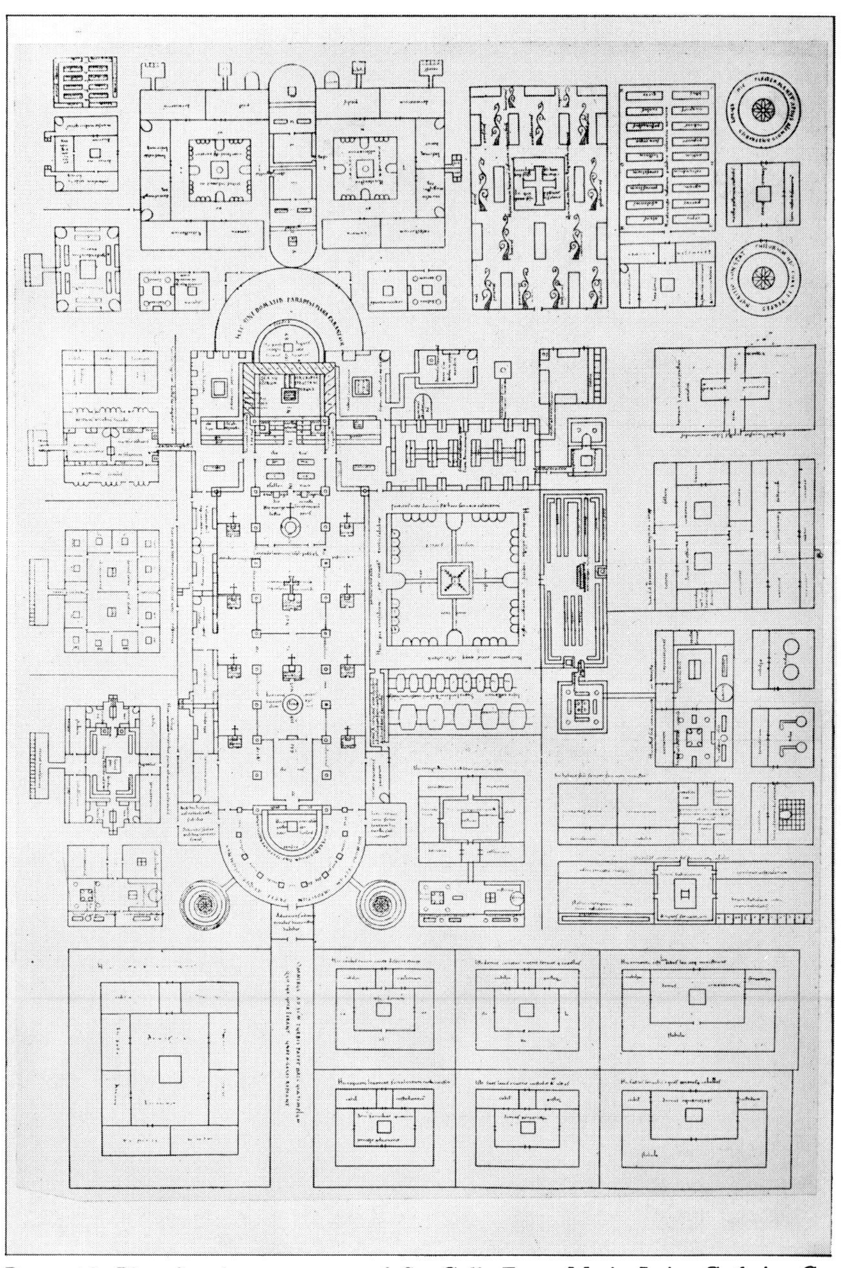

PLATE 13. Plan for the monastery of St. Gall. From Marie Luise Gothein, *Geschichte der Garten Kunst* (Jena, 1914), I, plate 124. Reproduced by permission of Eugen Diederichs Verlag, Düsseldorf. *See pp. 45–47.*

PLATE 14. The Villa Medici, Rome. From Giacomo Lauro, *Antiquae Urbis Splendor* (Rome, 1612–14). Reproduced by permission of the Rare Book Division, The New York Public Library, Astor, Lenox and Tilden Foundations. *See pp. 245–46, n. 72.*

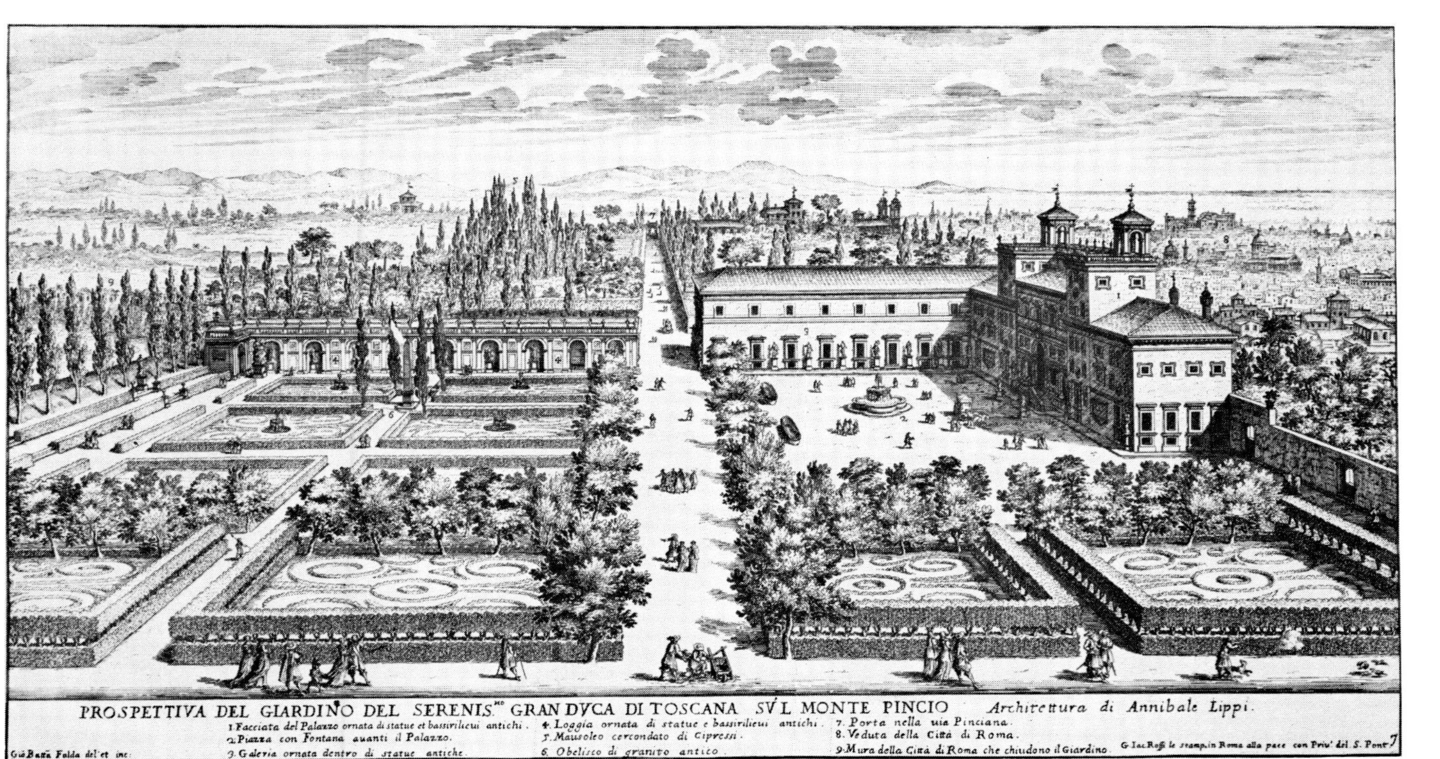

Plate 15. The Villa Medici, Rome. From G. B. Falda, *Li Giardini di Roma* (Rome? 168?), plate vii. Reproduced by permission of the Prints Division, The New York Public Library, Astor, Lenox and Tilden Foundations. *See pp. 245–46, n. 72.*

PLATE 16. The "Cleopatra" fountain in the *giardino segreto,* Cortile del Belvedere, Vatican. Drawing by Francisco da Holanda. The Escorial. *See pp. 164–65.*

PLATE 17. Mother of all things. From Francesco Colonna, *Hypnerotomachia Poliphili* (Paris, 1546). Reproduced by permission of the Spencer Collection, The New York Public Library, Astor, Tilden and Lenox Foundations. *See pp. 164–65.*

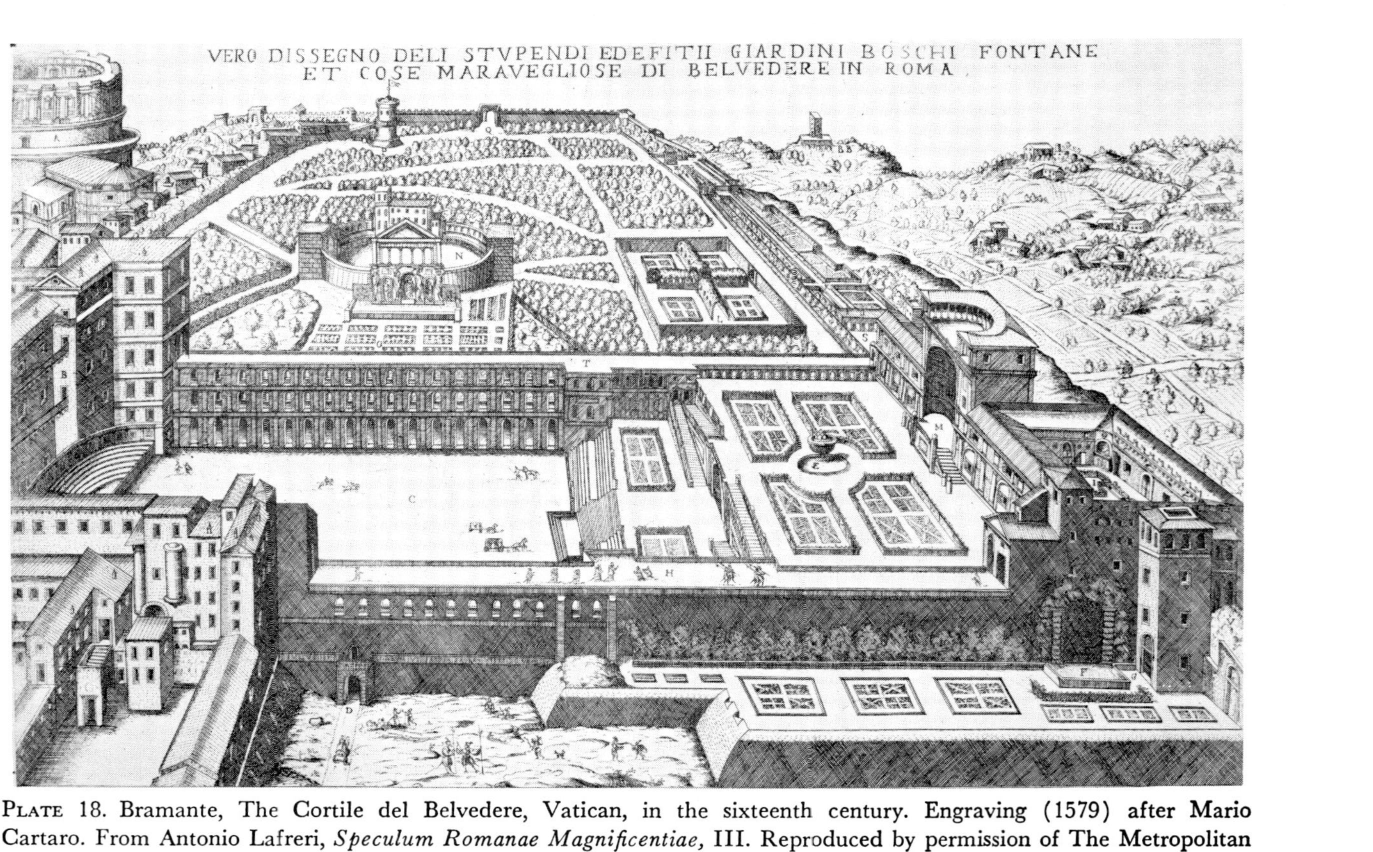

Plate 18. Bramante, The Cortile del Belvedere, Vatican, in the sixteenth century. Engraving (1579) after Mario Cartaro. From Antonio Lafreri, *Speculum Romanae Magnificentiae,* III. Reproduced by permission of The Metropolitan Museum of Art, Harris Brisbane Dick Fund, 1941. *See pp. 152–53, 162–63.*

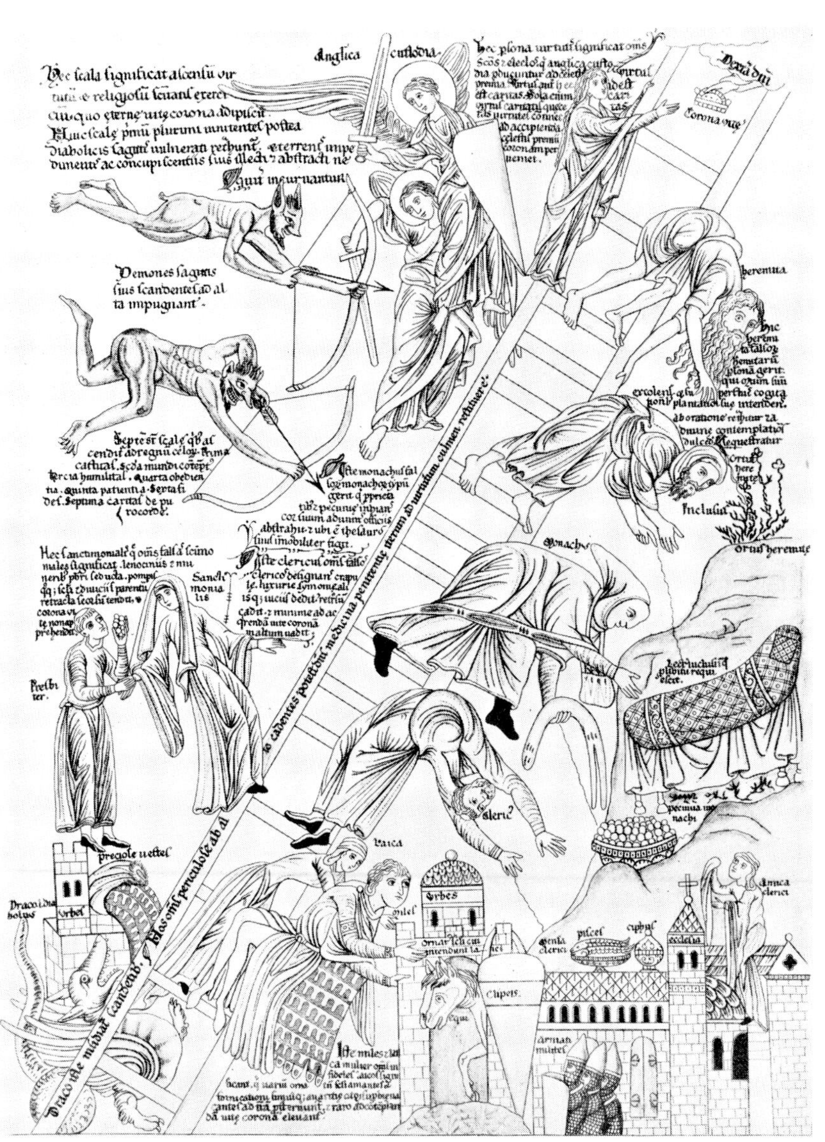

PLATE 19. The Ladder of Virtue. From Herrad of Landsberg, *Hortus Deliciarum,* in the edition of A. Straub and G. Keller (Strasbourg, 1901), fig. lvi. *See pp. 171–72.*

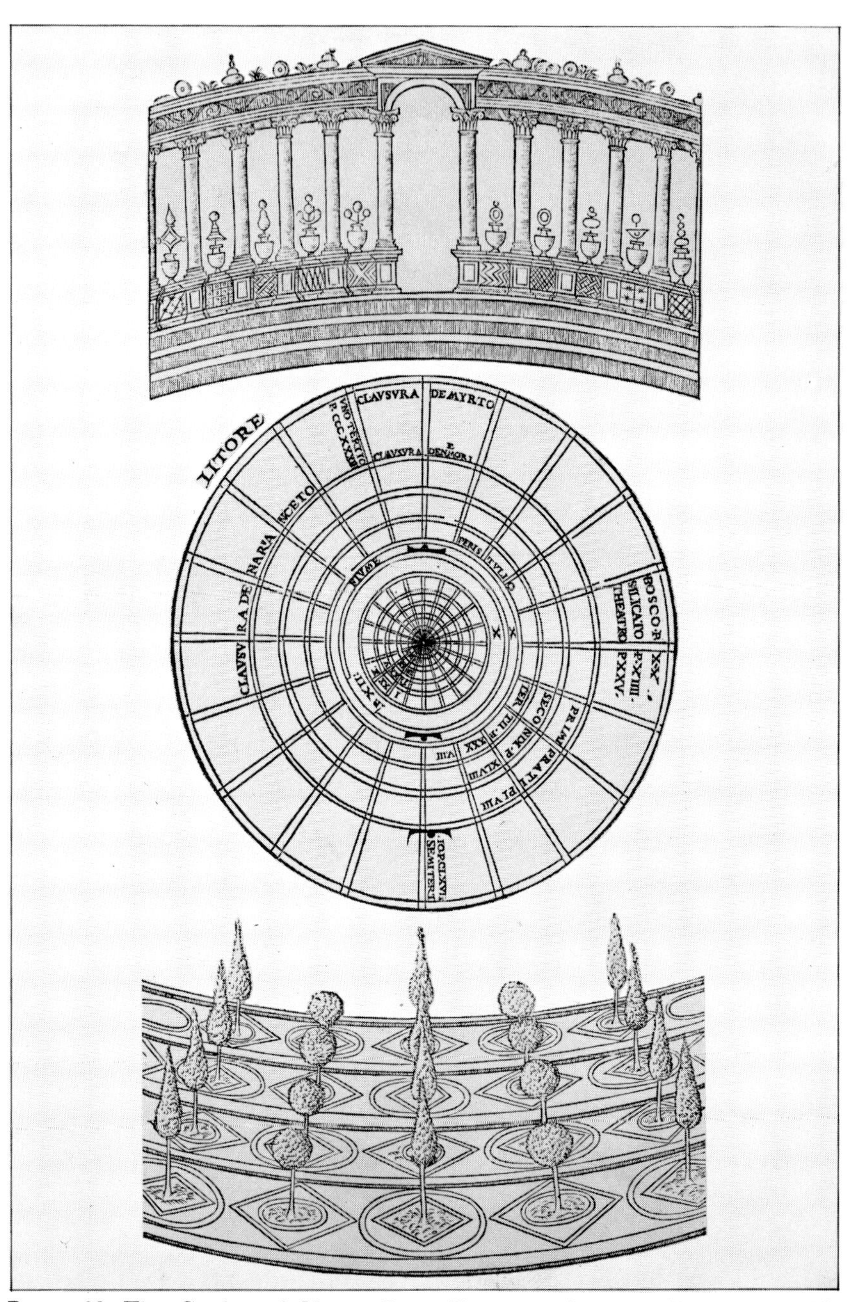

PLATE 20. The Garden of Venus. From Francesco Colonna, *Hypnerotomachia Poliphili* (Paris, 1546). Reproduced by permission of the Spencer Collection, The New York Public Library, Astor, Lenox and Tilden Foundations. *See pp. 182–85.*

we move toward the holy spot where love's god is most vigorously cultivated ("ubi viget maxime suo deo cultus" [st. 69]), is the imagery of fruition:

> Immortalis fieret ibi manens homo.
> Arbor ibi quelibet suo gaudet pomo . . . (st. 66)

(The man who remained here would be immortal, here where every tree rejoices in its fruit.)

The soul's answering harmony, it should be noted, is identical with the growth of its love, a point the English translator makes by transferring the sense of "accenduntur" to the preceding couplet, "in Cupid's flames increased were." The applause involved is nothing other than the soul's movement toward the good it perceives and seeks to embody; "accenduntur" assimilates this movement not only to Cupid's flames, but to the saint's love, enkindled by traces of the divine harmony and impelling him toward his heavenly homeland:

> My love is my weight! I am borne about by it, wheresoever I am borne. By your gift we are enkindled [*accendimur*] and we are borne upwards. We glow with inward fire and we go on.[106]

Thus inflamed, Phillis and Flora also go on, and the harmony that awaits them in the starlike choir of maidens is not a mathematical abstraction, but, like the hymning of the angels or the dance of the planets themselves,[107] a chorus of love and praise. In such a place as this—"ante dei vultus": before the very countenance of the god—the movements by which the soul is ordered cannot be distinct from its innermost feelings, just as those feelings will issue without partition or obstacle in movement toward the goal of all desire. Phillis and Flora will rediscover their soul's proper motion[108] (= emotion) in the dance of nymphs and satyrs who, celebrating Love in his own shrine, "keepe true measure with their feete,/That to the instruments do fleete": "Pedum servant ordinem et instrumentorum" (st. 70). The "true measure" of love's dance becomes, I suppose, a version of Augustine's *ordo amoris:* delight is the soul's "weight" and so by delight the soul is ordered.[109] But since the paradise to which Phillis and Flora are borne is a very earthly one, the dance is proclaimed by Bacchus—who in Macrobius presides over the descent of intoxicated souls to the lower world[110]—and made eccentric by a tipsy Silenus, who staggers and leaps among the dancers (st. 70). In the *Metamorphosis Goliae,* the intrusion of this enemy of "divine reason" (73) causes a violent debate, "for Pallas scorns what is pleasing to Venus" (155); but in the *Altercatio* the attendant gods dissolve in laughter.

The joke, of course, lies in the thoroughness with which the presumably clerical author applies the relevant doctrine and inverts all the usual discriminations.[111] This may be my excuse for seeming to be humorlessly intent in reading a rather slight poem and for appearing to ignore what might be considered its chief claim on our attention, its charm. The charm has been subjected to a certain rigor, however playful, and the romance motif of the birds' matins[112] has been provided with an intellectual structure, one that importantly keeps their hymn of joy or praise from being for Phillis and Flora merely a spectacle. The poet is not interested in teaching anyone about cosmic harmony; he is concerned, rather, to try out a way of feeling about the birds, about this spring morning, a way of experiencing this particular earthly paradise. The learned language of speculative music serves to discover new possibilities in the literary convention; and even where the theory is not so explicitly invoked as in the *Altercatio,* the same pattern of response may exist.[113]

Like the troubadour's spring morning, the lover's garden in the *Roman de la Rose* is not merely a pleasure in which he partakes. As we have already seen briefly, it is a concord in which his own heart must join:

Mout estoit bele l'acordance
De lor piteus chant a oïr;
Toz li monz s'en doit esjoïr.
Je endroit moi m'en esjoï
Si durement, quant je l'oï (484–88)

(Ful blisful was the accordaunce
Of swete and pitous song thei made,
For all this world it owghte glade.
And I mysilf so mery ferde,
Whan I her blisful songes herde) (496–500)

Hearing and feeling echo one another ("oïr . . . esjoïr," "esjoï . . . je l'oï") in a single harmony: *accordare* itself, as Leo Spitzer has suggested,[114] preserves this ambivalence between musical and psychological harmony, *chorda* (chord) and *cor* (heart). We can see why the birds' music should seem to Guillaume's hero, as it had to Phillis and Flora, like the song of angels (*Romaunt,* 671–72). The analogy expresses both his wonder and awe, and his sense that the garden is the place toward which he has been striving, the heart's homeland:

> For certys, as at my devys,
> Ther is no place in paradys
> So good inne for to dwelle or be,
> As in that gardyn, thoughte me. (651–654)

The confusion of these "spiritual angels" with "sereines de mer" (672–74) may indicate that Guillaume, if not his hero, is thinking of the bird-women who sing in Plato's spheres and continue to greet cosmic voyagers like Scipio or Alain de Lille's Prudence,[115] as well as of the mermaids who lure men to their death; in the context of the whole poem, of course, the bird song suggests both homecoming and temptation. In any case, it is in this harmony, heavenly or merely delusive, that the lover thinks to find his own true being. We might be tempted to see only a decorative sort of pathetic fallacy in the insistence that what the birds sing are courtly poems, their "serventois," "Lais d'amors e sonez cortois" (703–704). But such conceits, like all the later explicit allegory of assaults and stratagems, are supported and justified by the awakening heart's recognition of itself in the harmony that surrounds it: "the swetnesse of her melody/ Made all myn herte in reverdye" (719–20). No wonder then that the lover, like Phillis and Flora, is ready to accept Curtesie's invitation: "Come, and if it lyke you/To dauncen, dauncith with us now" (801–802).

Such moments are the musical equivalent of the lover's discovery of the garden reflected in the pool of Narcissus. It is just their objectivity, their openness to the world, that distinguishes his vision from the very different sort of dream we find in Tibullus, from whom Langlois thinks the Middle Ages "almost certainly inherited their concept of the paradise of love."[116] Sick in a foreign land, Tibullus longs for a place that is little more than the evoked opposite of his own turbulent situation. Exiled from family and from gods (he imagines Delia, chaste and poignantly irrelevant, in the service of powers to whom he can no longer appeal), he finds himself in the harsh age of Jupiter, whose emblem is the estranging sea and whose paths all lead to death:[117]

> nunc Jove sub domino caedes et vulnera semper,
> nunc mare, nunc leti mille repente viae.

(But now that Jupiter is Lord, there are wounds and carnage without cease; now the sea slays, and a thousand ways of sudden death.)

The paradise of love is imagined compensation, a reward to be granted the poet for all the privations he has suffered. What positive definition it has is purely in terms of feeling tone: the key words (60–64) are *dulce* (sweet), *tenui* (slender), *odoratis* (scented), *benigna* (kindly), *teneris* (delicate). The scene is in fact merely the negation of Tibullus' present existence, whose only foreseeable issue is the epitaph he consecrates to his pathless wandering in the fatal service of Messalla—from which only Venus can snatch him away:[118]

> HIC IACET IMMITI CONSUMPTUS MORTE TIBULLUS,
> MESSALLAM TERRA DUM SEQUITURQUE MARI.
> sed me, quod facilis tenero sum semper Amori,
> ipsa Venus campos ducet in Elysios. (55–58)

(Here lies Tibullus, ravished by death's hand, Messalla comrading o'er sea and land. But me, for I have been ever pliable to gentle love, shall Venus's self escort to the Elysian fields.)

"Ducet in Elysios" reverses "leti mille repente viae" in line 50 above, *Amori* transforms *mari,* and all the battles in which garlands are won are seen to be the engagements of Love:

> ac iuvenum series teneris immixta puellis
> ludit, et asidue proelia miscet amor. (63–64)

(Troops of young men meet in sport with gentle maidens, and Love never lets his warfare cease)

But this after all is only play. Since these fields grow out of no positive resources in the poet's present situation, but on the contrary are projected from his very deficiencies, what they embody is psychologically not very different from the wish for death, *rapax Mors* (65), under whose shadow the whole scene exists.

I do not mean by this merely that the Roman lover's paradise, unlike that of Phillis and Flora or of Guillaume's hero, is entered only after death, although this is important. Death, after all, may be conceived in more than one way. In Tibullus, it is not, despite the claim of *ducet,* a movement toward a pregnant futurity, as death might be (for example) in an atmosphere of Christian doctrine. It is, rather, a drift toward non-being, a drift backward in time to a place in which the confusions of time and of the self have not yet arisen. The association of a pastoral serenity and freedom with the poet's own childhood is explicit in Elegy 1.10, where in the face of war's ruptures and compulsions ("now I am dragged to war" [13]) Tibullus invokes the days when he had run freely, a tender child before the feet of his father's gods (16). The rigors of the present are countered by a playful devotion to the wooden deity who had nourished him—"Do not be ashamed to have been fashioned of an old tree trunk," he chides (17)—and by a daydream of Peace with her fruitful breast (68). In 1.3, the vision of Venus' paradise follows upon and serves the same function as another such vision of the Golden Age, a time in which the estranging sea had not yet broken the perfect harmony of man's existence. But now Tibullus is in the grip of the life which before he had merely dreaded, and the regressive tone of his imaginings is even more apparent. Where he is using the myth of the Golden Age more intellectually, he opposes a Virgilian picture of agricultural virtue to the rapacity of war: his relative detachment allows him this sort of didactic point. But in 1.3, where what is opposed seems to be the very condition of life itself, he reaches back before agriculture and even before animal husbandry to a bliss all but explicitly infantile, in which full-uddered ewes come unbidden to the happy swain:

ipsae mella dabant quercus, ultroque ferebant
obvia securis ubera lactis oves. (45–46)

(The very oaks gave honey, and with milky udders came the ewes unbidden to meet the careless swain.)

The topic becomes, in other words, a means of pure retrospection, rather an abdication of the present than any judgment passed on its shortcomings; and it is this gesture toward the past that is completed in the dream of Venus' paradise, where lovers play and crops spring uncultivated from the aromatic grass.

As we have remarked, the courtly lover's garden is also a dream, but its subjectivity is quite unlike that of Tibullus. Phillis and Flora are not escaping from their situation, but moving toward definitive judgment, "secundum scienciam et secundum morem" (according to knowledge and custom [st. 78]). The Amor to whom they appeal is a god of law and of rigorous judgments;[119] and although the basis for his decision in favor of the clerk is slyly omitted, it is dialectic that governs the relentlessly antithetical manner in which the whole poem pursues the fortunes of its two heroines, whose "sole *differentia* is the mode of their affections" (st. 5). The manner of the schools is less intrusive in the *Roman de la Rose* but a similar sort of intellectual wakefulness is not incompatible with the dream state it induces.[120] As we have seen, the experience of the lover strikes him with the force of an objective discovery, and he takes his stand in its reality, a reality he claims for his own:

Let whoso lyste a fol me calle.
For this trowe I, and say for me,
That dremes signifiaunce be (14–16)

Writing thus on Love's order, he makes the same claim for the seriousness of the romance he sets before the reader: there is not a word of falsehood in it (*Romaunt,* 2151–74). Just as the joy of Phillis and Flora comprehended the universal harmony of Love's paradise, so the poet's visionary spring song contains reality: it is a dream "Ou l'Art d'Amors est toute enclose" (38).

The allusion to the *Ars amatoria* should not make us forget that

Guillaume had available to him another notion of art, one more congruous than Ovid's daylight stratagems with dreams and dreaming—the learned dreams of men like Scipio or Boethius or Fulgentius. For the twelfth century, the arts are not a repertory of techniques, but man's hold on the very structure of reality; and their aim is the sort of apotheosis imagined by Martianus Capella: "they grant access to heaven, open the stellar regions to moral beings, and let faithful prayers ascend even to the bright ether."[121] The Ciceronian ideal of joining eloquence to wisdom becomes in Martianus a divine marriage and is transformed by the language of the mysteries into a myth of the soul's quest for its homeland:[122] a myth later writers concerned with re-enacting the marriage of Mercury and Philology use to define the seriousness of the claims they make for the liberal arts.[123] Martianus' seven maidens, for example, are assigned to attend the Lady Philosophy, who had come to Boethius in a dream with promises of escape and homecoming: "For I have swift and nimble wings which will ascend the lofty skies."[124] For Honorous of Autun, the arts are cities along the way from man's exile to his true home in Wisdom, at the beauty of whose king the sun and moon stand amazed.[125] Elsewhere the seven streams of the *Fons philosophiae* are conflated with the four rivers of Paradise; they may irrigate a "Christian Parnassus," or even more sensuously Virgilian landscapes, presided over by Mercury and Pan.[126] And in the *Anticlaudianus* the seven sisters attendant upon Wisdom construct the chariot in which Prudence, wearing the rent gown of Boethius' Philosophia, will "visit the stars and drink in the secret of God, moistening her lips at the divine fount."[127]

The theological justification for all this is a tradition, in Boethius and Martianus, in Hugh of St. Victor, in the theorists of Chartres, that builds upon an identification of the biblical Wisdom of God with the Platonic exemplar of all creation, the *Noys* who presides over man's perfection in the poems of Bernard Sylvester and Alain de Lille.[128] The origin of the arts, says Hugh of St. Victor, must be found in "that Wisdom in which the Form of the Perfect Good stands fixed" and in which man comes to recognize his own being.[129] But for our purposes, the important thing about these mythologies of knowledge is the way the arts are seen to converge on vision: on dreams (like Dante's) that are more intimately the self's possession than merely discursive understanding—"my vision was greater than our speech" (*Paradiso,* 33.55–56)—and whose contours the understanding can only incompletely fill in. The wisdom that contains all the arts ("scientiae thesaurus") is "the sun from which the mind becomes like day in the midst of shadows," a "rapturous paradise of the spirit" where man becomes a god.[130] Again and again, the value of the arts is seen to lie in the purchase they give on this elusive radiance. *Scientia* (knowledge) is the way to *sapientia* (wisdom), inhering in it as the physical inheres in the divine;[131] the operations of the seven sisters are various mirrors of the "simple and indivisible" "element" or "first principle" of true wisdom;[132] the lights of the various arts look forward to the illumination of glory, just as the six days of creation find their rest in a perpetual Sabbath;[133] Philologia, though wedded to language, is nevertheless crowned with a radiance that makes her an image of Pallas herself, "of the highest wisdom which is incorruptible and incomprehensible."[134] It is in such intuitions as these that we may perhaps discover the implications of Guillaume's claim to have found the art of love "enclosed" in a dream.[135]

Macrobius was among the first to describe systematically how philosophers might veil in fabulous narratives the arcana of their systems, an idea picked up enthusiastically by later writers, who developed, particularly in the twelfth century, a theory of the covering or *involucrum* in which truth might be enclosed.[136] The story of Scipio's dream, however, is no mere husk to be discarded, but, as Macrobius' own image suggests, a genuine *mysterium.* All the arts Macrobius expounds are contained in Scipio's dream, in the actual moment of altered vision, not as something hidden, but as something potential. What the general learns from his ancestor on their starry perch is quite literally a new perspective on the world; and all the scholarship his commentator musters (numerology, cosmography, ethics, theology of the soul) is the mind's attempt to grasp and fix in the understanding the vertigo and wonder of that celestial flight. In this Scipio's experience is like the dream of Hermes Trismegistus: "forthwith all things changed in aspect before me, and were opened out in a moment. And I beheld a boundless view; all was changed into light . . . and I marvelled when I saw it."[137]

Or we may be reminded of Dante, who tells of discovering in Boethius and Cicero confirmation for what had already been granted him as dream, "quasi come sognando," in the *Vita nuova,* and of accepting in the Lady Philosophy—even though "our speech . . . has not the power to report all that love says"—a consolation for the absent Beatrice.[138]

We have to do, in any case, with dreams that are not an escape from the self, but its fruition, and not a negation of the world, but the means by which its inner reality may be possessed: dreams, in short, by which one recognizes one's self in the cosmos and so discovers one's natural place.[139] The *locus amoenus* watered by the Fountain of Love may seem very different from those places sustained by the *Fons philosophiae,* but the relationship, in Love's realm, between the dream and the art it encloses, between vision and understanding, is similar to the pattern we have been considering.[140] For the rapt hero in Deduit's garden too the problem is to render in discursive order what is initially the undivided apprehension of a new life:

> I may not telle you all at ones;
> But, as I may and can, I shall
> By ordre tellen you it all. (710–12)

When later the god of love turns schoolmaster, it is precisely, Guillaume warns his readers, in order to expound the significance of the dream itself, to open up its hidden truth.

> For whoso wol the eendyng here,
> The craft of love he shall mowe lere,
> If that he wol so long abide,
> Tyl I this Romance may unhide,
> And undo the significance
> Of this drem into Romance.
> The sothfastnesse that now is hid,
> Without coverture shall be kid
> Whanne I undon have this dremyng,
> Wherynne no word is of lesyng. (2165–74)

> Qui dou songe la fin orra,
> Je vos di bien que il porra
> Des jeus d'Amors assez aprendre,

Por quoi il vueille tant atendre
Que j'espoigne e que j'enromance
Dou songe la senefiance:
La verité, qui est coverte,
Vos sera lores toute aperte
Quant espondre m'orroiz le songe,
Car il n'i a mot de mensonge. (2067–76)

Enromancer: it is a question, as in Dante, of lending speech to vision, of finding those words by which the dream may declare itself. Love's commandments for the *jeus* that are to follow may on occasion borrow from Ovid's more pragmatic notion of art. But they are first of all, for the lover as for the reader, an attempt to unfold in terms of behavior what has already been seized upon in vision as the goal for all striving: the vision epitomized in the moment at Narcissus' pool when the whole scene becomes the content of the lover's reflection. As Genius reminds him, no intuition in this life is perfect—the crystals reflect only a part of the garden at a time—and the devices of the discursive mind are never irrelevant, although they may be misdirected. But the imagination that informs Guillaume's vision is concerned, at its most fundamental level, not with strategies but with a kind of knowledge that is at once an apprehension of external reality and an ordering of the self. The religion of love in the *Roman de la Rose* has at least this in common with Dante's: it is not a matter only of intrigue, but of *observance,* the instrumentation of what has been seen.[141]

A second formula that epitomizes the distance between Deduit's garden and Tibullus' paradise is one having to do with the temporal dimension of the lover's adventure. Guillaume's dream is a prophetic dream, he tells us, every word of which comes true: a thrust into the future like the dream of Eden, which is no mere romantic nostalgia but an eschatological possibility. Our concern is not with retrogression but with the ongoing creation of the self. This sense of entering into a pregnant futurity, of the garden as a flowering of all the self's potentialities, is in the *Roman de la Rose* a structural fact, a quality of the narrative as we read it, not merely a sentence to be discovered beneath allegorical wrappings. But it aligns the courtly garden with certain other traditions, doctrinal and symbolic, of which the myth of the garden becomes a sort of narrative paradigm and which may in turn help to formulate what is involved in the myth. One image in particular must have come to Guillaume (and to Chaucer) with overtones that made it a nexus of this sense of renewal, the image of the proud earth's new garment.

3

Ovid had decked the Hours with all the colors of Flora's garden, and it has been supposed that these are the garments in which Botticelli's goddesses of cosmic springtime make their triumphant procession. Even maidens more humble, in the season when (as Lorenzo writes) "Flora adorns the world with flowers," may be encountered with crowns of blossoms, like Poliziano's Simionetta, and clad in gowns "di rose e fior depinta e d'erba."[142] Certainly the image of a flowery garment, at once the earth's quaint robe and the adornment of privileged mortals, seems to have engaged the imagination of many generations. Charles of Orleans' rondeau in celebration of the season's new "broderie / De soleil luyant, cler et beau" has been called "the most famous spring poem in French literature";[143] and the English herbalist Gerard transposes the figure to a more lordly register in order to urge upon his patron, Lord Burghley, the dignity of actual gardens:

> For if delight may provoke mens labour, what greater delight is there than to behold the earth apparelled with plants, as with a robe of imbroidered worke, set with orient pearles, and garnished with great diversitie of rare and costly jewels.[144]

I am not concerned here, though, with tracing the fortunes of this motif, but merely with establishing a context to suggest the sort of resonance it might have in the *Roman de la Rose*. Carolingian poets and singers of the *Carmina Burana* were constantly finding that spring clothed or adorned an awakened countryside. It is presumably to their example that Guillaume's "cointe robe" gives new life,[145] and they are of course to some extent just responding to hints in classical usage (*vestire, ornare, induere*), although the figure seems to have been much more popular with the medieval poets than it had ever been with Virgil, Ovid, or the writers *de re rustica*. But Guillaume's conversion of what was generally the *translatio* of a single word into an elaborate prosopopoeia of the earth's transformation suggests some heightened suggestibility to the figure; and the reasons for taking it seriously would appear to lie in a tradition that is not strictly literary.

If the twelfth century "discovered nature," if the poets associated with Chartres summoned up the goddess herself, Natura, resplendent in her garment of all living creatures, they did so under the auspices of a philosophy of creation. The new feeling for the natural world was not an absorption in particular beauties, not merely, as a recent historian has insisted, that "sentiment de la nature" no age has been entirely without. It was, rather, an intense questioning of the sources and the articulation of the world's wholeness, its identity.[146] Only when the "totality of the Universe" is felt as a living unity, at once a fact demanding explanation and a familiar presence, can Natura finally make her appearance, as she does in Bernard Sylvester's epic *De mundi universitate,* the epic of Creation. However the traditional forms may be strained by new learning, it is meditations on the Work of the Six Days that provide the vehicle for the intuition on which poets like Bernard or Alain de Lille are able to draw. And it is at the very beginning of the tradition of such meditations, in Basil's homilies *In hexaemeron,* that we may best see how the figure of the earth's garment becomes involved in a cosmic drama, one in which man has a crucial share. Basil's text, in Eustathius' Latin translation, was widely available in the twelfth century,[147] but I am concerned less with the source of the image than with the sensibility it incarnates when it arises in the context of Creation.

On the third day, Basil writes, God commanded the earth to bring forth its fruit.

> See how, at this short word, at this brief command, the cold and sterile earth travailed and hastened to bring forth its fruit, as it cast away its sad and dismal covering to clothe itself in a more brilliant robe, proud of its proper adornment and displaying the infinite variety of plants.

> respice quomodo, ex parva voce et praeceptione brevissima, tellus arida sterilisque repente parturiens et ad fetum fructiferationis impulsa, velut quodam luctuoso amictu deposito sumptisque laetioribus indumentis, et cultu proprii decoris exultans, omnia quae iussu caelesti conceperat effundebat.[148]

The exhortation to see this moment of parturition is not a rhetorical flourish. Basil stubbornly resists allegorization, by temperament, it would seem, as well as on principle (e.g., 9.1); his account of the Genesis story is omnivorously literal, full of the lore of herbals and bestiaries, and the work of the third day is visualized in terms of an actual springtime. Nevertheless, what he wrote is not natural history but a Lenten sermon, in which speaker and congregation alike strove to win back a Mosaic purity of apprehension. The author of Genesis had seen God, Basil tells his auditors, and they too must bring something of his "personal light" to the "contemplation of the wonders I have spread before your eyes" if they are to sense their own involvement with the scene, if they are to discern in the visible landscape of Eden the invisible presence of their own "first home."[149] As Augustine discovered, when all the abundance of the world is seen as a creation, as having been made, "it is as if morning dawned in the minds of those who contemplate" it.[150] For this dawning, we do not need Ambrose's explanation that the spring of Creation was a type of Christ's resurrection ("the passing over from vices to virtues, from the desires of the flesh to grace and sobriety of mind," etc.).[151] Basil is concerned with something prior to such rationalization, an immediate apprehension, a way of seeing.

To refer the stirrings of spring to the first spring is to see in them the sudden gratuitous immanence of the divine word, and so to discover our own stake in the renewal around us. The story of the Six Days opens out, as Basil says, upon the hidden mysteries of the holy of holies (2.1), and the greatest of these is the perpetuity of the relation between creation and creator.[152] *In the beginning God created heaven and earth.* "Astonishment at the thought checks my utterance," Basil exclaims (1.2), and it is just this mystery of beginnings that makes the story of Genesis so involving for later generations as well. "For before I was, you were, and I was nothing to which you could grant being. Yet, behold! I am. . . ."[153] What comes to birth in the scene Basil labors to put before the eyes of his congregation is being itself, and in the intuition he demands of them man and the world are fused in a single blossoming. The nature of this dawning awareness is already suggested in the exhilaration of Eustathius' "fructiferationis . . . exultens . . . effundebat," as it is in the Easter hymns of Fortunatus or Adam of St. Victor ("Novam creat creaturam . . . Mundi renovatio . . . Renovantur omnia"), or even in the triumphant "smale foules" of a Chaucerian spring, exulting in their escape from the snares and nets of winter: "The foweler we deffye, / And al his craft."[154]

To contemplate the Creation, in other words, is less to think about history than to look at the world in a particular way, *sub specie renovationis.* And such vision demands, as allegory or naturalism does not, a peculiar interchange between the seer and what is seen, the soul recognizing in the stirrings of the world the ground of its own being. In such moments of recognition the earth's bourgeoning garment becomes man's own adornment. We must consider what Basil's images suggest about the nature of this appropriation. In the contrast between *luctuosus amictus* and *proprius decor* two elements seem to be involved: one connected with the idea of changing garments, the other with what a garment itself may express. The first illuminates Creation by referring it to baptismal and other purifications; the second, in turn, defines purification by referring it back to the Work of the Six Days.

Apparently it was Philo who first rationalized the clothing taboos of pagan and Jewish mysteries and found in the animal skins Adam and Eve put on to hide their shame the "garment of flesh" whose shedding is the function, and reward, of the spiritual life.[155] Identified with the old Adam Paul insisted must be stripped away (Colossians 3:9–10, Ephesians 4:22–24), the tunics of skin become a common topic in the baptismal theology of the Fathers and also in accounts of monastic life, whose initiates must exchange them for a "vestis angelica."[156] For Basil's brother, Gregory of Nyssa, winning back Adam's original "tunic of light" is an important part of any spiritual return to Paradise;[157] and Ambrose prefaces his account of the sixth day of Creation with a warning that if his auditors are to recognize in Adam their own true beauty they must be ready to strip away the "amictus carnalis."[158] If in the twelfth century

Alain de Lille seemed more sanguine about the soul's fate in its "robe of flesh," Prudentia in her quest for the "new man" had still to be warned by the example of demons who have exchanged a "vestis decoris" (vestment of grace) for a "saccus doloris" (garb of lamentation).[159] What is important for our purposes in all this complex tradition, a veritable theology of vestments, is that purification is conceived as an exchange of garments, and not as what Plotinus calls an "entry into nakedness." In Plotinus, or in the "pessimistic gnosis" of the *Hermetica,* any garment whatever "grips to itself" and "holds down" the soul that needs to be divested "of all that we have put on in our descent" from the One.[160] What the Christian imagination characteristically seeks in Paradise, however, is a better or more fitting garment, "so that being clothed we shall not be found naked" (II Corinthians 5:3–4). This new garment may be identified with Sophia's "robe of honor" (a "garment of holiness" contrasted in Ecclesiasticus [14:17, 50:11] with the perishable garment of flesh), or it may be the raiment, redolent of frankincense, with which the Bridegroom of the Canticles arrays his beloved, her old "tunic" having been put off.[161] But in any case, the moment in which the initiate takes the luminous new garment is one in which (as Pseudo-Dionysius explains) "all that was disorder in him is reduced to order, what was unformed takes shape," so that "his life now shines with full light."[162] What is represented is the perfecting of the created self, not its undoing. Hugh of St. Victor explains that it is precisely in the ornaments bestowed by the Bridegroom, by which all that was unordered and uncomposed is reduced to form, *informis* (shapeless) to *formosus* (beautiful), that the soul comes to recognize her true beauty and worth, "dignitatem suam":

> How exalted and glorious [*decora*] you have been made my soul! What does such attire [*ornatus*] signify but that he who clothed you has been preparing you as his spouse for his bridal chamber? He knew for what sweet task you were destined and what raiment was needed [*novit qualis ornatus illud opus deceret*]; therefore, He gave what was fitting [*et ideo dedit quod decuit*].[163]

Hugh's wordplay serves to remind us of the connection between decoration and decorum, of the almost forgotten sense in which clothing does not conceal or abate but is the means by which a particular nature is fully realized.[164] Medieval aestheticians insist that "whatever makes a thing befitting [*decentem*] is called decoration [*decor*]";[165] and not only monks and kings, but also the heroes of romance often find in some final investiture the confirmation of the being they have striven to achieve.[166] It is just this emphasis and not fancy dress or holiday that we find in the passage from Basil—"oikeiois kosmois" (suitable ornaments), "cultu proprii decoris" (the adornment of its proper beauty)—as it is also in two passages that have been cited as approximations of Guillaume's description of the earth's new robe.[167] These passages, the first from Alain's philosophical epic, the second from a book of natural history, develop different tendencies in the hexaemeral tradition, but they have in common a way of apprehending the earth's new life:

> you would have thought that all the elements were keeping solemn festival, *renewing,* so to speak, *their own natures.* . . . The earth, lately stripped of its adornments by the thieving winter, through the generosity of spring, donned a purple tunic of flowers, that it might not, inglorious in ragged vestments, appear to the young virgin unbecomingly [*indecenter*].[168]

> And therfor in that tyme, al thynnges begynnyth to renoue and wix newe, and *returne Into estate.* . . . The humours of tren and herbis styeth up fro the rotis into the bowes, the seedis rysyth up, The cornes growyth, The medys wixen grene, the flowris coloureth the erthe, the tren clothyn ham wyth lewis, botonyth and spourgyth. . . . And al quyke thynges *takyth agayn thare vertues.* The byrdys syngyth, the nyghtyngall shewyth his organe notis, al the Erthe *rescewyth his anournement and his beaute,* and is like to a fayre yong man that arrayth hym well of al maner of anournement to shew hym-Selfe att the weddynge.[169]

"Vertues" gives a scientific twist to what Hugh's emphasis on *dignitas* and decorum renders on a political or moral level. But in both cases the concern is with the renewing of distinctive properties,[170] and it is this concern that defines the import of the garment that is taken on. This whole complex of ideas is in fact embodied and perpetuated in the word with which Basil describes the earth's new robe, *kosmos,* which signifies at once ornament and order, cosmetics and cosmos. The fact is worth noticing because the double sense of *kosmos* figures significantly in Christian thinking about the Creation; and the Latin *ornatus,* by which *kosmos* is often translated, seems to preserve of its range of connotation at least the fundamental notion of order.[171]

It was Pythagoras who first "gave the name of *kosmos* to the world," Plutarch informs us, "from the order and beauty of it, for so that word signifies"; and Plato had described how the demiurge embroidered heaven with stars "to be in very truth an adornment [*kosmos*] for it."[172] But Moses himself (Genesis 2:1) had written of the perfection of the heavens and earth "et omnis ornatus [*kosmos*] eorum." Creation does not stop short with an invisible and shapeless world, Basil explains, but proceeds to fit out the earth with fields of waving corn and meadows splendid with flowers; and in fact adorns each element with its own beauty:

> After the creation of the luminaries the waters are now filled with living beings and its own adornment is given this part of the world. Earth has received her ornament [*kosmos*] from her proper plants, the heavens have received the flowers of the stars, and, like two eyes, the great luminaries beautified them in concert.[173]

These ornaments, moreover, are "proper and natural" ones, and their abundance is what constitutes the perfection of which Moses spoke (2.1, 2.3). The Work of the Six Days does not merely accumulate beauties, for what Moses shows is how

> the finger of the supreme artisan [takes] possession of the substance of the universe, forming the different parts into one perfect accord, and making a harmonious symphony result from the whole.[174]

This sense of musical concordance is summed up epigrammatically by Bernard Sylvester: "ex partibus plenitudo," from many parts, a fullness.[175] As Basil indicates in the first sentence of the first homily, then, to account for the formation of a world (*kosmos, mundus*) is precisely to account for the process by which visible things are adorned (*diakosmēseōs, decorationem*). The ground of his whole vision of the Creation may be resolved into this single pun: making the ornament of the world, *kosmou kosmon*.[176]

The essential discovery is that to adorn a world is precisely to beworld it, to clothe it in its proper virtues and operations, to bring it to completion: the earth adorned is *terra composita*. The intuition implicit in this vocabulary was elaborated by Augustine and again by philosophers of the twelfth century into a theory of the stages of Creation—the exornation of the world.[177] As Hugh of St. Victor and the hexaemeral writers of Chartres explain, God desired for his creation not only being, but also beautiful being; and his ornaments—the "beautiful and fitting disposition" of all things—have this in common with the white garments granted initiates, that they confer upon what is "invisible and shapeless" its proper form:[178] "From a shapeless agitation he reduced all things to order."[179] Basil's image of the earth's new garb simply takes advantage of the pun implicit in *kosmos* to represent as investiture, as the ceremonial or baptismal assumption of proper dignities ("oikeiois kosmois"), what later writers considered the second movement of Creation: the moment when the poor bare existence of inform matter is adorned with its proper essence, when chaos becomes cosmos. In the twelfth century, poets elaborated this image in contexts more explicitly philosophical. Alain praises the power of God, whose word, enclosing things in number, measure, and weight, invests in "meliore toga" the "old mass, complaining of its ugly visage"; and Bernard Sylvester, like the author of the *Secreta secretorum,* imagines the world stripped of its "old cloak of blindness" and adorned for heavenly nuptials: the marriage of matter and form.[180]

Or rather, these festivities are a narrative equivalent for the abstract relation of matter and form: they render as temporal process and therefore allow us to understand dramatically what is for many theorists—William of Conches, for example, or Aquinas—simply a logical distinction between potency and act.[181] What must concern us here is not the doctrine of exornation, by no means as simple as I have made it sound nor one of which there was any unanimous understanding, but the devotional sense that underlies it. The distinction between creation and ornamentation builds on scriptural language and philosophical tradition (Genesis' double account of the Creation allows accommodation of the merely fabricating demiurge of the *Timaeus*);[182] but more than these speculative issues, it expresses a feeling for the gap between the bareness of our existence in a fallen and therefore uncreated world, and the fullness of being that is properly ours. As Hugh of St. Victor says, the stages of creation are an "example and lesson," instructing the soul to be content with no less than "beautiful being and happy being."[183] For Augustine, the second stage of Creation is a "conversion" of matter from a miserable to a blessed life, and Bonaventure too speaks of the "outcry" by which the very imperfection of matter rises toward God.[184] Calcidius had repeated the Aristotelian idea that matter desires *cultum ornatumque* "in the same way as the female desires the male," and this desire becomes in the cosmological epics of the twelfth century the prayer of matter for form, the longing of finite being for the "vestiture of features" by which its potencies may be realized: "in her confusion she prays for order, in her rudeness for form, in her horridness for beauty."[185]

This is why the image of the garment comes to define the point at which the individual and cosmic dramas intersect. What is lost in the Fall is man's garment of royal dignity, "regiae dignitatis amictus,"[186] and to re-enter Eden, as we have already seen Traherne insisting, is precisely to put on again all its perfections. The visionary poet of Alain's *De planctu Naturae* cannot but be abashed at the descent of the goddess, radiant in her robes of state, adorned with all the ornaments of creation he might have discovered in Basil—birds, fishes, animals, herbs, and trees.[187] And yet it is just the vision of this perfection, "woven without a seam,"[188] that holds out to earth the possibility of renewing her own ragged vestments so that, her "garment of delight" (*PL*, 210.440) restored, she might not appear inglorious before the virgin. Man himself is the only rent in Nature's garment; and now the silver splendor of the fountain itself bids him to drink (col. 442): an invitation expressed more sternly when Nature reminds him of the distinction between being and better being, and reproaches him for forgetting his own prayers for adornment (cols. 442, 445).

The nature of his involvement in the drama of Creation has been defined, perhaps more inwardly, in the long meditation on Creation in Augustine's *Confessions,* in his prayer for those garments of light that would enlighten his own darkness and make it as noonday (13.8.9). And it is Augustine too who asks the classical question for all those later writers who seek to clothe the soul in the flowers of paradise:

> But first "wash yourselves, be clean, take away the evil" from your souls and from the sight of my eyes, so that the dry land may appear. "Learn to do good, judge for the fatherless, defend the widow," so that the earth may bring forth the green herb and the tree yielding fruit. . . . "All these I have done," he says. Whence then so many thorns, if the earth is fruitful?[189]

It is this painful paradox, and also the possibility it implicitly recognizes, that lies at the heart of the notion of exornation.

Guillaume's hero, and I suppose this is largely the point, is less aware of what is problematic about the invitation of his May morning. Nevertheless, the image of the earth's changing garments introduces into the courtly garden the ambiance I have been trying to describe, the penumbra of ideas and aspirations associated with the doctrine of exornation; and this is important for two reasons. First, it alerts us to the possibility of taking seriously the lover's passion for dressing up. In this tradition sartorial images do not indicate superficiality or pretense (what is at issue after all is actuation), but merely the contingency of the goal, the sense that it is at once achieved and conferred—like the allegorical armor of Gawain or Tristan or like the imperial crown by which Charles hoped to remedy Naples' lack of an Adamic governor. It has to do with a sense of possibility, of dynamism. Where the soul's powers adorn it like an awe-inspiring garment, what is suggested is an openness of the self to whatever may be granted it, a self whose experience is not merely a rigid enforcement of prerogatives already held.[190] Now it is very possible we should have to say that Guillaume's hero was misguided if we were to judge by the standards of Alain de Lille (not to mention Hugh of St. Victor). The lover rejects a wintery Elde, but not the Old Adam, and he seems stubbornly devoted to his garment of flesh. But the endeavor itself is based on a vision as coherently imagined as that of the hexaemera.

Its starting place, in fact, is precisely that of Basil's third day:

These wodes eek recovern grene,
That drie in wynter ben to sene;
And the erthe wexith proud withalle,
For swote dewes that on it falle,
And the pore estat forget
In which that wynter had it set.
And than bycometh the ground so proud
That it wole have a newe shroud,
And makith so queynt his robe and faire
That it hath hewes an hundred payre
Of gras and flouris, ynde and pers,
And many hewes ful dyvers.
That is the robe I mene, iwis,
Through which the ground to preisen is. (57–70)

Li bois recuevrent lor verdure,
Qui sont sec tant come ivers dure;
La terre meïsmes s'orgueille
Por la rosee qui la mueille,
E oblie la povreté
Ou ele a tot l'iver esté;
Lors devient la terre si gobe
Qu'el viaut avoir novele robe;
Si set si cointe robe faire
Que de colors i a cent paire.
L'erbe e les flors blanches e perses,
E de maintes colors diverses,
C'est la robe que je devise,
Por quoi la terre miauz se prise. (53–66)

The earth's pride, like the lover's, has been criticized, but her dressing up is not after all without some justification. As Aquinas says, a woman may lawfully adorn herself to "manifest what becomes [her] estate," and the "quaintness" of earth's robe would be objectionable only if "superfluous and fantastic."[191] Her absentmindedness, to be sure, is rather sinister, since in a fallen world no new creation is absolute, which is just what the lover too is apt to forget, like many subsequent pastoral heroes. But in any case the new garb is associated with a new condition, however precariously possessed. Chaucer's "estat" seems a felicitous pun, and his version of the passage's final couplet calls our attention to another fruitful ambiguity. Neither *preisen* nor *prisier* distinguished clearly between praise, prize, and price, as if the praise of anything somehow emanated from its own worth (*pretium*), rather than being arbitrarily assigned; this sort of fusion was involved, I suppose, in the *pretz* that was the troubadour's reward, and the notion lingers in the *los e pris* (praise and worth) that l'Amant himself is seeking.[192] Classical rhetoricians betray a similar habit of thought when they speak of the ornaments by which speech is made more ample as its honors or praises:[193] if the earth prizes herself for her new gown, so splendid an adornment must also be her praise, "Through which the ground to preisen is." It would be difficult, I suppose, to demonstrate that Chaucer had all this in mind, but certainly a usage that identifies an enhancement of value with the wonder it elicits is appropriate for dealing with the adornment of a renewed world. In the springtime of creation, Alain reminds us, there is no praise without worth nor anything without praise ("Non ibi laus sine re, non res sine laude").[194] Hexaemeral writers insist that these lauds be offered back to their Creator, so that each of the world's ornaments becomes a voice in a chorus of universal adulation. The delighted earth of the *Roman* is doubtless more self-absorbed than the psalming birds or applauding islands of Ambrose's imagination,[195] but she is not merely showing off. Like the earth in an English version of the *Secreta secretorum,* what the lover's meadow puts on is its "worschippe and fairhede": its "worth-ship," the specific *dignitas* which is (in Portia's words) its "right praise and true perfection."[196]

The earth's robe inspires the lover, who loses no time in basting up his own sleeves (*Roman,* 97–99), and finds its archetype in the garments of the God of Love "nought yclad in silk . . . / But all in floures and in flourettes," in birds and beasts—like Nature herself, in all the variety of creation (890–917). This revelation—"He semede as he were an aungell / That doun were comen fro hevene cler" (916–17)—confirms in the lover a sense of his own possibilities. Like the earth at the beginning of his adventure, he wants to find for himself the "thing that hem sittyng is" and thereby win "loos and pris" (2309–10); the advice he gets from Love is simply the tropological application of all the splendid vestments he has seen: fair clothing and beautiful adornment, he learns, "A man amendith in myche thyng" (2258). The paradigm of the lover's whole venture in the garden, in other words—the emblem of that dawning self-discovery we have already considered—is Idleness' preoccupation with adorning herself "noblement." "Idleness," to be sure, may sound censorious, but Oiseuse is after all no very distant relative of Otium, who had defenders as well as detractors. She might, in any case, claim the authority of Alain's springtime, another "spendthrift" who "ennobles" the meadows with blooming garments of flowers, or indeed of Nature herself, whose garment granted to the miserable countenance of unformed matter also is designed to ennoble its wearer.[197] When later the validity of this venture is questioned, Le Jalous attacks fine clothes with a Boethian scorn for the man who looks in the wrong place for his proper ornaments. Recalling no doubt the traditional derivation of *nobilis* from *non vilis,* he wonders how something more "vile" than man, like the poor flower garlands of which ladies are so proud, can make him noble.[198] Or else his attitude is a more cynically reductive one, that of the uxorious husband, who sees in any attempt at adornment an investment in excess of the spiritual capital at hand:

> I waste my money when I buy you dresses of [expensive fabrics] . . . in which you ramble foolishly about, flirting and smirking, through the dust and mud, not caring a pin about God or about me. And then at night, when you lie beside me in bed, all nude, then you must not be touched. (*Roman,* 9079–90)

There is no point in adorning a dung heap, and no profit in *bel garnement* for one concerned rather with the rights of the marital bed than with courtly love, with keeping what he has rather than seeking what he has not. The issue resolves itself into a question of what possibilities are inherent in human feeling, and it is with the sense of these possibilities that the image of the earth's garment is involved.

The provenance of the image, furthermore, and the sensibility it embodies substantiate what we have seen about the forward thrust of the lover's journey, a thrust which is inherent in the quality of the poem's imagination and not merely in its story. The garden Guillaume imagines is no mere blur of sensuous reverie, as it is for Tibullus, and we may connect this fact with the way in which Guillaume thinks about adornment. Particularly at Chartres, the doctrine of exornation celebrates the moment at which each thing attains its fullest distinction from every other thing, becomes equal to itself, reaches its final "integrity of being."[199] The "nobilitas" that is the aim of all adornment is (as Dante says) "the perfection of its own nature in each thing"; and the "vileness" of matter is precisely the absence of form.[200] True beauty, Basil insists, is the beauty of Creation; and what pleases the eye of God (who "saw that it was good") is not a merely physical symmetry, but the light that streams from whatever "has achieved perfectly the realization of its end."[201]

No wonder, then, that Alain de Lille prays to the God of Creation, who orders all things by measure, number, and weight, for those words by which his own art may "ornament more perfectly the already created," and dress it more attractively in the "grace of form and species."[202] The aesthetic sensibility that derives *speciosa* from *species, formosa* from *formum,*[203] finds its perfect literary expression in the hexaemera's enthusiasm for the sheer variety of creation:

> What a difference He has foreseen among winged creatures! How He has divided them by kinds! How He has characterized each one of them by distinct qualities! (Basil, *Hexaemeron,* 8.8)

> What a variety in the disposition of their several parts! And yet how difficult it is to find the distinctive property of each of them, and to grasp the difference which separates them from other species. (Basil, *Hexaemeron,* 5.7)

This is a delight in plenitude sincerely devotional—"ex partibus plenitudo"!—yet all but indistinguishable from the mind's pleasure in its own activity, tracing out what Basil calls the "ingenious contrivances of creation" (*Hexaemeron,* 5.7). Classical rhetoric's habit of elaborate division and careful disposition becomes the means by which the poet imitates God's rhetoric and so brings his own matter to its proper ornament. This is what lies behind the pedantry and calculation of Matthew of Vendôme's manner, and makes it (as I have suggested) a suitable vehicle for the lover's sense of discovery. Matthew's typical *locus amoenus* is praised as the result of "nature's study"; as in the hexaemera, species are distinguished and given their proper characters, and the pleasures of the place are assigned to the five senses and the four elements.[204] This same feeling for the logical translucency of the Creation is expressed in the detailed specification of Nature's garment in Alain de Lille, in the "explication" of all the ordered offspring of matter's womb in Bernard Sylvester, and in the catalogues of birds and trees in Guillaume's garden.[205]

If the theory of exornation thus implies a theory of verbal ornament, it may be that the values perceived in the Work of the Six Days are most fully repossessed in the garden of rhetoric itself—where Matthew of Vendôme sees Philosophia refreshing herself amid the flowers of which Flora has woven the earth a new garment.[206] Matthew associates his three "redolences" of poetry—relish of thought (an "inner honeycomb"), polished words, and colors of rhetoric—with the creation of the microcosm: first the vital spirit, then the material body, and finally the behavior by which his potentialities are realized.[207] This may seem only an ingenious conceit, but it is not difficult to see how traditional rhetorical terminology corresponds to the language of the hexaemera.[208] Invention must be copious, and the "inner sweetness" of the "archetype," to be rendered sensible, must be "clothed" in language.[209] The *nitor* of polished words, a formal light of the sort Abbot Suger claimed for his work at St. Denis, banishes the *horrida inculta* with its festive brightness ("elucescit," "festivari").[210] And the colors of rhetoric, its ornaments, are the means by which the body of the discourse is adorned with variety and so attains its proper *dignitas*.[211] These links could be worked out more rigorously and at much greater length, but perhaps enough has been said to suggest why Guillaume's lover is concerned with the proper order of his discourse. His pleasure is an experience essentially structured, a delight taken in fruition, a "certain sweetness" (if I may borrow Aquinas' definition of all enjoyment) that is discovered in the last place.[212]

This derivation of "enjoyment" (*fruitio*) from "fruit" (*fructus*) may serve to remind us that the image of the garden is associated with these ideas of ornamentation not merely because Eden may be taken as the supreme adornment of the new creation. The developmental sense of medieval thought, its pressing toward perfection, its conversion of time to orderly process, has often been noted; and this sense provides medieval literature and art with some of its characteristic images: the ladder, the journey.[213] Since the eudaemonism that makes Eden a "Monopolie of al the pleasures and delights that are on earth, amassed together"[214] finds its object not in escape but in actualization, it is natural that Paradise should be above all the place in which things grow.

> if Paradise is a place where shrubs have an opportunity to blossom, then Paradise has a certain vital force which receives and multiplies seeds in which each and every virtue is planted. . . .[215]

Ambrose's language anticipates, as we shall see, the vision of the poets of the twelfth century: Bernard Sylvester's Granusion, so called because seeds of every living thing are perpetually nurtured there, or Alain de Lille's "secret place" of Nature, that "possesses in itself the power which is possessed by all other places."[216] What I want to consider is the way in which the myth of this cosmic garden is held in suspension by the very language in which the ongoing work of creation is assimilated to a metaphysics of matter and form, potency and act.

The classical notion of the ordered cosmos may be imagined not only in the familiar image of the cosmic city (of which Stoic sages claimed to be citizens), but also with an agricultural analogy. This is a particularly effective way of rendering the inwardness of the doctrine, establishing a perspective between the self and cosmic order conceived as that toward which all things grow:

> Again, it is undeniable that every organic whole must have an ultimate ideal of perfection. As in vines or in cattle we see that, unless obstructed by some force, nature progresses on a certain path of her own to her goal of full development . . . even so and far more in the world of nature as a whole there must be a process towards completeness and perfection.[217]

We have already remarked on the intricacy with which Cicero's doctrine of Nature is dependent upon the natural scene, but this agricultural bias belongs as much to the Latin language as to a particular philosopher.[218]

Kosmos is translated not only by *ornatus,* but also by *cultus* (e.g., Eustathius' "cultu proprii decoris"). The sort of punning this makes available may be suggested by the way Ambrose deals with the problem we have seen other hexaemeral writers confronting, why God should have created a world *incomposita* and without ornaments. God might immediately have clothed (*vestire*) the earth in flowers and fruits, Ambrose explains, but he wanted to demonstrate that the world was indebted to its Creator for such ornaments. But in one of those leaps of analogy Leo Spitzer has so eloquently admired, Ambrose goes on to explain the nature of this investment by evoking the atmosphere of the *Georgics* and its celebration of agriculture:

> The land was therefore unformed, since it was as yet unploughed by the industrious attentions of the farmer [*agricolae*], for the cultivator [*cultor*] had yet to appear. It was unformed because it was devoid of growing plants, the banks of streams lacked grassy slopes; the land was not shady with groves or productive of the fruits of the earth. . . . Correctly, then, was the land called unformed which was devoid of ornament [*ornatibus*] and which did not present to view the linked rows of budding vine shoots. God wished to show us that the world itself would have no attraction unless a husbandman [or creator: *operator*] had improved [or adorned: *ornasset*] it with varied culture [or beauty: *cultu*].[219]

The two senses of *cultus,* agricultural and cosmic, had already been mediated by the habitual use of the term to translate into the language of growth and fruition the Hellenic notion of education as self-creation (paideia); and Quintilian had borrowed the same connotations to insist that rhetorical ornament ("cultus ac nitor"), if properly cultivated, ought to bear fruit.[220] Throughout his *Hexaemeron,* Ambrose keeps returning to the language of the *Georgics* and to Virgil's sense of the incorrigible fruitfulness of the earth, "terra mater" full of the seeds of all things as Servius says.[221] The earth's garment is not merely imposed from without, but blossoms from within:

> The entire earth was now arrayed in this verdant garb of diverse plants. . . . The earth opening up the seeds [*semina resolvens*] gives life to everything. Then, under the command of God's word, it blossoms forth [*pullulabat*] at the gift of creative life. (*Hexaemeron,* 5.1.1)

This is the archetype that is implicated in the play on *cultus* and *operator.* The human cultivator (*operarius agrarius*) is discovered to participate in the work of the *Operator naturae,* creator of all things, whose ornaments ("cultivation") make the pullulating world a *hortus Dei.* Ambrose's vision seems to be implicit in his vocabulary. *Operatio* appears in the *Psychomachia* as Charity, and *Operator* elsewhere in Ambrose's own discussion is a term for the Creator (as opposed to a mere fabricator);[222] but here the word superimposes upon these meanings, or fuses with them, its classical suggestions of agricultural labor and also (given the context) of religious performance, ritual "work." Similarly, the meanings fused in *cultus* suggest that adornment is both cultivation and sacralization, a conferring of both being and holiness; and no more than the world—Ambrose cites the example of Lazarus—can man get along without such attention. The adornment of his own nature is at once a bourgeoning toward reality and his participation in the divine. We may be reminded, however distantly, of Phillis and Flora, who also discovered their proper cult flourishing in the midst of Love's garden.[223]

We must add another word to this verbal nexus. In the second book of the *Georgics,* Virgil had urged that plants which spring forth spontaneously at the call of nature be "divested" of their savagery ("silvestrem animum") by the energetic nurture ("cultus") of the husbandman; it is this nurture that is equated with clothing the land with vines and olives.[224] The passage is one of those that suggest to Servius the fruitfulness of "terra mater," and it may also anticipate Basil's account, in which God is gardener, of the changing vestments of earth. But what concerns us now is the poet's vocabulary. The "wildness" of the plants (*silvestrum*) is that of trackless woods (*silva*), whose fierce growth is unfruitful—"naturally harsh and sterile," Servius says, recalling an earlier passage in the *Georgics*—until grafted by man's care with "bud of nobler race."[225] Virgil's admiration for the gardener's skill (and Lucretius' before him)[226] was seized upon by other moralists than Polixines in *The Winter's Tale* to refute too easy claims for the primitive virtues of the "wildest stock," and their arguments find support in the ambiguities of *silva.* The word is simply the poet's term for *hyle,* Servius says, "that is, the congeries of elements, from which all things are brought to birth." It is through the obscure windings of matter and base desire that Aeneas pursues the golden bough of wisdom, by whose power their wildness may be brought to form and cultivation.[227] Gregory of Nyssa makes a similar discovery in the words of the Spouse's jubilant boast, "as an apple tree among the trees of the wood, so is my beloved among the sons" (Canticles 2:3). "Holy scripture is accustomed to use the word *woods* with reference to man's material existence," Gregory explains, which "becomes overgrown with all sorts of passions and [in which] dangerous wild beasts make . . . their lair."[228] Yet in the midst of this forest's sterile trees, a later commentator says, grows the fruitful tree that is Jesus Christ, who adorns them with his beauty, rejoices them with his odor, honors them with his fruit.[229]

The "poet's term"[230] is introduced into philosophical discourse by Calcidius, who seems to have been the first, in his commentary on the *Timaeus,* to render *hyle* by *silva,* rather than with the more technical and abstract *materia:*

> So the one possibility is that matter desires adornment and embellishment [*silva cultum ornatumque desideret*]; for it is misformed not . . . by nature, but by privation. For the ugliness of matter consists in this, that matter is deprived of adornment and form [*silvam cultu formaque indigere*]. . . . as we say that a thing that begins to be made, desires completion, so, I think, matter desires form; for it can only flourish [*florere*] if form joins it.[231]

This passage provides the terms with which the Chartrians elaborated their philosophy of Creation,[232] and the poet's language carries with it the poet's myth. Wild nature is cultivated—we have already seen, in Bernard Sylvester, the rankness of matter praying for such cultivation—and the garden flourishes out of the wilderness. This is the blossoming come upon by Virgil or by the Beloved of the Canticles. Such magical discoveries, in pious legend the prerogative of holy men and in romance the reward of knights,[233] are found to open upon the very structure of reality.

I should think that the discovery of this story implicit in *silva* and *cultus* would be important to thinkers or poets as the occasion, not so much for discovering new allegories in the matter of romance—medieval and Renaissance allegorists rarely need much occasion—as for feeling inherent in the vehicle itself, in wild places bourgeoning into civility, the pressure of the allegorical. And it might alert us not so much to specific didactic intentions as to habitual configurations of the imagination.[234] The conception of matter that medieval readers might have found in Calcidius, or in the Latin *Asclepius,* is itself, after all, one that eludes attempts at abstraction and turns of necessity toward "vague and obscure notion[s]"[235]—toward myth. As we have had occasion earlier to note, Plato provides later writers with images rather than with definitions. The *Asclepius* speaks of a *vis procreandi,* of the "womb" of matter, "most fertile for the conception of all things"; and Calcidius collects all the avatars of *silva:* "mother . . . nurse . . . womb of all generation." Matter seems to be imagined, in fact, less as a material than as a magically potent place (sometimes, Calcidius notes, it is called *locus*).[236] In the twelfth century, Bernard Sylvester's account of the Creation is preoccupied with the unfolding powers of just such places. The ornamenting of the macrocosm is imagined as a long parturition of the pregnant womb of matter, "generationis uterus indeffusus" (1.2.48); and man is instructed in his own seminal reparation of the world's mortality[237] by the example of Physis herself, whose Granusion, at once garden and "hidden womb" (2.9.22), blossoms perpetually under the fecundating influence of Nature, "mother of generation" (2.9.18–19, 31). The goal of both the great and the little cosmos is imaged forth in the creation of Paradise. Circumscribed with form (1.1.36), the rigid chaos of "silva" (1.1.18) blossoms into the happy woods ("felices silvas": 1.3.301, 329) of Eden, whose fruitful womb reproduces in a single spot all the riches of the world:

> Illic temperies, illic clementia caeli
> Floribus et vario gramine *praegnat* humum.
> *Nutrit* odora, *parit* species, pretiosa locorum
> Mundi delicias angulus unus habet. (1.3.319–22, my italics)

(There the temperance, there the clemency of the heavens, impregnates the earth with flowers and a multitude of grassy things. It nurses the scents and gives birth to spices [or species?],[238] that single nook which gathers together all the value of places, all the delights of the world.)

The poets of Chartres may borrow their dream of paradise from the literature of nostalgia, but they use this motif—in Bernard's Eden and Granusion, in Nature's garden of infinite possibility in the *Anticlaudianus* (1.57–60)—to express just the opposite, the blossoming of all things into reality. Another horticultural image reinforces this sense. The flourishing of form in and somehow from matter is a timeless one, but both Calcidius and Augustine, maybe taking a hint from the "seminia rerum" in Ovid's chaos, find its type in the germination of seeds: unformed matter is imagined as "the seed of heaven and earth."[239] And the process of its "unfolding" is extended imagistically to include all subsequent movement in time by the notion, successively Stoic, Neoplatonic, and Augustinian, of the seminal reasons, the seeds of all things whose blossoming is the subject of history, both natural and human.[240] "Obviously, from a single seed, according to the nature of each, crops can propagate crops, woods woods, herds herds, and peoples peoples, throughout the ages, so that there is not a single leaf or hair in all that rhythmic succession, the reason for which did not exist in the first single seed."[241] In the first instance, God is gardener, Dante's "ortolano eterno" (*Paradiso*, 26.64–65); in the other, it is the secondary agents of nature, performing what Bernard Sylvester calls the "opus nutriendis" (1.4.17), that lead the divinely impregnated potency to act. "As mothers are pregnant with their offspring, so is the world itself pregnant with the causes of all birth,"[242] and the divinely planted nursery of matter ("seminarium inditum") comes to form as a rose blossoms under the care of a husbandman.[243] The planting of the seed is the creative fiat at which the earth blossoms into its proper ornaments: a word that "became as it were a law of nature, and remained in the earth, imparting to it the power of bringing forth all being and yielding fruit in the future."[244] Thereafter, the role of Nature, Bernard's "mother of generation," is defined precisely by her striving to perpetuate this flourishing:

> The work of God is to create that which was not, whence we read, "In the beginning God created heaven and earth"; the work of nature is to bring forth into actuality that which lay hidden, whence we read, "Let the earth bring forth the green herb."[245]

The doctrine of the seminal reasons had already been pressed into service by the "intemperate vitalism"[246] of Plotinus' thought to visualize the cosmos as a Garden of Love; and Bernard Sylvester's own vision of universal germination has seemed to some scholars to be "bathed in the atmosphere of a fertility cult."[247] Without entering into the intricacies of this particular debate, we might suppose that it is in the nature of poetry to liberate mythic contents that are carried even by perfectly orthodox Christian doctrines: contents that are more than residual. As Calcidius explains, to image the potency of matter as that of a seed awaiting growth (rather than wax awaiting the impress of a seal) is to attribute to matter some vitality of its own, more than passive acquiescence to what is imposed from without.[248] It is the seminal reasons, Gerhart Ladner has argued, that give Augustine a model for imagining Creation as a calling of form up out of the void, rather than as a descent or a fall to matter: and thereby for conceiving Edenic reform not as "an undoing . . . of bodily creation but rather a continuation of creation in its entirety."[249] The intuition is of the fecundity of creation and also of time, perceived not as a formless falling away but as the very process by which form is progressively unfolded, a coming to birth. And it is within this fostering milieu that man pursues his own destiny, so that in the unflagging fruitfulness of created nature—in the miraculous power of seeds, "vim mirabilem seminum," flowing to us "as from a fountain"—Augustine (like Alain de Lille) finds at once the paradigm and the promise of our own spiritual flowering and regeneration.[250]

Some such intuition as this, I am suggesting, constitutes the relevance of the hexaemeral tradition to Deduit's garden, and also, to return to the starting place of our circuitous discussion, helps to account for the differences between Guillaume's paradise of love and its classical prototypes. I have been, as I warned I would be, interested less in the specific themes of Guillaume's poem than in the quality of imagination embodied in the image of love's garden. My assumption is that this image is not merely a literary topos or on the other hand—and this has been the point of my tentative and incomplete historical comparisons—an archetype rescued from some universal repository. It seems to me useful to consider it rather as a crystalization of a specific network of ideas and myths, as an imaging forth of a tradition of sensibility. Would it be going too far to say that the opening of the *Roman de la Rose* defines the nature and human possibilities of love by secularizing aspirations associated with hexaemeral speculation? This is doubtless too narrow a formula to account for the complexities of the courtly tradition; but it does seem to me profitable, in asking why love's garden should have so haunted Guillaume and his successors, to consider the ways in which l'Amant's discoveries are similar to those of Bernard Sylvester or of Basil. His experience, of course, is repeated by other lovers and in quite other gardens. Dante's Earthly Paradise is at once the cosmic garden of the hexaemera, "full of every seed" (*Purgatorio,* 28.119), and the poet's *cor gentil,* where the "good and wonderful seed" of the *Convivio* blossoms under the influence of love into all its actuality.[251] Dante's enthusiasm for the green shoots ("buone biade") put out by the noble heart encompasses and gives new life to the more purely schematic tradition of the tree or garden of virtues. In the springtime of the soul, too, "all quyke thynges takyth agayne there vertues," and the questor is fused with his goal. We have spoken before of the longing to put on all the fruitfulness of Eden. Now in effect, a purely eschatological futurity, the mere hope of restoration, has been linked to the unfolding of entelechy. The return to one's proper place is a kind of blossoming; and this is why, finally, Love's place is a garden.

V

Middle Ages and Renaissance

The Redemption of Space

In the preceding three chapters I have been trying to adumbrate a tradition of sensibility that has its roots in antiquity and continues to grow, with the impetus given it by Christian mythology, through the Middle Ages and the Renaissance. What, then, is new or distinctive in the aspiration Charles VIII discovers for himself in Naples? And furthermore why should we adduce to illuminate this newness—which we have especially wanted to associate with the experience of the Renaissance—a peculiarly mythological sensibility, the intuition of space as qualitatively determined and determining, when the innovation of Renaissance science seems to have been precisely to quantify and ultimately to devalorize man's relation to the cosmos?[1] This chapter discusses some differences between medieval and Renaissance gardens in order to suggest ways in which these questions might be answered.

We may begin, though, with a general observation. If the Renaissance is to be defined as a period of transition to the modern world, we must nevertheless be careful not to deny that transition a character of its own, not to treat it simply as an uneasy mixture of old and new. For Copernicus and Kepler, the new astronomical discoveries did not entail the rejection of the imaginative paradigms we have been considering. The sphere of the fixed stars may no longer have had a real function in Copernicus' system, but it was retained, however awkwardly, in order to be the place of the universe ("universi locus"), to express the sense that space is in its very nature what binds, encloses, "contain[s] and preserve[s] all things."[2] The vigor of Kepler's arguments against infinity springs precisely from the "secret, hidden horror" he sees in an "immensity, to which are denied limits and center and therefore all determinate places."[3] It is not true, he insists, that "there is no difference of one region or place from another" or that the universe is "everywhere similar to itself": "the army of the stars" "encloses" and "circumscribes" the world like a "wall or vault," and the solar system reposes in the very "bosom" of immensity.[4]

It is not the sense of cosmically ordered space that disappears in the new astronomy, but only the rigid barrier which in the Ptolemaic system isolated the sublunar world from the perfection of the heavens, the realm of striving and mutability from the incorruptible spheres where all things circle eternally back upon their beginnings. Copernicus accepts the Aristotelian idea that "if objects move or are moved from their natural place rectilinear motion supervenes";[5] his great discovery, implicit in the notion that the earth itself revolves, is that the things of the world are subject to a "double motion": not only the rise and fall by which individuals manifest their incompleteness, but also the circular motion—"the express image of the true felicity," Pico had called it, whose commencements are indistinguishable from its conclusions[6]—by which they participate in the perfection of the whole. If man will exercise his natural "affinity" with the heavens, and "face the facts . . . with both eyes open,"[7] he will discern the "admirable symmetry" and "clear bond of harmony" binding together all things[8] and will see that the earth too is in its "natural place and state." The universe is no longer a network of hierarchically distinguished places, but neither is it an amorphous expanse or the sheer distance of Pascal's nightmare. It is, rather, a work of art, "so bound together that nothing in any part thereof could be moved from its place without producing confusion of all other parts and of the Universe as a whole."[9] It is, we might say, a single place and wholly sacred: a "temple," as Copernicus says, ruled by the sun and "not unworthy of God's workmanship."[10] Kepler simply followed out the logic of this intuition when he installed in the very center of the solar system that deity whom earlier tradition had denied any involvement with space; the cosmos itself is discovered to be God's place.[11]

The Middle Ages, as we have seen, glimpsed this architecture and heard echoes of just such world harmonies. The crucial change is not so much in the topoi themselves as in what we might describe as the tone in which they are uttered, the way they are related to the data of everyday experience. It is of this change in tone, of this altered relation between paradigm and experience, that the peculiarly transitional moment of the new astronomy seems to me representative. New mathematical techniques may eventually become neutral instruments, but for Kepler they were predicated on the discovery that the soul bears within itself no dim recollection but the archetypes themselves, so that finally, he says, the world harmonies "become entirely soul."[12] In the Middle Ages man could not definitively inhabit the cosmic temple until he made his way from this fallen world to the City of Heaven—it is in Solomon's temple that the true music sounds, says Abelard[13]—and even at Chartres the pattern of the cosmos emerges only as we remove ourselves from the immediacy of the empirical.[14] These are questions of degree, of course, rather than absolute oppositions, and I suppose that all proto-renaissances are so called to the extent they entrust a dream of birth to the actual world, however that actuality may be characterized. Still, we may allow ourselves a formula, a perfectly familiar one, that may prove to have some heuristic value. What earlier ages attempted by ascesis, by excluding the data of immediate experience, the Renaissance characteristically achieves, as Copernicus' universe may testify, by an aesthetic integration. And in his own practical space, as we have had occasion to see in the first chapter of this essay, the gardener feels stirring a similar possibility. If Kepler claims, in a famous exchange with Robert Fludd, to touch God with his very hands, Leonard Mascall offers to put Nature, at least, in the grasp of the industrious husbandman.[15] Charles's adventure among the gardens of Naples is new, not in the longing for paradise, but in the awakening sense that such aspiration reveals no more than the contours of his present power. In what follows, I shall return to matters touched upon in the account of his discoveries, in order to see if by looking at some obvious differences in the design of medieval and Renaissance gardens we can define more closely this heightened sense of the availability of sacred space.

1

Even in the late Middle Ages, when the gardens of the *Roman de la Rose* and its progeny were flourishing in verse and floral motifs proliferated tapestries, manuscripts, and cathedrals,[16] actual gardens tended to be no more than a little green space, closed rigidly within walls or cloisters. The forms of the Renaissance garden remain essentially those of their medieval predecessors, but these forms are incarnated differently in the materials, particularly in space and in growing things, from which actual gardens are constituted. In horticulture as well as in astronomy, in other words, the central question is how far the cosmic paradigm is entrusted to the world in which men live. Nowhere is this more evident than in the Vatican's Cortile del Belvedere *(see Plate 18)*, where, between the pope's palace and a fifteenth-century villa on the hill behind, Bramante reconstituted for Julius II the gardens of Pliny and of imperial Rome. To Serlio his work seemed to mark the true rebirth ("suscitasse") of antique art,[17] and in order to indicate the nature of that birth, I can do no better, so suggestively has he formulated the terms, than to paraphrase the investigations of Robert Ackerman. Like the new villas of Naples and Florence, the old centrally oriented buildings are in Bramante's plan turned inside out, "to externalize them, so as to bring them into a physical relation with the surrounding space."[18] And now this space too becomes a positive presence; no longer a mere site for the buildings, it is a medium to be shaped and given form. This is the fundamental fact whose resonance we must try to assess: instead of being an "open area within a mass," the garden becomes a delimitation of the natural terrain itself.[19]

That it should be not a building but a garden, the prototype in fact of the great Roman gardens of the sixteenth century,[20] that seemed to the architects of the high Renaissance so crucial an innovation, testifies importantly to the nature of their ambitions. For Serlio, as for Ficino and Pico strolling near the villa of Leonardo Bruni, what was resuscitated with the antique art was not so much the body of a building as the quality of a place, a way of being related to the world. Pope Julius might have found precedent for the grandiosity of his schemes in classical writers' celebration of villas as embodiments of what we have already observed Wölfflin calling a "tectonic spirit."[21] Pliny the Younger, for example, had praised builders who drew upon resources "such as only nature could form," so that in the midst of "opere urbanissme" one is surprised by "ruris imitatio."[22] Tacitus marvelled at the skill and audacity of an art that could compel nature herself and construct for Nero a palace less notable for gems and gold than for "fields and lakes and . . . wooded ground alternating with clear tracts and open landscapes."[23] Now at the Belvedere, "where nature had formerly been avoided or overcome, it [is] . . . controlled; and a new kind of spatial expression [seeks] to domesticate the open air."[24] And this dream of possession and rebirth is, like Adam's dream or l'Amant's, one that has come true. The quality of the place is not sustained in a moment of vision like Petrarch's, ready to disintegrate at any instant into mere extension and subjective metaphor, but is fully realized by the certainties of art.

The disjunction earlier ages seem to have felt between the paradigmatic cosmos of the garden and the fallen world outside the wall suggests, more than a scrupulousness in marking off the precincts of the sacred, some fundamental distrust of space itself, at least of space as it now exists. We have considered, for example, how Guillaume de Lorris' Garden of Love captured the imagination of subsequent generations and we have offered some reasons for the power of the myth it embodies. But the conscious exclusions on the walls of Deduit's garden—Sorrow, Age, Poverty, all the works of time and imperfection—suggest in how hypothetical and even playful a way the ideal had in fact been imagined.[25] If such gardens seem more problematic in the Renaissance, it is not necessarily because Spenser or Tasso are more puritanically moralistic than Guillaume, but because they are more committed to imagining the realization of Love's garden in the actual world. Before his dream ends, in any case, Guillaume's hero is confronted with the radical contingency of Deduit's garden; however true it has been to his own life, before the divine and universal reality of Fairfield Park its joys become "queroles qui faillirent," dances that come to an end (20,353–55). The true garden, he is informed, is not square but round, and its reality, flowing from a triple rather than a double fountain, excludes precisely that plentitude of the merely natural in which the Lover had sought to discover his own being: as the contrasts between square and circle, dyad and trinity also suggest, it is "toute la terre/O ses richeces ancienes,/E toutes choses terrienes" to which its wall forbids admission.[26]

Jean de Meun does not, to be sure, dispense with the rhetoric of the *locus amoenus* in his attempt to conceive the experience of the faithful in the Shepherd's park (e.g., 20,647–59). This is what keeps the second garden from being merely a refutation of the first, and why the celebration of the timeless resting place may without absurdity be entrusted to a rather cynically naturalistic Genius. But for the natural experience to serve as an analogue of the divine, it must be purged not only of its temporality, but of its spatiality as well, a process that involves the poet in consciously paradoxical maneuvering. Images of process are used to suggest what is, in a world without "preterite, present, or a future tense" (20,023), essentially without alteration:

> If you say that the lambs on grass and flowers cannot forever graze, for they would soon devour them, then know that however much they graze and feed the grass and flowers forever are reborn. (19,975–980)

The satisfaction of earthly appetites expresses a state beyond the possibility of appetite; and in much the same way we are asked to imagine the beauties of a scene that is grasped somehow from no point of view. The lover does not see Fairfield Park half at a time, as he does Deduit's garden, reflected in the two crystals; gazing in the three-faceted carbuncle, he seizes the whole in a single act of comprehension that transcends mere direction:

> Always, in whatsoever place he may be, he sees all the beauties of the park, and knows them properly, and as they are in themselves. (20,571–74)

The task Jean sets his reader's imagination is similar to what the contemplative faces when he considers the book of creatures; and it is not surprising that we should find in the ordering of the monastery garden the same ambivalence toward spatial language we have observed in the *Roman de la Rose,* the same dialectic of the natural image and the meanings that must necessarily transcend it. This ambivalence is made explicit in the twelfth-century cloister at Vaison-la-Romaine, a garden that provides us with a convenient antithesis to Bramante's Belvedere. It is placed on the north of the cathedral so that an inscription may take advantage of traditional symbolism to represent the garden as a nest between the *terra diaboli* of the North and the sanctuary of the South:

> Obsecro vos fratres aquilonis vincite partes
> Secantes claustrum quia sic venietis ad austrum
> Trifida quadrifidum memoret succendere nidum
> Ignea bissenis lapidum sit ut addita venis
> pax huic domi

(I entreat you brothers to flee from the regions of Aquilo [the north wind] and seek out the cloister, for here you will come to Auster [the south wind]. May the triple [colonnade] remind you to inflame [with love] the fourfold nest so that the flame might find itself added to the twelve veins of stone: peace be to this house.)[27]

"Surge, Aquilo, et veni, Auster, perfla hortum meum": Awake, O north wind, and come thou south; blow upon my garden. Like the Beloved of the Canticles (4:16), the monks in their garden are suspended between the persecution of the world—the devil's cold weight, Augustine calls it—and the reviving breeze of the Spiritus Sanctus, blowing from the South ("the fiery region, and full of light") to melt the torpor of imprisoned souls.[28] The cloister is at once a refuge and a place of potential blossoming; and it is in the center of the cloister, from the monks' own "well of living waters," that the purifications are performed which will allow them to enter the House of God.[29]

The inscription itself, framed with acanthus, is handsomely classical in style,[30] and classical precedent might also be found for its nostalgia for the nest of the soul. Cicero, for example, speaks of Ulysses' seaborn longing for Ithaca, "lodged like a nest upon the roughest of small crags."[31]

And Ausonius discovers in his villa at Bordeaux, with its quadrangular walled garden full of roses, at once his homeland and the nest of his old age, "nidus senectae," the soul's natural place to which it returns from the life of the court.[32]

But the monk's true homeland is not to be discovered among the perishing roses of any merely terrestrial paradise; and the inscription in the cloister would seem to be intent on reminding him of the birds who nest, according to the Psalmist, in the Lord's tabernacle: "Yea, the sparrow hath found an house, and the swallow a nest for herself, where she may lay her young, even thine altars" (84:3). Into this tranquil scene, commentators like Gregory and Augustine introduce a distinction, crucial for the monastic life, between *domus* and *nidus*. Christ is the sparrow who rests safely in heaven; but just as the cloister is merely the access to the sanctuary (*domus Dei*), so the *nidus Ecclesiae* itself is not a place of origin or final rest, but merely a temporary shelter: "a house is chosen for eternity, a nest is put together for a time."[33] It is the strength of this promise that allows the faithful, "by use of frequent sighing,"[34] to build themselves their shelter in the midst of the cold wind of the world's persecutions. "In the nest, that is, in faith":[35] the cloister is in fact a sacred place only insofar as it provides an escape from physical to symbolic and internal directions. We have to do with the dimensions of a faith in things unseen, in the "future grace" of the Spirit's Auster, which will, as Augustine says, melt and irradiate the soul's present burdens to raise it far above "every image which the mind draws from the senses of the body."[36] The cloister is a vacancy in the physical, hollowed out by a sense of the contingency of the natural world that quite reverses the classical connotation of *nidus:* it becomes the promise of a "place" where all images are transcended.

This same merely conditional and ambiguous acceptance of the natural image may be seen in the cosmic structure of the cloister itself. The import and even the literal sense of the last two lines of the inscription at Vaison-la-Romaine have been disputed; but clearly they have in general to do with numerological symbolism, and Michel Rambaud has argued convincingly that the particular concept involved is that of incarnation.[37] The twelve "veins" of stone signify the union of the divine trinity and the created quaternity (a marriage of what Jean de Meun so emphatically distinguishes); and Rambaud catalogues all the ways in which the cloister may be seen to embody this dialectic of three and four. The four galleries are each divided by three main pillars; each gallery thus consists of four bays, and each of these communicates with adjacent buildings through three arcades or windows; within each bay, finally, the three arcades are separated by two double columns. Every part of the cloister, in other words, from the whole down to the smallest unit, is a "fourfold nest" inspired by three. And furthermore, the bays are grouped by four, the pillars by three, the arcades by three, and the double columns by two: a total, Rambaud remarks, of twelve. This numerological conceit may lead us to wonder if we have to do with the ingenuity of the medieval builder or of the modern commentator. But that the cloister raises such questions is precisely its point. The space is organized in such a way that its complexity as well as its unity can be grasped only in the mind. No single glance can seize its true dimensions, and Rambaud's last calculation takes leave of sensible experience altogether. We move, in Bonaventure's terms, from perception to judgment, from "place, time, and change" to what exists eternally.[38] The monk, like Phillis and Flora in the garden of a more secular love, may be inflamed ("succendere") by the earthly harmonies he perceives. But as Augustine concedes, the numbers received through the body—all the ravishing harmonies of the creatures from which he must finally turn in search of more spacious landscapes—are only "grudgingly" allowed to man's mortality;[39] and the devout soul at Vaison-la-Romaine is led beyond them, in meditation, to the divine. The natural man, flesh as well as spirit, is in the end excluded from a harmony only dimly adumbrated here below.

Such exclusions frequently have been observed in medieval art: either physical space is denied or else the onlooker is not included in the vision of its perfection. The walls of the early Christian basilica, for example, are apprehended less as structure than as a "screen . . . against a hostile or uncomprehending world"; and the "magic space" they enclose is defined by a splendid illusion of fresco or mosaic whose skill, like the carbuncle in Fairfield Park, is dedicated to liberating the devout from the "optical accidents of space" and the distractions of a particular point of view.[40] The Gothic cathedral sets out with a new confidence to realize concretely "the very laws that order heaven and earth."[41] But man remains a mere intruder in its impassively cosmic spaces, an order determined by the intellect, and making no concession to his physical presence or to the fallibilities and demands of the eye.[42] In a similar way, the world of Gothic painting and sculpture, a world of Edenic "consubstantiality" between figure and environment, is one "constructed without reference to the visual processes of the beholder and even without reference to his very existence."[43] The figures move horizontally within a purely symbolic space, contained between plinth and canopy, between the picture plane and the vibrating gold backdrop of Eternity, and make no gesture to include the beholder, although they may remind him of his final goal. Renaissance perspective is an attempt to break down these walls, to claim for the optical experience itself the unity and coherence the medieval artist had discovered in the merely ideal cosmos of his art and architecture.[44] What is involved is the redemption of the space of our fallen world, a rediscovery of its potential sacredness.

The orientation of medieval artists is exemplified by Cennini's remark that the painter's job is to "discover things not seen" (to suggest a mountain, it is sufficient to copy a rock),[45] and by the resolutely two-dimensional nature of their architectural renderings (geometry for the eye of God alone, to whom the building is offered).[46] For Alberti, however, the art of painting deals not with objects in their putative essentiality, but with "things seen," and no more than the hero of the *Roman de la Rose* does the artist hesitate to enact the fate of Narcissus, "embracing with art . . . what is presented on the surface . . . of the fountain."[47] Mathematicians may "measure with their mind alone the forms of things, separated from all matter," but the artist is concerned with a "more sensate Wisdom."[48] And yet Prospettiva, seated by Pollaiuolo among the liberal arts[49]—for her sake Leonardo claimed that painting was itself philosophy[50]—is not the least of Wisdom's handmaidens: more than a mere technique and not yet a surrender of art to a merely subjective "point of view." Perspective is above all that *commensuratio* (measurement) by which Piero della Francesca says, things may be "placed proportionately in their proper places [*luoghi loro*]."[51] It is this conviction that the natural place of things is to be found in the hitherto delusive world of appearances that is crucial. The accidents of space and vision, the diminution and foreshortening of objects as actually seen, are no longer dismissed as merely irrational variables.[52] The aim of the new art is not simply to create an illusion, but to discover the laws by which the ideal coherence of space—one might say the music of space—can be made visible; which is to say, the laws by which space and the figures it encloses are to be ordered with reference to the beholder himself, in the very act of perception. Man becomes the measure of all things, but Alberti gives *misura* a literal sense quite different from what was intended by the scepticism of Protagoras.[53] What is discovered is that the ratios that govern the operation of sight participate in the objective harmonies of the Platonists,[54] so that in the act of perception itself is to be found the ideal form of a painting, a building, or indeed, of a world. As Giulio Carlo Argan has suggested, perspective becomes the "process by which we reach the antique," whose beauty is nothing else than perfect proportion; and at the same time, the prototype of that new science which finds the mathematical regularity of Nature immanent in the act by which we scrutinize the world.[55] The new art of perspective is not a technique for painting pictures so much as it is a way of looking, the very "perfection of seeing"[56] that discovers the structure of the real immanent in experience itself. The space in which we actually live is found to be at once the antique world and the realm of Nature.

What is involved in this view is of course a new conception of space—infinite, homogeneous, mathematically neutral—which eventually will undermine altogether the cosmic sense of space as enclosing and somehow constitutive of being. Once the only limit is the horizon, one is forced to admit, with Cusanus and Bruno, that any "center" is merely subjective. Place itself (*locus*) becomes merely location (*locatio*), the mind's determination for its own ends.[57] Walpole seems to be aware of something like this when he connects the walled garden with the outmoded magic of the romances, "in which every entrance was guarded by nymphs or dragons."[58] In the age of Newton, however, the nymphs have departed, and the walls can be seen only as an antisocial act of partitioning, a "sumptuous and selfish solitude" (p. 11), or else a mere vacancy that rejects the true potencies of nature—the "dead walls of air" Marvell's Mower already objects to. Kent "leaped the fence," Walpole exults, "and saw that all nature was a garden" (p. 25); but the Eden he offers patrons of the new horticultural fashions is a peculiarly desacralized one, picturesque rather than ultimately real, revelatory not of man's being but of his sensibility.

Even in the Renaissance, the balance between illusionism and a concern for cosmic order was a delicate one.[59] Leonardo himself, near the end of his career, was noting the discrepancies between Alberti's artificial perspective and the actual functioning of the eye. Earlier studio traditions had been willing to permit the fact that vision is not static and that we see with two eyes rather than with one to violate the architectural stability of space, which in Alberti's ideal constructions is framed so hieratically by the picture plane. And they were ready to concede on empirical grounds what classical optics had always asserted, that the curvature of the eyeball itself distorts the regular recession of objects in space. The synthetic perspective for which Leonardo laid the theoretical groundwork freed the artist's visual experience from the constrictions of an artificial geometry, but at the expense of leaving him, as Kent's gardens do, once again outside the walls of the cosmos, forced to content himself with his own disorderly impressions.

But for the moment at least, artificial perspective seemed (as Berenson has said) "the art which humanizes the void, making of it an enclosed Eden"—a transformation not lost on pious observers in Alberti's own century, who moralized the new art to illustrate the perfect vision of the blessed.[60] The sense of enclosure is managed by a system that identifies the infinitely distant vanishing point of parallel lines with the center of the viewer's own visual experience.[61] There is still some controversy over the exact nature of Brunelleschi's famous panel of the Florentine Baptistery, but it may provide us with an emblem of the essential ambition of the new perspective. A tiny hole was bored through the centric point of the composition, so that a viewer gazing through the back of the panel could see, reflected in a mirror held at arm's length, the façade of the Baptistery from precisely the point Brunelleschi himself had observed it. Quite literally, then, the viewer's cone of vision, extending from his eye to the mirror, would be reflected by the spatial structure of the painting, receding toward infinity. It is to provide an equivalent mirroring of the eye by the vanishing point that Brunelleschi and Alberti work out their constructive techniques. Like Phillis and Flora in their dance, the individual is assimilated to a geometrical order that reveals not only the harmonies of the external world but also the true dimensions of his own experience: and the eye is reflected by infinity. The paradoxical dream of a boundless place, of an enclosure that orders without trammelling, is a recurrent one, surfacing in cosmic speculation—Anaximander's "unbounded" or the Christian Empyrean—and in mystical visions, like Poimandres' "boundless kosmos" of light.[62] Now, Brunelleschi's experiment might almost have been designed to exemplify Bruno's boast that when the "imaginary walls" of the cosmic spheres have been torn down, man will confront, not an alien void, but the image of his own magnitude; that man will appear to the infinite, as Ernst Cassirer has written, "at once as the enclosing and the enclosed."[63]

Bruno's heroic frenzies, to be sure, are impatient of any sensible horizon whatever, but it is not difficult to see in the Belvedere court a place that answers, in a more modest way, to such ambitions. It is a garden enclosed not so much by walls as by the structure of vision: by the fixed point of view of the pope's apartments and the imagined infinity of an architectural vanishing point, Bramante's neoclassical exedra.[64] The key to this evolution in garden design, which we have seen adumbrated in Naples and Florence, is the revival of Pliny's emphasis on the prospect—both of and from the garden.[65] Even in the fifteenth century, new demands for "royalty of sight"[66] had begun to convert the symmetries of the medieval garden plot, emerging from behind their walls and laid out in terraces, into an order comprehended in a single glance.[67] As the humanist Gianozzo Manetti proposed to King Alfonso in Naples, if the eye could grasp in a single glance, "in uno aspectu," what the mind knows of the landscape's beauty, then man, "living and looking," would discover a sensible measure of his own greatness.[68] Vision is after all, a later writer observes, a "usurping Sence" that "can endure no narrow circumcription; but must be fed both with extent and variete";[69] and what is most poignant even for Satan in Eden's "goodly aspect" is the "sudden view of all this World *at once*."[70] The virtuous gardener begins to understand that he need not be excluded from this unity. The view itself, Alberti says, should smile the good host's welcome to his guests; as in Pliny's Tuscan villa, "everything is offered to the eyes."[71] And what is already thereby implied is the extension of this empire out into the prospect beyond the limits of the garden, until the eye loses itself in distance.[72] Pliny has described one such view—"at your feet, the sea; at your back, villas; and above, the woods"—and Palladio, to take but a single instance, tells how the Villa Rotunda is oriented to take advantage of the "theater" of views that extend through the distance to the horizon itself.[73] The garden's boundaries no longer fence it from a radically different world outside, but serve instead to localize a potency which is now perceived to be universal. The difference is perhaps like the difference between the monk's garden in the wilderness, "cut off from all the world," and Flora's "hortus in agris," a perpetual blossoming in the midst of the very fields, made fruitful by her power, that constitute the dowry of the goddess.[74]

Bramante's design (*see Plate 18*) anticipates the vocabulary of sixteenth-century gardens by completing this double process of assimilation, the garden extending itself to include the world at the same time it fuses with the experience of the beholder. Three great terraces convert the natural irregularity of the site into architectural volume, and an axial organization replaces the conglomerative mode of the earlier Renaissance and of the Vatican's own earlier gardens.[75] Without losing their cosmic quadrangular design, the terraces become constituents of vision, receding planes bordered by porticoes, like the checkered ground of Renaissance stage perspectives. Nor is it merely accidental that the lower terrace should in fact have become the first permanent theater of the Renaissance. At Poggio Reale too, as later at the Farnesina, it seemed natural to devote to spectacle and festivity the privileged spaces of the new villa architecture; and if artificial perspective finds its purest flowering in scenographic art, the reason must be sought in the special sort of theatricalization it bestows upon experience.[76] Vitruvius describes how decorators of the classical villas Bramante was emulating borrowed from the scenic façade of the satyr play those "ports, promontories, shores, rivers, fountains, temples, mountains, herds, and even shepherds" which, painted or constructed or carved in living foliage, turned their gardens into what a modern commentator has called "tableaux projected in three dimensions."[77] The attitude we may detect here, as in the passage already cited from Palladio, is one that takes the natural world, the world of physical space, as the scene of human activity: not an alien or indifferent background, but the context or environment in which human gestures assume their truest form. Filarete had already remarked on the way in which the soul is led by the grandeur of church architecture to discover its own unrecognized potentialities: "We Christians build our churches high, so that those who enter feel themselves elevated and the soul can rise to the contemplation of God."[78] At the Belvedere, it is exterior space that accomplishes this definition. Situated in the papal apartment of which Raphael's frescoes make "one ideal temple of the human mind,"[79] the eye is led by the garden's center-accents through three circles, all concentric to the self, until it comes to rest in an infinity at once spatial and historical: the exedra that is both the meeting place of parallel lines and the resuscitation of the Temple of Fortuna at Palestrina.[80]

The power and harmony of mind celebrated in Raphael's Stanza della Segnatura find in the Belvedere court at once a physical manifestation and (in the radical sense) their definition. Pope Julius' hundred-year project for the transformation of Rome states more amply what we have seen adumbrated at Naples and Florence and translated into the homelier imagery of English prodigy houses: the dream of a secular book of creatures, the reading of which carries us, not away from the world, but toward a more complete possession of it. Laneham's remark about Kenilworth may bear repeating, so neat an adaptation is it of the traditional way of speaking of the garden of this world as an unfolding of God: "argument most certein of a right nobl minde, that in this soort could haue thus all contriued."[81] But perhaps we should cite the more dignified authority of Manetti, who already in Alfonso's Naples had found in such activities of man as the planting of tall trees or the construction of large buildings at once the symptom of his thirst for immortality and the objectified image, the definition, of his nature: homes, towns, cities, all the second creations of man's culture, these are ours, Manetti says, they constitute humanity.[82]

2

Behind the exedra, with its reminiscences of Roman temple architecture, is the spiritual center of the Belvedere gardens and, indeed, probably the occasion for the whole project: the *giardino segreto* designed to house the papal collection of classical statuary. This inner court, the first museum of the Renaissance, seems to have been conceived also as a sacred grove, whose visitors are warned in an inscription over the entrance by the sibyl's words to Aeneas: "procul este prophani" (let the profane keep their distance).[83] We have already seen in the case of Ficino how readily the dream of antique harmonies could translate itself into a rediscovery of a sacred landscape. Now, in laying out the pope's viridarium, Bramante everywhere associates the astounding images of antiquity (the astonishment is amply registered in visitors' accounts) with the energies of the natural world. Cypresses had been imported so that the informal gardens to the west would correspond to Pliny's specifications, and tourists comment on the beauty of the vista as well as on the profusion of growing things.[84] The Laocoön and the Apollo Belvedere are themselves set in niches painted with arbors full of birds and flowers.[85] And in the most elaborate niche of all, Cleopatra drowses, like a nymph beside her sacred pool, in a grotto planted with real foliage, while water flows from her breasts into a sarcophagus adorned with the exploits of Trajan.[86] To Pico's nephew, Gianfrancesco, the garden with its "altars" to pagan deities seemed, indeed, "the grove of Venus and Cupid," but, in sad contrast to the plane tree by the Ilissus, little more thereby than a Circean garden where men are turned to brutes; inspired perhaps by Mantegna's *Minerva,* he set about writing his own verses "De Venere et Cupidine expellendis."[87] To other visitors, however—which may suggest a paganism less reprehensible—the Venus Felix standing amidst fragrant citrus seemed to be presiding over the "sacred orchards" of the Hesperides, whose fruit (it has been supposed) she originally received from the Cupid upon whom she smiles.[88] (*See Plates 16–17.*)

Gianfrancesco Pico's account of the Cleopatra fountain recalls a similar fountain in Francesco Colonna's romance, *Hypnertomachia Poliphili* (1499), and a historian has suggested that Bramante remembered this strange work, full of architectural lore and hermetic secrets, when he transformed the dying queen into an image of that fruitfulness Colonna explicitly connects with the Mother of All Things.[89] The adventures of Poliphilus, in any case, may be taken as a parable of Pope Julius' own endeavor, as indeed of Petrarch at Vaucluse or of Ficino or of Mantegna at Lago di Garda. Colonna's hero encounters the Mother of All Things, watering with her breasts a verdant landscape, only after he has emerged from an obscure cavern, a "fearefull hell, darke hollownesse, and dreadfull place," whose labyrinthine ways remind him of the labors of Daedalus, Psyche, or the hero of Apuleius' *Metamorphoses*.[90] What he undergoes is an initiation, one that takes him in progressive stages through the realm of the senses to the cosmic garden of Venus herself. This penetration into the fecund source of Nature leads Poliphilus to a discovery of his own true nature, and (more unexpectedly perhaps) to a grasp of the secrets of classical architecture. Poliphilus is rewarded with the love of the nymph Polia—the image of himself whom he loves but has not hitherto possessed—only when, passing through a landscape of monuments and gardens, he finally becomes worthy of such a place as Venus' amphitheater, where all the glories of the Roman Colosseum are born anew.

The lover's characteristic thrust toward self-realization becomes in Colonna a quest for the very architecture (= *archē*) of the soul, which is discovered in the sacred place where antiquity and nature blossom together. Just this fusion of ideas, self and architecture, nature and the ancient world, defines the peculiar sacredness of Julius' grove at the Belvedere. Images of antiquity seem to manifest in the permanence of stone the regenerative power of Nature itself, and in such places—the perfected world where Apollo now makes his home, one poet claims[91]—man also returns to his own true dimension. The physical and spiritual fecundity suggested by the Cleopatra fountain (and by the garden as a whole) testifies at once to the personal grandeur Julius has achieved and to the potency of his efforts at classical revival. Nor is this only a matter of symbolism. The architectural use of water, playing over statuary and out of grottoes, was something new; and visitors praise Julius, in language reminiscent of Pliny's celebration of Roman aqueducts, for the power and skill—leveling hills and filling valleys—by which he provides this display.[92] It is in fact the restoration of the aqueducts, beginning with Alberti's work for Julius' predecessor, Nicholas V, that finally makes the hills of ancient Rome once again habitable; this quite literal association with reviving antiquity gives a special resonance to fountains celebrated elsewhere more playfully or in a more purely pastoral mode. Frontius had shown that water was the gift of emperors; and as if to confirm Pontano's advice to King Alfonso, Sixtus V by the end of the sixteenth century "distinguished himself from all other pontiffs and rivalled the ancient Caesars" with the new Acqua Felice, which springs triumphantly through Roman arches and leads its subterranean waters (according to Tasso) to the light of the sun that shone on Augustus.[93] Water, and especially the play of water in fountains, becomes, as no visitor of even contemporary Rome needs to be persuaded, the sensible measure of the vitality of the antique world. This intuition is worked out most elaborately, I suppose, at the Villa d'Este, where water playing from the grotto of a many-breasted Diana of Ephesus originally made harmonies on the famous water organ, and streams flowing from a hundred fountains connect the Fountain of Tivoli, where a sibyl pays tribute to the lord of the villa, with that of a reborn Roma Triumphans.[94] At the Belvedere, the Mother of All Things is a source, not only of grass and orange trees, but of all that is suggested by Trajan's exploits as well. (Since Frontius had served under Trajan, it is appropriate that the fountain should have reminded Gianfrancesco Pico of ancient aqueducts.) An adulatory poet, admiring the way Cleopatra was turned into a river, had already praised Julius as another Caesar, second only in years, who leads to Rome the waters of the Nile; and shortly after the pope's death a statue of Nile himself was recovered to match the Tiber already on display.[95] The two great river gods, each bearing a cornucopia, faced each other across the court's central fountain, and together they may be taken to define the components of Julius' imperial ambition: the flood of the perpetually reborn

Eternal City, the spontaneous and inexhaustible fertility the Egyptians called god.

The emphasis on fecundity, of course, is apt to be found in any *locus amoenus* since the garden of Alcinoüs; even the Church, according to Rabanus Maurus, is a garden because something is always growing there.[96] The pope's garden, however, as an early traveler remarked, is "loca amplissima & amena dorico more constructa," built in the Doric style.[97] The immediate reference of this last phrase is probably to the loggia west of the garden, but we might find suggestions for a wider application in another, more precise description of the statuary court:

> paved in squares of tiles, laid on end, and in every square a beautiful orange tree grows out of the pavement, of which there are a great many [*gran copia*] arranged in perfect order [*con perfetto ordine*].[98]

If the whole place seems of a Doric or classical perfection, it is perhaps because it answers so completely to the norms, ultimately rhetorical ones, by which the Renaissance liked to define the structure of nature itself. "The soul is delighted by all copiousness and variety," Alberti says, but copiousness "without dignity" is a "dissolute confusion"; and his prescriptions for villa gardens include, along with suggestions for pavement, statues, and artificial grottoes, rules for the proper order—no random grove—in which trees should be planted.[99] The insistence on both *copia* and *ordo,* on sensuous variety and intellectual precision, may indicate, furthermore, another way in which the Renaissance garden embodies the change in attitude or expectation we have been trying to define. And once again, what is new is not the ideal, but the extent to which the design of actual gardens entrusts this ideal to the real world: where exactly is the order discerned, and how is it related to the variety?

As we have already seen, one tradition that might reinforce the urgency of these norms is that of hexaemeral meditations on the Creation. For writers from Basil to Milton, Eden is God's garden because it unites plenitude with unity; just as accounts of later gardens, by encyclopedists and travelers as well as poets and theologians, tend to unite hyperbole with rigid partition. "What can your eye desire to see, your eares to heare, your mouth to taste, or your nose to smell," asks the Elizabethan gardener, William Lawson, "that is not to be had in an Orchard, with abundance of variety?"[100] We may prefer the more flexible pleasures of the classical landscape to this pedantic assurance that each of the senses is systematically gratified, in which Lawson unconsciously follows not only Matthew of Vendôme's advice to poets in search of their own "copie," but also the way in which philosophers like Anselm or Albertus Magnus proceeded when they wanted to consider gardens.[101] But as we have suggested, this invasion of poetry by dialectic is appropriate when the *locus amoenus* is to be read like a book, the poet contributing merely a gloss; and when the deity discovered in its sensuous variety is not the embodiment of regressive fantasy, but the power that brings all things to their fruition.

It is this power, that of "nature . . . full of so many works, ample in so many good things," which was celebrated at the end of the twelfth century in Peter Riga's *De ornatu mundi.*[102] As the title suggests, the classical *locus amoenus* seems here to be associated directly with the Work of the Six Days, so that it becomes "paradisus Dei," full of perfumes and the honey-sweating trees of traditional millennial imaginings. And like Venus's paradise in Claudian, its walls are adorned with the precious art of Mulciber, the bringer of civilization.[103] In such a place, Nature's copiousness must go hand in hand with her artfulness:

> Hic experta fuit natura quid ars sua posset,
> Et, quanto potuit, pinxit honore locum.
> Non stillavit in haec loca quaedam gloria rerum,
> Sed quasi cum nimbo copia fluxit opum. (9–12)

(Here Nature tested what her art might do, and, as greatly as she could, she adorned the place with every beauty. Nor in this place did the glory of things come in a trickle; but as from a storm cloud, the plenty of her works poured forth.)

It is in this art the poet humbly petitions to share (1–6). His most intricate dialectical permutations—"Here the nard casts forth its odor, the rose blooms, the bird sings; the one gives pleasure to the nose, the other to the eyes, to the ears the last" (55–56)—only translate into the poet's own ornament ("cultum sermonis"[1]) the care with which the grove itself has been cultivated and brought to its proper perfection: no mere retreat, but like the lover's garden, the veritable "rosa mundi" (169). But as I have already suggested, the essentially analytic manner of Peter Riga or of Matthew of Vendôme means that order is discovered in the sensuous experience only as we move away from that experience: an order less of *res* than of *verba,* one we are convinced of rather than perceiving directly. If Peter is more insistent than Guillaume de Lorris in warning his readers to fly to the "sacred rose" that is man's proper simple (171–80), it is precisely because he adheres more rigidly to the rhetorician's paradigm, rejecting all the seductions of narrative that might sink him in mere perception. We are not surprised to discover at the end of the poem that the true garden is the Word Himself: "it flourished in heaven, on earth it withered" (177). Just as the poet's language transcends those things which it orders in the reader's mind, so finally the true Word transcends the world altogether.

Variety and order are the two poles on which the twelfth-century vision of Nature turn, but the style of imagination exhibited by Peter Riga, or by Bernard Sylvester's similar verses on the exornation of the world (1.3), seems to relate these terms in an irreducibly vertical way. A recent commentator has argued, eloquently and learnedly, that in the thought of Bernard at least there is an "existential" impulse that would see "the archetype latent in the empirical manifestation"; but he concedes that the rhetorical tradition gives Bernard no language by which such a unity might actually be imagined.[104] The rhetorical style, indeed, is entirely adequate to its own particular vision of the world and makes it seem almost inevitable, in fact, that this vision should be imposed: the exhortation of Peter Riga's last lines has been implied all along in his way of seeing the world's garden. The story of the feeling for nature in the Middle Ages is long and obscure, and rather than entering into it here, I should like to mention just two other instances of a pronounced verticality in medieval gardens—one sacred and one secular, one from the twelfth century and one from the sixth—which may provide us with a pair of emblems with which to frame this characteristic imaginative style: a worldly monk who tumbles into his garden plot, and the wiser courtier who offers up his flowers to a virgin queen.

Herrad of Landsberg's "spiritual encyclopedia" of the late twelfth century, the *Hortus deliciarum,*[105] may represent for us the monastic art and rhetoric that attempt to appropriate from the world's landscape whatever remains unimpaired and to make of the cloister a paradise regained. Like the gardens of Albertus Magnus in *De vegetabilibus,* the *Hortus deliciarum* is dedicated to health and pleasure.[106] Both the famous illustrations and Herrad's Latin verses are permeated with the imagery of the Canticles, which turns Mount Hohenburg into something very like its prototypes in Goliardic parody, a garden of the gods in which troops of maidens, blooming like flowers, perform their sacred rites and live in perpetual song: "Gaude laeta/ Canta sueta/ Cohors virginum . . . /Bibant, bibant,/Vivant, vivant,/Omnes aeternaliter."[107] Monastic florilegia or books of devotion like the *Speculum virginum* (c. 1070–1150) had already insisted that the holy reading was an opportunity to "wander through fields joined one with another, delight in varied flowers . . . and glory in weaving for [oneself] a crown of many colors."[108] What such images involve is not merely the pleasure of metaphor, but the conviction that since divine learning is the mirror in which virgins may discover their proper adornment,[109] education must be imagined as exfoliation, the blossoming of the soul's true being. The *Hortus deliciarum* expands upon these "spiritual paradises" to include among its *deliciae* the honey of the philosophers as well as of the fathers,[110] but it is with the inwardness of her encyclopedic lore that Herrad is most concerned. The tract itself is not merely a source of information, but, as its readers are instructed, a canticle to be revolved in one's heart until all the data of universal history and twelfth-century science come to be understood in their bearing upon the economy of salvation.[111] And this inwardness is to be grasped, this act of assimilation to be accomplished, not in terms of philosophical system, nor even primarily of dogma, but precisely through the images by which the treatise is adorned. These images, visual and verbal, do not merely illustrate ideas; they become, as Fritz Saxl has said, primary symbols, the very act by which the mind envisions the intertwined harmonies of microcosm and macrocosm.[112] The seven arts, it is discovered, flow, as do the four virtues in another illustration, from the rivers of Paradise;[113] and the pastoral landscape of the Canticles becomes the means by which the garden of hexaemeral learning, the vision of the world's integrity in its first creation, is claimed as a resource of the self. The soul, in other words, seems to draw from knowledge of the world that same nourishment, "as from a sweet honeycomb" (p. 126), earlier monastic readers had found in their devotions. The world becomes the soul's garden.

Yet we are unlikely to confuse the cloister of Mount Hohenburg with the gardens discovered by Phillis and Flora, or by the lover in the *Roman de la Rose*. Herrad is as careful as Peter Riga to insist that the flower that does not fade is seen only *sub figura* (p. 134), and that it will be enjoyed only when the flood of this world has safely been navigated. The glimpse of the rivers of Paradise, caught in *remoto speculo* (pp. 129, 132), is valuable precisely so far as it guides the nuns in their dangerous voyage "upon earthly waters" (p. 123) to the place where they shall be seen *in oculo*. Herrad's style relentlessly suspends the nuns between antitheses—exile and homecoming, labor and rest, dolor and remedy, heat and shade—so that what is important is less the place their flesh inhabits than the direction in which their will is moved; "Quaerite, sperate, scitote, tenete, vocate" (seek, hope, inquire, persist, call [p. 126]). Like the nest of Vaison-la-Romaine, this world's *Hortus deliciarum* becomes a summons to what lies beyond, a spoken word whose promise liberates from the "sad prison" of all space (p. 126): the visual symbol of this is the ladder of love on which, in one of Herrad's illustrations, monks and laymen alike must scramble toward their true reward. There are two cities, Augustine had explained, "una in *re* huius saeculi, altera in *spe* Dei."[114] It is by the constant repetition of the "certain hope" of seeing the Word face to face, the "verus sponsus nunc absconsus" (the true spouse, now hidden [pp. 127, 129–30, 132]), that the nuns are led in their climb from the world of mere things. If the flower of this world, whether of the cloister garden or of the library, "admonishes the pious mind with many arguments,"[115] the argument and the flower are quite distinct, and the penalties for confusing them are severe. The monk who pauses on his trip up Herrad's ladder to cultivate his own garden plot ("tending his garden and attending with superfluous thoughts to his own planting") falls as surely as those distracted by any worldly pleasure from the true *dulcedo* of divine contemplation.[116] (*See Plate 19.*)

We may seem by now to have strayed from actual gardens to their use as symbolic shorthand for sensuous or natural experience in general, although I think this is a distinction Herrad would not have recognized. Gardens, after all, are a temptation as actual as the beds and baskets of gold toward which other men topple from Herrad's slippery ladder. John Cassian had in fact seen a peril in even the smallest garden plot, and in the thirteenth century, when the nuns of St. Lambert wanted to picnic in a meadow near in the infirmary, their Provincial reminded them of such warnings.[117] Adam sinned in a garden, Christ was betrayed in a garden, such places are dangerous; and yet the nuns' superior concedes the reasonableness of the request, for blooming flowers and singing birds are an image of heavenly blessedness. It is the actual garden of the cloister that must speak, if anything will, of the longed-for Eden—to those who know how to heed its message. Fritz Saxl cites the example of a monk who appended to his diagram of Bonaventure's *Lignum vitae* a sketch of a monk writing at the foot of a tree, and also these verses which seem to make of some actual garden the scene of the whole drama of redemption:

> Adam the clerk was writing under a tree,
> Of how the first Adam sinned through a tree,
> And the last Adam, born of a Virgin,
> Repaired the harm of the first, on a tree.[118]

It is the intensity of the hope of Adam, the clerk, that makes his immediate place transparent to a mystery beyond all places, and so preserves him from the fall of Herrad's monk, or of the first Adam.

Fortunatus, too, was concerned with *dulcedo* and with the uses of actual gardens, gardens which, like his own rhetoric, served to soften and humanize both the barbarities of Merovingian courts and the austerities of Queen Radegunde's monastic retreat.[119] His occasional verse is precisely a verse to create occasions, to appropriate for culture the actual fabric of social life. It is through the inspiration of Childebert's garden that naked power may be celebrated in images of sweetness and growth (just as Venus and Cupid deck with flowers the marriage bed of Sigebert and Brunhild);[120] and thus Virgilian topics blossom again, however precariously, in the barbarian forest that earlier had threatened to rob the young poet's verse of all its flowers.[121] And it is the sensuous appeal of the monastery gardens at Poitiers, the "copia florum" heaped on banquet table or altar, the multitude of *deliciae* that makes Fortunatus' head reel and his heart stir with love (11.11, 11.24), which helps to define what critics have often called a nascent rhetoric of courtly sentiment.[122] The terms in which Fortunatus might have wanted to be praised are perhaps suggested by his eulogy to a clerical friend:

> Propelled by a happy breathing, the breeze of your refreshing [*recreabilis*] opinion soothed our ears; and caressed with a gentle motion, with a rustling sound, this messenger of sweet flowers, freighted with all the odors of the paradisal garden, perfumed our very nostrils with its aromatic breath, proclaiming appropriately that, just as in the beginning, eastward in Eden, so in a later age and in a different place, God would plant Elysium (5.1)

Yet for all this willingness to partake of the garden of this world—for which he was suspect in his own lifetime and frequently since[123]—the posture in which we remember Fortunatus and in which he may be taken to complement Herrad's unfortunate monk is the one where he assumes to offer up the product of his garden to a higher beauty:

> O regina potens, cui aurum et purpura vile est,
> Floribus ex parvis te veneratur amans.
> Et si non res est color, attamen ipse per herbas,
> Purpura per violas, aurea forma crocus.
> Dives amore Dei, vitasti praemia mundi,
> Illas contemnens, has retinebis opes.
> Suscipe missa tibi variorum munera florum,
> Ad quos te potius vita beata vocat.
> Quae modo te crucias, recreanda in luce futura,
> Aspicis, hinc qualis te retinebit ager.
> Per ramos fragiles, quos nunc praebemus olentes,

Perpende hinc, quantus te refovebit odor,
Haec cui debentur, precor, ut cum veneris illuc,
Meque tuis meritis dextera blanda trahat.
Quamvis te spectet paradisi gratia florum,
Istae vos cupiunt iam revidere fores.
Et licet egregio videantur odore placere,
Plus ornant proprias, te redeunte, comas.

(O mighty queen, to whom gold and purple are of little worth, with a few flowers your lover reveres you. And though color has no substance, yet it is present through these growing things—purple in violets, and the crocus with its golden form. Rich in the love of God, you have shunned the world's rewards; despising that wealth, you will keep this. Take up the gift of varied flowers I send you, flowers to which your blessed life summons you yet more strongly. You who now mortify yourself in order to be made anew in the light that is to be, descry from these what fields will henceforth receive you. From these fragile branches, which now we offer in all their fragrance, judge how great a perfume will then refresh you. I pray that when you, to whom these things are due, have come to that place, your sweet right hand may through your merits draw me thither. However much the grace of the flowers of Paradise may be awaiting you, though, these doors even now long to see you again. And though they seem to please with their uncommon fragrance, these flowers, when you return, adorn more fairly their own blossoming.)[124]

The gerundive mode of the ninth line is the natural expression of a rhetoric built habitually around a distinction between the wealth of the world and of God, the one "vile" and inchoate, the other fully actualized, completed with all its ornaments. Dante's dreamer will discover the flourishing of his proper nobility (*non vile*) in the garden of his natural life, but Fortunatus is again and again brought short in his enjoyment of the queen's fruits and flowers by the reaches of time that separate them from the eternal roses and lilies of the true "locus puellarum" where, like Herrad's nuns, flower-gathering virgins serve their Lord.[125] Even the more secular sweetness of King Childebert's garden is subject to the same dialectic. It blossoms in his honor, Fortunatus assures the king's widow, and its health-giving plants draw their sweetness from the hands that planted them. As in the gardens of Alcinoüs or of Pope Julius, the fecundity of growing things, "paradisiacal roses," vines, and fruit trees, memorialize the regal potency of their cultivator; but to the king himself, the garden is only a starting place:

> Hinc iter eius erat, cum limina sancta petebat,
> Quae modo pro meritis incolit ille magis.
> Antea nam vicibus loca sacra terebat amatus,
> Nam tamen assidue templa beata tenet (6.8; *PL*, 88.226)

(From here went his path, when he was seeking the holy threshold, where now for his merits he prefers to dwell. For your beloved formerly wore out the sacred precincts with coming and going, but now he holds eternally to the blessed temples.)

The *locus sacer* of the garden, like the monk's cloister, is no more than an antechamber to the temple itself, where the blessed Childebert at last enjoys that true health figured only conditionally by the roses, however paradisiacal, of this world.

The queen's own flowers, Fortunatus tells us in another poem, are heaped on the altar of the monastery. Even in the spring, when the Lord has vanquished Tartarus, and every other woman wears a sweet-smelling rose, "you who are fragrant only for Christ donate these first fruits [*primitias*] to the holy temple" (8.12). *Primitias* seems to make of Radegunde's natural blooms a liturgical sacrifice, and so may serve to explicate her role in "O regina potens," where in her retreat she participates in Christ's passion to be renewed with Him in the springtime of another world (line 9). We might recall Marvell's search, in "The Coronet," through "every Garden, every Meadow" to find a proper garland for divinity. His puritan conscience will allow him no such intermediary as Fortunatus adores but must crown the Savior Himself; his necessary failure is felt the more strongly, and characteristically it is not the poverty or insignificance of his matter that concerns Marvell but the snake twined about its root. The only course open to the poet is to convert his praise to sacrifice, and—like Radegunde, although the tone is very different—let his flowers wither so that they "May crown thy Feet, that could not crown thy Head."

Fortunatus' gesture, however, is not a sacrificial one, but that of a weak man who must be coaxed into heaven: his offering does not reject the blandishments of the senses but devotes them to their proper use. Color may in itself be nothing, but because the queen does not reject such gifts Fortunatus' veneration can be nurtured by his sentiments—

finding analogies in purple and gold, in all the *dulcedo* of the garden—and clothe itself in the rhetoric of a lover. And in turn, this rhetoric is itself the means by which the earthly delights of Radegunde's garden, properly weighed by the poetic act (line 12), are consecrated to the service of a higher vision. It is precisely when the flowers cease to be mere things, and are offered up to the true beauty from which they receive their adornment, that they become a call to the soul, drawing it up, as Fortunatus hopes to be drawn, to its proper beatitude. But like God's own rhetoric in the Book of Creation itself, what all this represents is accommodation to the weakness of the flesh. Next to Radegunde's Christian heroism, or Marvell's, the devotions of Fortunatus must seem of a pastoral simplicity and weakness. It is in this tender sense of the fragility of his few flowers (line 2)—a poor gift, he says elsewhere, from a humble garden (8.11)—that Fortunatus anticipates what seems particularly important in the medieval attitude toward nature, whether it manifests itself in the first tentative shoots of monastic calligraphy or lingers in the "little briddes" and "swote grasse" of Chaucer. The sensibility is one that reveals itself in Fortunatus not only by such details as balancing *olentes* and *fragiles* (line 11), but also by the whole posture he assumes at Poitiers: the little brother in Christ,[126] fondly inebriated with those delights in which the queen indulges him and which she has herself long since transcended.

Gregory the Great introduces from aesthetics the traditional distinction between color and form to illustrate the folly of those who dwell on literal meanings to the exclusion of allegorical ones, and to signalize his own determination to push on beyond the merely sensuous raptures of the garden of the Canticles.[127] His remarks come to mind because, like Fortunatus (who dedicated his poems to him), Gregory thinks that the sensuous glow of color is in itself nothing, a mere husk, at most a rhetorical gesture toward the transcendent reality of form. At Vaison-la-Romaine, as we have seen, it is the form of the garden that directs the mind away from earthly shadows to cosmic reality. Color and other sensuous delights may very well be a distraction, as they are for Herrad's monk; at best, as in a twelfth-century description of the gardens and fields of Clairvaux, they are a pastoral ministry to the weak or a solace to the ill.

Exclaiming over the amenities of the place ("multum amoenitatis") and distributing them to the various senses, the monastic author of this description is at the same time careful to ascribe to them their proper use: raising the mind, inflaming ("accendat") the soul to its proper *dulcedo*. The odors remind him of the vestments of Jacob; the colors, of Solomon. And so, he says, "while I profit from the ministry of the outdoors, not a little do I delight in the mystery of what is hidden away."[128] The frequency with which monastery gardens were placed adjacent to the infirmary has a certain emblematic value that may define for us the nature of this external ministry. Flowers were praised originally for their medicinal value, and the physician might often, as he did at St. Gall, have his own garden, blooming with roses and lilies.[129] But by the twelfth century, gardens were beginning to be referred to as places of delight, and it is the rhetorician's full panoply of sensuous pleasures that is seen at Clairvaux as a special ministry to the infirm:

> Within this enclosure, many and various trees, prolific with every sort of fruit, make a veritable grove, which lying next to the cells of those who are ill, lightens with no little solace the infirmities of the brethren [*infirmitates fratrum non mediocri levat solatio*], while it offers to those who are strolling about a spacious walk, and to those overcome by the heat, a sweet place for repose [*suave reclinatorium*]. The sick man sits upon the green lawn [*sedet aegrotus cespite in viridi*], and while inclement Sirus burns the earth and dries the rivers, he is secure, hidden, and shaded from the heat of the day, the leaves of a tree tempering the heat of that fiery star; for the comfort of his pain [*ad doloris sui solatium*], all kinds of grass are fragrant in his nostrils. The lovely green of herb and tree nourishes his eyes and, their immense delights hanging and growing before him, well might he say, "I sat down under his shadow [*sub umbra aboris illius*] with great delight, and his fruit was sweet to my taste" [Canticles 2:3]. The choir of painted birds caresses his ears with sweet modulation, and for the care of a single illness the divine tenderness provides many consolations [*ad unius morbi remedium, divina pietas multa procurat solatia*], while the air smiles with bright serenity, the earth breathes with fruitfulness, and the invalid himself with eyes, ears, and nostrils, drinks in the delights of colors, songs, and perfumes. (*PL*, 185.569)

The author does not miss the analogy between the shelter afforded the monks from the day's sun and labor and the merciful protection from her own weakness the Beloved of the Canticles finds beneath the tree of her Lord—"in the shadow of faith, in the repose of the spiritual life."[130] But more important than this exegetical point is the way in which, throughout the passage, solace and infirmity, solace and dolor, are linked as complementary aspects of a single situation. Partly the author is merely echoing the language of monastic regulations—"the frail and infirm are to be provided with solace, so that they may bear their sufferings without dejection"[131]—but the basis in feeling for such regulations was established much earlier, in a passage that crystallizes all of Augustine's passionate ambivalence about the natural world. Having catalogued the blessings of the earthly life, including all the "manifold and various loveliness of sky, and earth, and sea," he goes on to say that these "are but the solace [*solacia*] of the wretched and condemned," a feeble image of the rewards (*praemia*) of the life to come.[132] The same sensibility is still at work when Bonaventura, reducing the arts to theology (and so to the context of man's fallen state), converts the Horatian *utile* and *dulce* to "comfort" and "consolation."[133] "Sedet aegrotus cespite in viridi": the sick man sits upon the green lawn. The greenness is not denied, but it takes on the pathos of all our sickness, a pathos still implicit in the solace troubadours and courtly lovers were finding at about this time in pleasances and gardens of love, the "recompense for all their pains" but at best a fleeting joy.

Some such intuition as this seems to be implicated in the design of the gardens as well. Even Robert of Artois' great park at Hesdin, modeled though it seems to have been on the imperial paradises of the East, was suffused with the consciously factitious glamour of Celtic faerie, with the same air of bright make-believe as Chrétien de Troyes (for example) uses to qualify Erec's quest for the enchanted "joie de court." There is something conditional about the way in which these "gardens of wonder," full of "things new and strange that seem miraculous to the common man,"[134] respond to their own aspirations, as there is in attitudes toward courtly love itself. We may concentrate on some recurring features. Just as the cosmic order of the garden is walled off from real space, it is also isolated, as the mind's own discovery, from the internal space of one's sensuous delight. Order is the rigid demarcation of wall, fence, or cloister. Within these rigidities, however, the solace of monk or lover is found in a quite random profusion of turf, flower, and water. The flowery mead of poets and illuminators is a lush carpet on which one reposes, the image, in Albert the Great as well as at Clairvaux, of an allowed suspension of responsibility, an invitation "ad delectabiliter quiescendum," to a delicious relaxation.[135] Flowers are scattered in these tiny meadows or turf seats or pleached trellises with a truly pastoral sweetness and inconsequence; or else, particularly in late medieval tapestries or illuminations, they swarm with a wildness that threatens to obliterate form altogether.[136] Trees are valued for the coolness of their shade (at Clairvaux, a place to hide, a respite from the sun and from the vigilant weeding demanded by soil that threatens always to revert to its native wildness); and if they are clipped, it is not to express the grandeur of regularity but to provide triple wreaths from which artificial fruit can be hung for May holidays.[137]

Gerhart Ladner has called to our attention the way in which the fifteenth-century revival of classical grotesques crystallizes a new feeling for the structural elements in floral ornament, the feeling that makes the first printed title pages (for example) so strikingly different from the "planless proliferation of Gothic ornament."[138] We may see in the new fashion an altered sense of the possibilities inherent in the natural world itself. The new motifs were dug up with Nero's Golden House in the 1480s, and they continued to be associated with the sort of hidden and secret places ("occulto luogo e riposto") from which they took their name: baths, garden rooms, and sacred grottoes of the emperors, places involved in the "mysteries of the most antique philosophy."[139] Raphael's completion of Bramante's loggia adjacent to the papal apartments was to be experienced from within as a sort of rhythmic frame for the landscape beyond; and it is appropriately for this passageway, with its view over the Roman hills and its illusionistic pergolas, that Raphael and Giovanni da Udine designed the grotesques in which Vasari later discovered all the wonders of creation, "as many varieties as Nature herself has been able to create."[140] The pieties of "Raphael's Bible" are framed with blooms of every country and every season, an abundance "without end" presided over by the same goddess, Mother of All Things, who reposes among the streams and orange trees of the *giardino segreto.* Diana of Ephesus was reborn in European art, in fact, under the auspices of just these fantasies,[141] at the Vatican and also at the Villa Madama—another "earthly paradise" where, at the end of the century, Guarini still could find the "onley nook o'th' iron world" where "the golden age retir'd."[142] But Raphael's vision of this deity is a sober one. In the Stanza della Segnatura the goddess of universal fecundity serves as a seat for Philosophy herself, and in the copiousness of the Vatican loggia at least one critic has seen "reason made evident in order."[143] After all, what Vitruvius seems most to have objected to in the new ornamental style was precisely the way it attributed an architectural order and stability to the exuberant forms of the nautral world, insinuating a vision whereby a reed might support a roof, and a slender, flexible stalk, a human figure.[144] Such possibilities became actual in Raphael's loggia, where later observers saw "all sorts of flowers that might with their verdancy render charming a loggia, distinguished in a most beautiful order"[145]—trees, tendrils, and growing things all serving with a remarkable new confidence to articulate the fundamental geometry of the architecture itself.[146] The same spirit animates Giovanni's decoration of Raphael's loggia at the Villa Madama. If in their later development grotesques came to express "the extravagant and even demonic vitality of nature,"[147] the birds, beasts, fruits, and flowers of Giulio de' Medici's villa opened upon an order suggestive of a very different sort of intoxication: the intricate geometry of gardens Raphael had designed so as to arrange on a single axis a perfect square, a perfect circle, and the oval of a classical hippodrome.[148]

Even before such major statements, printed title pages had begun to popularize the new ornamental style, developed in Venetian circles under the spell of a romantic archeology that was typified in an earlier generation by Felice Feliciano (who led Mantegna on his expedition on Lake Garda) and which found its "perfect flower," according to a recent historian, in the dreamer of the *Hypnerotomachia Poliphili,* "Francisco Columnae Antiquario."[149] Colonna himself not only decorates his monuments and temples with grotesque ornament, which seems to have been imitated by later artists and printers, but also cites individual motifs as hieroglyphics or involves them allegorically in the action of his story.[150] What is striking for our purposes is the frequency with which the mystery veiled by these images is a sense of order working itself out through vital process. The ceremonial ox's skull is adorned with foliage to serve as an emblem of Patientia, encountered by Poliphilus just as he is about to enter upon his initiation, through the five senses, into the garden of Venus—an appropriate encounter, if the bucranium, as some modern historians have claimed, was originally connected with Eleusis.[151] Earlier, with two instruments of husbandry, the same image had symbolized labor and, in particular, the creative labor of God in nature.[152] Below the skull in the tablet dedicated to Patientia is the dolphin and anchor that Aldus Manutius had found on a coin of Titus, whose message is an elegant expression of the paradox inherent in all natural growth and maturation:[153] *festina lente.* To make haste slowly would inevitably be Poliphilus' mode of progress through this land of "sweet liberties," where Queen Eleuterilida rules over "the wealth of nature."[154] Finally, a ewer borrowed from classical ornament also serves to figure the initiate's gradual ("paulatim") progress through this kingdom, proceeding like a plant beneath the watering can, "poco a poco."[155] At the end of this growth, in a ceremony that prepares him to enter Cythera, the vase of the soul blossoms with the sacred rose tree, a naturalistic tree of life that continued to flourish in grotesques and in sixteenth-century devices and emblems.[156]

We have the impression, turning the pages of Colonna's romance, that the ornaments of title pages, monumental pilasters, or garden loggias assume before our eyes a narrative life and begin to act out the destiny inherent in the mystery of their form. Poliphilus' adventures seem once again a sort of mythological projection of the aspirations of new architectural styles. He might appear to leave Reason behind him when he reverses Hercules' choice and plunges through a gate sacred to the Mother of Love into a garden realm very different from the temporary retreat allowed the stoic hero. The triumphs here are all of Love, cosmic rapes and Vertumnus' fruitful pursuit of Pomona; and the religion is that of Priapus. Yet the place in which Poliphilus finally arrives is no formless deceptive isle of Acrasia, no Bower of False Bliss. As in the *Roman de la Rose,* we are made constantly aware that the lover's progress is toward the very center of reality, for everything in this circular garden tends toward the navel, "il mediano umbilico," of the "mysterious island, fecund with every vernal delight" (Ui^{v}): a place where "nymphs of the center," revealed in their ravishing nudity, dance intricately in honor of the progenitress of all things.[157] Venus' realm is in fact an immense formal garden, an elaborately geometrical fantasy in the manner of Plato's Atlantis, whose concentric circles had already been utilized to express the cosmic ambitions of Hadrian's villa gardens at Tivoli[158] and were to appear again in the squared circles of the first botanical gardens at Padua[159]—where Colonna's interest in all the variety of the Six Days' Work and his faith in its essential order were implemented in practice many years before Francis Bacon proposed a college for this purpose, or rather a temple, in a new Atlantis. (*See Plate 20.*)

We may see in Colonna's garden a first imagining of the possibility Bacon turns into a program: bringing the hexaemeral garden of Nature down from the realms of Platonic abstraction or Christian ascesis it had inhabited in Martianus Capella, Bernard Sylvester, or Alain de Lille, situating it firmly in the empirical world, replacing the poets' abstractions with the many-breasted goddess herself. The focus of Cythera is no longer the stone tablet of the laws which had marked the exact center of Atlantis' sacred precincts but the fountain of Venus, a source at once cosmic in its magic geometry and explicitly sexual in its veil the lovers find they must rend. It has frequently been observed that Colonna's discovery of the past has more in common with the Arcadian visions of Poliziano or Sannazaro than with the more abstract rationalism usually attributed to Alberti.[160] What is new about the pastoral impulse in the Renaissance, what makes it paradoxically a major form, is not merely the assertion of nature as a norm of order. It is, rather, the attempt of poets and playwrights, however problematic these attempts may on occasion seem, to discover this order in immediate sensation, in the playful sensuousness of the pastoral itself, its imagery no longer transparent to the sort of learned allegory that prevents Niccolò Niccoli (for example) from finding in Petrarch's eclogues anything at all "that smells of the pastoral or sylvan."[161] The *Hypnerotomachia,* to be sure, is scarcely straightforward; but surely the burden of its mystery and the largest significance of Colonna's alchemical pedantry lies in just this: the language of transcendence—in this case, the narrative language of vision and initiation—is applied not to a flight from the material world but to its transmutation; and the eternal is discovered, as Paracelsus later stipulated it must be, not through but in the natural world.[162] Otto Benesch has written suggestively of connections between Paracelsus and the new feeling for nature in painters like Altdorfer,[163] but perhaps we may once again let the Elizabethan gardener Leonard Mascall speak for us. The art of gardening, he says, is one by which "not only we may see with our eyes, but also feele with our handes in the secrete workes of nature . . . [her] diversitie of shootes, blossoms, & buds, in divers kindes."[164] Formally his remark is no more than a repetition of Homer's fertility topos; even the Carolingian Rabanus Maurus (as we have seen) knew that a garden, like a church, is a place where something always grows. But the sensibility revealed in Mascall's remark is rather different. Unwittingly, one supposes, he realizes the dream of Hermes Trismegistus[165] and feels, even more literally than Kepler, the orderly profusion of nature at his very fingertips.

This sense of order implicit in sensuous experience is as present in Poliphilus' way of experiencing the isle of Cythera as it is in the plot of the romance. The quality of sensibility is important because Colonna is not merely a storyteller, but also a projector of actual renaissances, a visionary architect of palaces, monuments, and (most of all) gardens.[166] Like the green center of her amphitheater, Venus's whole garden realm is designed "not merely to stupify the intellect, but to confound the senses" (Yvi^{r}). Again and again Poliphilus uses what Curtius calls the inexpressibility trope to suggest the "ineffable pleasure" (Yvii^{r}) of colors, scents, and the bare breasts of amorous nymphs; the senses are enticed and assaulted (Vi^{r}), surrounded and overwhelmed until the lover no longer knows in what manner he exists (Yvii^{r}). But in this stupefaction, consciousness is not lost; or rather, if the old self is obliterated, a new one is discovered. The beauty of the island works like poetry to charm and to civilize because, like poetry, its delights even when most seductively sensuous are merely the rhetorical extensions, the effect, of an implicit order. Cythera is the place in which the wild and tactless heart, "silvacola & inepto core" (Tvii^{v}), comes to be cultivated.

The "alma dea della natura" everywhere performs "con ordine," "decentissimamente (Ti^{v}). The ground is "leveled and equal" (Svi^{v}), the shore lined with a mineral "not broken, not brittle, not muddy, but translucent, intact, without flaw, like a lucid and ingenious crystal" (Svii^{r}). The water is without refraction, so that objects within are in no way distorted, and whatever is presented to it, as if to answer Nature's complaint in Jean de Meun, is reflected with a perfect integrity (Tviii^{v}). The air is "saluberrimo, purgatissimo, atque purissimo, & longe lucidissimo, liberamente ad gli ochii provi[s]io, levissimo & coaequabile, & invariabile cum grande amoenitate" (very healthy, very clear, very pure, lucid to great distances so that the eye might have free passage, very light, very equal, invariable in its loveliness [Ti^{r}]). The emphasis always falls on the philosopher's *aequalitas,* integrity of being; and on the lucidity that makes this order accessible to experience. Although (in accordance with Pliny's requirements) rings of boscage and meadow alternate with the more formal perfections of topiary and parterres, it is clear that what Colonna had in mind is the simultaneity of variety and unity, of sensuous luxuriance and intellectual precision, a simultaneity that scarcely needs explicit remarking since it is the almost automatic reflex of his way of seeing. Everywhere nature's utmost care ("praecipuo studio") goes together with her bounty and profusion ("congesticiamente") (Ti^{r}); and if every branch is garnished with flowers, each leaf and blossom, so evenly are they trimmed, contribute to the perfect form of the whole (Svii^{r}).

The design of the garden is a fantastic elaboration of the medieval motifs of square enclosure and central accent. Around the amphitheater in the very center of the island are three rings of quadrangular parterres and figured pavements planted in the manner of Julius' statuary court. Closer to the circumference are three circles of *prati,* enclosed carpets of green like medieval walled gardens, connected by a network of rose-covered pergolas whose intersections are marked by pavilions and cenotaphs.[167] The trapezoidal shape of each garden, Colonna is careful to specify, is simply the deformation of a perfect square, for in this sacred place the quadrangles must acknowledge the domination of the center toward which they tend (Ti^{v}). Each has its own center accent (fountain or topiary work), an entrance in the exact center of each side, and in each corner an elevation, like a medieval mount, constructed of four terraces (squares, circles, or triangles) and centered by a tree clipped into a crown, a hemisphere, or a sphere.

The garden is the nursery of the gods and their abode, "alumno degli dii & statione" (Svi^{v}), a phrase that recalls both Plato's "nurse of all being," and Colonna's own "Mother of All Things," who had been borrowed to preside over the Belvedere's statuary court. In order to embody this myth, Colonna calls up the same sense of cosmic reticulation of space we have already observed at Vaison-la-Romaine or at St. Gall, but with this important difference: form is not embodied in the mind or on the page, but in the living stuff of the garden itself, in "green fortifications" (Svii^{r}) and growing walls with every flower in place. The plants and flowers Poliphilus enjoys, like those of the Orti Oricellari or of Lorenzo's botanical garden at Careggi, are weighted with all the dignity of antique heroes and classical learning. The pedantry with which he catalogues the rarities from Pliny and other authorities ("a most celebrated tree" and every bird studied by man [Uvi^{v}]) testifies to his wonder at encountering in the real world, as he approaches the center of the garden, the plenitude and variety he had discovered hitherto only in the literature of the ancients: Venus's realm is "statione & convento" (Uvii^{r})[1] of all nature's works, their adopted land and place of assembly. And he finds this blossoming not scattered at random on lawns but ordered in the mystery of circle, square, and endless knot or (in the parterre nearest Venus's fountain) in the heraldry of the gods themselves. These emblems celebrate Jove's eagle as the dispenser of the divine bounty by which all things are nourished; and the plants of which they are composed, perennially flowering, continually green and uniform, pay their own tribute to the "design of fruitful nature" (Uvi$^{r\text{-}v}$).

We may sense a similar tribute in Giovanni Rucellai's account of his gardens at the Villa Quaracchi near Florence. He catalogues all its "beautiful and pleasing features"—varieties of trees, abundance of fruit and scented flowers, shady walks and perpetual green—with the iterative enthusiasm of the hexaemeral writers, and indeed he begins his notes by saying that he calls the place "lo spechio," the mirror.[168] The villa and its gardens were designed, presumably by Alberti, a few years before Colonna's romance, and many of its details are similar to those of the gardens Poliphilus visits: pergolas of carefully trimmed trees, espaliers twined with vines and roses, and (above all) the fantastic elaboration of trimmed boxwood.

The topiary art may have survived in some rudimentary way throughout the Middle Ages,[169] but it becomes important again in the Renaissance because it is no longer felt to be merely fanciful: if classical texts could not supply the skill, they could give that skill a new authority. Pliny's gardens were, like those of Cyrus, orderly as well as fragrant; and the *opus topararius* was employed (to cite Vitruvius again) to make the whole external world of "ports, promontories, shores, rivers, fountains, temples, mountains, herds, and even shepherds" the scenic backdrop of country pleasures.[170] To Stoic critics this was a mad or childish presumption, to prefer pitiable imitation to the actual cosmos.[171] But Nero leveled whole towns on Palatine Hill to adorn his "golden domain"[172] with a pond as great as a sea, a landscape of field, forest, and meadow where "every variety" of wild or domestic animal wandered in peace (as they do in Colonna's Cythera), and finally a moving dome of the heavens beneath which the emperor himself dined—all this in order "to be housed like a human being."[173]

Giovanni Rucellai leveled no towns, of course, but it is just the tone of Vitruvius' catalogue that we find in his breathless account of boxwood trimmed into

> ships, galleys, temples, basins and columns, vases, urns . . . men, women, heraldic lions with flags of the commune, monkeys, dragons, centaurs, chameleons, diamonds, little sprites with bows, trophies, horses, asses, oxen, dogs, stags, birds, a bear and a wild boar, dolphin, jousters, archers, a harpy, philosophers, Popes, Cardinals . . . and a few other similar things.[174]

These figures ("and a few other similar things"!) do not merely offer pleasure to the eye and consolation to the body; they substantiate, in their profusion, the claims of a garden that festoons its espaliers with the family's coat of arms as well as with roses and that aims at extending its largesse to the whole surrounding countryside. As in a poetical account of the later gardens of Caprarola, trees offer their "crowns of wonderful art" to the honor of the Lord who planted them.[175] Nero was scarcely an acceptable authority for such pretensions, but it does not seem to me farfetched to detect in Giovanni's enthusiasm for the world mirrored in his garden—not to mention Pope Julius's grandiose scheme for the Belvedere Cortile, which was in fact to be portrayed as an artificial lake, reminiscent of Nero's maritime spectacles[176]—something of the Roman emperor's passion to test the limits of his humanity. In realizing such impulses, knots and topiary play a part, humble but emblematic of a confidence in man's ability to discover in the external world, in nature as actually experienced, an order proportionate to his own aspirations. The topiary gardener, writes Pontano, by uniting nurture and nature, human skill and the constructive processes of time, succeeds in converting "the formless mass into shapes of beauty":[177] in leading *silva* to its proper ornament. In remarking on the *copia* and *ordine* of the orangery's checkerboard plantation, the Venetian ambassador was perhaps in his own way expressing some such sense of creational integrity restored.

Abbreviations Used in the Notes

AB	*Art Bulletin*
AJP	*American Journal of Philology*
CSEL	*Corpus Scriptorum Ecclesiasticorum Latinorum* (Vienna, 1866—)
ELH	*English Literary History*
JHI	*Journal of the History of Ideas*
JWCI	*Journal of the Warburg and Courtauld Institutes*
MGH	*Momumenta Germaniae Historica* (Hannover-Berlin, 1826—)
MLN	*Modern Language Notes*
MP	*Modern Philology*
PL	*Patrologia Latina,* ed. J. P. Migne (Paris, 1844–90) Cited by volume and column.
PMLA	*Publications of the Modern Language Association*
SP	*Studies in Philology*

Notes

Notes to the Preface

1. Fulke Greville, "A Treatie of Humane Learning," 1.158–59, cited in Edward Tayler, *Nature and Art in Renaissance Literature* (New York, 1964), p. 32.

2. A. Bartlett Giamatti, *The Earthly Paradise and the Renaissance Epic* (Princeton, N.J., 1966); Stanley Stewart, *The Enclosed Garden* (Madison, Wis., 1966); Paul Piehler, *The Visionary Landscape* (London, 1971). Eugenio Battisti's learned and suggestive article "*Natura Artificiosa* to *Natura Artificialis*" (in *The Italian Garden,* First Dumbarton Oaks Colloquium on the History of Landscape Architecture ed. David R. Coffin [Washington, D.C. 1972]. pp. 1–36) came to my attention only after work on this essay was substantially completed.

Notes to Chapter I

1. Philippe de Chennevières, *Archives de l'art français* (Paris, 1851–52), I, p. 274; cf. Paul Pélicier's edition of Charles's letters (Paris, 1903), IV, pp. 187–88.

2. His letter to Sir Thomas Browne, in *The Works of Sir Thomas Browne,* ed. Geoffrey Keynes (London, 1931), VI, p. 301.

3. Henry More, cited in Maren-Sofie Røstvig, *The Happy Man* (Oslo, 1954), I, p. 181.

4. Evelyn, in Røstvig, I, p. 185.

5. Chennevières, I, p. 275. For an interesting treatment of a related theme, see A. Dupront, "Espace et humanisme," *Bibliothèque d'Humanisme et Renaissance,* VIII (1946), pp. 7–104.

6. Erich Auerbach, "Philology and *Weltliteratur,*" *The Centennial Review,* XIII (1969), p. 14.

7. Briçonnet's letter, Chennevières, I, p. 275.

8. Ernst Kantorowicz, *Frederick the Second* (London, 1931), p. 220. It is in fact

by way of Naples that the notion of the pleasure garden first reached the West from the twelfth century onward; see Margurite Charageat, *L'Art des jardins* (Paris, 1962), pp. 80–92; Pierre Grimal, *L'Art des jardins* (Paris, 1953), pp. 53–58; and Georgina Masson, *Italian Gardens* (New York, n. d.), pp. 47–51.

9. J. W. Spargo, *Virgil the Necromancer* (Cambridge, Mass., 1934), pp. 12, 14–15, 22, 23, 33, 122, etc.; also pp. 304–11 on the diffusion of the tales.

10. At Ziza in Palermo an inscription boasts: "It is the terrestrial paradise that here opens before your eyes. Here reigns the king who aspires to glory. And this château is called the glorious." Margurite Charageat, "Le Parc d'Hesdin," *Bulletin de la Société de l'Histoire de l'Art Français,* 1950 (Paris, 1951), pp. 99–100.

11. Pietro de Crescenzi, *Trattato della agricoltura,* trans. Bastiano de' Rossi (Milan, 1805), II, pp. 330–31 (Bk. VIII, Chap. III).

12. Charles Trinkaus, *In Our Image and Likeness* (Chicago, 1970), pp. 246–47.

13. Giovanni Pontano, *I tratti delle virtue sociali,* ed. F. Tateo (Rome, 1965), p. 137 (*De splendore,* VII). Cf. George L. Hersey, *Alfonso II and the Artistic Renewal of Naples 1485–1495* (New Haven, Conn., 1969), pp. 22, 59.

14. Grimal, *L'Art des jardins,* pp. 61–62, calls Hesdin "the *mise en scène* of the Celtic enchanted garden."

15. Brunetto Latini, *Li livres dou trésor,* ed. F. J. Carmody (Berkeley, Calif., 1948), p. 126. Cf. Charles Davis, "Il buon tempo antico," *Florentine Studies,* ed. Nicolai Rubinstein (Evanston, Ill., 1968), pp. 46–47.

16. P. O. Kristeller, *Studies in Renaissance Thought and Letters* (Rome, 1956), pp. 406–410.

17. Hersey, *Alfonso II,* pp. 1–5, 18–26.

18. Francesco Guicciardini, *History of Italy,* trans. John R. Hale (New York, 1964), p. 86 (Chap. I).

19. E. H. Gombrich, *Norm and Form* (London, 1966), pp. 29–34; Gerhart Ladner, "Vegetation Symbolism and the Concept of Renaissance," *De artibus opuscula XL: Essays in Honor of Erwin Panofsky,* ed. Millard Meiss (New York, 1961), pp. 303–22; Elizabeth Armstrong, *Ronsard and the Age of Gold* (Cambridge, Eng., 1968), pp. 1–9; Harry Levin, *The Myth of the Golden Age in the Renaissance* (Bloomington, Ind., 1969), pp. 32–57.

20. Poliziano, *Giostra,* 1. 4. A similar motif is found on at least one of Lorenzo's medals; Cornelius von Fabriczy, *Italian Medals,* trans. G. W. Hamilton (London, 1904), p. 120; Ladner, "Vegetation Symbolism," p. 316, n. 59. One might also mention the olive-wreathed Pallas in Botticelli's painting, which used to be associated specifically with Lorenzo's Naples expedition; Edward Armstrong, *Lorenzo de' Medici and Florence in the Fifteenth Century* (New York, 1896), p. xii; and (for a more recent assessment) Rudolf Wittkower, "Transformations of Minerva in Renaissance Imagery," *JWCI,* II (1938–39), p. 200.

21. E.g., the remarks made by the Ferrarese ambassador in 1475 on the connection between Lorenzo's political strength and the reputation won by his elaborate entertainments; Armstrong, *Lorenzo de' Medici,* pp. 100–101. Cf. Machiavelli's *History of Florence,* VIII, vii, on the uses of pageantry; and VIII, iv, on the Naples trip.

22. It was in the "Orti Oricellari" of Lorenzo's brother-in-law, Bernardo Rucellai—gardens ornamented with classical statuary and growing every plant mentioned in classical literature—that the heirs of Ficino's academy, in a time of dislocations, developed the myth of Lorenzo's golden age (a time of peace, liberty, and leisure for the mind) and the political theory of the "harmony of discords" by which he had established it. Felix Gilbert, "Bernardo Rucellai and the Orti Oricellari," *JWCI,* XII (1949), pp. 101–31; Bernardo Rucellai, *De bello Italico* (London, 1733), pp. 4–5. Before the uncertainties of fortune had forced Rucellai to "retire to his flowering garden" (Gilbert, p. 109), he had been Florence's ambassador to Naples, met Pontano, and presumably savored those harmonies Serlio was to take as the paradigm of all the delight civil strife had forever lost for Italy. Years later, Bernardo's own gardens still reminded Machiavelli of "some princes in the kingdom of Naples, who take much delight in planting groves, and shady arbors, in the ancient manner"; Machiavelli, *The Art of War,* trans. Neal Wood (New York, 1965), p. 10.

23. Alfred von Reumont, *Lorenzo de' Medici,* trans. R. Harrison (London, 1876), I, p. 411.

24. Sebastiano Serlio, *Tutte l'opere d'architettura et prospetiva* (Venice, 1619; facs. ed., Ridgewood, N.Y., 1964), pp. 121–23. Cf. Roberto Pane, *Architettura del Rinascimento in Napoli* (Naples, 1937), pp. 15–26.

25. Hersey, *Alfonso II,* p. 60, n. 12.

26. Per Gustaf Hamberg, "The Villa of Lorenzo il Magnifico at Poggio a Caiano," *Figura* (n.s.), I (Stockholm, 1959), pp. 76–87; Rudolf Wittkower, *Architectural Principles in the Age of Humanism,* 2nd ed. (New York, 1965), pp. 70–76.

27. James S. Ackerman, "Sources of the Renaissance Villa," *The Renaissance and Mannerism,* Acts of the 20th International Congress of the History of Art (Princeton, N.J., 1963), p. 9.

28. Leon Battista Alberti, *Ten Books on Architecture,* trans. James Leone, ed. J. Rykwert (London, 1955), p. 194 (IX, iv).

29. Serlio, *Tutte l'opere,* p. 122.

30. Alberti, *Ten Books,* p. 104 (V, xvii), p. 189 (IX, ii).

31. André Chastel, *Art et humanisme à Florence au temps de Laurent le Magnifique* (Paris, 1961), pp. 151–56; Hersey, *Alfonso II,* pp. 18–21, 63.

32. Chastel, *Art,* pp. 218–25.

33. The trope is an old one: see, e.g., E. H. Gombrich, "Alberto Avogadro's Description of the Badia of Fiesole and of the Villa of Careggi," *Italia medioevale e umanistica,* V (1962), pp. 217–29; esp. p. 228: "Digna suis dominis, atria digna deis" ("Courtyards worthy of their masters, worthy of the gods"). Also Fritz Baumgart, "La Caprarola di Ameto Orti," *Studj Romanzi,* XXV (1935), pp. 77–179.

34. Vincenzio Giustiniani's demand for garden architecture, cited in Heinrich Wölfflin, *Renaissance and Baroque,* trans. Kathrin Simon (Ithaca, N.Y., 1966), p. 151. For a similar remark by Aretino, see Lionello Puppi, "The Villa Garden of the Veneto," in *The Italian Garden,* First Dumbarton Oaks Colloquium on the History of Landscape Architecture, ed. David R. Coffin (Washington, D.C., 1972), p. 95.

35. Ackerman, "Sources," pp. 8–9; Chastel, *Art,* p. 168, ff.; J. Schultz, "Pinturic-

chio and the Revival of Antiquity," *JWCI,* XXV (1962), pp. 35–55; Gombrich, *Norm and Form,* p. 119; A Richard Turner, *The Vision of Landscape in Renaissance Italy* (Princeton, N.J., 1966), pp. 193–212. The Poggio Reale was in fact frescoed to commemorate Alfonso's victory over the barons whose revolt had interrupted its construction. But the presence of these frescoes on the outside of the villa turns it into a sort of pageant spectacle, perhaps even a witty allusion (as a recent critic has suggested) to just those fortresses rendered unnecessary by Alfonso's prowess; Hersey, *Alfonso II,* pp. 60, 65, 69–70, and n. 63.

36. Michael Levey, *Painting at Court* (New York, 1971), Chapter II; Gustave Gruyer, *L'Art ferrarais* (Paris, 1897), I, p. 465; Werner Gundersheimer, *Ferrara: The Style of a Renaissance Despotism* (Princeton, N.J., 1973), pp. 242–44, 267; Otto Pächt, "Early Italian Nature Studies and the Early Calendar Landscape," *JWCI,* XIII (1950), pp. 13–47.

37. André de la Vigne, *Le Vergier d'honneur,* in William Roscoe, *The Life and Pontificate of Leo the Tenth,* rev. by Thomas Roscoe (London, 1846), I, pp. 496–97. The full text is in *Archives curieuses de l'histoire de France,* ed. M. L. Cimber (Paris, 1834), ser. I, vol. I, pp. 334–36.

38. Pontano, *Lepidina,* 5.12–13, translated in Hersey, *Alfonso II,* p. 20; cf. pp. 19–21, 60–63, 95–97.

39. M. Verino, cited in William Roscoe, *The Life of Lorenzo de' Medici* (Philadelphia, 1803), II, p. 183. Pontano reminds his pupil Alfonso that "certain great lords among the Romans got praise for their water system above all else" and suggests that such works will "commend the magnificentia of the man who commissions it" (*De magnificentia,* VIII); cited in Hersey, *Alfonso II,* p. 95.

40. Poliziano, *Ambra,* lines 599–603; trans. Roscoe, *Lorenzo,* II, pp. 186–87.

41. Roscoe, *Lorenzo,* II, pp. 60–61, 184; Armstrong, *Lorenzo,* pp. 232–33. For the collector's passion, cf. Dupront, pp. 25–40.

42. Vasari's *Lives* of Pontormo, del Sarto, and Franciabigio; F. M. Clapp, *Jacapo Carucci da Pontormo* (New Haven, Conn., 1916), pp. 28 ff., 175; S. J. Freedberg, *Painting of the High Renaissance in Florence,* 2nd ed. (New York, 1972), I, pp. 481–82, 632.

43. Ibid., p. 564.

44. Dante, *Purgatorio,* 28.77–78; *De monarchia,* 3.16.

45. The standard account is H. François Delaborde's *L'Expédition de Charles VIII en Italie* (Paris, 1888). For Charles as Augustus and Charlemagne: Donald Weinstein, "The Myth of Florence," *Florentine Studies,* ed. Rubinstein, pp. 15–44; Eva Borsook, "Decor in Florence for the Entry of Charles VIII of France," *Kunsthistorisches Institut in Florenz, Mitteilungen,* Vol. I, Part II (Dec., 1961), pp. 106–22. Cf. *The Memoirs of Philip de Commines,* trans. A. R. Scoble (London, 1912), II, pp. 145, 149, 153–54; Guicciardini, *History of Italy,* I. ix, for portents.

46. Ernest Lavisse, ed., *Histoire de France* (Paris, 1903), V^1, p. 36. An Italian observer, though, has said that Charles was greeted in hostile silence; Erasmo Pèrcopo, "Per l'entrata solenne di Carlo VIII in Napoli," *Studi di storia napoletana in onere di Michelangelo Schipa* (Naples, 1926), pp. 347–51.

47. Percy Ernst Schramm, *Sphaira-Globus-Reichsapfel* (Stuttgart, 1958), pp.

123, 130, and figs. 83–85. The orb would have been highly visible to Charles in the frieze at the Castle Nuovo in which Alfonso I had commemorated the inauguration of Aragonese rule in Naples and claimed Hercules, on account of his association with Parthenope, as his own "mythical ancestor and forerunner"; see George Hersey, *The Aragonese Arch at Naples, 1443–1475* (New Haven, Conn., 1973), pp. 36–40; also Hersey, *Alfonso II,* pp. 101–106; and for the coronation of Alfonso II, Jean Burchard, *Diarium,* ed. L. Thuasne (Paris, 1884), II, p. 154.

48. Schramm, pp. 32–35, 71–73.

49. Marie Luise Gothein, *A History of Garden Art,* trans. Mrs. Archer-Hind (New York, 1928), I, pp. 391–94.

50. Lavisse, V[1], p. 158.

51. Gothein, I, p. 391; Franco Simone, *The French Renaissance,* trans. H. Gaston Hall (London, 1969), pp. 39–42.

52. Gothein, I, p. 391.

53. Marc-René Jung, *Hercule dans la littérature française du XVIe siècle* (Geneva, 1966), pp. 38–39. Somewhere in the background of such celebrations was probably the old tradition that claimed for the French nobility in general and for Charlemagne in particular the blood of Hector and Hercules; e.g., Lemaire de Belges, *Oeuvres,* ed. J. Stecher (Louvaine, 1882), II, p. 469.

54. Frances Yates, "Queen Elizabeth as Astraea," *JWCI,* X (1947), p. 60 and fig. 19a; Schramm, p. 120.

55. S. Tolkowsky, *Hesperides* (London, 1938), p. 120.

56. Gothein, II, p. 5; Tolkowsky, p. 200.

57. *De hortis Hesperidum,* 1.46–52. Text in Giovanni Pontano, *Carmina,* ed. B. Soldati (Florence, 1902).

58. E.g., *De amore conjugali,* I, v–vi; I, viii; II, ii–iv. Even here, though, there is some suggestion that it is the husbandry of prudent lovers, uniting sentiment with modesty, that guarantees them golden apples (II, iv, 11–14, 47–48).

59. *De hortis Hesperidum,* 2.407–431.

60. *Ibid.,* 1.168–77. Francesco had been celebrated as liberator and restorer of Italy; Delaborde, pp. 624–25.

61. Particularly in the Augustinian tradition, the second phase of creation is the summoning (*revocatio*) of inform matter to assume its proper ornaments and perfect form; e.g., Gerhart Ladner, *The Idea of Reform* (Cambridge, Mass., 1959), pp. 167–85; Etienne Gilson, *The Christian Philosophy of Saint Augustine,* trans. L. E. M. Lynch (New York, 1960), pp. 197–209; a concise later statement is in Hugh of St. Victor, *De sacramentis,* 1.1.3. Rudolf Wittkower, "Chance, Time, and Virtue," *JWCI,* I (1937–38), pp. 313–21, traces the way in which the old enmity between virtue and fortune is joined, in the Renaissance, by a new emphasis on their cooperation: "Virtute duce, comite fortuna" (with virtue as guide and fortune as companion); cf. Erwin Panofsky, *The Iconography of Correggio's Camera di San Paolo* (London, 1961), pp. 60–66. Such mottoes become commonplace on the title pages of garden books; e.g., Jacques Dalechamps, *Histoire générale des plantes* (Lyons, 1616): "In Virtute et Fortuna."

62. See Erwin Panofsky, *Hercules am Scheidewege* (Berlin, 1930), pp. 145–50,

for the golden apples as a symbol of virtue and therefore an attribute of Hercules Prodicius. For the Middle Ages, the apples represented the "golden ornament of learning"; but the Renaissance recalled that the grove had been consecrated to Venus (cf. Servius on the *Aeneid,* 4.484) and set itself the task of liberating its fruits from the custody of vice.

63. E.g., Augustine, *The City of God,* 4.20–21.

64. *Regrets,* sonnet 172 (Hercules made himself god by the force of his own virtue); cited in Jung, *Hercule,* p. 136. Cf. Marcel Simon, *Hercule et le Christianisme* (Paris, 1955), pp. 82–83. Ripa, *Iconologie* (Paris, 1644), pp. 197–98, sees in the three apples the sign of virtue's ability to lift man "above the mortal condition and make him almost an angel."

65. Lactantius, *The Divine Institutes,* 6.3. For Petrarch, see esp. Theodore Mommsen. "Petrarch and the Story of the Choice of Hercules," *JWCI,* XVI (1953), pp. 178–92. (My whole summary in this paragraph is much indebted to Mommsen's article.)

66. Julia Cartwright, *Isabella d'Este* (New York, 1923), I, p. 126.

67. For citrus and the iconography of the Virgin: Tolkowsky, pp. 173–79. The motif was a special favorite of Mantegna.

68. Louis Réau, *Iconographie de l'art chrétien* (Paris, 1955–59), II[2], cols. 112–20, for the history of the type; esp. his remarks on the variation represented by Mantegna's madonna: "the protection of the Madonna of Mercy restricts itself to a donor; the Mother of All becomes the Mother of One."

69. Paul Kristeller, *Andrea Mantegna,* trans. S. A. Strong (London, 1901), p. 308 ff.

70. St. Michael and St. George; Kristeller, *Mantegna,* p. 312.

71. The coral hanging from the bower has the same implication. E. Tietze-Conrat, *Mantegna* (New York, 1955), p. 195, cites the tradition that sees coral as protection against diabolic monsters.

72. Kristeller, *Mantegna,* p. 313, for the connection with the Enclosed Garden. Compare Tietze-Conrat, p. 25: "Earth and humanity are linked with the heavenly sphere; the bower in which the figures are gathered opens toward the sky."

73. Cartwright, *Isabella d'Este,* p. 125.

74. Peter Hirschfeld, *Mäzene: Die Rolle des Auftraggebers in der Kunst* (Munich, 1968), p. 123.

75. Edgar Wind, *Bellini's Feast of the Gods* (Cambridge, Mass., 1948), p. 4, n. 3, suggests links between the Grotta, Mantegna's *Madonna,* and Correggio's trellis ceiling at San Paolo; the relation between the first two, it should be admitted, is largely conjectural. Cf. Kristeller, *Mantegna,* pp. 346–47; and for important modification of the traditional reconstructions, Egon Verheyen, *The Paintings in the Studiolo of Isabella d'Este at Mantua* (New York, 1971), pp. 1–21, 52–55. The connection between the *Camera di San Paolo* and the trellis in Mantegna's altarpiece is widely acknowledged; and Panofsky, in *Correggio,* pp. 5, 17, 98, has noted the similarities between Isabella's literary and artistic program for the Grotta and that of Gioanna di Piacenza. Also among the progeny of Mantegna's arbor is Raphael's ceiling for the garden loggia of the Farnesina, frescoed, like Isabella's

cloistered garden at Belriguardo, with the story of Cupid and Psyche; the floor plan of the villa suggests Peruzzi's attention to the innovatory schemes of the Poggio a Cajano and the Poggio Reale, and his *Sala delle Prospettive* converts the whole vast structure into "an ephemeral garden pavillion," where (according to a contemporary poet) Venus finds her favorite haunt; see Oskar Fischel, *Raphael,* trans. Bernard Rackham (London, 1948), p. 166; Gundersheimer, pp. 258–61; Turner, pp. 201–203; Christoph Frommel, *Die Farnesina und Peruzzis architektonisches Frühwerk* (Berlin, 1961), pp. 39, 89–97.

76. Millard Meiss, *Painting in Florence and Siena after the Black Death* (Princeton, N.J., 1951), p. 149.

77. Bernard of Clairvaux, *De aquaeductu* (*PL,* 183.437 ff.).

78. Henry Hawkins, *Partheneia sacra* (*1633*) (Aldington, Kent, 1950), esp. pp. 9, 211–21.

79. Panofsky, *Correggio,* pp. 1–6.

80. Julia Cartwright, *Italian Gardens of the Renaissance* (London, 1914), p. 54.

81. Wind, *Bellini,* pp. 18–19; Panofsky, *Correggio,* p. 13.

82. Chennevières, p. 275; my italics.

83. Cartwright, *Italian Gardens,* p. 54.

84. E.g., Verheyen, pp. 30–51; E. H. Gombrich, *Symbolic Images* (London, 1972), pp. 82–84.

85. Wind, *Bellini,* pp. 27–35, 46–47; Panofsky, *Correggio,* p. 10. As Correggio's program makes clear, the realm of the new Diana must at least begin with the four elements of the physical world; Panofsky, p. 99.

86. Panofsky, *Correggio,* p. 11. Pico cites this line from Virgil's *Eclogues* (3.60) in *Heptaplus,* trans. Douglas Carmichael (New York, 1965), p. 148 (VII, proem). Virgilian commentators were unanimous in identifying Jove with the *anima mundi;* e.g., *Opera Vergiliana* (Lugduni Batavorum, 1575), sig. Ciii. And the Hermetic literature—or that part of it concerned with an "optimistic gnosis"—is replete with assertions that all things are full of, or manifest, or are God; *Hermetica,* ed. Walter Scott (Oxford, 1924), I, pp. 155, 159, 185, 223, 327; Giordano Bruno, *The Expulsion of the Triumphant Beast,* trans. A. D. Imerti (New Brunswick, N.J., 1964), p. 235: "nature is God in things."

87. Wölfflin, p. 149.

88. David Coffin, *The Villa d'Este at Tivoli* (Princeton, N.J., 1960), pp. 78–92.

89. The abstractions to be represented were Liberality, Wisdom, Nobility, Valor, Compassion, Justice; and Arts, Tongues, Sciences, Arms, Peace, and Laws. See Vasari's life of Tribolo; Bertha Wiles, *The Fountains of Florentine Sculptors* (Cambridge, Mass., 1933), pp. 24 ff., 33 ff. Cf. Ronald Martin Steinberg, "The Iconography of the Teatro dell' Acqua at the Villa Aldobrandini," *AB,* XLVII (1965), pp. 453–63.

90. Coffin, p. 88.

91. *Mother Hubberds Tale,* 1169–88. For Spenser and Burghley: Harold Stein, *Studies in Spenser's Complaints* (New York, 1934), pp. 78–100; John Buxton, *Elizabethan Taste* (London, 1963), p. 58.

92. John Summerson, "Theobalds: A Lost Elizabethan Palace," *The Listener,*

LIII (1955), pp. 567–68; Summerson, "The Building of Theobalds," *Archaeologia,* XCVII (1959), pp. 107–26; Conyers Read, *Lord Burghley and Queen Elizabeth* (New York, 1960), pp. 121–24. Wolsey had drawn inspiration from Italian design, but did not apparently follow any specific model; e.g., Derek Clifford, *A History of Garden Design* (New York, 1953), p. 88.

93. Gombrich, *Norm and Form,* pp. 39–40; cf. Puppi, esp. pp. 100–102.

94. Lawrence Stone, *The Crisis of the Aristocracy 1558–1641* (Oxford, 1965). Cf. Marc Girouard, *Robert Smythson and the Architecture of the Elizabethan Era* (London, 1966), p. 32.

95. J. H. Hexter, *Reappraisals in History* (Evanston, Ill., 1961), p. 102.

96. Summerson, "Theobalds," p. 568. On Burghley House, see Christopher Hussey, "Burghley House," *Country Life,* CXIII (1953), esp. pp. 1828–32, 1962–65.

97. Read, *Burghley,* p. 123.

98. Summerson, "The Building of Theobalds," pp. 122–23; cf. his "Theobalds," p. 568. For a similar pleasure house at Elvetham, see John Nichols, *The Progresses and Public Processions of Queen Elizabeth* (London, 1823), III, p. 101. The ruler's insignia affixed to a tree has cosmological overtones in a number of legends, e.g., those clustering around the return of Frederick II; see Ladner, "Vegetation Symbolism," p. 312, note 39.

99. Summerson, "The Building of Theobalds," p. 120; Nichols, III, pp. 241–42; Stone, *Crisis,* p. 23, cites other examples of the fashion, which is recommended in Alberti, *De re aedificatoria,* IX, iv. For Alberti in England, see John Summerson, *Architecture in Britain, 1530–1830,* 5th ed. (Baltimore, 1970), p. 56; and more generally, Frances Yates, *Theatre of the World* (Chicago, 1969).

100. Buxton, p. 49, quotes Hatton's remark that he is leaving his "other shrine, I mean Holdenby, still unseen until that holy saint may sit in it, to whom it is dedicated"; cf. p. 51 on Wollaton; also Girouard, p. 78 ff.

101. Nichols, III, p. 108. This theme of pastoral "incarnation" is developed with particular elaborateness in 1591 at Elvetham, where the queen's departure leaves the landscape desolate: "For how can Sommer stay, when Sunne departs?" (ibid., III, pp. 120–21); cf. III, pp. 113, 118–19; also Churchyard's greeting in Suffolk in 1579: "The deaw of Heaven droppes this day on dry and barren ground,/Wherefore let fruteful heartes, I saye, at drumme and trumpet sound" (ibid., II, p. 182).

102. *The Dramatic and Poetical Works of Robert Greene and George Peele,* ed. A. Dyce (London, 1874), pp. 578–79 ("The Gardener's Speech").

103. E.g., Nichols, II, pp. 180–81.

104. *Robert Laneham's Letter,* ed. F. J. Furnivall (New York, 1907), p. 47.

105. *The Works of George Gascoigne,* ed. J. W. Cunliffe (Cambridge, Eng., 1910), II, pp. 100–101; cf. II, pp. 122–24.

106. *Laneham,* ed. Furnivall, p. 53.

107. Read, *Burghley,* p. 123. For Nicholas Bacon's own gardens, see Nichols, II, pp. 58–59.

108. See Miles Hadfield, *Gardening in Britain* (London, 1960), pp. 53, 57–61;

also B. D. Jackson's "Life of William Turner" in the Ray Society facsimile edition of Turner's *Libellus re herbaria* (London, 1965), pp. 17–20.

109. Burghley's son, Robert Cecil, traded Theobalds to James I for Hatfield House, where he continued to employ leading gardeners: Salomon de Caus and John Tradescant (who later became Charles I's gardener); see Hadfield, pp. 65–67.

110. John Gerard, *The Herball* (London, 1597), A2^{r-v}.

111. Thomas Hill ("Didymus Mountaine"), *The Gardeners Labyrinth* (London, 1594), "Dedication to William Cecil, Lord Burghley": "but surceasing to travise farther in this terrestriall *Gardeners Labyrinth,* I wish unto your honour by dayly Prayer, the fruition of the Heavenly Paradise, craving of the Omnipotent & provident God, the guider of that gorgeous Garden, that he would vouchsafe to graunt unto you, the sweete savour of his chiefe fragrant flouers."

112. Rembert Dodoens, *A Niewe Herball,* trans. Henry Lyte (London, 1578), iii^{v}.

113. See, for this tradition, Paul H. Johnstone, "In Praise of Husbandry," *Agricultural History,* XI (1937), pp. 80–95; and "The Rural Socrates," *JHI,* V (1944), pp. 151–75. Also Røstvig, I, pp. 71–116.

114. William Lawson, *A New Orchard and Garden* (London, 1638), p. 2. Compare Richard Surflet's prefatory letter to his translation (revised by Gervase Markham) of Jean Liébault and Charles Stevens, *Maison rustique* (London, 1616): "there is never a precept of paynefull toyle and laborious husbandrie throughout the Whole Booke, but it soundeth an alarum and proclaimeth an open defiance against thee as a Sluggard" (A3^{v}).

115. Lawson, *New Orchard,* p. 40. Cf. Gervase Markham, *The English Husbandman* (London, 1635), p. 4: "it is most necessary for keeping the earth in order, which else would grow wilde and like a wildernesse, brambles and weedes choaking up better Plantes, and nothing remaining but a Chaos of confusednesse."

116. Lawson, *New Orchard,* p. 69. Cf. Gervase Markham, *A Way to Get Wealth* (London, 1631), part II, pp. 1–2.

117. Surflet, *Maison rustique,* A2^{r}.

118. Lawson, *New Orchard,* pp. 39, 41.

119. *PL,* pp. 185.569 (cf. Wisdom 4:3).

120. See Peter Ure's New Arden edition of *King Richard II* (Cambridge, Mass., 1956), li–lvii.

121. Lawson, *New Orchard,* p. 69; Surflet, *Maison rustique,* A4^{r}. The debate over grafting that worried Perdita (in *The Winter's Tale*) is conducted in these terms—the Fall and what man can do about it; see, e.g., Lawson, pp. 43–44.

122. Surflet, *Maison rustique,* A1^{r}; he cites Pico, among others. Cf. Hugh Platt, *Floraes paradise* (London, 1608), pp. 1–16, for an elaborate "Philosophicall Garden" as a counterpart to practical advice for gardeners. Charles Singer points out that invocations of pagan earth deities are preserved in several medieval herbal manuscripts, invocations that "preserve something of the . . . atmosphere in which the herbal first took its rise"; "The Herbal in Antiquity," *Journal of Hellenic Studies,* XLVII (1927), pp. 47–48.

123. Leonard Mascall, *A Booke of the Arte and Maner How to Plante and Graffe All Sorts of Trees* (London, 1575), "Dedication." But Mascall might have found a similar sentiment in the *Hermetica;* see Scott's edition, I, p. 159.

124. Lawson, *New Orchard,* pp. 52, 63–64; cf. pp. 9, 24, 26.

125. Markham, *Way to Get Wealth,* part V., pp. 4–5.

126. Ambrose, *Hexaemeron,* 3.9.38; cf. Augustine, *De Genesi contra Manichaeos,* 1.16.26 (*PL,* 34.185). For a summary of the problem, see John Calvin, *Commentaries on the Book of Genesis,* trans. John King (Edinburgh, 1847), I, pp. 173–75.

127. John Parkinson, *Paradisi in sole* (London, 1629), "To the Courteous Reader."

128. Ibid.

129. Surflet, *Maison rustique,* A1^{v}.

130. Platt, *Floraes,* A3^{v}; also Hugh Platt, *The Jewell House of Art and Nature* (London, 1594), B3^{r}. Cf. Alberti, *De re aedificatoria,* V, xiv.

131. John Trevisa, *Medieval Lore from Bartholomew Anglicus,* ed. Robert Steele (London, 1924); esp. the Prologue.

132. Parkinson, "To the Courteous Reader." Even when giving utilitarian directions, Parkinson does not call up the Fall, but only suggests how more "graceful and fruitful" forms may be obtained (p. 548).

133. The prefatory poem by "Guilielmus Brodus Pharmaeopaeus": "Totus inest horto mundus; at iste libro" (The whole world is in your garden; and likewise in this book).

134. See Wilfred Blunt, *The Art of Botanical Illustration* (London, 1950), esp. pp. 45–56; Pächt, esp. pp. 25–37; also William M. Ivins, Jr., *Prints and Visual Communication* (Cambridge, Mass., 1953), pp. 21–50.

135. The tree that withers when Adam falls flourishes again in the crucifixion. See E. S. Greenhill, "The Child in the Tree," *Traditio,* X (1954), pp. 323–71; Rose J. Peebles, "The Dry Tree: Symbol of Death," in *Vassar Medieval Studies,* ed. C. F. Fiske (New Haven, 1923), pp. 59–79. Ladner, "Vegetation Symbolism," p. 314, points out Dante's pivotal role in secularizing the Holy Cross legend, so that the figure of the dry tree which flourishes could be used with the "connotation of natural rather than supranatural renewal." In emblem books, the image is moralized by such mottoes as "Deo Volente," "Prospiciente Deo," or simply "Spes." See Joachim Camerarius, *Symbolorum & emblematum ex re herbaria* (Nuremberg, 1593), emblem 3; also 5, 31, 66; cf. *Omnia Andreae Alciati emblemata* (Paris, 1583), pp. 131, 159; Guy de Tervarent, *Attributs et symboles dans l'art profane 1450–1600* (Geneva, 1958), cols. 989–91. For an application of this motif to the iconography of actual gardens, see Eugenio Battisti, "*Natura artificiosa* to *Natura artificialis,*" in *The Italian Garden,* First Dumbarton Oaks Colloquium on the History of Landscape Architecture, ed. David R. Coffin (Washington, D.C., 1972), pp. 22–23.

136. Joachim Camerarius, *De re rustica* (Nuremberg, 1596): "Omnia Florebunt Prospiciente Deo." Cf. Pietro Andrea Mattioli, *Kreutterbuch* (Frankfort, 1586), where the garden enclosed flourishes out of *spes* "wan Gott wil"; under the aegis of the Virgin banishing the snake, Solomon with his book and Adam with his hoe

reap the benefits of Flora and Pomona. Also Johann Coler, *Oeconomia ruralis et domestica* (Frankfort, 1672), where the enclosed garden is composed of the four elements from the Tetragrammaton. (*See Plates 9–10.*)

137. The four plants in the foreground of Sweert's garden are associated with the four continents; see the more elaborate use of the motif in John Parkinson's *Theatrum botanicum* (London, 1640). (*See Plate 8.*)

138. See p. 13 for the Virgin. Flora is pictured with a bare breast as "mother of flowers" (*Fasti,* 5.183); see Julius Held, "Flora, Goddess and Courtesan," *De artibus,* ed. Meiss, p. 206.

139. Giles Fletcher's "Christ's Victory in Heaven," st. 28 in the *Poetical Works,* ed. F. S. Boas (Cambridge, Eng., 1908), p. 25. Cf. Hawkins, *Partheneia,* pp. 13–14; Edgar Wind, *Pagan Mysteries in the Renaissance,* 2nd ed. (New York, 1968), p. 137.

140. For the Virgin with sun and moon, see Meiss, *Painting in Florence and Siena,* p. 154. The mythographers explain that Apollo carries a bow and arrows to express "the forcible vertues of the sunnes transparent raies" by which all things are engendered and maintained; Diana or the moon, particularly in her role as Lucina, is associated with moisture and humidity; see Cartari's *Fountain of Ancient Fiction,* trans. Richard Linche (London, 1599), E4^{r-v}, E3^{v}–F4^{r}, H1^{r}. For Ceres' key, which opens Earth's bosom after winter has locked it: Cartari, M4^{r}.

141. Wittkower, "Transformations of Minerva," p. 197: "alma Minerva/Mortales cunctis artibus erudiens." Wittkower notes the association of Minerva-Wisdom with dry and flourishing trees. Cf. Flora and Minerva on the title page of William Turner, *A New Herball* (London, 1551).

142. E.g., Mattioli (note 136, above); also Gerard, *The Herball* (London, 1597); Rembert Dodoens, *Stirpium historiae* (Antwerp, 1616); Parkinson, *Theatrum botanicum.*

143. Power subject to us: Otto Brunfels, *Herbarum* (Argentoratium [Strasbourg], 1530).

Notes to Chapter II

1. A. O. Lovejoy, *The Great Chain of Being* (Cambridge, Mass., 1936), p. 127, translating Pascal, *Pensées,* frag. 72 (my italics).

2. *De rerum natura,* 1.958–87. For the history of this figure in antiquity, see F. M. Cornford, "The Invention of Space," in *Essays in Honor of Gilbert Murray* (London, 1936), pp. 215–35.

3. Pascal, *Pensées,* frag. 348 (Lovejoy, p. 127).

4. Cornfold, "The Invention of Space," p. 219. This shift is one that has occupied Ernst Cassirer, especially in *The Individual and the Cosmos in Renaissance Philosophy,* trans. Mario Domandi (New York, 1964), to which my whole argument is obviously much indebted.

5. Friedrich Solmsen, *Aristotle's System of the Physical World* (Ithaca, N.Y., 1960), p. 141.

6. *Physics,* 212a20. I have used the translation by R. P. Hardie and R. K. Gaye in *The Works of Aristotle,* ed. W. D. Ross (Oxford, 1930).

7. Solmsen, p. 141, remarks that this is a falsification of the original doctrine, although Lucretius unwittingly accepts it. See Aristotle, *Physics,* 4.5–8.

8. For the tendency to conflate *chora* (room) with *topos* (place), see the notes of P. H. Wickstead and F. M. Cornford in their Loeb edition of Aristotle's *Physics* (London, 1929), I, pp. 272, 288; also Cornford, *Plato's Cosmology* (London, 1937; rpt. New York, 1957), p. 200.

9. Aristotle, *Physics,* 212b18–20; Cassirer, *Individual and Cosmos,* p. 181. P. O. Kristeller, *Eight Philosophers of the Italian Renaissance* (Stanford, 1964), pp. 103–104, has pointed out the significance of the introduction (by Telesio in the 16th century) of the new term, *spatium.*

10. *Physics,* 208b15–20. For center and limit: *On the Heavens,* 308a15 ff., and Pierre Duhem, *Le Système du monde* (Paris, 1913–59), I, pp. 200–201. Cf. Duhem, VII, pp. 158–302, for the special emphasis on the cosmic center in medieval cosmology.

11. Cicero, *De re publica,* 6.15.15, a passage amplified by Macrobius (*Commentary on the Dream of Scipio,* 1.14) and still echoed by Copernicus (Alexandre Koyré, *From the Closed World to the Infinite Universe* [Baltimore, Md., 1957], p. 33). Cf. Cicero, *De natura deorum,* 2.37.94–95, which Petrarch found to be written "almost in a Catholic manner" ("Of His Own Ignorance," in *The Renaissance Philosophy of Man,* ed. E. Cassirer, P. O. Kristeller, and J. H. Randall, Jr. [Chicago, 1948] pp. 80–85); and more generally, Otto von Simson, *The Gothic Cathedral,* 2nd ed. (New York, 1962), pp. 29–39.

12. E.g. Augustine, *Confessions,* 11.5.7: cf. Etienne Gilson, *The Christian Philosophy of Saint Augustine,* trans. L. E. M. Lynch (New York, 1960), p. 191.

13. E.g., Honorius of Autun, *Expositio in Cantica Canticorum,* 5 (*PL,* 172.432); Arnold of Bonneval, *De operibus sex dierum,* prologue (*PL,* 189.1515–16); both cited in M. D. Chenu, *La Théologie au douzième siècle* (Paris, 1957), pp. 22–23, 26; cf. Brian Stock, *Myth and Science in the Twelfth Century* (Princeton, N.J., 1972), p. 126, n. 10. Leo Spitzer, *Studies in Historical Semantics* (New York, 1948), pp. 265–66, has noted that Alain de Lille, in dealing with God's ordination of the world, changes the scriptural "disposuisti" to "claudens," converting an arrangement to an enclosure.

14. Stock, p. 21 and figs. III, a,b,c; Harry Bober, "An Illustrated Medieval Schoolbook," *Journal of the Walters Art Gallery,* XIX–XX (1956–57), pp. 65–97.

15. Edgar Zilsel, "Copernicus and Mechanics," *JHI,* I (1940), p. 115.

16. Laurence Ecker, "Place Concept in Chinese," *Language,* XVI (1940), p. 23.

17. Duhem notes that the tradition of the *Physics* was not dissociated from that of the categories in considering the nature of place, although the Middle Ages finally introduced a distinction between *locus* (place: the environing body) and *ubi* (where: a property of the object itself); I, p. 43 ff., and III, p. 194 ff.

18. See E. R. Curtius, *European Literature and the Latin Middle Ages,* trans. Willard Trask (New York, 1953), pp. 195–96, for the rhetorical tradition of the "pleasant place" (*locus amoenus*), and its punning identification with love.

19. *On the Heavens,* 310a30–311a14; trans. from Loeb edition, ed. W. K. C. Guthrie (Cambridge, Mass., 1939).

20. Solmsen, pp. 128–30; cf. Thomas S. Kuhn, *The Copernican Revolution,* 2nd ed. (New York, 1959), pp. 95–99.

21. Solmsen, pp. 125–27, 270–72. The pun available in "in principium" (or *archē*) allowed for a similar demythification of biblical cosmogony. E.g., Ambrose, *Hexaemeron,* 1.4.12, based on Basil, *Hexaemeron,* 1.1. The theme is elaborately developed in Augustine; see *Confessions,* 12.28.39; also *PL,* 34.174, 222, 247. Cf. Stock, pp. 19–21, for this mechanism at Chartres.

22. *Physics,* 208b28–35; cf. Solmsen, p. 130.

23. The epithets are collected in Calcidius' commentary on the *Timaeus;* J.C.M. Van Winden, *Calcidius on Matter, His Doctrine and Sources* (Leiden, 1959), p. 46. Cf. Stock, pp. 104–105.

24. For Anaximander, see Cornford, "Invention of Space," pp. 226–27; Werner Jaeger, *The Theology of the Early Greek Philosophers* (Oxford, 1936), p. 30. Cf. Solmsen, pp. 119–22; Spitzer, *Studies,* p. 184.

25. *Timaeus,* 33b–34b (trans. Cornford, *Plato's Cosmology,* pp. 54–58). For "the encompassing," cf. Cornford, "The Invention of Space"; Jaeger, *Theology,* p. 30.

26. Jaeger, *Theology,* pp. 20, 198, n. 5, for *physis* as substance and origin; also Ernst Cassirer, *The Philosophy of Symbolic Forms,* trans. Ralph Manheim (New Haven, Conn., 1955), II, p. 50. For "principle" as "seed," see Charles H. Kahn, *Anaximander and the Origins of Greek Cosmology* (New York, 1960), p. 98; also "Of Those Sentiments Concerning Nature with Which Philosophers Were Delighted," in *Plutarch's Morals,* ed. W. W. Goodwin (Boston, 1870), III, p. 107.

27. Cassirer, *Symbolic Forms,* II, p. 37; cf. Ernst Cassirer, *Language and Myth,* trans. Susanne Langer (New York, 1946), pp. 32–34.

28. The epigram is traditionally attributed to Thales (Aristotle, *De anima* 411a7); cf. Cassirer, *Individual and Cosmos,* pp. 148–152, on the connection between empiricism and animism.

29. Cassirer, *Symbolic Forms,* II, p. 74; cf. Owen Barfield, *Saving the Appearances* (London, 1957).

30. Mircea Eliade, *Patterns in Comparative Religion,* trans. Rosemary Sheed (New York, 1958), pp. 242–45.

31. Cicero, *De natura deorum,* 2.33.83; cf. Spitzer, *Studies,* pp. 183–84; also p. 192, citing Lucretius: "aether pascit" (the air nourishes).

32. For the cosmic egg: Spitzer, *Studies,* p. 184; also Don Cameron Allen, "A Note on Lyly's Midas," *MLN,* LX (1945), pp. 326–27, and LXI (1946) pp. 503–504. Plutarch's "Of Isis and Osiris" (*Moralia,* pp. 351–84) is an elaborate mythologization of Aristotle's description of matter as "matrix or womb" (*Physics,* 192a13–25); cf. A. A. Barb, "Diva Matrix," *JWCI,* XVI (1953), pp. 193–238; Edgar Wind, *Pagan Mysteries in the Renaissance,* 2nd ed. (New York, 1968), p. 137, n. 27.

33. G. Van der Leeuw, *Religion in Essence and Manifestation,* trans. J. E. Turner, 2nd ed. (New York, 1963), p. 47; cf. Eliade, *Patterns,* p. 13; Cassirer,

Language and Myth, p. 66; Cassirer, *Symbolic Forms,* II, pp. 73–81; Rudolf Otto, *The Idea of the Holy,* trans. J. W. Harvey, 2nd ed. (New York, 1950), p. 27.

34. Seneca, *Letters,* 41.3; cf. Petrarch, *The Life of Solitude,* trans. J. Zeitlin (Urbana, Ill., 1924), p. 298.

35. F. M. Cornford, *From Religion to Philosophy* (London, 1912; rpt. New York, 1957), pp. 31–35; Cassirer, *Symbolic Forms,* II, pp. 97–100.

36. Mircea Eliade, *The Sacred and the Profane,* trans. Willard Trask (New York, 1959), pp. 21–22; Van der Leeuw, p. 393.

37. Van der Leeuw, pp. 49–50, for this etymology.

38. Cornford, *From Religion to Philosophy,* pp. 1–72.

39. Cassirer, *Language and Myth,* p. 33; and his *Symbolic Forms,* II, pp. 34–37.

40. Van der Leeuw, pp. 29–36, 543–55; Jaeger, *Theology,* p. 79; Lucien Lévy-Bruhl, *How Natives Think,* trans. L. Clare (New York, 1966), pp. 22–117.

41. Edith Cobb, "The Ecology of Imagination in Childhood," *Daedalus,* LXXXVIII (1959), p. 540. Jean Piaget has utilized Lévy-Bruhl's "participation mystique"; e.g., *The Child's Conception of the World,* trans. J. and A. Tomlinson (London, 1929), p. 132.

42. For the theology of Paradise in what follows, I have relied mainly on Gerhart Ladner, *The Idea of Reform* (Cambridge, Mass., 1959); George H. Williams, *Wilderness and Paradise in Christian Thought* (New York, 1962); Jean Daniélou, "Terre et paradis chez les pères d'église," *Eranos Jahrbuch,* XXII (1953), pp. 433–72; Anselm Stolz, *The Doctrine of Spiritual Perfection,* trans. A. Williams (St. Louis, 1938).

43. For the Christian eudaemonism that identifies pleasure and fruition, see John Burnaby, *Amor Dei* (London, 1938), p. 86 ff; also, on the idea of perfection, Morton Bloomfield, *Piers Plowman as a Fourteenth-Century Apocalypse* (New Brunswick, N.J., 1962), esp. pp. 49–50.

44. This vocabulary is pervasive; e.g., Stolz, p. 102; Etienne Gilson, *The Mystical Theology of Saint Bernard,* trans. A. H. C. Downes (London, 1940), p. 45; Charles Singleton, *Journey to Beatrice, Dante Studies II* (Cambridge, Mass., 1954), p. 274 (on Bonaventure). Also Pierre Courcelle, "Tradition néo-platonicienne et traditions chrétiennes de la 'Region de dissemblance'," *Archives d'Histoire Doctrinale et Littéraire du Moyen Âge,* XXXII (1957), pp. 5–33; and more generally, Gerhart Ladner, "*Homo Viator:* Medieval Ideas on Alienation and Order," *Speculum,* XLII (1967), pp. 237–59.

45. Evelyn Underhill, *Mysticism* (New York, 1940), pp. 154–62; Van der Leeuw, pp. 317–22.

46. Burnaby, p. 90, notes the parallel between *Ennead* 1.6.8 and the usages in *De doctrina Christiana,* 1.10, *The City of God,* 9.17, etc. (cf. *De beata vita,* 1.1–5; *Confessions,* 7.21.27). For gnosticism, Hans Jonas, *The Gnostic Religion* (Boston, 1958), pp. 48–99.

47. *Confessions,* 13.9.10; I have used John K. Ryan's translation (Garden City, N.Y., 1960); cf. *The City of God,* 11.28, and *Epistles,* 55.10.18; also Etienne Gilson, *The Christian Philosophy of St. Augustine,* p. 134 and n. 29.

48. W. J. Roche, "Measure, Number, and Weight in St. Augustine," *New Scholasticism,* XV (1941), pp. 350–76.

49. Augustine, *Contra Faustum,* 20.5 (*PL,* 42.391): "omnia congruenter locis suis et ordinibus faciens atque disponens" (making and disposing all things in conformity with their proper places and order). General treatments of the return to Eden and its relation to the tradition of weight and natural place are in Bloomfield, *Piers,* pp. 44–67; Joseph A. Mazzeo, *Structure and Thought in the Paradiso* (Ithaca, N.Y., 1958), Chapter III; cf. Jean Leclercq, *The Love of Learning and the Desire for God,* trans. C. Misrahi (New York, 1962), pp. 39–40, for weight and natural seat in Gregory.

50. Thomas Browne, *The Garden of Cyrus,* I, in the Everyman's Library edition of *The Religio Medici and Other Writings* (London, 1906), p. 180.

51. S. K. Heninger, Jr., "Some Renaissance Versions of the Pythagorean Tetrad," *Studies in the Renaissance,* VIII (1961), pp. 7–35, remarks that Browne's quincunx is "in fact, a continuous tetrad" (p. 32); cf. Leo Spitzer, *Classical and Christian Ideas of World Harmony* (Baltimore, 1963), pp. 64–70; Lactantius, *Institutes,* 2.10(9). Howard Rollin Patch, *The Other World* (Cambridge, Mass., 1950), pp. 154 ff., surveys the iconography of Eden's four rivers; for their elaboration in the hexaemeral tradition, see (for example): Ambrose, *De Paradiso,* 3.13–23; Augustine, *City of God,* 13.21.

52. Cassirer, *Symbolic Forms,* II, pp. 97–100, 146–47; cf. Lévy-Bruhl, pp. 185–90. As Morton Bloomfield has pointed out to me, however, the sanctity of four may be connected rather with the dimensionality of objects than with the coherence of space. See Philo, *On the Creation of the World,* 49–52; Mary Ewer, *A Survey of Mystical Symbolism* (London, 1933), pp. 104–112. In any case (as Miss Ewer makes clear) the number four has to do with the peculiarly spatial nature of the created world, the final manifestation of Godhead.

53. Hugo Rahner, "The Christian Mystery and Pagan Mysteries," in Joseph Campbell, ed., *Pagan and Christian Mysteries* (New York, 1963), pp. 178–96 (I quote from p. 185); cf. Jean Daniélou, *The Theology of Jewish Christianity,* trans. John A. Baker (London, 1964), pp. 274 ff. Browne (*Garden of Cyrus,* IV) coins "decussation" from the Latin of Justin Martyr, who seems to have been the first to apply Plato's figure to the Cross; see R. A. Norris, *God and World in Early Christian Theology* (New York, 1965), p. 56.

54. Philo, *On the Creation of the World,* 78; translation in Vol. I of the Loeb edition of F. H. Colson and G. H. Whitaker (Cambridge, Mass., 1949). For the spatial character of cosmic harmony, see Spitzer, *World Harmony,* p. 5: like mana, harmony is the ground both of the world soul and of the individual man, and this identity is what constitutes the sacredness of man's existence in Eden. Obviously, too, the position of Eden, on a high mountain that unites cosmic realms, makes it a center in Eliade's sense; see *Cosmos and History,* trans. Willard Trask (New York, 1959), pp. 12–21; also Daniélou, "Terre et paradis," pp. 442–43; Singleton, *Journey to Beatrice,* pp. 141–46.

55. Philo, *On the Creation of the World,* 142. For the symbolism of Adam's

name: M. L. W. Laistner, *Thought and Letters in Western Europe,* 2nd ed. (Ithaca, N.Y., 1957), p. 240; esp. Augustine, *Enarrationes in Psalmos,* 95.15 (*PL,* 37.1236), where the context of this symbolism is a play on the connections between a single place and the whole world.

56. Edmund Spenser, *The Faerie Queene,* 6.4.28, a lesson exemplified by Calidore on Mt. Acidale. For the theory, see Eliade, *Patterns,* pp. 382–85; and for the practice, Patch, *The Other World,* Chapter V.

57. *Paradise Lost,* 10.303; Ephraem of Syria, *Select Metrical Hymns,* trans. Henry Burgess (London, 1853), p. 114 (*Hymns on Paradise,* 1). Cf. Bloomfield, *Piers,* p. 48; also Spitzer, *Studies,* p. 265, for the "boxed-in" feeling in the Middle Ages.

58. Philo, *Allegorical Interpretation,* 1.65–66; cf. Ambrose, *De Paradiso,* 3.18.

59. E.g., Gregory of Nyssa, *From Glory to Glory,* ed. and trans. Jean Daniélou and Herbert Musurillo (New York, 1961), p. 228. For later uses: Stanley Stewart, *The Enclosed Garden* (Madison, Wis., 1966), pp. 50–59.

60. Mary Irma Corcoran, *Milton's Paradise Lost with Reference to the Hexameral Background* (Washington, D.C., 1945), p. 17.

61. Ambrose, *Hexameron, Paradise, and Cain and Abel,* trans. John Savage (New York, 1961), p. 288 (*De Paradiso,* 1.1).

62. Pseudo-Tertullian, *De judicio Domini,* in Arturo Graf, *Miti, leggende e superstizioni del Medio Evo* (Turin, 1892), p. 197.

63. Dracontius, *De laudibus Dei,* 1.183, 187 (ed. F. Vollner, in *MGH,* XIV [Berlin, 1905]). Cf. Patch, *The Other World,* pp. 139–40.

64. Claudius Marius Victor, *Alethia,* 1.224. Text edited by Carolus Schenkl (*CSEL,* XVI, Part 1 [Vienna, 1888]); cf. the French translation and commentary on the Prayer and lines 1–170 of Book One by P. F. Hovingh (Groningen, Neth., 1955).

65. Godfrey of Viterbo, *Pantheon,* in Graf, p. 209.

66. Hippolytus, cited in Daniélou, "Terre et paradis," p. 443. Cf. II-*Enoch* 8.1–8 and I-*Enoch* 25.4–8 (both cited in Daniélou, "Terre et paradis," p. 434). Avitus speaks of Eden as the "secret place of Nature" (*Poematum,* 1.193–94; ed. R. Peiper, *MGH,* VI, Part 2 [Berlin, 1883]), a phrase later echoed by Alain de Lille to describe Nature's garden—like Eden, a sacred source—in the *Anticlaudianus,* 1.55–56 (text edited by R. Bossuat [Paris, 1955]). Also *Architrenius,* in Thomas Wright, *Anglo-Latin Satirical Poets* (London, 1872), I, p. 251; cf. Paul Piehler, *The Visionary Landscape* (London, 1971), p. 88.

67. Theodore of Mopsuestia, cited in Daniélou, "Terre et Paradis," p. 444; *Purgatorio,* 28.77–78 ("luogo eletto / all'umana natura per suo nido").

68. Sir Walter Raleigh, *Works* (Oxford, 1829), II, p. 77.

69. Patch, *The Other World* (p. 139) notes the formulaic rigidity in descriptions of Paradise. Arnold Williams, *The Common Expositor* (Chapel Hill, N.C., 1948), may be consulted for the dangers of literalism.

70. Peter Sterry (17th cent.), quoted in Louis Martz, *The Paradise Within* (New Haven, Conn., 1964), p. 33.

71. Origen's homily on Numbers 16, cited in Daniélou, "Terre et Paradis," pp. 432–33.

72. Origen, *On First Principles,* ed. G. W. Butterworth (New York, 1966), pp. 89–94 (*De principiis,* 2.3.6–7). For Origen's ambivalence toward the material world, see Norris, pp. 141–56; Ladner, *Reform,* pp. 70–75. For the later history of the tradition of the upper world, see Jerome Taylor, ed., *The Didascalicon of Hugh St. Victor* (New York, 1961), p. 190, n. 56; William Nelson, *The Poetry of Edmund Spenser* (New York, 1963), pp. 220–21. F. M. Cornford, *Principium sapientiae* (Cambridge, Eng., 1952), p. 174, links Anaximander's "boundless" with a similar idea.

73. *Paradise Lost,* 11.836–38; cf. Corcoran, p. 32.

74. For purposes of exhortation, of course, it might always have proved useful to throw the emphasis on the former rather than on the latter—on psychology rather than myth. Milton's attitude has precedent in a remark like that by Ernaldus in his twelfth-century hexaemeron: "non felicem facit locus, sed vita" (not place but life makes felicity [*PL,* 189.1546]). But the assumption here is that life is dependent on place; the act of Creation, in Ernaldus' account, consists of assigning to the things of nature not only "duties" and "congruent measure" but also "propria loca, et nomina" (proper places and names [*PL,* 189.1515]). Cf. *Paradiso,* 1.55–57, for the link between *virtù* and man's proper place. Milton, in asserting that virtue is brought to place, in effect denies any distinction between Eden and the places of the fallen world.

75. This has frequently been remarked. E.g., J. B. Broadbent, *Some Graver Subject* (New York, 1960), pp. 169–201; Frank Kermode, "Adam Unparadised," in *The Living Milton,* ed. Frank Kermode (London, 1960), pp. 85–123; Maynard Mack, "Introduction," *English Masterpieces IV: Milton* (Englewood Cliffs, N.J., 1961), pp. 19–21.

76. *Du Bartas, His Divine Weekes and Works,* "Eden," 220 ff., in Joshua Sylvester, *The Complete Works,* ed. Alexander Grosart (Edinburgh, 1880).

77. "Eden," 300 ff.; cf. Stolz, p. 20.

78. "Eden," 87–88. The same figure appears on the title page of Calvin's commentary on Genesis (Geneva, 1564; reproduced in John King's translation [Edinburgh, 1847]), although here the image is made to look ahead to the tree of the second Eden, that of the crucifixion: "Rami ut ego insererer defracti sunt" (The branches were pruned away in order that I might be grafted on).

79. Augustine, *De Genesi ad litteram,* 8.8.15–16 (*PL,* 34.379).

80. Thomas Traherne, *Centuries,* 1.29. I have used the text in *Centuries, Poems, and Thanksgivings,* ed. H. M. Margoliouth (Oxford, 1958). Cf Martz, pp. 35–102.

81. Ephraem of Syria, *Hymns on Paradise,* 9.5–6; trans. from Daniélou's French version, "Terre et paradis," p. 434.

82. See note 54, above.

83. For a survey of this tradition, see Ruth Wallerstein, *Studies in Seventeenth-Century Poetic* (Madison, Wis., 1950), Chapter VIII; also Martz, Chapters I–II.

84. See Patch, *The Other World,* Chapter V; also Corcoran, p. 27.

85. Daniélou, "Terre et paradis," p. 435.

86. Ambrose, *Hexaemeron,* 6.2.3 (trans. Savage, p. 229). Cf. Traherne, *Centuries,* 1.6: "It [the world offered by God] will make you to see your own Greatness."

87. *Centuries,* 1.3, 1.15, *et passim.* Cf Romans 4:13; I–Corinthians 3:21–22.

88. For the hexaemera: Corcoran, pp. 1–40; Frank E. Robbins, *The Hexaemeral Literature* (Chicago, 1912); Watson Kirkconnell, *The Celestial Cycle* (Toronto, 1952). For Bible epics: A. Bartlett Giamatti, *The Earthly Paradise and the Renaissance Epic* (Princeton, N.J., 1966), pp. 67–83; Curtius, pp. 458–62; many of the texts are conveniently assembled in Graf, *Miti, leggende e superstizioni.* Cf. Patch, *The Other World.*

89. Basil, *Hexaemeron,* 8.8; translation in *Letters and Select Works,* trans. Blomfield Jackson for *Nicene and Post-Nicene Fathers,* 2nd ser., Vol. VIII (New York, 1895), p. 101.

90. Orientius, *Commentary,* 1.109. The text has been edited by Robinson Ellis in the *CSEL* series, Vol. XVI, Part 1 (Vienna, 1888); cf. the edition with English commentary by Mildred Dolores Tobin (Washington, D.C., 1945). The same remark appears in Dracontius, *De laudibus Dei,* 1.176; and in Claudius Marius Victor, *Alethia,* Prayer, 32–33.

91. E.g., Dracontius, *De laudibus Dei,* 1.348–58; Victor, *Alethia,* Prayer, 32–33, 50–55. Hovingh, p. 83, catalogues Victor's frequent use of *munus* (gift), *dos* (dowry), *largitas* (bounty). Cf. Ambrose, *De Paradiso,* 4.3–4 (where nature's gifts are her "voice"; compare Philo, *On the Creation,* 79) and also 3.65.

92. Lovejoy, p. 49.

93. Victor, *Alethia,* Prayer, 41–44.

94. E.g., in Dracontius, *De laudibus Dei,* 1.427–48, our first parents enjoy a pastoral freedom from shame ("wandering through flowers") since all things are made for their use; while in a fallen world (Ambrose, *Hexaemeron,* 5.1.2) nature's plenty evokes only envy and greed. Cf. Prudentius, *Liber cathemerinon,* 3.106–107: the implicit contrast is between the use of a familiar servant and the idolatry of a fallen world. II–Corinthians 6:10 had defined the Christian as one who has nothing, but (like the Senecan wise man: *De beneficiis,* 7.1–12) possesses all things; and Augustine finds the distinction between using and enjoying the key by which man may return to his "native country" (*De doctrina Christiana,* 1.3–5). Cf. Corcoran, p. 21.

95. The related topic of "much in little" has been treated in Kitty Scoular, *Natural Magic* (Oxford, 1965), pp. 38–117.

96. *Natural History,* 23.2.2; Loeb edition, ed. H. Rackham (Cambridge, Mass., 1950). For stoic devotion to the gifts of nature, see, e.g., Cicero, *De finibus,* 4.14.37, *De legibus,* 1.8.25.

97. Otto, p. 36.

98. E.g., Dracontius, *De laudibus Dei,* 1.118–37, on the gift of light by which all things are constituted; or Victor, *Alethia,* Prayer, 50–55, where creation is the "gift of being." Also Ambrose, *Hexaemeron,* 5.1.1.

99. Dracontius, *De laudibus Dei,* 1.176, 198. After the Fall, according to Ernaldus, man lacks the garment of royal dignity, "amictus regiae dignitatis" (*PL,* 189.1546);

for the transformation of this conceit into the garment of Nature (e.g., in the *Anticlaudianus*), as well as for its baptismal use, see below, Chapter IV.

100. Hugh of St. Victor, *Dialogue Concerning the Earnest Money of the Soul,* trans. Kevin Herbert (Milwaukee, Wis., 1956); Claude Chavasse, *The Bride of Christ* (London, 1940).

101. *Purgatorio,* 28.92–93; Avitus, *Poematum,* 1.191–92.

102. E.g., Virgil, *Georgics,* 2.323; Lucretius, *De rerum natura,* 1.250, 2.991. For Proba ("Maro mutatus in melius") see Curtius, p. 459.

103. Daniélou, "Terre et paradis," pp. 442–43.

104. Avitus, *Poematum,* 1.212; Du Bartas, "Eden," 99, 346–47.

105. E.g., Philo, *On the Creation,* 25.78; Avitus, *Poematum,* 2.3–4, 2.172; cf. Robbins, p. 33, n. 1, for several examples. Hovingh, p. 121, notes the relation to this tradition of Victor's account of man in Eden as "the lord for whom everything was prepared" (*Alethia,* 1.142).

106. *Phaedrus,* 247a–248c; Herman L. Sinaiko, *Love, Knowledge, and Discourse in Plato* (Chicago, 1965), pp. 61–72. Frank Kermode, *Shakespeare, Spenser, Donne* (New York, 1971), pp. 84–115, traces the literary fortunes of the Platonic banquet, and especially of its corruption, the banquet of the senses. Chapman's version, "Ovid's Banquet of Sense," takes place in another garden, but one which preserves of Eden (if we are to accept Kermode's reading) only its dangerous seduction; the more usual interpretation has been to see in the poem an attempt to recover the Adamic talent for possessing the spiritual in the material.

107. Luke 13:29. See Walter Lowrie, *Art in the Early Church,* 2nd ed., rev. (New York, 1965), pp. 51–53; Lowrie, *Action in the Liturgy* (New York, 1953), pp. 91–94, explains the Eucharistic banquet as a recovery of the Edenic communion with the Creator in the creature. Monastic and mystic writers frequently identify the heavenly food that does not satiate (see Stolz, p. 17) with the banquet of the original garden, God's own "table"; e.g., Nicholas of Clairvaux (*PL,* 184.1058, drawing on Bernard, *PL,* 183.663), cited in Jean Leclercq, *La Vie parfaite* (Paris, 1948), p. 165; also Bonaventure, "The Tree of Life," in *Mystical Opuscula,* trans. José de Vinck (Paterson, N.J., 1961), p. 99.

108. E.g., Avitus, *Poematum,* 2.3; Basil, *Hexaemeron,* 2.1; Ambrose, *Hexaemeron,* 3.8.35, "ubertas fecundae matris" (the fruitfulness of the teeming mother [*PL,* 14.170]); Ephraem, *Metrical Hymns,* p. 113. On the "realm of unremitting plenty" ("ubertatis indeficientis") in Augustine, see Kenneth Burke, *The Rhetoric of Religion* (Boston, 1961), pp. 117–22, and Chapter II, *passim.*

109. Philo, *On the Creation,* 45.133, trans. Colson and Whitaker (Loeb edition), p. 105. Cf. J. C. Plumpe, *Mater Ecclesia* (Washington, D.C., 1943), for the relation between Christian images and the classical mother of all things (*mater = materia*); the mother's bare and streaming breast serves to figure the Virgin, the Mother Church, and Caritas, as well as the pagan Cybele.

110. Nicholas of Clairvaux, cited in R. E. Kaske, "Langland and the *Paradisus Claustralis,*" *MLN,* LXXII (1957), pp. 481–83.

111. Early instances are Jerome, *Epistles,* 125.7, and Caesarius of Arles (d. 542), *Opera,* ed. G. Morin (Turnabout, Belg., 1953), pp. 932–33 (Sermon 234.1). For

general accounts, see Bloomfield, *Piers*, pp. 44–67; Ladner, *Reform, passim;* Williams, *Wilderness and Paradise*, pp. 28–64; also several studies by Jean Leclercq: *La Vie parfaite* (Paris, 1948); *La Spiritualité de Pierre de Celle* (Paris, 1946); *Pierre le Vénérable* (Abbaye S. Wandrille, France, 1946); *The Love of Learning and the Desire for God* (New York, 1962); "Les Deux Compilations de Thomas de Perseigne," *Mediaeval Studies*, X (1948), p. 207 ff.

112. For the relation of monastic *otium* and the Sabbath, see Leclercq, *Pierre de Celle*, p. 82 ff.

113. Ladner, *Reform*, pp. 319–77. Cf. Leclercq, *La Vie parfaite*, pp. 168–69. Morton Bloomfield in "Joachim of Flora," *Traditio*, XIII (1957), p. 281, n. 36, has traced this emphasis back to Pseudo-Dionysius' notion that the heavenly hierarchy is reflected in the earthly.

114. See, for example, Leclercq, *Pierre le Vénérable*, p. 126; Leclercq, *Pierre de Celle*, pp. 84–85.

115. See especially Leclercq, *The Love of Learning*, pp. 11–17, *et passim.*

116. For the late Latin feeling for nature, see Philip Schuyler Allen, *The Romanesque Lyric* (Chapel Hill, N.C., 1928), and also his *Mediaeval Latin Lyrics* (Chicago, 1931). For the pagan "inclination to retirement" and its links with monasticism, see André Festugière, *Personal Religion among the Greeks* (Berkeley, Calif., 1954), pp. 53–67.

117. Jerome, *Epistles*, 125.11; cf. E. K. Rand, *Founders of the Middle Ages* (Cambridge, Mass., 1928), p. 119.

118. Augustine, *De ordine*, 1.2.4 (*PL*, 32.980); trans. R. P. Russell (*Divine Providence and the Problem of Evil*) in the Fathers of the Church series (New York, 1948). Cf. *Epistles*, 10.2 (*PL*, 33.74): "Otio deificari" (to be sanctified in retirement).

119. So he describes the project of his retreat in *De beata vita*, 1.1–5.

120. See *Contra academicos*, 3.4.9; *De ordine*, 1.8.25.

121. Marie Luise Gothein, *A History of Garden Art*, trans. Mrs. Archer-Hind (New York, 1928), I, p. 171, notes that *hortus* generally refers to a villa garden. I have used the following general accounts for Augustine: R. J. Halliburton, "The Inclination to Retirement—The Retreat of Cassiciacum and the 'Monastery' of Tagaste," *Studia Patristica V, Texte und Untersuchungen*, LXXX (Berlin, 1962), pp. 329–40; F. Van der Meer, *Augustine the Bishop*, trans. B. Battershaw and G. R. Lamb (London, 1961), pp. 207–17; Gerald Bonner, *St. Augustine of Hippo* (London, 1963), pp. 92–115; Ladner, *Reform*, pp. 352–56; Rand, pp. 251–84.

122. See Leclercq, *The Love of Learning*, p. 108. Williams, *Wilderness and Paradise*, notes the use by early universities of a paradise ideology inherited from the monasteries (esp. pp. 167–68).

123. Leclercq, *Pierre le Vénérable*, p. 103, a conscious play upon the usual polarity of *negotium* and *otium*. For monastic use of these Ciceronian terms, see Hans Baron, "Cicero and the Roman Civic Spirit in the Middle Ages and Early Renaissance," *Bulletin of the John Rylands Library*, XXII (1938), pp. 72–97; also Leclercq, *Pierre de Celle*, p. 82 ff.; *The Love of Learning*, pp. 73, 145–46.

124. Etienne Gilson, " 'Sub umbris arborum,' " *Mediaeval Studies,* XIV (1952), pp. 149–51.

125. Basil, *Epistles,* 14, cited in Kenneth E. Kirk, *The Vision of God,* 2nd ed. (London, 1932), p. 308.

126. Evans, *Art in Mediaeval France* (Oxford, 1948), p. 64; Simson, *The Gothic Cathedral,* p. 44 and note 58; Leclercq, *The Love of Learning,* p. 137. Leclercq, *La Vie parfaite,* p. 44 ff., cites John Chrysostom, who defines monks as "the inhabitants of mountains."

127. I have used the translation in Leclercq, *The Love of Learning,* p. 136.

128. *PL,* 172.590. Cf. Peter Damian on Cluny as a "garden of delights," cited in Kenneth J. Conant, "Iconography and Sequence of the Ambulatory Capitals at Cluny," *Speculum,* V (1930), p. 286.

129. Alicia Amherst, *A History of Gardening in England* (New York, 1910), p. 14.

130. Gulielmus Durandus, *The Symbolism of Churches and Church Ornaments,* trans. J. M. Neale and B. Webb (Leeds, 1843), Chap. I, Sections 42–43. The four sides represent contempt of self and of the world, love of God and of our neighbor; the trees and herbs are virtues; the well "the dew of God's heavenly gifts"; and so on.

131. The attribution to Hildebert is Joan Evans' in her *Life in Medieval France,* 3rd ed. (New York, 1969), pp. 54–55. Migne includes this *Laus vitae monasticae* among the works of Geoffery of Vendôme (*PL,* 141.373).

132. A. Kingsley Porter, *Medieval Architecture* (New York, 1909), p. 63 ff. For a somewhat different theory, see Joan Evans, *The Romanesque Architecture of the Order of Cluny* (Cambridge, Eng., 1938), pp. 135–36.

133. Honorius, *De claustro* (*PL,* 172.590); cf. Williams, *Wilderness and Paradise,* pp. 47–48.

134. Michel Rambaud, "Le Quatrain mystique de Vaison-la-Romaine," *Bulletin Monumental,* CIX (1951), p. 171. Gothein, I, p. 174, cites William Rufus on the roses at Romsey; also Gladys Taylor, *Old London Gardens* (London, 1953), p. 15. Cf., however, Wolfgang Sörrensen, "Garten und Pfanzen im Klosterplan," in *Studien zur St. Galler Klosterplan,* ed. J. Duft (Saint Gallen, Switz., 1962), pp. 196, 235–36.

135. Gregory of Nyssa, *From Glory to Glory,* p. 130.

136. *De claustro animae,* 4.29 (*PL,* 176.1168). Traditionally assigned to Hugh of St. Victor; see Kaske, p. 482.

137. John Theodore De Bry, *Florilegium renovatum* (Frankfort, 1641), fig. 1 (1st ed., Frankfort, 1612). For De Bry and his circle (including the "Vitruvian" gardener, Salomon de Caus), see Frances Yates, *Theatre of the World* (Chicago, 1969), pp. 70–72; also her *The Rosicrucian Enlightenment* (London, 1972), pp. 11–13, 67, 70–73, 80. Cf. Gothein, II, pp. 26–27.

138. The Persian "paradise," from which the basilica's atrium seems to have taken its name and possibly its design, was explicitly cosmological in its plan. What struck Xenophon was the geometrical rigor of Cyrus' garden (*Oeconomicus,* 4.16 ff.); and, from what can be inferred from rugs and tapestries, the typical way of

disposing such gardens was in four squares, with the emperor's pleasure dome at the intersection of the canals or alleys—rivers of paradise. See Pierre Grimal, *L'Art des jardins* (Paris, 1954), p. 21 ff.

139. Cf. Richard Krautheimer, *Studies in Early Christian, Medieval, and Renaissance Art* (New York, 1969), pp. 121–22, for John the Scot's account of the "vibrations" awakened in him by the number eight.

140. For a convenient summary of the tradition, see Edgar de Bruyne, *The Esthetics of the Middle Ages,* trans. E. B. Hennessy (New York, 1969), pp. 48–55; Bruyne, *Etudes d'esthétique médiévale* (Bruges, 1946), II, pp. 343–70; also Simson, pp. 21–50.

141. *De claustro animae,* 4.31 (*PL,* 176.1168–69). For *aequalitas,* Bruyne, *Etudes,* II, p. 272, also Index, s.v., "aequalitas."

142. R. Glaber's treatise on the "divine and abstract quaternity of the world," cited in Joan Evans, *Clunaic Art of the Romanesque Period* (Cambridge, Eng., 1950), p. 110 ff.

143. Text and discussion in Paul Frankl, *The Gothic* (Princeton, N.J., 1960), pp. 76–77. For medieval builders: Frankl, *The Gothic,* pp. 48–110; Frankl, "The Secret of the Medieval Masons," *AB,* XXVII (1945), pp. 46–60; J. S. Ackerman, "'*Ars sine scientia nihil est,*'" *AB,* XXXI (1949), pp. 84–111; Simson, pp. 3–20. For romanesque: Kenneth John Conant, *Carolingian and Romanesque Architecture,* 3rd ed. (Baltimore, 1974), pp. 478–79; also Conant, "Medieval Academy Excavations of Cluny, IX: Systematic Dimensions in the Buildings," *Speculum,* XXXVIII (1963), pp. 1–45.

144. For Vitruvius and the Middle Ages: Frankl, *The Gothic,* pp. 88, 102; cf. Roger Hinks, *Carolingian Art* (Ann Arbor, Mich., 1962), p. 110.

145. Robert Willis, "Description of the Ancient Plan of the Monastery of St. Gall in the Ninth Century," *Archaeological Journal,* V (1848), pp. 85–117; cf. J. M. Clark, *The Abbey of St. Gall as a Centre of Literature and Art* (Cambridge, Eng., 1926), pp. 71–90; F. Cabrol and H. Leclercq, *Dictionnaire d'archéologie chrétienne et de liturgie* (Paris, 1907–53), VI[1], cols. 80–106.

146. Walter Horn and E. Born, "The 'Dimensional Inconsistencies' of the Plan of St. Gall," *AB,* XLVIII (1966), pp. 285–308; also H. Reinhardt, "Der St. Galler Klosterplan," *Historischer Verein des Kantons St. Gallen, Neujahrsblatt,* XCII (1952), p. 19.

147. Reinhardt, pp. 18–25; Simson, p. 18, n. 40; but cf. Horn, "Dimensional Inconsistencies," pp. 297–99.

148. Wolfgang Braunfels, *Monasteries of Western Europe,* trans. Alastair Laing (Princeton, N.J., 1972), p. 46. Walter Horn has argued, though, that *exemplata* has the sense of a "copy" of a previous plan, rather than "making as an example"; see "The Plan of St. Gall—Original or Copy?" in *Studien zur St. Galler Klosterplan,* ed. Duft, pp. 79–102. For the author of the plan, see Walter Horn, "On the Author of the Plan of St. Gall and the Relation of the Plan to the Monastic Reform Movement," in *Studien,* ed. Duft, pp. 103–27.

149. Clark, *Abbey of St. Gall,* p. 74.

150. Horn, "Dimensional Inconsistencies," pp. 290–91; Horn, "On the Author," pp. 103–27; Braunfels, pp. 37–46.

151. Horn, "On the Author," p. 109.

152. Willis, p. 90; his own conclusions seem systematically to reverse those of his predecessors; cf. Sörrensen, pp. 195–96.

153. See the remarks on St. Gall in Conant, *Carolingian and Romanesque Architecture,* p. 56.

154. Interpreters of Ezekiel 40:47 said that the atrium of the heavenly temple was a square of one hundred cubits in order to signify perfection; e.g., Gregory, *Homiliarum in Ezechielem,* 2.10.17–18 (*PL,* 76.1067–68); *De claustro animae,* 4.31 (*PL,* 176.1169). Is this veneration for the number 100 a reason why a monastic commentator should say that "it is generally held that the cloister should be 100 feet square" (cited in Horn, "Dimensional Inconsistencies," p. 296)? At St. Gall the 100-foot-square cloister represents a fusion of the two basic square modules employed in the plan, 40 and 2½.

155. For the monastic schedule and the layout of the cloister, see R. Liddlesdale Palmer, *English Monasteries in the Middle Ages* (London, 1930), Chapter VI, *passim,* and esp. pp. 112–14; also pp. 48–49; cf. Kenneth John Conant, *Benedictine Contributions to Church Architecture* (Latrobe, Pa., 1949), p. 19; Braunfels, *passim.*

156. Jean Leclercq, "Le Cloître est-il un paradis?" in *Le Message des moines à notre temps* (Paris, 1958), p. 145; cf. Stolz, pp. 42–43, 46.

157. Williams, *Wilderness and Paradise,* Chapter II, collects a number of texts.

158. The two stages are clearly distinguished by D. A. Underwood, "The Fountain of Life," *Dumbarton Oaks Papers,* V (1950), pp. 41–138. The texts are Romans 6:3–4, and John 3:5 (as Underwood notes, the King James version fails to render the Vulgate properly: *renatus*).

159. Cloistered paradise and paradise of delights: the terms are Jean Leclercq's (*La Vie parfaite,* pp. 164–65), although he does not link them to baptismal theology; cf. Stolz, pp. 30–31. *Paradisum deliciarum* is from Latin versions of the Septuagint, Genesis 2:15; see Corcoran, pp. 20–21.

160. I take this account of the term from Cabrol and Leclercq, III[2], cols. 1991–92.

161. Honorius, *De claustro,* p. 149 (*PL,* 172.590).

162. *Laus vitae monasticae, PL,* 141.373–74.

163. Samuel Chew, *The Pilgrimage of Life* (New Haven, Conn., 1962), fig. 13. For the significance of the compasses, which Chew fails to note, see Simson, p. 35. Roche, pp. 352–55, identifies measure, the initial act of creation and the one on which all subsequent acts rest, with the act of limiting, of establishing boundaries. Cf. Alain's "sub numero claudens" (enclosing in number), cited in Spitzer, *Studies,* pp. 265–66.

164. Cabrol and Leclercq, III[2], 1998 ff.; also Richard Krautheimer, *Early Christian and Byzantine Architecture* (Baltimore, 1965), pp. 249–50; Braunfels, pp. 14–15 (Braunfels, however, says the engraving is of Watopedi, also on Mt. Athos). For tholos and Fountain of Life, see Underwood.

165. More recent scholarship seems to have settled on a tree, an evergreen cited in Charlemagne's *Capitulary on Villas;* the significance of the center points in the hospital and novitiate, however, remains in doubt, and a recent commentator has suggested they are wells; Reinhardt, p. 11, Sörrensen, pp. 195, 197–99.

166. The symbolisms of fountain and tree are too complex to enter into here. There is a good survey of the former in Underwood, "The Fountain of Life"; and of the latter in Gerhart Ladner, "Vegetation Symbolism and the Concept of Renaissance," in *De artibus opuscula xl: Essays in Honor of Erwin Panofsky,* ed. Millard Meiss (New York, 1961), pp. 303–22; cf. Jean Daniélou, *Primitive Christian Symbols,* trans. D. H. Hunter (Baltimore, Md., 1964), pp. 25–41.

167. Eusebius, *The History of the Church,* 10.4, cited in J. G. Davies, *Origin and Development of Early Christian Architecture* (New York, 1953), p. 98 ff.

168. Ernst Schlee, *Die Ikonographie der Paradiesesflusse* (Leipzig, 1937), pp. 133–46; Cabrol and Leclercq, II², 1955–69; E. Baldwin Smith, *Architectural Symbolism of Imperial Rome and the Middle Ages* (Princeton, N.J., 1956), pp. 27–30.

169. E.g., Louis Hautecoeur, *Les Jardins des dieux et des hommes* (Paris, 1959), p. 100; Mario Praz, *Studies in Seventeenth Century Imagery,* 2nd ed. (Rome, 1964), pp. 16–17, n. 1; also fig. 9, p. 44.

170. Durandus, *The Symbolism of Churches,* 1.42–43; Honorius, *PL,* 172.590.

171. Sörrensen, pp. 253–62: the tree of life in which the fruits of perpetual health [or salvation] are redolent.

172. Underwood, p. 55. Cf. Rahner, "The Christian Mystery," p. 201, for citations from the Eastern Fathers, Pseudo-Dionysius, and Augustine ("vulva matris aqua baptismatis": their mother's womb is the water of baptism).

173. Braunfels, p. 234.

174. Frank Crisp, *Mediaeval Gardens* (London, 1924), pp. 13, 51–53. George Kernodle, *From Art to Theater* (Chicago, 1944), p. 67, notes that a fountain alone was often used in processions to represent a garden.

175. Crisp. figs. 236–237.

176. Andreas Capellanus, *The Art of Courtly Love,* trans. John Jay Parry (New York, 1941), p. 68; cf. A. J. Denomy, "An Inquiry into the Origins of Courtly Love," *Mediaeval Studies,* VI (1944), p. 178, who cites the same figure from the Provençal poet Marcabrun.

177. Gothein, fig. 133.

Notes to Chapter III

1. Ernst Robert Curtius, *European Literature and the Latin Middle Ages,* trans. Willard Trask (New York, 1953), pp. 193–94.

2. Matthew of Vendôme, *Ars versificatoria,* 1.109, in Edmund Faral, *Les Arts poétiques du XIIe et du XIIIe siècle* (Paris, 1924), p. 147. Cf. Paul Piehler, *The Visionary Landscape* (London, 1971), p. 89.

3. Curtius, pp. 183–202, on the rhetorical tradition of the *locus amoenus* or pleasance; also Thomas G. Rosenmeyer, *The Green Cabinet* (Berkeley, 1969), pp. 198–202.

4. Rosenmeyer, p. 201.

5. *Phaedrus,* 247–250; trans. W. C. Helmbold and W. G. Rabinowitz (New York, 1956), pp. 29–33; cf. R. Hackforth, Plato's *Phaedrus* (Cambridge, Eng., 1952), pp. 80–81, on the "place" of Being; also Paul Friedländer, *Plato: An Introduction,* trans. Hans Meyerhoff (New York, 1958), p. 194. Mircea Eliade notes the relation between shamanistic ecstasy and the return to Paradise; "The Yearning for Paradise in Primitive Tradition," *Diogenes,* III (Summer, 1953), pp. 18–30.

6. Girolamo Fracastoro, *Naugerius: sive De poetica dialogus,* ed. and trans. Ruth Kelso (Urbana, Ill., 1924), pp. 50–52 (154 r-v). For *Turrius,* see Baxter Hathaway, *The Age of Criticism* (Ithaca, N.Y., 1962), pp. 318–28.

7. Edward Hutton, *Country Walks about Florence* (New York, 1908), pp. 1–30, for the *Decameron;* Georgina Masson, *Italian Gardens,* (New York, n.d.), p. 52, for Naples and the *Amorosa visione.*

8. *Decameron,* 4. introduction. 35–36; ed. V. Branca (Florence, 1965).

9. "Conclusione dell' autore," 7–8.

10. 7. introduction. 4–6. Cf. *Filocolo,* 4.14, 4.72; text in Boccaccio, *Opere Minori,* ed. M. Marti (Milan, 1969).

11. Lines 49–52; cf. Winthrop Wetherbee, *Platonism and Poetry in the Twelfth Century* (Princeton, N.J., 1972), pp. 128–34; also pp. 146–51 on Matthew of Vendôme (*Ars versificatoria,* 2.2.)

12. E.g., Charles Singleton, "On Meaning in the Decameron," *Italica,* XXI (1944,) pp. 117–24; Aldo Scaglione, *Nature and Love in the Late Middle Ages* (Berkeley, 1963), p. 64; Edith Kern, "Gardens in the *Decameron Cornice,*" *PMLA,* LXVI (1951), pp. 505–523.

13. *Amorosa visione,* 22.62–63; cf. Ovid, *Metamorphoses,* 3.466: "inopem me copia fecit" (plenty makes me poor). For the *Genealogy,* see Louis Vinge, *The Narcissus Theme in Western European Literature,* trans. R. Dewsnap and N. Reeves (Lund, Sweden, 1967), pp. 103–105; D. T. Starnes and E. W. Talbot, *Classical Myth and Legend in Renaissance Dictionaries* (Chapel Hill, N.C., 1955), p. 197. For the world as a mirror in gnostic/Neoplatonic thought: Vinge, pp. 37–40.

14. *Filocolo,* 4.43; trans., *Thirteene Most Pleasant and Delectable Questions . . . Englished by H. G.* (1566), ed. Edward Hutton (London, 1927).

15. Cited in Erwin Panofsky, *Renaissance and Renascences in Western Art,* 2nd ed. (New York, 1969), pp. 13–14.

16. Marie Luise Gothein, *A History of Garden Art,* trans. Mrs. Archer-Hind (New York, 1928), I, p. 242.

17. *Epistolae metricae,* 3.1, 3.4; both passages in Ernest Hatch Wilkins, *Petrarch at Vaucluse* (Chicago, 1958), pp. 51, 58–59.

18. A different disposition of man, of water, of the earth itself: *Epistolae variae,* 42 (Wilkins, *Vaucluse,* p. 70); text in Konrad Burdach and Paul Piur, *Briefwechsel des Cola di Rienzo* (Berlin, 1912), III, p. 94 ff.

19. *Epistolae familiares,* 13.8.15. Text in *Le familiari,* ed. Vittorio Rossi and Umberto Bosco (Florence, 1933–42); trans. in Wilkins, *Vaucluse,* pp. 122–23.

20. Cicero associates *angustus* with Attic as opposed to Asiatic style and, more generally, with philosophy as opposed to rhetoric; *Brutus,* 84.289, *Orator,* 33.117. For *plenus* and *copia: De oratore,* 1.13.59.

21. E.g., *Familiares,* 13.12.5; *Bucolicum carmen,* 3.117; *Vita solitaria,* in *Prose,* ed. G. Martellotti, et al. (Milan, 1955), pp. 296, 358–60, 366, 556 (*The Life of Solitude,* trans. Jacob Zeitlin [Urbana, Ill., 1924], pp. 105, 152, 157, 291). For a history of the punning sense of *cultus,* see Henri Marrou, *Saint Augustin et la fin de la culture antique* (Paris, 1938), Appendix A.

22. Morris Bishop, *Petrarch and His World* (Bloomington, Ind., 1963), p. 13, translating *Epistolae seniles,* 1.3.

23. *Rime,* 142.5–9. Text edited by Ferdinando Neri, in Petrarca, *Rime, Trionfi, e poesie latine* (Milan, 1951).

24. The Coronation Oration is translated in E. H. Wilkins, *Studies in the Life and Works of Petrarch* (Cambridge, Mass., 1955), pp. 300–13; cf. Petrarch, *Rime,* 7, 8, 9; also *Bucolicum carmen,* 3. For love as actualization, not mere passion but a sprouting of the seeds of virtue, see *Petrarch's Secret,* trans. William H. Draper (London, 1911), p. 121; text in *Prose,* ed. Martellotti, p. 144.

25. *Rime,* 186.9–11. Cf. Aldo Bernardo, *Petrarch, Scipio, and the Africa* (Baltimore, Md., 1962), pp. 48–49.

26. The laurel [or Laura] gave me my name, laurel my fame, laurel my wealth: *Bucolicum carmen,* 10.376–77. Text with English translation and notes may be found in Thomas Bergin, *Petrarch's Bucolicum Carmen* (New Haven, Conn., 1974).

27. Pierre de Nolhoc, *Pétrarque et l'humanisme,* 2nd ed. (Paris, 1907), II, p. 263 ("solemnissime"), p. 267 ("sacrarum arbuscularum").

28. *Petrarch's Secret,* pp. 134–35 (*Prose,* ed. Martellotti, p. 159). Augustine remarks that the laurel unites both poetic and imperial ambitions.

29. *Familiares,* 11.12.10. For Petrarch's gardens, see de Nolhoc, II, pp. 259–68; E. H. Wilkins, *The Life of Petrarch* (Chicago, 1961), Index, s.v., "gardens and planting."

30. *Familiares,* 16.6.24; cf. J. H. Whitfield, *Petrarch and the Renascence* (Oxford, 1943), p. 90.

31. Petrarch, *Life of Solitude,* p. 158 (*Prose,* ed. Martellotti, p. 368). Cf. *Familiares,* 13.8.13–16 (Wilkins, *Vaucluse,* pp. 122–23). For the bookplate: Wilkins, *Life,* p. 23.

32. *Familiares,* 7.15.2. Cf. *Rime,* 114.5–6: "as Love invites me, now rhymes and verses do I pluck, now plants and flowers."

33. Petrarch, *Life of Solitude,* p. 157 (*Prose,* ed. Martellotti, p. 366).

34. *Familiares,* 10.4.11; *Posteritati,* in *Prose,* ed. Martellotti, p. 12; *Epistolae variae,* 42 (Burdach, *Briefwechsel,* p. 96).

35. *Posteritati,* in *Prose,* ed. Martellotti, pp. 12, 16. Cf. *Rime,* 186; *Africa,* 9.237–45; and the discussion in Bernardo, pp. 48–49.

36. *Bucolicum carmen,* 3.89–92, 111–12; 1.34; Bergin, *Petrarch's Bucolicum Carmen,* p. 218, note to line 34.

37. Morris Bishop, *Letters from Petrarch* (Bloomington, Ind., 1966), p. 9, translating *Posteritati* (*Prose,* ed. Martellotti, p. 13); cf. *Familiares,* 8.3.11–12.

38. Quotation from Bishop, *Letters,* p. 19 (*Familiares,* 1.1.22). In *Petrarch's Secret,* the controlling image seems to be Plato's charioteer, interpreted through the Augustinian notion of the soul's weight; e.g., pp. 25, 38, 65, 129–30, 189 (*Prose,* ed. Martellotti, pp. 46, 60, 86, 152–54, 212). Cf. *Bucolicum carmen,* 8.10–11, 10.14–15; also *Familiares,* 15.4.10–14, 17.5.1–3, *Seniles,* 9.2 (all three letters in Bishop, *Letters,* pp. 135, 150, 260).

39. Stephen Gilman, *The Art of La Celestina* (Madison, Wis., 1956), p. 167.

40. O hills, valleys, rivers, woods, fields/ O witnesses of my grievous life: *Rime,* 71.37–38; cf. e.g., 37.32; 125.8–9, 66–78; 288.

41. E.g., ibid., 22, 23, 28, 35, 176, 189.

42. Ibid., 128.82–83; cf. 50, 280, 281, 320, 327.

43. Ibid., 85.3, 243.14, 188.13.

44. Ibid., 34, 160, 162, 165, 192, 243, for example.

45. Ibid., 306.12: "santi vestigi"; cf. 162.4; also *Bucolicum carmen* 3.97.

46. *Paradise Lost,* 11.333.

47. Leo Spitzer notes the "spiritual climate" suggested in courtly literature by the lady's "air" and says that Petrarch's "divine woman becomes more and more similar to a pagan goddess of nature." *Studies in Historical Sematics* (New York, 1948), p. 260. Also D. S. Carne-Ross, "The One and the Many," *Arion,* V (1966), p. 207.

48. *Familiares,* 21.13.10; cf. Whitfield, pp. 87–88.

49. Ibid., 17.5.1–3 (Bishop, *Letters,* p. 150).

50. *Life of Solitude,* p. 298 (*Prose,* ed. Martellotti, p. 564); also *Familiares,* 16.6.23. The tempest-harbor images are pervasive. For some examples: *Petrarch's Secret,* pp. 39, 94 (*Prose,* ed. Martellotti, pp. 62, 116); *Epistolae variae,* 13.42, *Familiares,* 15.8.4–5, 16.6.25, *Exul ab Italia* (all in Wilkins, *Vaucluse,* pp. 13, 69, 104–105, 107, 171–72, 179); also *Familiares* 21.13.11 (Bishop, *Letters,* p. 176).

51. E.g., *Familiares,* 15.8.4: "inopi et angusto" (poor and narrow). Cf. Hans Baron, "Franciscan Poverty and Civic Wealth as Factors in the Rise of Humanistic Thought," *Speculum,* XIII (1938), pp. 1–37.

52. E.g., *Familiares,* 16.6.24 (Wilkins, *Vaucluse,* p. 171).

53. *Familiares,* 11.4.2. Morris Bishop's translation (*Letters,* p. 105) cannot reproduce the verbal enclosure of Petrarch's Latin: "To the Closed Valley I came as a boy . . . To the Closed Valley I came as a youth. . . . To the Closed Valley I came as a man." Cf. *Familiares,* 11.12.1, for a similar sentiment. Even when fortune drives him away from Vaucluse, he continues to dream of flowery recesses, "loca florea circum" (*Bucolicum carmen,* 8.126).

54. *Seniles,* 10.2 (Wilkins, *Vaucluse,* p. 206).

55. *Epistolae variae,* 42 (see Burdach's note, *Briefwechsel,* pp. 94–95); also *Epistolae metricae,* 3.1.

56. E. H. R. Tatham, *Francesco Petrarca, the First Modern Man of Letters* (London, 1925–26), II, pp. 60–61.

57. *Life of Solitude,* p. 299 (*Prose,* ed. Martellotti, p. 566); Petrarch is citing Seneca's *Epistles,* 41.

58. *Familiares,* 11.12.1–6, *Seniles,* 10.2, *Familiares,* 21.13.11 (Bishop, *Letters,* pp. 106, 268, 176).

59. *Bucolicum carmen,* 10.15; *Familiares,* 19.16.8 (Bishop, *Letters,* p. 162). Cf *Familiares,* 11.1.1–2 (Bishop, *Letters,* p. 103).

60. See Wilkins, *Vaucluse,* p. 179: "This shall be fatherland and Helicon. Here have I brought the muses to find rest" (*Exul ab Italia*). Also *Familiares,* 15.3.14: "Hic michi Roman, hic Athenas, hic patriam ipsam mente constituo" (Here I constitute in my mind my Rome, my Athens, my very fatherland).

61. *Familiares,* 15.3.14; cf. ibid., 8.3.12.

62. G. Billanovich, *Petrarca letterato* (Rome, 1957), I, pp. 193–98, has attempted to redate the letter and to argue that the incident it recounts is a wholly fictitious one, intended to symbolize and commemorate the conversion of Francesco's younger brother. The theory, however, has not been universally accepted; for a summary of the controversy, see Hans Baron, *From Petrarch to Leonardo Bruni* (Chicago, 1968), pp. 17–23. For my own purposes, it is the nature of the fiction Petrarch chose, if fiction it be, that is significant. Many images of spiritual mountain climbing have been assembled by Conrad Rawski, ed., *Petrarch: Four Dialogues for Scholars* (Cleveland, 1967), pp. 187–88.

63. *Familiares,* 4.1; translation by Hans Nachod, in *The Renaissance Philosophy of Man,* ed. Ernest Cassirer, P. O. Kristeller, and J. H. Randall, Jr. (Chicago, 1948), p. 44. Petrarch is quoting Seneca, *Epistles,* 8.5.

64. *Renaissance Philosophy,* ed. Cassirer, et al., pp. 41–42.

65. Gilman, p. 247, n. 30, notes the same association of the ravages of fortune with a "special dimensionality of landscape" in the prologue to the second part of Petrarch's *De remediis fortunae.*

66. *The Life of Solitude,* p. 154 (*Prose,* ed. Martellotti, p. 362).

67. *The Life of Solitude,* p. 158 (*Prose,* ed. Martellotti, p. 366).

68. Drayton's *Poly-Olbion,* cited in Marjorie Nicolson, *Mountain Gloom and Mountain Glory* (Ithaca, 1959), p. 54. For Petrarch and the monastic sense of nature, see Etienne Gilson, "Sur deux textes de Petrarch," in *Studi petrarcheschi,* VII, ed. U. Bosco (Bologna, 1961), pp. 35–50; and Hugh Richmond, *Renaissance Landscapes* (The Hague, Neth., 1973), pp. 38–55.

69. Jean Leclercq, *Pierre le Vénérable* (Abbaye S. Wandrille, France, 1946), pp. 94–95, citing Peter's *Epistles,* 1.20 (*PL,* 189.89 ff.): "pro angustia cellae, latitudinem coeli" (for the narrowness of the cell, the latitude of the heavens).

70. Nicolson, *Mountain Gloom,* p. 49; the whole text is in E. T. McLaughlin, *Studies in Medieval Life and Literature* (New York, 1894), p. 6. Cf. Johan Nordström, *Moyen âge et renaissance* (Paris, 1933), pp. 133–34, 136, for some similar experiences.

71. See *Epistolae metricae,* 3.1 and 3.4 (Wilkins, *Vaucluse,* pp. 51–55, 58–60).

72. Peter La Primaudaye, *The French Academie,* trans. T. B. (London, 1614), A8r; *Love's Labors Lost,* 1.1.25; for Savonarola, whose *De veritate prophetica* begins under a plane tree outside Florence, see Edgar Wind, *Pagan Mysteries in the Renaissance,* 2nd ed. (New York, 1968), p. 186.

73. Tacitus, *De oratoribus,* 1.12; cited in Rosenmeyer, p. 198.

74. *Phaedrus,* 229b–e, 230b–c. For Boreas and Oreithyia, see Apollonius of Rhodes, *The Voyage of Argo,* trans. E. V. Rieu (London, 1959), p. 41.

75. Both cited in André Pézard, "Nymphes platoniciennes au paradis terrestre," in *Medioevo e Rinascimento, Studi in onore di Bruno Nardi* (Florence, 1955), II, p. 553.

76. *Phaedrus,* 229c; Karl Kerényi, *Eleusis,* trans. R. Manheim (New York, 1967), p. 45.

77. For *Phaedrus* and the development of literary pastoral, see Clyde Murley, "Plato's *Phaedrus* and Theocritean Pastoral," *Transactions of the American Philological Association,* LXXI (1940), pp. 281–95; Charles Segal, "Nature and the World of Man in Greek Literature," *Arion,* II (1963), pp. 45–46; Adam Parry, "Landscape in Greek Poetry," *Yale Classical Studies,* XV (1957), pp. 18–19; Richard Cody, *The Landscape of the Mind* (Oxford, 1969), p. 4 ff.

78. *Phaedrus,* 235c–d; cf. 238c–d; 262d; 278b; 279b; Hackforth, pp. 14–15; F. M. Cornford, *Principium sapientiae* (Cambridge, Eng., 1952), pp. 66–75.

79. *Phaedrus,* 259a–d; cf. Hackforth, p. 118. For cicadas, Rosenmeyer, pp. 134–35; Don Cameron Allen, *Image and Meaning* (Baltimore, 1960), pp. 83–86.

80. *Phaedrus,* 250b–c, for mystery language; for noon, Rosenmeyer, pp. 88–89.

81. Hackforth, p. 87, n. 1.

82. Diogenes Laërtius, *Lives of Eminent Philosophers,* 3.7; Loeb translation by R. D. Hicks (London, 1925).

83. Ibid., 4.1.

84. *Oedipus at Colonus,* 668–719; cf. 14–20. The association occurs to Cicero in *De finibus,* 5.1.3.

85. Charles Picard, "Dans les jardins du héros Academos," *Institut de France, Séance Publique Annuelle des Cinq Académies du Jeudi 25 Octobre 1934, Discours* (Paris, 1934), p. 49. Cf. H. I. Marrou, *A History of Education in Antiquity,* trans. George Lamb (New York, 1964; Mentor Edition), pp. 103–104; Jean Delorme, *Gymnasion* (Paris, 1960), pp. 37–42, 337–44.

86. Franz Cumont, *Recherches sur le symbolisme funéraire des romains* (Paris, 1942), Chapter IV, for the Muses; and for philosophical adaptations of these themes, Pierre Boyancé, *Le Culte des Muses chez les philosophes grecs* (Paris, 1937), esp. pp. 155–84, 249–97, 350. A more sceptical survey of the scanty direct evidence is in Harold Cherniss, *The Riddle of the Early Academy* (Berkeley, 1945), Chapter III; cf. Eduard Zeller, *Plato and the Older Academy* (London, 1888), p. 25.

87. *Phaedo,* 61a, 84e–85b, 110a; cf. *Cratylus,* 405, for Apollo and purification. Cf. Cornford, *Principium sapientiae,* pp. 66–106. For Plato's heroization: Boyancé, pp. 267–68. For Neoplatonism and theurgy: Wind, *Pagan Mysteries,* pp. 1–16;

Joseph Bidez, "La Liturgie des mystères chez les Néoplatoniciens," *Académie Royale de Belgique, Bulletin de la Classe des Lettres,* 1919, pp. 415–30; E. R. Dodds, *The Greeks and the Irrational* (Berkeley, 1964), pp. 283–311.

88. Picard, p. 61.

89. Delorme, pp. 334–35.

90. Justius Lipsius, *Two Bookes of Constancie,* "Englished by John Stradling," ed. by Rudolf Kirk (New Brunswick, N.J., 1939), p. 134. Lipsius' own more individualistic stoic retreat is also the "house of [his] Muses," and he assimilates it to the tradition of the Academy and of the contemplative raptures of the *Phaedrus* (pp. 135–37).

91. "Tanta vis admonitionis inest in locus": Cicero, *De finibus,* 5.1.1–2; Loeb translation by H. Rackham (London, 1914).

92. For Cicero's use of his Academy as a place for philosophical disputations, see (for example) *Tusculan Disputations,* 2.3.9. For the Hermathena, *Ad Atticum,* 1.1.5; trans. L. Constans (Paris, 1962); cf. Pierre Grimal, *Les Jardins romains* (Paris, 1943), p. 386. The statue was the gift of Atticus, whose own pleasure garden at Epirus was an "Amalthaeum," sacred to Amalthea, the nymph who nursed Zeus on Mt. Ida; see Grimal, p. 320 ff. Cicero wrote to Atticus (1.16.18) for details of the garden's layout and also for information about the nymph herself, in order to build his own "Amalthaeum" at Arpinum. Cf. *Ad Atticum,* 2.1.11, and the discussion in Gothein, I, p. 80.

93. Grimal, *Les Jardins romains,* Chapter X, traces the popularity in Rome of these motifs.

94. Cf. Michel Ruch, *Le Préambule dans les œuvres philosophiques de Cicéron* (Paris, 1958), pp. 80–85; Grimal, *Les Jardins romains,* pp. 383–87.

95. *De oratore,* 2.5.20; Loeb translation by E. W. Sutton and H. Rackham (Cambridge, Mass., 1942). The dramatic structure of the prologue has been studied in Ruch, pp. 185–202.

96. *De oratore,* 1.7.24; *Theatetus,* 173d. Cf. Jean-Marie André, *L'Otium dans la vie morale et intellectuelle romain* (Paris, 1966), pp. 306–310.

97. E.g., *De officiis,* 3.1.1: "in leisure to think about business, and in solitude to speak with [one's] self"; *De re publica,* 1.17.27: "never doing more than when doing nothing, never less alone than when alone." Cf. Grimal, *Les Jardins romains,* p. 385; also André Festugière, *Personal Religion among the Greeks* (Berkeley, Calif., 1954), pp. 53–67, on retirement into oneself.

98. *Brutus,* 2.8, for the distinction between "moderate and honest *otium*" and "inertia" (laziness) or "desidia" (idleness). For "otium cum dignitate": André, *L'Otium;* E. Remy, "Dignitas cum otio," *Le Musée Belge,* XXXII (1928), pp. 113–27; Ruch, p. 83 ff., C. Wirszubski, "Cicero's *Cum dignitate otium:* A Reconsideration," *Journal of Roman Studies,* XLIV (1954), pp. 6–13.

99. *De oratore,* 2.87.358; the image of the wax tablet is found at 2.86.354; cf. *Rhetorica ad Herennium,* 3.17.30, and Quintilian, *Institutes,* 11.2.21–22.

100. *Rhetorica ad Herennium,* 3.19.31–32; Quintilian, *Institutes,* 11.2.21–22. On the importance of visualization, see esp. Frances Yates, *The Art of Memory* (Chicago, 1966), pp. 19–20, 23–24.

101. Johannes Romberch, *Congestorium artificiose memorie* (Venice, 1533), 29r; cf. Frances Yates, "The Ciceronian Art of Memory," in *Medioevo e Rinascimento, Studi in onore di Bruno Nardi* (Florence, 1955), II, pp. 889–90.

102. Yates, *Art of Memory,* pp. 75, 87 (Albert the Great), 142 (Camillo), 117 (Publicius), 197–227 (Bruno). Cf. D. P. Walker, *Spiritual and Demonic Magic from Ficino to Campanella* (London, 1958), pp. 126–44.

103. *De oratore,* 2.87.357. This sentiment is reformulated by Aquinas in terms of the scholastic theory of the fantasy and then much repeated in later memory books: "simple and spiritual intentions slip easily from the soul unless they are as it were linked to some corporeal similitudes" (Yates, *Memory,* p. 85).

104. Aristotle, *Topics,* 163b24–30. Cf. Yates, *Memory,* pp. 45–46.

105. Jacobus Publicius, *Oratoriae artis epitome* (Venice, 1485), F5r ("De ordine locorum"). For the merging of systems of memory and invention: Walter J. Ong, *Ramus, Method, and the Decay of Dialogue* (Cambridge, Mass., 1958), p. 280; Robert Klein, "The Figurative Thought of the Renaissance," *Diogenes,* XXXII (Winter, 1960), esp. pp. 107–109; Robert Klein, *La Forme et l'intelligible* (Paris, 1970), pp. 79–82; Yates, *Memory,* pp. 186–87, 228–38.

106. See Ong, p. 104 ff., for the spatial nature of the places, as opposed to the vestigially aural character of the categories.

107. *De oratore,* 2.39.162; *Topica,* 2.7; *De oratore,* 2.34.146.

108. Ibid., 2.39.162; 2.34.146. Cf. *De inventione,* 2.14.46: "nascentur" (are born). Cicero would seem to take seriously, in other words, the root sense of "genera causae": the kinds of argument represent a diversity of births.

109. Pietro Bembo, *Gli Asolani,* trans. Rudolf Gottfried (Bloomington, Ind., 1954), pp. 39, 99.

110. Baldessare Castiglione, *The Book of the Courtier,* trans. Thomas Hoby (London, 1928), pp. 17, 297. Cf. Rosalie Colie, *The Resources of Kind* (Berkeley, 1973), p. 113.

111. *De senectute,* 1.3; Loeb translation by W. A. Falconer (London, 1923). Cf. Pierre Grimal, "De Lucilius à Cicéron: caractères généraux du dialogue romain," *L'Information Littéraire,* VII (1955), pp. 195–96, for the authority of historical figures.

112. *De amicitia,* 1.4; Loeb translation by W. A. Falconer (London, 1923).

113. *De Legibus,* 1.7.21: *vis, mens, numen*; cf. *De natura deorum,* 2.38.98, where nature's testimony, apprehended directly by the eye, renders subtle discussion superfluous. Alexander Litman, *Cicero's Doctrine of Man and Nature* (New York, 1930), explains how for Cicero nature became primarily a moral or aesthetic category.

114. *De natura deorum,* 2.32.82, 2.33.83; Loeb translation of H. Rackham (London, 1933).

115. *De legibus,* 1.8.25; Loeb translation by C. W. Keyes (London, 1928).

116. Ibid., 2.2.4, 2.2.5, 2.3.6, 2.2.5.

117. Mircea Eliade, *The Sacred and the Profane,* trans. Willard Trask (New York, 1959), p. 24; *De legibus,* 2.2.4.

118. See Millard Meiss, *Andrea Mantegna as Illuminator* (New York, 1957),

pp. 55–56; Panofsky, *Renaissance and Renascences,* p. 173. The text is in Paul Kristeller, *Andrea Mantegna* (London, 1901), pp. 472–73.

119. Desiderius Erasmus, *Ten Colloquies,* trans. Craig R. Thompson (New York, 1957), p. 132; cf. Johan Huizinga, *Erasmus and the Age of Reformation,* trans. F. Hopman (New York, 1957), p. 104.

120. Erasmus, *Ten Colloquies,* pp. 131–33; the whole dialogue is elaborately organized around images of feasting, sacred and profane; see, for example, pp. 141–43, 161, 171.

121. I follow the summary in Alfonso Lazzari, *Ugolino e Michele Verino* (Turin, 1897), pp. 69–70; cf. Nesca Robb, *Neoplatonism of the Italian Renaissance* (London, 1935), pp. 159–61.

122. Marsilio Ficino, *Opera omnia* (Basel, 1576; fasc. ed., Turin, 1959), pp. 616–17.

123. P. O. Kristeller, *The Philosophy of Marsilio Ficino,* trans. Virginia Conant (New York, 1943), p. 23; citing Ficino, *Opera,* p. 944.

124. Arnaldo della Torre, cited in André Chastel, *Marsile Ficin et l'art* (Geneva, 1954), p. 17, n. 16.

125. Ficino, *Opera,* p. 493; also Raymond Marcel, *Marsile Ficin* (Paris, 1958), pp. 161, 288; Kristeller, *Philosophy of Marsilio Ficino,* p. 22.

126. The bust was supposed, furthermore, to have been discovered in the ruins of the original Academy; see André Chastel, *Art et humanisme à Florence au temps de Laurent le Magnifique* (Paris, 1961), p. 72. For the symposia, see Ficino's *De amore,* 1.1 (*Opera,* pp. 1320–21); for the society of the Academy, Chastel, *Marsile Ficin,* pp. 7–56, and Robb, pp. 57–89.

127. Kristeller, *Philosophy of Marsilio Ficino,* p. 22.

128. Ficino, *Opera,* p. 805; E. H. Gombrich, *Symbolic Images* (London, 1972), pp. 31–81.

129. In the preface to his translation of Plotinus (*Opera,* p. 1537), Ficino reproaches both the poets who obscure truth with impious fables and the peripatetics who try to divorce philosophy and religion; see Eugenio Garin, *Italian Humanism,* trans. Peter Munz (New York, 1965), pp. 88–94.

130. Chastel, *Marsile Ficin,* pp. 45, 47; Gombrich, *Symbolic Images,* pp. 123–95; Klein, *La Forme et l'intelligible,* pp. 65–88; Eugenio Garin, *Portraits from the Quattrocento,* trans. Victor and Elizabeth Velen (New York, 1972), pp. 142–60.

131. Nancy Struever, *The Language of History in the Renaissance* (Princeton, N.J., 1970), pp. 70–71, notes the "inseparability of rational doctrine and irrational matrix . . . in the Humanists' concept of translation. Without its penumbra of affective form the doctrine is not fully intelligible; Plato was a personality as well as a mind."

132. Ficino, *Opera,* p. 844, cited in Chastel, *Art et humanisme,* p. 228.

133. Lorenzo de' Medici, *Altercazione,* 1.11, 1.26, 2.1–6; text in Attilo Simioni, ed., *Opere* (Bari, 1914). Cf. Chastel, *Marsile Ficin,* pp. 23, 33, n.1.

134. Robb, pp. 90–175. The bucolics of Naldo Naldi, which render in terms of pastoral allegory the vicissitudes of Lorenzo and his circle, have been seen as the

first important impulse in the Renaissance revival of pastoral that comes to fruition in the works of Pontano and Sannazaro, singers of Neapolitan gardens; see Alice Hulubei, "Naldo Naldi," *Humanisme et Renaissance,* II (1936), pp. 169–86, 309–29.

135. For Ficino's use of the idea of natural place see Kristeller, *Philosophy of Marsilio Ficino,* pp. 171–99; representative instances are in *Opera,* pp. 315, 675–76, 753. For the influence of the monastic tradition, see Kristeller, *Studies in Renaissance Thought and Letters* (Rome, 1956), pp. 99–122, 355–72.

136. Cosimo's gift of the villa at Careggi might have recalled his own boyhood days under the tutelage of Roberto de' Rossi, whose villa gardens are the scene of the second of Leonardo Bruni's *Dialogi,* and whose banquets (like Ficino's) were said to be "philosophical affairs." But Rossi, in turn, had first acquired his devotion to the speculative life—no mere Ciceronian retreat but an academic *vita solitaria* that earned his circle the criticism of the more civic minded—at the feet of Marsili. In an era rife with controversy the author of the *Paradiso degli Alberti* (c. 1425) finds it natural to put the ideas of his own time in the mouth of this friar of the preceding century (1380s), for much the same reason, perhaps, as he places his improbably harmonious debate between humanists, champions of the vulgar tongue, and scholastic mathematicians in the paradise gardens of a country villa: as in Cicero's dialogues, speaker and place lend their authority to a vision of the intellectual life and link it with the graceful re-creations of the *Decameron.* For Cosimo and Rossi, see Kurt S. Gutkind, *Cosimo de' Medici* (Oxford, 1938), pp. 4–5; Hans Baron, *The Crisis of the Early Italian Renaissance,* 2nd ed. (Princeton, N.J., 1966), pp. 320–21, 324–25. For the influence of Marsili, see Robb, p. 32; B. L. Ullman, *The Humanism of Coluccio Salutati* (Padua, 1963), p. 117. On the *Paradiso degli Alberti:* Baron, *Crisis,* pp. 81–93; also Baron, *Humanistic and Political Literature in Florence and Venice at the Beginning of the Quattrocento* (Cambridge, Mass., 1955), pp. 13–37.

137. Ficino, *Opera,* p. 609; trans. in Kristeller, *Philosophy of Marsilio Ficino,* p. 296.

138. Cf. Eduard Fraenkel, *Horace* (Oxford, 1957), pp. 211–13; also André, *L'Otium,* pp. 469–70. Text and translation from the Loeb edition of C. E. Bennett (New York, 1930).

139. Ficino in his exposition of Epicurus (*Opera,* p. 1009) distinguishes *gaudium* from *laetitia,* the former being a joy purely of the mind, the latter more closely associated with the senses. The relevant passages in Cicero are *De finibus,* 2.4.13–14, 3.1.1, 3.10.35; *Tusculan Disputations,* 4.31.66, 4.6.11–14.

140. Steele Commager, *The Odes of Horace* (New Haven, Conn., 1962), p. 333.

141. "Canzona di Bacco," in *Opere,* ed. Simioni, II, p. 250. The connection with Ficino's wall is made, e.g., by Chastel, *Marsile Ficin,* pp. 18–19, nn. 21, 29.

142. The inscription of the villa Borghese; see Gothein, I, pp. 333–34, and also Heinrich Wölfflin, *Renaiisance and Baroque,* trans. Kathrin Simon (Ithaca, N.Y., 1966), pp. 159–60, for the Latin text. At San Vigilio visitors were exhorted to leave all troubles behind in town, to partake in "honest play," to fill their arms with "boughs, flowers, and fruit"; see Gothein, I, p. 243.

143. Pico della Mirandola, "On the Dignity of Man," in *Renaissance Philosophy,* ed. Cassirer, p. 234.

144. Ficino, *De amore,* 2.2, 2.5, 5.2 (*Opera,* pp. 1324, 1336, 1335); trans. Sears Jayne, *Marsilio Ficino's Commentary on Plato's Symposium* (Columbia, Mo., 1944). Cf. Kristeller, *Philosophy of Marsilio Ficino,* p. 145, for the connection with the message of the Academy's wall; and more generally, Wind, *Pagan Mysteries,* pp. 36–52; Erwin Panofsky, *Studies in Iconology* (New York, 1939), pp. 129–69.

145. Ficino, *Opera,* p. 921; cf. p. 315, for God as "the great wealth and the greatest pleasure"; also Charles Trinkaus, *In Our Image and Likeness* (Chicago, 1970), pp. 492–93. "Mystical hedonism" is from Wind, *Pagan Mysteries,* p. 51; cf. pp. 53–80; also Chastel, *Marsile Ficin,* pp. 81, 121–28.

146. Ficino, *Opera,* p. 523; Horace, *Odes,* 2.3.1–4.

147. Cf., for symbol and intuition, Gombrich, *Symbolic Images,* pp. 145–60; Klein, *La Forme,* pp. 65–88.

148. Ficino, *Opera,* pp. 1129–30; cf. Chastel, *Marsile Ficin,* pp. 30–32.

149. Ficino, *Opera,* p. 965; trans. in Arturo Fallico and Herman Shapiro, *Renaissance Philosophy: The Italian Philosophers* (New York, 1967), p. 119.

150. *Opera,* p. 807; cf. Gombrich, *Symbolic Images,* pp. 45, 159–60. In another letter, Ficino says that if he could "point out with the finger" vice would appear "a wild forest bristling with sharp thorns," and virtue "a well cultivated and fertile field" (*Opera,* pp. 834–35); see Gombrich, *Symbolic Images,* p. 208.

151. *Opera,* p. 1324; Panofsky, in *Studies,* p. 141, n. 41, notes that the use in this passage of *allicit* (attracts) recalls the derivation of *kallos* (beauty) from *kalein* (to call).

152. Kristeller, *Studies,* pp. 99–122.

153. *Odes,* 2.3.1–4 (trans. Bennett); cf. Commager, pp. 243–306.

154. Ficino, *Opera,* p. 632; cf. Kristeller, *Philosophy,* pp. 295–96.

155. Ficino, *Opera,* p. 315; cf. "Five Questions Concerning the Mind" (*Opera,* p. 675 ff.) in *Renaissance Philosophy,* ed. Cassirer, pp. 193–212, for a succinct statement of the dilemma. Also Trinkhaus, pp. 489–98; Garin, *Portraits,* pp. 146–48.

156. Live today, we must live today, that he might live today and joy in the present: Ficino, *Opera,* pp. 646, 632; *Supplementum Ficinianum,* ed. P. O. Kristeller (Florence, 1937), I, pp. 60–61.

157. Antiphon to the Magnificat at Christmas Vespers (cf. Luke 2:11); Luke 23:43. Cf. Jean Daniélou, *From Shadows to Reality,* trans. Wulstan Hibberd (London, 1960), p. 24: "the essence of the Christian message is the *Hodie of* Paradise"; also Karl Löwith, *Meaning in History* (Chicago, 1949), pp. 182–90; and Gerhart Ladner, *The Idea of Reform* (Cambridge, Mass., 1959), pp. 64–65, 144, 291–92.

158. Ficino, *Opera,* p. 728. Cf. Chastel, *Marsile Ficin,* p. 9, and his *Art et humanisme,* pp. 228–29.

159. Ficino, *Opera,* p. 844 ("Hoc est Marsilii voluntas nostra sicut in coelo fit hodie, ita fieri & in terra"); cf. note 185 below.

160. I rely mainly on Walker, *Spiritual and Demonic Magic;* Frances Yates, *Giordano Bruno and the Hermetic Tradition* (Chicago, 1964); and Raymond Klibansky, Erwin Panofsky, and Fritz Saxl, *Saturn and Melancholy* (London, 1964).

161. Ficino, *Opera,* pp. 805, 807; Gombrich, *Symbolic Images,* pp. 41–45; Chastel, *Marsile Ficin,* p. 31.

162. Ibid., p. 909; cf. Chastel, *Art et humanisme,* p. 151.

163. Ibid., pp. 520–21; cf. Chastel, *Marsile Ficin,* pp. 103–104.

164. Chastel, *Art et humanisme,* p. 151.

165. Yates, *Giordano Bruno,* p. 77; cf. Gombrich, *Symbolic Images,* pp. 174–75 (on *The Birth of Venus*).

166. E.g., Ficino, *Opera,* p. 564, cited in Klibansky, p. 268; cf. Walker, pp. 12–24.

167. These images may be traced in C. G. Jung, *Psychology and Alchemy,* trans. R. F. C. Hull (London, 1953). For the rose of the philosophers, pp. 74–75 and figs. 29, 30, 37, 83; for the philosophical tree, identified, as in Raymond Lull, with the Tree of Life, pp. 245, 265–66, 335–36.

168. See Frances Yates, "The Art of Ramon Lull," *JWCI,* XVII (1954), esp. pp. 144–51, 153–55.

169. See, for example, Paracelsus, *Selected Writings,* ed. and trans. J. Jacobi (New York, 1951), pp. 103, 177, 181, 182–83, 184, 185, etc. For the link with Ficino: Klibansky, p. 267.

170. Walker, pp. 97–101.

171. Hugh Platt, *Floraes paradise* (London, 1608), pp. 1–16. Cf. M. Caron and S. Hutin, *The Alchemists* (New York, 1961), p. 143, for alchemists as "celestial gardeners" in a very realistic sixteenth- or seventeenth-century garden.

172. Ficino, *Opera,* p. 573: "quasi quidam agricola est, certe quidam mundicola est." For "divinus agricola": *Opera,* p. 318; cited in Trinkaus, p. 496.

173. Pico, "On the Dignity of Man," in *Renaissance Philosophy,* ed. Cassirer, p. 249.

174. Especially Walker, pp. 43–53, 75–84. Cf. Yates, *Giordano Bruno,* pp. 80–83, for the distinctions between medieval and Renaissance.

175. Cited in Walker, pp. 32–33 ("cognatum coeli vim").

176. E.g., Pico, "On the Dignity of Man," in *Renaissance Philosophy,* ed. Cassirer, pp. 246–49. Cf. Yates, *Giordano Bruno,* pp. 67–68, for the distinction between demons and "mundana numina"; and Chastel, *Marsile Ficin,* pp. 64–79, for angelic and demonic in Ficino; also Walker, pp. 45–53.

177. Walker, pp. 75–84, 112–26; p. 19 for Ficino's lyre. On magic and art, cf. Klein, *La Forme et l'intelligible,* esp. pp. 41–44, 161–70.

178. Ficino, *Opera,* p. 496; cited in Walker, p. 3.

179. See Rosemond Tuve, *Seasons and Months* (Paris, 1933), Chap. I.

180. Alesandro Braccesi, *Descriptio horti Laurentii Medicis,* in William Roscoe, *The Life of Lorenzo de' Medici* (Philadelphia, 1803), III, pp. 327–29.

181. Ficino, *Opera,* p. 608; cf. Wind, *Pagan Mysteries,* p. 39.

182. Wind, *Pagan Mysteries,* esp. pp. 36–52.

183. Natalis Comes, *Mythologiae* (Venice, 1567; facs. ed., New York, 1976), p.

129 (4.15); cf. Vincenzo Cartari, who identifies the Graces with the Hours and crowns them with flowers: *Imagini delli dei de gl'antichi* (Venice, 1647), pp. 225–26, and figure 87; also Starnes and Talbot, pp. 88–89, 92. The names of the graces are discussed by Ficino in *De amore,* 5.2.

184. Ficino, *Opera,* p. 844; cf. *Opera,* p. 502, where the example of David, the singer of cosmic harmonies, is claimed for Ficino's own health-giving regimen of perambulations through "amoena prata" and tuneful praise of gardens and groves.

185. Ibid., pp. 843–44: "Agriculturae literarumque studia invicem feliciter coniunguntur" (The study of agriculture and of letters, each in its turn, joined happily together); cf. p. 608: "in the domain of Careggi for the sake of cultivating not the fields only but the soul." See Chastel, *Art et humanisme,* pp. 226–33, for Pan-Saturnas and punning on Cosimo-cosmos; for patrons as Pan in Hellenistic rhetoric, Rosenmeyer, pp. 244–45.

186. Chastel, *Art et humanisme,* p. 149.

187. Ficino, *Opera,* pp. 893–94; cf. Chastel, *Art et humanisme,* pp. 148–49, and his *Marsile Ficin,* p. 147. Pico's remark may remind us that the magus too claims that "feelings and conceptions of our souls can by the force of the imagination be rendered volatile and corporeal"; Fabio Paolini, in Walker, p. 136.

188. For Colonna, see below, Chapter V. For Filarete: *Treatise on Architecture,* trans. and ed. John R. Spencer (New Haven, Conn., 1965), pp. 6–10, 23–25; for other magic harts, see Howard Rollin Patch, *The Other World* (Cambridge, Mass., 1950), p. 244 ff.; also D. C. Allen, *Image and Meaning,* pp. 99–104. For both Colonna and Filarete, cf. Anthony Blunt, *Artistic Theory in Italy, 1450–1600,* 2nd ed. (Oxford, 1956), pp. 39–44.

Notes to Chapter IV

1. The relevant texts are Servius' commentary on *Aeneid,* 6.638, 5.734. For the association of love with the rhetorical tradition of the *locus amoenus* (the pleasance), see E. R. Curtius, *European Literature and the Latin Middle Ages,* trans. Willard Trask (New York, 1953), pp. 192, 197, n. 22; also J. A. W. Bennett, *The Parliament of Fowls* (Oxford, 1957), p. 70.

2. Pierre Grimal, *Les Jardins romains* (Paris, 1943), pp. 44–104; cf. Julius Held, "Flora, Goddess and Courtesan," in *De artibus opuscula XL,* ed. Millard Meiss (New York, 1961), pp. 201–218.

3. Pseudo-Lucian, "Affairs of the Heart," 12–17; in N. D. Macleod, *Works of Lucian* (Cambridge, Mass., 1947), VIII, pp. 167–79. Macleod (p. 148) notes the relation to Achilles Tatius.

4. *Modern Painters,* 4.13; cf. Grimal, *Les Jardins romains,* pp. 69–72.

5. Marsilio Ficino, "Five Questions Concerning the Mind," trans. J. L. Burroughs, in *The Renaissance Philosophy of Man,* ed. Ernst Cassirer, P. O. Kristeller, J. H. Randall, Jr. (Chicago, 1948), p. 200.

6. Howard Rollin Patch, *The Other World* (Cambridge, Mass., 1950); A. C. L. Brown, *Ywain, A Study in the Origins of Arthurian Romance* (Boston, 1903).

7. Petronius, *Satyricon,* 127; I have used William Arrowsmith's free but suggestive translation (Ann Arbor, Mich., 1960). Cf. Curtius, pp. 195–96.

8. Fernando de Rojas, *The Spanish Bawd* (*La Celestina*), trans. J. M. Cohen (Baltimore, Md., 1964), pp. 231–32. Cf. Longus, *Daphnis and Chloe,* 2.3–7; Achilles Tatius, *Clitophon and Leucippe,* 1.15–19.

9. Juvenal, *Satires,* 3.10–20; cf. Martial, *Epigrams,* 3.58.45–51. Pliny, *Natural History,* 19.19.50; Loeb trans. of H. Rackham (Cambridge, Mass., 1950).

10. For Massys, see Held, pp. 216–17; Georgina Masson, *Italian Gardens* (New York, n.d.), p. 238. A sixteenth-century poet claims to find the fountain of Venus at the Farnese Villa in Caprarola a dangerous influence; Fritz Baumgart, "La Caprarola di Ameto Orti," *Studj Romanzi,* XXV (1935), p. 102.

11. F. A. Wright, *Works of Liudprand of Cremona* (New York, 1930), pp. 207–208, 256–57; cf. Reto Bezzola, *Les Origines et la formation de la littérature courtoise en occident* (Paris, 1944–63), I, p. 245, n. 2.

12. *The Travels of Sir John Mandeville,* ed. A. W. Pollard (London, 1900), pp. 183–84. Cf. Patch, *Other World,* p. 160; Marie Luise Gothein, *A History of Garden Art,* trans. Mrs. Archer-Hind (New York, 1928), I, p. 160.

13. Albertus Magnus, "De vegetabilibus," 7.1.14, in *Opera omnia,* ed. A. Borgnet (Paris, 1891), X, pp. 293–94: "delectabiliter quiescendum." *Delectatio* (delight, charm) is the word about which Albert's whole discussion revolves. For the Eastern influence in medieval gardens, see Gothein, I, p. 190 ff.; Pierre Grimal, *L'Art des jardins* (Paris, 1954), pp. 51–66.

14. Gothein, I, p. 190; *Roman de la Rose,* ll. 592–93.

15. E.g., Achilles Tatius, *Clitophon and Leucippe,* 1.15: pleached alleys, vines, shadow play. Longus, *Daphnis and Chloe,* 4.2–3: perspective, crossed alleys. For the garden at Asolo, see Pietro Bembo, *Gli Asolani,* trans. Rudolf Gottfried (Bloomington, Ind., 1954), pp. 13–14; for Bembo's own gardens, Julia Cartwright, *Italian Gardens of the Renaissance* (London, 1914), pp. 135–64; Louis Hautecoeur, *Les Jardins des dieux et des hommes* (Paris, 1959), p. 79.

16. Bembo, *Gli Asolani,* in *Opere in Volgare,* ed. M. Marti (Florence, 1961), 1.18 (p. 38), 2.21 (p. 99), 2.13 (p. 86); trans. Gottfried, pp. 39, 99, 115.

17. Bembo, *Gli Asolani,* 1.4 (p. 17), 1.6 (pp. 18–19); trans. Gottfried, pp. 13–15.

18. Cf. Paul Piehler, *The Visionary Landscape* (London, 1971), esp. pp. 13–19.

19. For love as natural movement, see J. A. Mazzeo, *Structure and Thought in the Paradiso* (Ithaca, N.Y., 1958), pp. 50–83; also N. J. Perella, *The Kiss, Sacred and Profane* (Berkeley, 1969), p. 90 ff.; Eric D'Arcy's introduction to Thomas Aquinas, *Summa theologiae* (New York, 1967), XIX (*The Emotions*). Pierre Rousselot, *Pour l'histoire du problème de l'amour au moyen âge* (Münster, 1908), has attempted to distinguish this "physical" theory from an "ecstatic" one, but his argument is attended by a certain ambiguity. Partly what is involved is a theoretical distinction of the sort Nygren and others later drew between Eros and Agape (see

note 31, below). More often, though, Rousselot seems to be setting the lover's sensibility over against theoretical definitions of his passion. Lovers in a Platonic tradition may be going home, but they will experience this enhancement of their own beings as rapture, ecstasy, possession. The image of the lover's journey of discovery, of self-discovery, is one that cuts across theoretical distinctions in order to seize upon the inwardness of his experience; and it is with this image I shall be primarily concerned.

20. For "coaptation" between the lover and his goal, see Aquinas, *Summa,* I–II, qq. 23, 26–28 (and Mazzeo, *Structure,* pp. 64–65). The object instills in the lover a resemblance that inclines the lover toward it so that the resemblance may be perfected. The circular movement that results is parallel to procession and return in Neoplatonic accounts of creation, a process that is figured by Venus' attendant graces; on this, see Edgar Wind, *Pagan Mysteries in the Renaissance,* 2nd ed. (New York, 1968), pp. 26–52.

21. Peter Dronke, *Medieval Latin and the Rise of European Love-Lyric,* 2nd ed. (Oxford, 1968), pp. 136–58; James Eustace Shaw, *Guido Cavalcanti's Theory of Love* (New York, 1958). Also Maurice Valency, *In Praise of Love* (New York, 1958), p. 205 ff.; and John Charles Nelson, *The Renaissance Theory of Love* (New York, 1958), pp. 34–44.

22. *Convivio,* 3.3: bodies "have love for the place where their generation is ordained, and in which they increase, and from which they have vigour and power. Wherefore, we see the loadstone always receives power from the place of its generation"; trans. E. P. Sayer, *The Banquet of Dante Alighieri* (London, 1887). Cf. *Purgatorio,* 17–18, for "natural" love.

23. *Paradiso,* 1.56–57; *De monarchia,* 3.16; trans., H. W. Schneider, *On World Government* (New York, 1957), p. 78.

24. Valency, pp. 158–59; cf. René Nelli, *L'Erotique des troubadours* (Toulouse, 1963), pp. 169–74; and especially, A. J. Denomy, "*Jois* among the Early Troubadours," *Mediaeval Studies,* XIII (1951), pp. 177–217. Even when the lover's joy is in opposition to the state of the actual world, it is from the landscape he takes his vocabulary of growth and blossoming.

25. Bernart de Ventadorn, Appel no. 39; text and translation in Alan Press, *Anthology of Troubadour Lyric Poetry* (Austin, Tex., 1971).

26. E.g., Jaufré Rudel, Jeanroy no. 1, in Press, *Anthology,* pp. 38–39; Rudel, no. 3, in Denomy, "*Jois,*" p. 187. Medieval Latin poets, too, rejoiced *with* the landscape (*congaudete*); see James Wilhelm, *The Cruelest Month* (New Haven, Conn., 1965), p. 107; cf. Dronke, p. 392.

27. Peire d'Auvergne, Del Monte no. 15, in Press, *Anthology,* pp. 92–93. Cf. Rudel, no. 4, in Denomy, "*Jois,*" p. 186; Peire Rogier, Appel no. 5, in Denomy, p. 204.

28. E.g., Guillaume de Poitou, Jeanroy no. 9, in Denomy, "*Jois,*" p. 181; Bernart, no. 42, in Denomy, p. 195; Peire d'Auvergne, no. 6, in Denomy, p. 200.

29. Rudel, no. 2, in Press, *Anthology,* pp. 30–31.

30. Especially Rudel, no. 2, in Press, *Anthology,* pp. 30–31; cf. Rudel, no. 1, in

Press, pp. 36–37; Marcabrun, Dejeanne no. 40, in Press, pp. 50–51. For the birds' Latin, see Leo Spitzer, *Classical and Christian Ideas of World Harmony* (Baltimore, Md., 1963), pp. 55–58, 175–78; also Dronke, p. 121, n. 1.

31. This conflict of physical and personalistic terms would be one way of understanding the Eros-Agape opposition; see Anders Nygren, *Agape and Eros,* trans. P. S. Watson (Philadelphia, 1953); M. C. D'Arcy, *The Mind and the Heart of Love,* 2nd ed. (New York, 1956). The problem of deriving an ethic from physics has been touched upon by John Burnaby, *Amor Dei* (London, 1938), p. 89; cf. Etienne Gilson, *The Christian Philosophy of Saint Augustine,* trans. L. E. M. Lynch (New York, 1960), p. 137 ff.

32. Aquinas, *Summa,* I–II, q. 27, a. 3.

33. Plato, *Phaedrus,* 255d; trans. W. C. Helmbold and W. G. Rabinowitz (New York, 1956). Cf. Thomas, *Summa,* I–II, q. 28, a. 2, for the mutual indwelling of the lovers, both in apprehension and in appetite: in both cases, the image of the beloved is for each an image of his own good and therefore his own possibility.

34. Most notoriously, F. R. Leavis, *The Common Pursuit* (London, 1952), p. 145; for courtly egoism, D. W. Robertson, *A Preface to Chaucer* (Princeton, N.J., 1962), p. 94.

35. Cf. Henri Frankfort, et al., *Before Philosophy* (Baltimore, Md., 1964), p. 12: "for modern, scientific man the phenomenal world is primarily an 'It'; for ancient—and also for primitive—man it is a 'Thou.' "

36. Bernart de Ventadorn, no. 44; trans. André Berry, *Florilège des Troubadours* (Paris, 1930). Hildegard of Bingen, cited in Dronke, p. 68.

37. Cf. Kittly Scoular, *Natural Magic* (Oxford, 1965), p. 172.

38. Charles Williams, *The Figure of Beatrice* (London, 1943), p. 176. For "speculation" in Dante, see Mazzeo, *Structure,* pp. 11–24; also his *Medieval Cultural Tradition in Dante's Comedy* (Ithaca, N.Y., 1960), pp. 56–132.

39. The flowers and the grass and whatever shines or is beautiful to see: Cavalcanti's "Avete 'n voi." For noetic language and love poetry, see Dronke, pp. 57–97; "new life" is from p. 74 and "Avete 'n voi" is cited on p. 142. Cf. Henry Corbin, *Avicenna and the Visionary Recital,* trans. Willard Trask (New York, 1960), pp. 267–70.

40. Leone Ebreo, *Dialoghi d'amore,* ed. C. Gebhardt (Heidelberg, 1929), pp. 22^{v}–26^{r}; trans. E. Friedeberg-Seeley (London, 1937), pp. 39–48.

41. *Gli Asolani,* 2.20 (ed. Marti, p. 160); trans. Gottfried, p. 190.

42. Georgio Vasari, *Lives,* trans. Gaston de Vere (London, 1912–14), IV, p. 109.

43. *Gli Asolani,* 2.20 (p. 160); trans. Gottfried, pp. 189–90.

44. Kenneth Clark, *Landscape into Art* (Boston, 1961), pp. 55–57, notes both the continuity with Gothic style and the change.

45. Etienne Pasquier (end of sixteenth century), cited in Alan M. F. Gunn, *The Mirror of Love* (Lubbock, Tex., 1952), p. 45.

46. Robertson, *Preface,* p. 198; cf. John W. Fleming, *The Roman de la Rose* (Princeton, N.J., 1969), pp. 55–56.

47. *The Romaunt of the Rose,* lines 21–23, in *The Works of Geoffrey Chaucer,*

ed. F. N. Robinson, 2nd ed. (Boston, 1957). The French text is cited from Guillaume de Lorris and Jean de Meun, *Le Roman de la Rose,* ed. Ernest Langlois (Paris, 1914–24).

48. Williams, *Figure of Beatrice,* p. 7.

49. *Romaunt,* 33–34; *Roman,* 31–33.

50. Both C. S. Lewis and Charles Muscatine insist upon a connection with the romance tradition; see *The Allegory of Love* (Oxford, 1936), p. 127, and *Chaucer and the French Tradition* (Berkeley, 1957), pp. 13–14. For the self-realization theme in the romances, see Reto Bezzola, *Le Sens d'aventure et de l'amour* (Paris, 1947), esp. pp. 81–88.

51. *Romaunt,* 729; *Roman,* 714. Yvain, too, finds a "chemin à destre" (lines 180–81); cf. Erich Auerbach, *Mimesis,* trans. Willard Trask (Princeton, N.J., 1953), pp. 128–29; and for the sacredness of the right hand, Robert Hertz, "La Prééminence de la main droite," in *Mélanges de sociologie religieuse et folklore* (Paris, 1928), pp. 99–129.

52. Cf. Gunn, p. 102.

53. Yvain makes the same sort of decision when he takes the adventure of the magic well for his own, and the choice demands the same sort of doubling in the structure of the romance: first we hear about the adventure, then we see it.

54. For the birds: *Romaunt,* 71–81 (the actual May), 100–108 (in the dream of the May morning), 492–508 (heard from outside the garden), 655–684 (within the garden, where they seem like angels). For the earth's garment, *Romaunt,* 56–70, 890–917. In an Old French prototype, *Florance et Blancheflor,* what the hero, or rather, heroine, encounters is a castle of roses; the sense of discovering the epitome of the May morning is the same; William A. Neilson, *The Origins and Sources of the Court of Love* (Boston, 1899), p. 36.

55. *Altercatio Phyllidis et Florae,* ed. A. Bömer, *Zeitschrift für deutsches Altertum,* LVI (1918), stanza 69; "Circa silve medium locus est occultus,/Ubi viget maxime suo deo cultus" (In the midst of the woods is a secret spot where reverence to their god thrives most vigorously). The vitalism implicit in "viget" is underlined by a variant reading noted by Bömer: "ibi viret [grows green] maximus suus deo cultus."

56. Matthew of Vendôme, *Ars versificatoria,* 1.107–108, in Edmund Faral, *Les Arts poétiques du XIIe et du XIIIe siècle* (Paris, 1924), pp. 146–47.

57. Rudel, no. 2, in Press, *Anthology,* pp. 30–31; cf. Wilhelm, *The Cruelest Month;* Rosemond Tuve, *Seasons and Months* (Paris, 1933).

58. E.g., the catalogues of birds and of trees; *Romaunt,* 655 ff., 1355 ff. "Unspoken energy" is from Muscatine, *Chaucer,* p. 31.

59. Bezzola, *Sens,* p. 41 ff., notes the device of withheld identity in the romances, and connects it with the theme of self-realization.

60. Most elaborately in Bonaventure, e.g., *Itinerarium,* Prologue 4, 2.13, *et passim.* For the tradition see Mazzeo, *Cultural Tradition,* pp. 15–16, 35–36, 40–41; Ruth Wallerstein, *Studies in Seventeenth-Century Poetic* (Madison, Wis., 1950), pp. 180–277. Frederick Goldin, *The Mirror of Narcissus in the Courtly Love Lyric*

(Ithaca, N.Y., 1967), Chapter I, connects the *speculum* tradition with the Narcissus story.

61. Bernard Sylvester, *De mundi universitate,* 2.9.79–83; ed. C. S. Barach and J. Wrobel (Innsbruck, 1876).

62. Bernart, no. 43; cf. C. S. Lewis, *The Allegory of Love,* pp. 128–29; also Goldin, pp. 92–107; Wilhelm, pp. 158–59; Louise Vinge, *The Narcissus Theme in Western European Literature,* trans. R. Dewsnap and N. Reeves (Lund, Sweden, 1967), p. 71.

63. Rose of the world, mirror of all things: "Si linguis angelicis," *Carmina Burana,* no. 50, sts. 8, 12; text in *Carmina Burana,* ed. J. A. Schmeller (Stuttgart, 1847). Cf. Dronke, pp. 181–92 for the *flos florum* (flowers of flowers) topos; also Mazzeo, *Structure,* p. 133: "It was Beatrice, herself a surpassing *speculum,* who guided Dante through the universe of *specula.* . . ."

64. Cf. Erich Köhler, "Narcisse, la fontaine d'Amour, et Guillaume de Lorris," *Journal des Savants,* April–June, 1963, pp. 86–103.

65. E.g., "Si linguis angelicis," st. 33. The linking of *dulce* and *amarus* became proverbial; see Wind, *Pagan Mysteries,* p. 161 ff., also Dronke, p. 329.

66. E.g., *Romaunt,* 497 (though the word may have the force of "tender" or "merciful" as one might hope one's lady would be); cf. Dronke, p. 392, for love's "plaintive melody."

67. *Romaunt,* 1539–42; cf. Vinge, pp. 65, 84–85.

68. Goldin, pp. 21–52, for theme of "birth of self-consciousness through love"; cf. G. Van der Leeuw, *Religion in Essence and Manifestation,* trans. J. E. Turner, 2nd ed. (New York, 1963), pp. 286–87.

69. *Roman,* 1607: "Mais de fort eure m'i mirai"; I follow Goldin's translation, p. 57: "I saw myself there."

70. Andreas Capellanus, *The Art of Courtly Love,* trans. John Jay Parry (New York, 1941), p. 28 (1.1) Cf. D. W. Robertson, "The Subject of the *De Amore* of Andreas Capellanus," *MP,* L (1953), pp. 145–61; also Robertson, *Preface,* pp. 72–88; Charles Dahlberg, "Macrobius and the Unity of the *Roman de la Rose,*" *SP,* LVIII (1961), pp. 578–80.

71. *Summa,* I–II, q. 26; cf. Mazzeo, *Structure,* pp. 63–65, 189.

72. *Purgatorio,* 18.23–26; cf. Charles Singleton's commentary (Princeton, N.J., 1973), pp. 413–15.

73. Bernard of Clairvaux, *Steps of Humility,* 10.28; trans. G. B. Burch (Cambridge, Mass., 1940). Cf. R. T. Schoek, "Andreas Capellanus and St. Bernard of Clairvaux," *MLN,* LXVI (1951), pp. 295–300. We have already seen Petrarch wrestling with Augustine's strictures on this subject; e.g., *De vera religione,* 39.72 (*PL,* 34.154): "Noli foras ire . . . in interiore homine habitat veritas" (do not wish to go abroad, truth lies within man); cf. *Confessions,* 10.6.8–10, 10.34.51–10.35.57.

74. Dronke, pp. 318–31, however, denies parodic intent and takes the poem "almost as an emblem of . . . the poetry of *amour courtois*" (p. 330). The relation to the *Roman de la Rose* was noted by Ernest Langlois, *Origines et sources du Roman de la Rose* (Paris, 1891), pp. 45–46.

75. *Roman,* 20,279–20,682 for Genius' attack, 18,153–18,298 for deceptive mirrors, 19,895–19,906 for God as the perfect mirror; cf. Gunn, p. 268, n. 117; Gérard Paré, *Le Roman de la Rose et la scholastique courtoise* (Ottawa, 1941), pp. 107–108.

76. Higden's Chronicle, 7.22 (Rolls Series 41, VIII, 55); John Trevisa's translation.

77. Cf. Charles Muscatine, "The Emergence of Psychological Allegory in Old French Romance," *PMLA,* LXVIII (1953), pp. 1160–1182; also Donald Stone, Jr., "Old and New Thoughts on Guillaume de Lorris," *Australian Journal of French Studies,* II (1965), pp. 157–60.

78. A. Bartlett Giamatti, *The Earthly Paradise and the Renaissance Epic* (Princeton, N.J., 1966), p. 66.

79. Gunn, p. 112.

80. Ulrich of Strassburg, for example: "For *kalos* meaning 'good' and *kallos* meaning 'beautiful' are taken from *kalo* which is to 'call' or 'cry' "; cited in Ananda Coomaraswamy, *Figures of Speech or Figures Thought* (London, 1956), p. 53; cf. Augustine, *Confessions,* 10.6.9, *De libro arbitrio,* 2.16.43. For general surveys: Mazzeo, *Structure,* pp. 68–83; Robertson, *Preface,* pp. 65–80.

81. *Altercatio,* st. 66.

82. Cf. Erich Auerbach, *Literary Language and its Public in Late Latin Antiquity and in the Middle Ages,* trans. Ralph Manheim (New York, 1965), pp. 195–96, n. 7.

83. This habit of deriving behavior from the perception of an objective *mysterium* has a close analogue in medieval exegetical practice. The tropological sense is derived from, and understood as a participation in, the timeless reality that binds together the literal, the allegorical, and the anagogical events: *faciendum* (what must be done), in other words, is derived from the (timeless) *factum* (what has been done). See Henri de Lubac. *Exégèse médiévale* (Paris, 1959–64), I, pp. 549–57, 621–33.

84. Langlois, *Origines,* pp. 9–10, 78; cf. Giamatti, pp. 49–53; Lewis, pp. 73–76. E. Faye Wilson, "Pastoral and Epithalamium in Latin Literature," *Speculum,* XXIII (1948), pp. 35–57, spells out the continuity.

85. Line 281; text and translation in the Loeb edition by Maurice Platnauer (London, 1922). For the political import of the poem, see Alan Cameron, *Claudian, Poetry and Propaganda at the Court of Honorius* (Oxford, 1970), pp. 99–102; cf. Dronke, pp. 193–94.

86. Wilson, pp. 53–57. Cf. Muscatine, "Psychological Allegory"; Erich Auerbach, *Dante: Poet of the Secular World,* trans. Ralph Manheim (Chicago, 1961), esp. p. 94; also Auerbach, *Literary Language,* p. 300.

87. Faral, *Arts poétiques,* p. 149 (lines 51–52, 57–58).

88. It is not clear, however, whether or not the poet of the *Altercatio* could actually have used Matthew. Wilson dates the poem around 1150; Faral, *Arts poétiques,* puts the *Ars versificatoria* "before 1175."

89. The formulaic pairing of sight and sound, bough and bird, is common: e.g., *Romaunt,* lines 493, 689–90. Or the units may be larger, as in the description of the

May morning: 50–70 sight, 71–89 sound. Before the account of Love's entourage, the lover describes the sounds of the garden (645–722); afterwards, its sights (1349–1438).

90. Leo Spitzer, *Essays on English and American Literature* (Princeton, N.J., 1962), pp. 200–216.

91. F. M. Cornford, *Plato's Cosmology* (London, 1937; rpt. New York, 1957), p. 144 (*Timaeus*, 41d–42d).

92. Macrobius, *Commentary on the Dream of Scipio,* trans. W. H. Stahl (New York, 1952), p. 124 (1.9.3).

93. E.g., Bernard Sylvester, *De mundi universitate,* 2.10.54; cf. 2.4.49. For the tradition of Martianus in the twelfth century: Wilson; Winthrop Wetherbee, *Platonism and Poetry in the Twelfth Century* (Princeton, N.J., 1972), esp. 74–151. Wilson, p. 57, cites Neckham's commentary on Capella for *corpora stellarum.* Cf. Dante, *Purgatorio,* 31.106, and André Pézard, "Nymphes platoniciennes au paradis terrestre," in *Medioevo e Rinascimento, Studi in onore di Bruno Nardi* (Florence, 1955), II, p. 543 ff.

94. *Altercatio,* sts. 61–63. The rather free translation by "R.S." (London, 1598) is in *The Latin Poems Commonly Attributed to Walter Mapes,* ed. Thomas Wright (London, 1841), pp. 368–69.

95. *Metamorphosis Goliae Episcopi,* lines 31–32; text in *Latin Poems Commonly Attributed to Walter Mapes,* ed. Wright; cf. Wetherbee, pp. 127–34, 220. Line 24 of the *Metamorphosis* is identical with the *Altercatio's* line (st. 61.4) on the intervals.

96. *Altercatio,* st. 54; cf. Wetherbee, 222–23.

97. Martianus Capella, *De nuptiis Philologiae et Mercurii,* 1.11–12; ed. Adolph Dick (Leipzig, 1925), p. 11: "the song of the heavens." Medieval commentators insist upon the divinity of this melody; e.g., Johannes Scotus Erigena, *Annotationes in Marcianum,* ed. Cora Lutz (Cambridge, Mass., 1939), p. 115.

98. For nightingales and cosmic harmony, see Spitzer, *World Harmony,* p. 54 ff.

99. Edmund Faral, *Recherches sur les sources latines des contes et romans courtois du moyen âge* (Paris, 1913), p. 202, notes that the emphasis on instrumental music is an innovation in the usual pattern of the earthly paradise. For the merging of classical, biblical, and medieval instruments in musical symbolism, see John Hollander, *The Untuning of the Sky* (Princeton, N.J., 1961), esp. pp. 43–51, 128–45.

100. For David's music, Charles de Tolnay, "Music of the Universe," *Journal of the Walters Art Gallery,* VI (1943), pp. 83–104.

101. For cosmic music and the angelic choir, see Spitzer, *World Harmony,* p. 35; Tolnay, p. 90.

102. Spitzer, *World Harmony,* p. 5.

103. Manfred Bukofzer, "Speculative Thinking in Medieval Music," *Speculum,* XVII (1942), p. 180, cites the fourteenth century *Speculum musicae:* "Music in general, taken objectively, extends itself as it were to all things." Cf. Spitzer, *World Harmony,* pp. 34–35; and for a clear summary, Hollander, pp. 20–51. Cf. Boethius, *De musica,* 1.9–11, 28 (*PL,* 63.1176–77, 1193).

104. Macrobius, *Commentary,* p. 195 (2.3.7).

105. Neckham's commentary on Capella, cited in Wilson, p. 57.

106. Augustine, *Confessions,* 13.9.10; trans. John K. Ryan (Garden City, N.Y., 1948). At Vaison-la-Romaine, a monastery garden performs just the same function as Love's garden in the *Altercatio,* "inflaming" the minds of the monks by its intimations of divine harmony; see Chapter V.

107. The dance of the planets is mentioned in the *Timaeus,* 40c, elaborated by Plotinus, 4.4.33, preserved in Calcidius, 124, and used to adorn Nature's crown in Alain de Lille (*PL,* 210.434). For Christian usages, see Spitzer, *World Harmony,* pp. 27–28.

108. Cf. *Timaeus,* 90c–d: "The motions akin to the divine part in us are thoughts and revolutions of the universe; these, therefore, every man should follow and [correct] those circuits in the head that were deranged at birth, by learning to know the harmonies and revolutions of the world"; trans. Cornford, *Plato's Cosmology.*

109. Augustine, *City of God,* 15.22; *De musica,* 6.11.29. Spitzer, *World Harmony,* p. 60, applies this notion to the joy of the troubadours.

110. Macrobius, *Commentary,* p. 135 (1.12.8). The strictly literary authority for including Bacchus and Silenus in Love's entourage would appear to be the Fescennine side of the classical epithalamium—e.g., the cortege in Sidonius Apollinaris cited by Faral (*Recherches,* pp. 202–203). But when this tradition is interpreted in terms of cosmic harmony, Bacchus and his cohorts figure the fall of the soul to merely fleshly harmonies or, more generally, the fall of form to matter. The bowl of Bacchus that Macrobius has in mind is the constellation Crater, from which the soul, intoxicated by the influx of matter, begins its descent: the drunkenness over which Bacchus presides, in other words, is part of the astral symbolism we have already observed in the poem. His cup may be remembered, too, in the chalice of love Phillis and Flora see the Graces bearing before Cupid. According to Servius and others, the Graces are the offspring of Bacchus, and we may remember their own association with allegories of cosmic procession and return. See D. T. Starnes and E. W. Talbot, *Classical Myth and Legend in Renaissance Dictionaries* (Chapel Hill, N.C., 1955), pp. 251–52; also Wind, *Pagan Mysteries,* Chapter III. In the Renaissance, Bacchus continues to figure the visible incarnation of invisible mysteries, as he did for Pico; and his cup appears in other romantic *loci amoeni,* often with an effect more sinister than here: e.g., the bowl of Genius and the golden cup of Acrasia in the Bower of Bliss (*The Faerie Queene,* 2.12.49, 53).

111. R. S. Haller, "The *Altercatio Phyllidis et Florae* as an Ovidian Satire," *Mediaeval Studies,* XXX (1968), pp. 119–33; cf. Robertson, *Preface,* pp. 126–34, for earthly inversions of cosmic music and cosmic dance.

112. Brown, *Yvain,* pp. 82–94; Patch, *The Other World,* Index, s.v., "birds."

113. Cf. Spitzer, *World Harmony,* pp. 169–70: "Once we have realized the importance of *musica mundana* for the medieval world, we should not allow ourselves henceforth to take lightly any allusions to music in the literary works of the Middle

Ages, to accept them as mere metaphors, or even as *topoi* in the sense of Curtius. There is always behind them a universal and transcendent meaning which reminds the reader of the whole, unsecularized complex of world harmony accessible as well to feeling as to reason." Which is not to say, I take it, that these possibilities of response are always, or equally, activated by every literary work.

114. Ibid., pp. 84–86.

115. Macrobius, *Commentary,* pp. 193–94 (2.3.1), citing Plato's *Republic,* 617b; Alain de Lille, *Anticlaudianus,* ed. R. Bossuat (Paris, 1955), 1.92, 4.389; cf. Hugo Rahner, *Greek Myth and Christian Mystery,* trans. B. Battershaw (New York, 1963), p. 355, for the traditional double nature of the sirens.

116. Langlois, *Origines,* p. 10, n. 1; also Neilson, p. 12.

117. Tibullus, *Elegies,* 1.3.49–50; text and translation in the Loeb edition, ed. J. P. Postgate (London, 1928).

118. See 1.1.53 for the identification of Messalla with the active life (wandering over land and sea) that Tibullus would reject in favor of love and pastoral retirement.

119. *Altercatio,* st. 77: "Amor habet iudices, Amor habit iura:/Sunt Amoris iudices Usus et Natura" (Love has judges, Love has laws; the judges of Love are Custom and Nature).

120. For dream narrative as an "authenticating" device, see Morton Bloomfield, *Piers Plowman as a Fourteenth-Century Apocalypse* (New Brunswick, N.J., 1962), pp. 11–13; also his "Authenticating Realism and the Realism of Chaucer," *Thought,* XXXIX (1964), pp. 335–58. Fleming, p. 54, thinks l'Amant's dream is a nightmare or *insomnium,* but there is not much evidence the lover was in love before his dream, and he says explicitly that it all came true afterwards; so on two counts it does not fit Macrobius' definition (*Commentary,* 1.3.3–5).

121. Martianus Capella, *De nuptiis Philologiae et Mercurii,* 2.126, cited in Wetherbee, p. 88.

122. Pierre Courcelle, *Late Latin Writers and their Greek Sources,* trans. H. E. Wedeck (Cambridge, Mass., 1969), pp. 214–19, 222–23, 296–99; also G. Nuchelmans, "Philologia et son mariage avec Mercure jusqu'à la fin du xiie siècle," *Latomus,* XVI (1957), pp. 84–107.

123. Wetherbee, pp. 26–27, citing Thierry of Chartres,

124. Boethius, *Consolation,* IV, met. 1; trans. in the Loeb edition of H. F. Stewart and E. K. Rand (Cambridge, Mass., 1918). For the association with Martianus: Howard Rollin Patch, *The Tradition of Boethius* (New York, 1935), p. 61; Marie-Thérèse d'Alverny, "La Sagesse et ses sept filles," *Mélanges F. Grat* (Paris, 1946), I, pp. 245–78.

125. *De animae exilio et patria, sive De artibus* (*PL,* 172.1241–46), esp. Chaps. I, XII. See the discussion in Robert D. Crouse, "*Honorius Augustodunensis:* The Arts as *Via ad Patriam,*" in *Arts libéraux et philosophie au moyen âge,* Actes du Quatrième Congrès International de Philosophie Médiévale (Montreal, 1969), pp. 531–39.

126. Godfrey of St. Victor's *Fons philosophiae,* cited in Patch, *Boethius,* p. 89; cf.

Adolf Katzenellenbogen, *The Sculptural Programs of Chartres Cathedral* (Baltimore, Md., 1959), p. 21, citing John of Salisbury, *Polycraticus* 7.10. For "Christian Parnassus": d'Alverny, pp. 260–62.

127. Alain de Lille, *Anticlaudianus,* 1.313–15, 2.106–107; trans. W. Hafner Cornog (Philadelphia, 1935), p. 67. At Chartres the seven arts frame the scene of the incarnation itself, each sister hovering over the writer she most notably inspires, *auctores* who assume the posture of Evangelists taking dictation from the Holy Spirit; see Katzenellenbogen, *Sculptural Programs,* p. 21; also Curtius, pp. 51–52, 57–58.

128. See Jerome Taylor's Introduction and notes to his translation of Hugh of St. Victor's *Didascalicon* (New York, 1961), esp. pp. 175–82; also Wetherbee, esp. pp. 11–125, and Brian Stock, *Myth and Science in the Twelfth Century* (Princeton, N.J., 1972).

129. *Didascalicon,* 1.1 (trans. Taylor, p. 46).

130. *De planctu Naturae,* pr. 6 (trans. Moffat, p. 65; *PL,* 210.464–65).

131. Honorious, *De animae exilio,* Chap. I; *PL,* 172.1241.

132. Alain de Lille, *Anticlaudianus,* 2.325–79 (trans. Cornog, pp. 73–75).

133. Bonaventure, *De reductione artium ad theologiam,* 6–7; translation in *Medieval Philosophy,* ed. Herman Shapiro (New York, 1964), p. 374.

134. Martianus Capella, *De nuptiis,* 1.40, 2.114 (ed. Dick, pp. 25, 48); cf. the commentaries of Remigius of Auxerre, ed. Cora Lutz (Leiden, 1962), pp. 112–13, and of Dunchad, ed. Cora Lutz (Lancaster, Pa., 1944), p. 13; also Wetherbee, pp. 86–88.

135. The phrase seems to have been carefully preserved by the poem's commentators; see Gunn, pp. 31, 34, 36, 45.

136. Macrobius, *Commentary,* 1.2.1–17. For the *involucrum* see Stock pp. 31–63; Wetherbee, pp. 36–48; Lubac, II, pp. 182–208 (esp. pp. 194–97).

137. *Poimandres,* 4; *Hermetica,* ed. Walter Scott, (Oxford, 1924), I, p. 115.

138. *Convivio,* 2.12, Canzone 2; cf. Auerbach, *Dante,* p. 71.

139. E.g., Hugh of St. Victor, *Didascalicon,* 1.1 (trans. Taylor, p. 47); Wetherbee, p. 21, citing Adelhard of Bath.

140. Cf. Stock, pp. 11–31, on the relation of myth to encyclopedia; Pichler, esp. pp.19, 84–110, on the relation between landscape and dialogue.

141. *Observance,* from *servare:* (1) to watch, to look at, and (2) to guard, to keep. Cf. Gunn, p. 73.

142. Painted with roses and flowers and with grass: Poliziano, *Giostra,* 1.43; cf. 1.47; Lorenzo is quoted in Wind, *Pagan Mysteries,* p. 116. For Ovid and the Hours, see Erwin Panofsky, *Renaissance and Renascences in Western Art,* 2nd ed. (New York, 1969), pp. 192–93. Cf. E. H. Gombrich, *Symbolic Images* (New York, 1972), pp. 31–81.

143. Wilhelm, p. 240.

144. John Gerard, *The Herball* (London, 1597), a2^{r}.

145. Tuve, *Seasons and Months,* p. 111, n. 31; many instances in Tuve, e.g., pp. 15, 75, 83–84, 201, 204, 208; or in Helen Waddell, *Medieval Latin Lyrics,* 5th ed. (London, 1948), pp. 142, 156, 212, 220.

146. M.-D. Chenu, *La Théologie au douzième siècle* (Paris, 1957), pp. 19–51 ("La Découverte de la nature"); also Stock, pp. 19–31, 64–65; Wetherbee, pp. 28–36. Cf. George D. Economou, *The Goddess Natura in Medieval Literature* (Cambridge, Mass., 1972).

147. For the currency of Basil in the twelfth century (from which six mss. survive), see E. Amand de Mendieta and S. Y. Rudberg, *Ancienne version latine des neuf homélies sur l'Hexaéméron de Basil de Césarée, Texte and Untersuchungen,* LXVI (Berlin, 1958), 17–18. Also Watson Kirkconnel, *The Celestial Cycle* (Toronto, 1952), p. 491, for his later popularity.

148. *Homilies on the Hexaemeron,* 5.2. English translation by Blomfield Jackson from *Letters and Select Works, Nicene and Post-Nicene Fathers,* 2nd ser., Vol. VIII (New York, 1895). Cf. for text, translation, and notes, *Homélies sur l'Hexaéméron,* ed. Stanislas Giet (Paris, 1950). Latin is cited from Eustathius' more or less contemporary translation (c. 400), edited by de Mendieta and Rudberg (note 147, above).

149. Basil, *Hexaemeron,* 1.1, 6.1. Cf. Jean Daniélou, *Platonisme et théologie mystique* (Paris, 1944), pp. 203–204; Giet, *Homélies,* p. 91, n. 4; John F. Callahan, "Greek Philosophy and the Cappadocian Cosmology," *Dumbarton Oaks Papers,* XII (1958), esp. pp. 32, 49–50 Also Beryl Smalley, *The Study of the Bible in the Middle Ages,* 2nd ed. (Oxford, 1952), pp. 11–12 on Origen; and Gerhart Ladner, *The Idea of Reform* (Cambridge, Mass., 1959), pp. 78–79 on Basil's contemporary, St. Ephraem.

150. *The City of God,* 11.29; trans. Marcus Dods (New York, 1950).

151. Ambrose, *Hexaemeron,* 1.4.13–14; trans. in Fathers of the Church series by John Savage (New York, 1961).

152. Cf. Chenu, p. 293, n. 1.

153. Augustine, *Confessions,* 13.1.1 (trans. Ryan, p. 335); cf. Gilson, *Augustine,* p. 203.

154. Adam of St. Victor, *Liturgical Poetry,* ed. and trans. Digby Wrangham (London, 1881), I, pp. 57, 77; *The Legend of Good Women,* F 130–39.

155. J. Quaestan, "A Pythagorean Idea in Jerome," *AJP,* XLIII (1942), pp. 207–15; Jean Daniélou, *The Theology of Jewish Christianity,* trans. John A. Baker (London, 1964), p. 326 ff; André Festugière, *La Révélation d'Hermès Trismégiste* (Paris, 1949–54), III, pp. 144–48.

156. E.g., Jean Leclercq, *La Vie parfaite* (Paris, 1948), p. 19; Basil, *Ascetic Works,* trans. W. K. L. Clarke (London, 1925), p. 141; Dionysius, *Ecclesiastical Hierarchy,* 536b, in Denys Rutledge, *Cosmic Theology,* (London, 1964), p. 183.

157. Daniélou, *Platonisme,* pp. 30–32, 48–60. Also Ladner, *Reform,* p. 157, n. 14, and p. 176, n. 27; Ladner, "The Philosophical Anthropology of St. Gregory of Nyssa," *Dumbarton Oaks Papers,* XII (1958), pp. 90–91.

158. Ambrose, *Hexaemeron,* 6.5.39; *PL* 14.256.

159. Alain de Lille, *Anticlaudianus,* 4.292–93, 5.229, 7.66 (trans. Cornog, pp. 98, 108, 130).

160. *Ennead,* 1.6.7; trans. Stephen MacKenna, 2nd ed., rev. B. S. Page (London, 1956). *Hermetica,* 7.2–3 (ed. Scott, I, p. 173); cf. 10.16–21, however, for garments

of fire. Also André Festugière, *Corpus Hermeticum* (Paris, 1945–54), I, pp. 82–83; J. M. Rist, *Plotinus, the Road to Reality* (Cambridge, Eng., 1967), p. 188 ff.

161. Canticles 4:11, 5:3; Gregory of Nyssa, *From Glory to Glory,* ed. and trans. Jean Daniélou and Herbert Musurillo (New York, 1961), pp. 226, 250–51.

162. *Ecclesiastical Hierarchy,* 404c, in Rutledge, *Cosmic Theology,* p. 82.

163. Hugh of St. Victor, *Soliloquium de arrha animae; PL,* 176.954, 960–61; trans. Kevin Herbert, *Soliloquy on the Earnest Money of the Soul* (Milwaukee, Wis., 1956), pp. 15, 23–24.

164. Ananda K. Coomaraswamy, "Ornament," *AB,* XXI (1939), pp. 375–82; also Angus Fletcher, *Allegory* (Ithaca, N.Y., 1964), pp. 108–46.

165. Ulrich of Strasburg, in Coomaraswamy, "Ornament," p. 380.

166. For clothes symbolism in the romances, see Bezzola, *Sens d'aventure,* pp. 122 ff., 235; also Bloomfield, *Piers Plowman,* p. 108.

167. Langlois cites the first in his notes to the *Roman de la Rose.* The second is cited by Tuve, *Seasons and Months,* p. 63 (although this particular passage is a fifteenth-century version of the seventh- or eighth-century handbook, could hardly be a source, and may in fact reflect a Chaucerian influence in its diction).

168. *De planctu Naturae,* pr. 2 (trans. Moffat, pp. 19–21; *PL,* 210.440). My italics.

169. Robert Steele, ed., *Three Prose Versions of the Secreta Secretorum,* Early English Text Society, extra series, LXXIV (London, 1898), pp. 243–44. My italics.

170. For *virtus-proprietas-dignitas,* see Leo Spitzer, *Studies in Historical Semantics* (New York, 1948), p. 256, n. 19.

171. Coomaraswamy, "Ornament," pp. 380–81.

172. William Goodwin, ed., *Plutarch's Morals* (Boston, 1870), III, p. 132 ("Sentiments Concerning Nature," 2.1); an etymological lesson often repeated, e.g., *Asclepius,* 10; Origen, *De principiis,* 2.3.6. Plato, *Timaeus,* 40a (trans. Cornford, p. 118); cf. Edgar de Bruyne, *Etudes d'esthétique médiévale* (Bruges, 1946), II, p. 258.

173. *Hexaemeron,* 7.1; cf. 2.1, 2.3. The invisible and shapeless earth is from the Septuagint Genesis 1:2; on the influence of the Latin rendering of this verse ("invisibilis et incomposita") see Aquinas, *Summa,* I, q. 66, a. 1, and William Wallace's notes in his translation, *Summa theologiae* (New York, 1967), X (*Cosmogony*), p. 173.

174. *Hexaemeron,* 1.7; also 3.10. Cf. Plotinus, *Enneads,* 3.2.13; Augustine, *Confessions,* 13.28.43.

175. Bernard Sylvester, *De mundi universitate,* ed. C. S. Barach and J. Wrobel (Innsbruck, 1876), 1.2.130.

176. Cf. René Roques, *L'Univers dionysien* (Paris, 1954), Chapter I, and esp. pp. 50–53.

177. Gilson, *Augustine,* pp. 197–209; C. J. O'Toole, *The Philosophy of Creation in the Writings of St. Augustine* (Washington, D.C., 1944); J. M. Parent, *La Doctrine de la création dans l'école de Chartres* (Paris, 1938); Bruyne, *Etudes,* II, Chapter VI; Etienne Gilson, "La Cosmogonie de Bernardus Silvestris," *Archives D'Histoire Doctrinale et Littéraire du Moyen Age,* III (1928), pp. 5–24.

178. Hugh of St. Victor, *De sacramentis,* 1.1.3–4, 6; *PL,* 176.187–91; trans. Roy J. Deferrari (Cambridge, Mass., 1951), pp. 8–11.

179. Parent, p. 158, citing William of Conches ("ex inordinata jactatione redegit in ordinem").

180. Alain de Lille, *Anticlaudianus,* 5.291–92 (trans. Cornog, p. 119); Bernard Sylvester, *De mundi universitate,* 1.2.95–96, 180–89; cf. 1.1.40; also Alain de Lille, *De planctu Naturae,* pr. 3 (trans. Moffat, pp. 24–25; *PL,* 210.442–43).

181. Since for Aquinas matter and form are inseparable, the temporal process of distinction and ornamentation is not a progressive access to being, but only a matter of sorting and grouping what is already fully created. The beauty of ornament becomes therefore a matter of the "extrinsic." *Summa,* I, q. 70, a. 1; also Etienne Gilson, *The Philosophy of St. Bonaventure,* trans. Dom Illtyd Trethowan (London, 1938), p. 275.

182. I.e., Genesis 1:2–31 seems to recapitulate what is complete in 1:1. This invites conflation with the *Timaeus,* "heaven and earth" being identified with matter and intelligible form; see Parent, *passim,* and Pierre Duhem, *Le Système du monde* (Paris, 1913–59), II, p. 427 ff.

183. *De sacramentis,* 1.1.3 (trans. Deferrari, p. 9); cf. Taylor, ed., *Didascalicon,* pp. 227–28.

184. Augustine, *De Genesi ad litteram,* 1.5.10; O'Toole, pp. 22–23. Gilson, *Bonaventure,* pp. 272–75.

185. Bernard Sylvester, *De mundi universitate,* 1.1.20–21; cf. Alain de Lille, *Anticlaudianus,* 5.277–305; "vestiture of features" is from Alain's *De planctu Naturae,* pr. 3 (trans. Moffat, p. 24; *PL,* 210.442). Calcidius cites and explains Aristotle, *Physics,* 192a13, in paragraphs 286–87; in J. C. M. Van Winden, *Calcidius on Matter, His Doctrine and Sources* (Leiden, 1959), pp. 82–90; the idea was elaborated by Plutarch, *Moralia,* 372e–f, 770a–b.

186. Ernaldus, *Hexaemeron* (twelfth century), *PL,* 189.1546.

187. Pr. 1, met. 2 (*PL,* 210.435–39; trans. Moffat, pp. 11–18). In such images as the garments of Alain's Nature, we see the fusion of the notion of the earth's ornaments with another, related tradition, one that finds in the created world the garment or veil of the immanent Logos; for some instances see H. A. Wolfson, *Philo* (Cambridge, Mass., 1947), I, p. 332; *Asclepius,* 17b (Scott, I, p. 327); Macrobius, *Commentary,* 1.2.17; Lubac, I, pp. 121–22, citing Scotus Erigena; Roques, p. 55, citing Pseudo-Dionysius. In general, the garment is worn by the Logos when what is emphasized is the brilliance of its transcendence, from which human eyes must be veiled; the garments are the earth's when what is emphasized is the splendor of some transforming immanence: Natura, Alain says, is brighter than her garments. Cf. Scoular, pp. 23–25.

188. Trans. Moffat, p. 13; *PL,* 210.436. For a similar connection between Nature's garment, perpetually rewoven in spite of Antropos' malice, and the earth's own garment, joyfully cured of "the harmys and gret damage" of winter's rage, see John Lydgate, *Reson and Sensuallyte,* ed. E. Sieper (London, 1901), lines 101–436.

189. *Confessions,* 13.19.24 (trans. Ryan, p. 350).

190. See Rosemond Tuve's suggestive remarks on virtues as adornment in *Allegorical Imagery,* pp. 40–41.

191. Aquinas, *Summa,* II–II, q. 169, a. 2, cited in Coomaraswamy, "Ornament," p. 381.

192. E.g., *Roman,* 1139, 2194, 5233.

193. Walter J. Ong, *Ramus, Method, and the Decay of Dialogue* (Cambridge, Mass., 1958), pp. 277–79; the notion of praise emanating from its object is Ong's, though he is not concerned with the linguistic ambiguity.

194. *Anticlaudianus,* 7.90.

195. Ambrose, *Hexaemeron,* 5.12.36, 3.5.23; cf. Spitzer, *World Harmony,* pp. 20–28.

196. *Merchant of Venice,* 5.1.108; *Secreta secretorum,* ed. Steele, p. 73.

197. *De planctu Naturae,* met. 2, pr. 3 (*PL,* 210.439, 442; trans. Moffat, pp. 18, 24).

198. *Roman de la Rose,* 9050–62; for *nobilis-non vilis,* Isadore of Seville, *Etymologies,* 10.184, Compare Boethius, *Consolation,* II, pr. 5: "Art thou thyself adorned with May flowers? Or doth thy fertility teem with the fruits of summer? . . . Why embracest thou outward goods as if they were thine own? . . . you, who in your mind carry the likeness of God, are content to take the ornaments of your excellent nature from the most base and vile things" (trans. Steward and Rand, pp. 199, 203).

199. Bruyne, *Etudes,* II, pp. 272–73.

200. *Convivio,* 4.16 (trans. Sayer, p. 226).

201. Basil, *Hexaemeron,* 2.7, 3.10, 4.6; cf. Callahan, pp. 50–51.

202. *Anticlaudianus,* 5.278–305, 3.136–50 (trans. Cornog, pp. 110, 81).

203. Mazzeo, *Structure,* pp. 70–73 (Augustine); Bruyne, *Etudes,* II, pp. 255–60 (Chartres), III, p. 101 (Alexander of Hales); Coomaraswamy, *Figures,* pp. 46–47 (Ulrich of Strasburg, Aquinas, Dionysius).

204. Matthew of Vendôme, 1.111 (ed. Faral, pp. 148–49).

205. *De planctu Naturae,* pr. 1, met. 2; *De mundi universitate,* 1.2.212, 1.3 (cf. Stock, pp. 126–27); *Roman de la Rose,* 643 ff., 1328 ff.

206. Matthew of Vendôme, 2.1–5 (ed. Faral, pp. 151–52).

207. *Ibid.,* 2.9, 1.33, 3.50–52 (ed. Faral, pp. 153, 117, 179–80).

208. Bruyne, *Etudes,* I, p. 36; also his *Esthetics of the Middle Ages,* trans. E. B. Hennessy (New York, 1969), Chap. I; cf. Scoular, Chap. I, esp. p. 5, for similar links in Elizabethan literature.

209. Geoffrey of Vinsauf, 43–61 (ed. Faral, pp. 198–99); cf. Bruyne, *Etudes,* II, pp. 27–28, 31, 33.

210. Matthew, 2.11 (ed. Faral, p. 154); cf. Matthew, 3.2 (ed. Faral, pp. 167–68) for *verba polita.* "Horida inculta" is from Cicero, *Orator,* 11.36; for *nitor-cultus-horridus,* cf. Cicero, *Brutus,* 57.238; Quintilian, 8.3.61, 10.1.124, 11.1.48; and for later uses, Bruyne, *Etudes,* I, p. 53 ff., II, p. 34. On light aesthetics: Mazzeo, *Tradition,* pp. 56–90; Erwin Panofsky, ed., *Abbot Suger on the Abbey Church of St. Denis and its Art Treasures* (Princeton, N.J., 1946).

211. *Rhetorica ad Herennium,* 4.13.18: "To confer distinction [*dignitas*] upon

style is to render it ornate, embellishing it by variety"; cf. Bruyne, *Etudes,* I, pp. 56, 60; also Charles Sears Baldwin, *Medieval Rhetoric and Poetic* (New York, 1928), pp. 216, 219. For the relation of *dignitas* to Matthew's "colors," see Bruyne, *Etudes,* II, p. 35.

212. Aquinas, *Summa,* I–II, q.11, a.1.

213. E.g., George Poulet, *Studies in Human Time,* trans. E. Coleman (Baltimore, Md., 1956), pp. 5–6; Bloomfield, *Piers Plowman,* Chapter II, esp. p. 53; Jean Daniélou, *From Shadows to Reality,* trans. Wulstan Hibberd (London, 1960), pp. 22–47.

214. Henry Hawkins, *Partheneia sacra,* cited in Scoular, p. 164.

215. Ambrose, *De Paradiso,* 1.6; trans. John J. Savage, *Hexameron, Paradise, and Cain and Abel* (New York, 1961), p. 289.

216. *De mundi universitate,* 2.9.15–19; *Anticlaudianus,* 1.55–57 (trans. Cornog, p. 53).

217. Cicero, *De natura deorum,* 2.13.34–35; Loeb translation by H. Rackham (London, 1933). Cf. Hans Jonas, *The Gnostic Religion* (Boston, 1958), p. 244.

218. Henri Marrou, *A History of Education in Antiquity,* trans. George Lamb (New York, 1964; Mentor Edition), pp. 311–12.

219. Ambrose, *Hexaemeron,* 1.8.28 (*PL,* 14.137–38): "Ostendere enim voluit Deus, qui nec mundus ipse haberet gratium, nisi eum vario cultu operator ornasset." Trans. Savage, pp. 30–31.

220. For *cultus* and "cultivation": Henri Marrou, *Saint Augustin et la fin de la culture antique* (Paris, 1938), Appendix; Harry Levin, "Semantics of Culture," *Daedalus,* XCIV (1965), p. 1 ff.; Stock, esp. pp. 68 ff., 80–81, 86–87.

221. See his commentaries on *Georgics,* 2.11, 49; in *Servii Grammatici . . . commentarii,* ed. G. Thilo and H. Hagen (Leipzig, 1878–1902), III, pp. 219, 222. For "terra mater," cf. Ambrose, *Hexaemeron,* 3.8.35. For Ambrose and Virgil, see M. D. Diederich, *Vergil in the Works of St. Ambrose* (Washington, D.C., 1931), pp. 6–32, and esp. pp. 25–26; also the annotations in Savage's translation of the *Hexaemeron.*

222. Prudentius, *Psychomachia,* 573; Loeb edition, edited by H. J. Thomson (Cambridge, Mass., 1953). Ambrose, *Hexaemeron,* 2.1.2 (*PL,* 14.145): "operator naturae" vs. "inventor figurae."

223. Cf. *Asclepius,* 8–9, for the notion that the earth's "cultivation" is entrusted to man; here too *cultus* is associated with worship.

224. *Georgics,* 2.35–52; Loeb edition, ed. H. R. Fairclaugh (London, 1918).

225. Servius' gloss to Georgics, 2.51 (ed. Thilo and Hagen, III, p. 222); Virgil sees in the "asperity" of *silva* the very origins of agriculture—*Georgics,* 1.152. Cf. Polixines' argument in *The Winter's Tale,* 4.4.88 ff.

226. See *De rerum natura,* 5.1361–78, for the gardener's taming of "wild fruits." Cf. Erwin Panofsky, *Studies in Iconology* (New York, 1939), pp. 40–43.

227. Servius on *Aeneid,* 1.314 and 6.131. The more elaborate reading of the bough as wisdom is from the Renaissance commentator, Jodocus Badius. All three are cited in William Nelson, *The Poetry of Edmund Spenser* (New York, 1963), pp. 158–59; cf. p. 218, for Landino's use of this tradition in his commentary, where

silva equals *matter* equals *mater;* Piehler, p. 77, cites Bernard Sylvester's commentary: *in silvam* = "in the collection of temporal goods."

228. Gregory of Nyssa, *From Glory to Glory,* p. 174.

229. Guillaume de St. Thierry, *Commentaire sur le Cantique des Cantiques,* trans. M. Davy (Paris, 1958), pp. 121–23.

230. So Isadore of Seville observes, agreeing with Servius: *Etymologies,* 13.3.1.

231. Calcidius, paragraph 287. The Latin text is from *Timaeus, a Calcidio translatus commentarisque instructus,* ed. J. H. Waszink (London, 1962); translation from Van Winden, pp. 88–89.

232. For Calcidius' influence on Bernard Sylvester's doctrine of ornamentation, see Theodore Silverstein, "The Fabulous Cosmogony of Bernardus Silvestris," *MP,* XLVI (1948–49), p. 95 ff.; Gilson, "Cosmogonie de Bernardus Silvestris"; Stock, pp. 106–112, 126, *et passim.*

233. See for example the instances in Patch, *The Other World* (Index, s.v., "forest"). Brunetto Latini's *Tesoretto,* XIX, shows how this traditional romance motif may be moralized explicitly as a progression from matter to form; see Edith Kern, "Gardens in the *Decameron Cornice,*" *PMLA,* LXVI (1951), p. 521. Giordano Bruno reverses the pattern when he contrasts man's original state, gardener of the Tree of Life in Paradise, with his present subjection to women: "chaos of irrationality, wood [*hyle*] of wickedness, forest [*selva*] of ribaldry, mass of uncleanliness"; *Cause Principle, and Unity,* trans. Jack Lindsay (New York, 1962), pp. 117–18.

234. Cf. Piehler, pp. 72–78 *et passim;* Wetherbee, p. 226, and the studies, cited there, of Leo Pollman, esp. *Das Epos in den romanischen Literaturen* (Stuttgart, 1966), pp. 87–88.

235. Calcidius, *Commentary,* 274 (trans. Van Winden, p. 49).

236. *Asclepius,* 14b, 15 (trans. Scott, I, pp. 313–15); cf. Stock, pp. 104–105. Calcidius, *Commentary,* 273 (trans. Van Winden, p. 46).

237. See 2.14.153–80; e.g., lines 161–62: "the unconquered ones fight death with the weapons of generation, repair nature and perpetuate the species."

238. Here as elsewhere I have consulted both Winthrop Wetherbee's complete translation of Bernard's *Cosmographia* (New York, 1973), and the extensive translations in Stock (here, pp. 134–35).

239. Calcidius, *Commentary,* 310; Augustine, *De Genesi ad litterum, liber imperfectus,* 3.10, 4.12 (*PL,* 34.224). Cf. O'Toole, p. 18; also Augustine, *De Genesi contra manichaeos,* 7.11 (*PL,* 34.178). Gilson, *Augustine,* p. 345, n. 32, notes that doctrinally this is an accidental usage; imaginatively, however, it seems important.

240. I have used Gilson, *Augustine,* pp. 206–209; O'Toole, pp. 70–83; Gilson, *Bonaventure,* Chapter X. Walter Clyde Curry, *Shakespeare's Philosophical Patterns* (Baton Rouge, La., 1937), Chapter II, has a quick convenient survey, but he seems to confuse the seminal reasons with the "seed of heaven and earth" that Augustine and others thought to find in inform matter. The doctrines must remain distinct, although, as I have suggested, they coincide in a single image and may therefore be taken to represent similar imaginative intuitions. Cf. Nelson, *Spenser,* p. 210 ff; Robert Ellrodt, *Neoplatonism in the Poetry of Spenser* (Geneva, 1960), Chapter IV.

241. Augustine, *De vera religione,* 42.79; trans. John H. S. Burleigh, in *Augustine's Earlier Writings* (London, 1953); cf. *De Genesi ad litteram,* 4.33.51 (*PL,* 34.318); also *De Genesi ad litteram,* 5.23.45 (in Ellrodt, p. 78, n. 117); *De trinitate,* 3.8.13 (in Curry, pp. 35–36).

242. Augustine, *De trinitate,* 3.9.16, cited in Gilson, *Augustine,* p. 345, n. 36.

243. Gilson, *Bonaventure,* pp. 298–303; cf. Augustine, *City of God,* 12.25, for Nature as farmer.

244. Basil, *Hexaemeron,* 5.1 (I follow Giet's French version, p. 279); cf. 7.2, 5.10. Basil's enthusiasm for the fruitfulness of the imminent "command" sometimes makes him sound as if he were speaking of the Stoic world soul (Giet, p. 320), a danger he is at pains to avoid, e.g., in 8.1. See Giet's introduction, p. 30 ff., for the similarity of this notion to that of the seminal reasons and for its influence on Augustine.

245. Hugh of St. Victor, *Didascalicon,* 1.9; trans. Taylor, p. 55. Hugh is following Calcidius, who says that "seeds are the origin and beginning of the works of nature" (*Commentary,* 23).

246. Emile Bréhier, *The Philosophy of Plotinus,* trans. Joseph Thomas (Chicago, 1958), p. 58. See *Enneads,* 3.5.9, for the identification of Plato's Garden of Plenty and Poverty with the blossoming of seminal reasons; also *Enneads,* 3.1.7.

247. Curtius, p. 112. Cf. Aldo Scaglione, *Nature and Love in the Late Middle Ages* (Berkeley, 1963) for the "naturalism" of Chartres, and of courtly literature as well.

248. Calcidius, 310 (trans. Van Winden, pp. 150–51). Cf. Gilson, *Bonaventure,* p. 294 ff.; also Maurice de Wulf, *History of Medieval Philosophy,* trans. E. C. Messenger (London, 1925), I, p. 366.

249. Ladner, *Idea of Reform,* p. 184; cf. Gilson, *Bonaventure,* pp. 304–305.

250. Augustine, *City of God,* 22.24. The basis for connecting physical generation and spiritual regeneration—the translation in The Fathers of the Church series (New York, 1954), p. 483, makes this connection particularly explicit—is I-Corinthians 3:7.

251. *Convivio,* 4.20–22; cf. 4.17–18 for virtues as branches of the single root or trunk of nobility. Cf. Piehler, esp. pp. 131–34, for similar images in the *Commedia.*

Notes to Chapter V

1. Joan Gadol, *Leon Battista Alberti, Universal Man of the Early Renaissance* (Chicago, 1969), esp. Chap. IV.

2. Alexandre Koyré, *From the Closed World to the Infinite Universe* (Baltimore, 1957), p. 33; Thomas S. Kuhn, *The Copernican Revolution,* 2nd ed. (New York, 1959), pp. 145, 149; also Edward Rosen, ed., *Three Copernican Treatises,* 2nd ed. (New York, 1959), pp. 143–44.

3. Koyré, p. 61.

4. Ibid., pp. 62, 76, 78.

5. Kuhn, pp. 152–53; cf. Stephen Toulmin and June Goodfield, *The Fabric of the Heavens* (New York, 1961), pp. 173–74.

6. Pico della Mirandola, *Heptaplus,* 7. proem; trans. Douglas Carmichael (New York, 1965), p. 151. Cf. Toulmin and Goodfield, p. 96.

7. Rosen, p. 145; Kuhn, p. 154.

8. Kuhn, pp. 179–80.

9. Ibid., p. 142.

10. Ibid., pp. 179–80; Rosen, pp. 143–45.

11. Gerald Holton, "Johannes Kepler's Universe," in *Toward Modern Science,* ed. Robert Palter, 2nd ed. (New York, 1969), pp. 477–78.

12. Ibid., p. 482; see Kepler, *Gesammelte Werke* (Munich, 1940), VI, p. 725: "nec imago sint veri sui Paradigmatis, sed ipsum suum veluti Paradigma."

13. Cited in Otto von Simson, *The Gothic Cathedral,* 2nd ed. (New York, 1962), pp. 37–38.

14. Edgar de Bruyne, *Etudes d'esthétique médiévale* (Bruges, 1946), II, pp. 278–89; Winthrop Wetherbee, *Platonism and Poetry in the Twelfth Century* (Princeton, N.J., 1972), pp. 35–36; but cf., for an opposing view, Brian Stock, *Myth and Science in the Twelfth Century* (Princeton, N.J., 1972), pp. 280–81.

15. For Kepler and Fludd, W. Pauli, "The Influence of Archetypal Ideas on the Scientific Theories of Kepler," in C. G. Jung and W. Pauli, *The Interpretation of Nature and the Psyche* (New York, 1955), p. 209; cf. Holton, p. 484; Erwin Panofsky, "Artist, Scientist, Genius," in *The Renaissance: Six Essays,* 2nd ed. (New York, 1962), pp. 121–82. For Mascall, see Leonard Mascall, *A Booke of the Arte and Maner How to Plante and Graffe All Sorts of Trees* (London, 1575), "Dedication," (p. 21 above.)

16. Joan Evans, *Nature in Design* (London, 1933), pp. 46–106; also her *Pattern, A Study of Ornament in Western Europe* (Oxford, 1931), I, pp. 40–81.

17. Cited in James S. Ackerman, *The Cortile del Belvedere* (Vatican City, 1954), p. 121. My understanding of Bramante's design is based mainly on Ackerman's book, and also his essay, "The Belvedere as a Classical Villa," *JWCI,* XIV (1951), pp. 70–91.

18. Ackerman, *The Cortile,* pp. 121–22.

19. Ibid., pp. 121–22; cf. James S. Ackerman, *The Architecture of Michelangelo,* 2nd ed. (Baltimore, Md., 1971), pp. 25–32; also Eugenio Battisti, "*Natura artificiosa* to *Natura artificialis,*" in *The Italian Garden,* First Dumbarton Oaks Colloquium on the History of Landscape Architecture, ed. David R. Coffin (Washington, D.C., 1972), pp. 1–36.

20. On the influence of the Cortile, see Ackerman, *Cortile,* pp. 140–41; Derek Clifford, *A History of Garden Design* (New York, 1953), pp. 36–39; Marie Luise Gothein, *A History of Garden Art,* trans. Mrs. Archer-Hind (New York, 1928), I, pp. 230–31.

21. See above, p. 14.

22. "In the midst of this elegant regularity you are surprised by the imitation of the negligent beauties of rural nature": Pliny the Younger, *Letters,* 5.6; Loeb edition, ed. W. M. L. Hutchinson (London, 1915), pp. 390–91; cf. pp. 379, 383.

23. Tacitus, *The Annals,* 15.42; Loeb edition, trans. John Jackson (Cambridge, Mass., 1956).

24. Ackerman, *Cortile,* pp. 121–22.

25. Donald Stone, "Old and New Thoughts on Guillaume de Lorris," *Australian Journal of French Studies,* II (1965), pp. 157–70; Paul Piehler, *The Visionary Landscape* (London, 1971), pp. 98–105; Donald Howard, *The Three Temptations* (Princeton, N.J., 1966), pp. 109–10; cf. Fritz Saxl, "Pagan Sacrifice in the Italian Renaissance," *JWCI,* II (1939–40), p. 363.

26. All the world and its ancient riches and all earthly things:*Roman de la Rose,* ed. E. Langlois (Paris, 1914–24), 20, 312–14. Cf. D. W. Robertson, "The Doctrine of Charity in Medieval Literary Gardens," *Speculum,* XXVI (1951), pp. 24–49. For the dyad as matter: Hugh of St. Victor, *Didascalicon,* ed. Jerome Taylor (New York, 1966), pp. 66, 200; also Vincent Hopper, *Medieval Number Symbolism* (New York, 1938), pp. 47, 101, 117. For the square of creation, see n. 37 below.

27. Michel Rambaud, "Le Quatrain mystique de Vaison-la-Romaine," *Bulletin Monumental,* CIX (1951), p. 157. Archeologists have not agreed on the proper rendering of the last three lines; I cite only one of the possibilities mentioned by Rambaud.

28. Augustine, *Epistles,* 140.22.55 (*PL,* 33.561), cf. Gregory, *Moralia, PL,* 76.436; Rabanus Maurus, *Allegoria, PL,* 112.860; *Glossa ordinaria, PL,* 113.1152. Rambaud, p. 163, cites earlier use of this symbolism in cloister decoration.

29. Rambaud, p. 171, notes the use of a central fountain for ablutions, and remarks that it is on such occasions that the inscription could be read (i.e., while the reader is within the court, facing the sanctuary). Gregory, *Moralia,* 31.46.92–93 (*PL,* 76.623), finds a specifically baptismal sense in the "Auster" of Job 39:26.

30. See L.-H. Labaude, "La Cathédrale de Vaison," *Bulletin Monumental,* LXIX (1905), pp. 306–314. Rambaud, pp. 161–63, notes the classicism of the inscription's vocabulary.

31. Cicero, *De oratore,* 1.44.196; Loeb edition, ed. E. W. Sutton and H. Rackham (Cambridge, Mass., 1942).

32. Ausonius, *Moselle,* p. 449. I am assuming, if only for its emblematic value, the tradition that connects Ausonius with the famous *De rosis* ("Ver erat et blando"). For the villa at Bordeaux, see *Domestica,* 1 ("De herediolo"); also Helen Waddell, *Mediaeval Latin Lyrics,* 5th ed. (London, 1948), p. 289.

33. Augustine, *Enarrationes in Psalmos,* 83.7 (*PL,* 37.1060–61). Christ the Sparrow is in Gregory's *Moralia,* 19.27.48 (*PL,* 76.128–29.) Both passages are cited in the *Glossa ordinaria, PL,* 113.985–86. Cf. Numbers 24:21. Rambaud cites Job 29:18, but the passage from the Psalms corresponds much more closely to the actual situation of the cloister; and the former (the "nest" of Job's upright mind) is explained by Gregory in terms of the latter. I.e., the "soul of the saintly man" (see Rabanus Maurus, *PL,* 112.1006) is derived from the integrity of the Church, its proper place.

34. Gregory, *Moralia,* 19.27.48 (*PL,* 76.128).

35. *Glossa ordinaria, PL,* 113.986.

36. Augustine, *Epistles,* 140.22–23 (*PL,* 33.560–62); trans. Wilfrid Parsons (New York, 1953), pp. 103–107.

37. See Rambaud, pp. 165–69, for number symbolism in the Augustinian tradition; also Hopper, pp. 83–84.

38. Bonaventure, *The Mind's Road to God,* trans. George Boas (New York, 1953), p. 18. Cf. Edgar de Bruyne, *Esthetics of the Middle Ages,* trans. E. B. Hennessy (New York, 1969), pp. 109–17; also Richard Krautheimer, *Studies in Early Christian, Medieval, and Renaissance Art* (New York, 1969), pp. 120–21, 130.

39. Augustine, *De musica,* 6.11.33; trans. R. C. Taliaferro (New York, 1947), p. 358; *Confessions,* 10.6.8–10, 10.8.15. For time and space in Augustine, Gerhart Ladner, *The Idea of Reform* (Cambridge, Mass., 1959), pp. 203–212, 220.

40. Walter Lowrie, *Art in the Early Church,* 2nd ed., rev. (New York, 1965), pp. 95–97; Simson, pp. 3–11; Otto Demus, *Byzantine Mosaic Decoration* (Boston, 1955), pp. 31–34.

41. Simson, p. 39. For this distinction between romanesque and gothic, see ibid., pp. 3–20, 211–31; and more briefly, Lowrie, *Art,* pp. 94–96.

42. Erwin Panofsky, *Renaissance and Renascences in Western Art,* 2nd ed. (New York, 1969), pp. 28–29; James S. Ackerman, " '*Ars sine scientia nihil est,*' " *AB,* XXXI (1949), pp. 106–108; Rudolph Wittkower, *Architectural Principles in the Age of Humanism,* 2nd ed. (New York, 1965), pp. 158–61.

43. Erwin Panofsky, *Early Netherlandish Painting* (Cambridge, Mass., 1953), I, p. 17. Cf. Panofsky, *Renaissance and Renascences,* pp. 132–33.

44. Cf. Panofsky, *Renaissance and Renascences,* p. 133: " 'modern' . . . space could come into being only when the high-medieval sense of solidity and coherence, nurtured by architecture and sculpture, began to fuse with what little had been preserved, throughout the centuries, of the illusionistic tradition established in Graeco-Roman painting."

45. See Elizabeth Holt, *A Documentary History of Art* (Garden City, N.Y., 1957–1958), I, p. 137, for Cennini's remarks. Also, for discussion, Giulio Carlo Argan, "The Architecture of Brunelleschi and the Origins of Perspective Theory in the Fifteenth Century," *JWCI,* IX (1946), pp. 96–121.

46. See Simson, p. 13; and n. 42 above. Erwin Panofsky, *Meaning in the Visual Arts* (Garden City, N.Y., 1957), p. 83, observes a similar situation in Villard de Honnecourt's canon of proportions, where "the schema almost completely renounced . . . the object."

47. Leon Battista Alberti, *On Painting,* trans. J. R. Spencer (New Haven, Conn., 1956), pp. 64, 68.

48. Ibid., p. 43; cf. Gadol, pp. 66–69.

49. Gadol, p. 132; Robert Klein, "Pomponius Gauricus on Perspective," *AB,* XLIII (1961), pp. 211–13.

50. Holt, I, p. 277.

51. Piero della Francesca, *De prospectiva pingendi,* ed. G. Nicco Fasola (Florence, 1942), p. 63; Holt, I, pp. 256–57. See esp. Rudolf Wittkower, "Brunelleschi and 'Proportion in Perspective'," *JWCI,* XVI (1953), pp. 275–91; Erwin Panofsky, *The Codex Huygens and Leonardo da Vinci's Art Theory* (London, 1940), esp. p. 106.

More general accounts in Gadol, Chaps. II–III; Richard Krautheimer and Trude Krautheimer-Hess, *Lorenzo Ghiberti,* 2nd ed. (Princeton, N.J., 1970), pp. 229–53.

52. Cf. Wittkower, "Brunelleschi," p. 276.

53. Gadol, p. 68.

54. Wittkower, "Brunelleschi," pp. 285–87.

55. Argan, pp. 96–97; cf. Gadol, pp. 66–67. Ghiberti on beauty as proportion is cited in Wittkower, "Brunelleschi," p. 279.

56. Ernst Cassirer, *The Individual and the Cosmos in Renaissance Philosophy,* trans. Mario Domandi (New York, 1964), p. 158 (citing Leonardo).

57. Ibid., p. 180; cf. Dorothea Singer, *Giordano Bruno, His Life and Thought* (New York, 1950), p. 58; Gadol, esp. pp. 149–57.

58. Horace Walpole, *History of Modern Taste in Gardening,* in Isabel W. U. Chase, ed., *Horace Walpole: Gardenist* (Princeton, N.J., 1953), pp. 12–13.

59. Panofsky, *Codex Huygens,* pp. 99, 106; John White, *The Birth and Rebirth of Pictorial Space,* 2nd ed. (London, 1967), esp. pp. 125, 194, 207–215; also for a survey of recent scholarship, Robert Klein, *La Forme et l'intelligible* (Paris, 1970), pp. 283–93.

60. Michael Baxandall, *Painting and Experience in Fifteenth Century Italy* (Oxford, 1972), pp. 103–105; Bernard Berenson, *Italian Painters of the Renaissance* (New York, 1957), p. 199. Cf. Fritz Saxl, *Lectures* (London, 1957), p. 115.

61. Cf. Timothy Kitao, "Prejudice in Perspective: A Study of Vignola's Perspective Treatise," *AB,* XLIV (1962), pp. 173–94, esp. pp. 176, 178.

62. *Hermetica,* 1.7; ed. Walter Scott (Oxford, 1924).

63. Cassirer, *Individual and Cosmos,* pp. 188–91.

64. Ackerman, *Cortile,* p. 123.

65. Esp. *Epistles,* 2.17, 5.6.

66. Henry Wotton, *Elements of Architecture* (1624), cited in B. Sprague Allen, *Tides of English Taste* (Cambridge, Mass., 1937), I, p. 126; cf. *The Prose Works of Sir Philip Sidney,* ed. Albert Feuillerat (Cambridge, Eng., 1912), I, p. 91; also Marc Girouard, *Robert Smythson and the Architecture of the Elizabethan Era* (London, 1966), pp. 86–88.

67. Louis Hautecoeur, *Les Jardins des dieux et des hommes* (Paris, 1959), p. 113; Clifford, p. 33.

68. *De dignitate et excellentia hominis,* cited in Charles Trinkaus, *In Our Image and Likeness* (Chicago, 1970), p. 246. Cf. Cicero, *De natura deorum,* 2.39.99, where the same notion is used to illustrate the discovery of divine reason.

69. Wotton, in Allen, *Tides,* I, p. 126.

70. *Paradise Lost,* 3.540–54 (my italics); cf. Marjorie Nicholson, "Milton and the Telescope," *ELH,* II (1935), pp. 1–32.

71. *Epistles,* 5.6 (ed. Hutchinson, p. 388). *De re aedificatoria,* 9.2; trans. James Leoni, *Ten Books on Architecture,* ed. J. Rykwert (London, 1955).

72. This is the basis of Alberti's delight in a *camera obscura* device; see Kenneth Clark, *Leon Battistia Alberti on Painting* (London, 1945), p. 5. The new development is neatly, if belatedly, exemplified by two prints of the Villa Medici in Rome, reproduced as Plates 14 and 15 in this book. The earlier shows the parterres,

seen from a high point of view, pressed up against the villa and embraced by its arcades like an outdoor living room. In the later print the angle of vision is somewhat lower, and one looks down the cross axis of the garden so that the whole layout appears as a perspective composition leading through the formal garden to the bosco and finally to the soft hills beyond. This sort of transition is basic in baroque gardens; e.g., the Villa Aldobrandini in Frascati. Cf. on this whole topic, Battisti, pp. 24–29.

73. Pliny, *Epistles,* 2.17 (ed. Hutchinson, p. 160); James S. Ackerman, *Palladio* (Baltimore, Md., 1967), p. 70.

74. Ovid, *Fasti,* 5.209; K. E. Kirk, *The Vision of God,* 2nd ed. (London, 1932), p. 308, for Basil's garden. Cf. Battisti, p. 16.

75. Ackerman, *Cortile,* pp. 122–24; cf. Hautecoeur, p. 116.

76. André Chastel, "Cortil et théâtre," in *Le Lieu théâtral à la renaissance* (Paris, 1964), pp. 41–47; Klein, *La Forme et l'intelligible,* pp. 294–309; Ackerman, *Cortile,* pp. 124–25.

77. Vitruvius, *On Architecture,* 7.5.2; Loeb edition, trans. Frank Granger (London, 1931); Pierre Grimal, *L'Art des jardins* (Paris, 1954), p. 25. Cf. Vitruvius, 5.6.9; Pliny the Elder, *Natural History,* 16.60.140, 35.37.117. The reciprocal influences of painting, theater, and the *opus topiarius* are traced in Pierre Grimal, *Les Jardins romains* (Paris, 1943), pp. 93–101, 285–89, 364–65.

78. Cited in Wittkower, *Architectural Principles,* p. 10.

79. S. J. Freedberg, *Painting of the High Renaissance in Rome and Florence,* 2nd ed. (New York, 1972), I, p. 116.

80. Ackerman, "The Belvedere as Classical Villa," pp. 85–86.

81. *Robert Laneham's Letter,* ed. F. J. Furnivall (New York, 1907), p. 53.

82. Trinkaus, pp. 240, 247.

83. Hans Henrick Brummer, *The Statue Court in the Vatican Belvedere* (Stockholm, 1970), pp. 239–40.

84. Ackerman, "The Belvedere," pp. 84–85; *Cortile,* pp. 34–35.

85. Brummer, pp. 41–42, figs. 36, 52.

86. Ibid., p. 168 ff.; also Otto Kurz, "Huius nympha loci," *JWCI,* XVI (1953), pp. 171–77; Elisabeth MacDougall, "*Ars Hortulorum:* 16th Century Garden Iconography and Literary Theory in Italy," in *The Italian Garden,* First Dumbarton Oaks Colloquium on the History of Landscape Architecture, ed. David R. Coffin, (Washington, D.C., 1972), pp. 53–57. The same statue was not finally identified as Ariadne until the eighteenth century; Brummer, p. 154.

87. On the Expulsion of Venus and Cupid: E. H. Gombrich, *Symbolic Images* (London, 1972), pp. 102–108.

88. A tactful interpretation of a poem dedicated to the Medici pope, Leo X; see Brummer, pp. 230–37, and also p. 126 for the apple as attribute of Venus Felix.

89. Gombrich, *Symbolic Images,* pp. 105–106.

90. My citation is from the anonymous Elizabethan translation, *The Strife of Love in a Dream* (1592), ed. Andrew Lang (London, 1890), p. 74; cf. p. 76.

91. Brummer, pp. 225–26; cf., for this complex of ideas, Gerhart Ladner,

"Vegetation Symbolism and the Concept of Renaissance," in *De artibus opuscula XL: Essays in Honor of Erwin Panofsky,* ed. Millard Meiss (New York, 1969), pp. 303–22.

92. Ackerman, *Cortile,* p. 143; cf. Pliny, *Natural History,* 36.24.123.

93. Leopold Ranke, *The History of the Popes,* trans. E. Foster (London, 1847), I, p. 361; cf. Frontius, *Aqueducts,* 2.103, 105; also 2.89, 93. For Pontano, see Chap. I, n. 39, above.

94. David Coffin, *The Villa d'Este at Tivoli* (Princeton, N.J., 1960), pp. 17–19, 87.

95. Brummer, pp. 192, 221–22.

96. Rabanus Maurus, *De universo,* 19.9 (*PL,* 111.530).

97. Ackerman, *Cortile,* p. 143.

98. Ibid., p. 34; cf. p. 145 for Latin text.

99. Alberti, *De re aedificatoria,* 9.4; Alberti, *On Painting,* pp. 75–76. Cf. Baxandall, *Painting,* pp. 133–37; also his *Giotto and the Orators* (Oxford, 1971), Chap. III.

100. William Lawson, *A New Orchard and Garden* (London, 1638), p.70: "For whereas every pleasure commonly filles some one of our sences, and that onely, with delight, this makes all our sences, swim in pleasure and that with infinite variety, joyned with no less commodity." Cf. Battisti, pp. 4–5.

101. Anselm cited in Kenneth Clark, *Landscape into Art* (Boston, 1961), p. 2; Albertus Magnus, *De vegetabilibus,* 7.1.14, in *Opera omnia,* ed. A. Borgnet (Paris, 1891), X, p. 293 ff.

102. *De ornatu mundi,* lines 163–64; text in *PL,* 171.1235–38. The poem is associated in manuscript with a *De operibus sex diem* and *De ordine mundi,* which deals with the possibility of man's return to creational integrity. Cf. Ernst Robert Curtius, *European Literature and the Latin Middle Ages,* trans. Willard Trask (New York, 1953), p. 198.

103. *De ornatu mundi,* pp. 93–98; cf. Erwin Panofsky, *Studies in Iconology* (New York, 1939), pp. 35–39, for Vulcan.

104. Stock, p. 128.

105. The illustrations are edited by A. Straub and G. Keller (Strassburg, 1901); Herrad's verses are cited from C. M. Engelhardt, *Herrad von Landsperg* (Stuttgart, 1818).

106. Engelhardt, p. 121: "The verses of Abbess Herrad, with which she lovingly salutes the little maidens of Hohenburg and to faith and delight in their true spouse healthfully invites them [*ad veri sponsi fidem dilectionemque salubriter invitat*]"; cf. Albertus Magnus, *De vegetabilibus,* 7.1.14.

107. Engelhardt, pp. 128, 131 ("Rejoice and sing, O happy, familiar troupe of maidens. . . . Let everyone drink, let everyone drink eternally! Let everyone live, let everyone live eternally!"); cf. p. 121.

108. *Speculum virginum,* cited in Arthur Watson, "The *Speculum Virginum* with Special Reference to the Tree of Jesse," *Speculum,* III (1928), pp. 446–47. Cf. Adolf Katzenellenbogen, *Allegories of the Virtues and Vices in Medieval Art*

(London, 1939), for all three illustrated books considered here. For the florilegium, as well as for the monastic *lectio* in general, see Jean Leclercq, *The Love of Learning and the Desire for God,* trans. C. Misrahi (New York, 1962), pp. 186–88.

109. Watson, pp. 446–47.

110. See Engelhardt, pp. 125–26: like "a little bee inspired by God," Herrad has gathered together from the "various flowers of holy scripture and of the philosophers . . . a single fragrant honeycomb."

111. See Engelhardt, p. 121; cf. p. 125 and compare Leclercq, *Love of Learning,* p. 188.

112. Fritz Saxl, *Lectures,* p. 228 ff.; also his "A Spiritual Encyclopedia of the Later Middle Ages," *JWCI,* V (1942), pp. 82–134; R. Will, "Le Climat religieux de *l'Hortus deliciarum* d'Herrade de Landsberg," *Revue d'Historie et de Philosophie Religieuses,* XVII (1937), pp. 522–66, esp. pp. 543–44.

113. Straub and Keller, eds., *Hortus deliciarum,* fig. xi. Cf. L. D. Ettlinger, "Muses and Liberal Arts," in *Essays in the History of Art Presented to Rudolf Wittkower,* ed. D. Fraser, H. Hibbard, M. Lewine (London, 1967), II, pp. 29–35; also Katzenellenbogen, *Allegories,* fig. 68, for the "mystical paradise" in the *Speculum virginum.*

114. One in the things of this world, the other in the hope of God: Augustine, *City of God,* 15.21 (*PL,* 41.466).

115. Engelhardt, p. 135. Bernard speaks of the literal sense of scripture as a garden; *Cantica canticorum: Eighty-Six Sermons on the Song of Solomon,* trans. J. J. Eales (London, 1895), I, p. 238.

116. Straub and Keller, eds., fig. lvi. Cf. F. Chatillon's review in *Revue du Moyen Age Latin,* II (1946), pp. 81–84, for an explication of this plate; also John Rupert Martin, *The Illustration of the Heavenly Ladder of John Climacus* (Princeton, N.J., 1954), esp. pp. 10–19.

117. Kirk, p. 258; Wolfgang Sörrensen, "Garten und Pfanzen im Klosterplan," in *Studien zur St. Galler Klosterplan,* ed. J. Duft (Saint Gallen, Switz., 1962), p. 259.

118. Saxl, "Spiritual Encyclopedia," p. 113 and plate 27b.

119. For *dulcedo* and Fortunatus' culture-creating role, see esp. Reto Bezzola, *Les Origines et la formation de la littérature courtoise en occident* (Paris, 1944–63), I, pp. 41–76; also D. Tardi, *Fortunat* (Paris, 1927), esp. pp. 52–53. Dissenting views are in Curtius, pp. 412–13; Peter Dronke, *Medieval Latin and the Rise of European Love-Lyric,* 2nd ed. (Oxford, 1968), pp. 206–209.

120. Fortunatus, *Miscellaneorum,* 6.2, 6.8; text in *PL,* 88.204–208, 226; cf. 1.18–20, 9.3; and for the mixed nature of what the poet had to work with, Gregory of Tours, *History of the Franks,* trans. O. M. Dalton (Oxford, 1927), I, pp. 61–62.

121. Prologue to the *Miscellaneorum, PL,* 88.62–63.

122. See Bezzola, *Les Origines,* I, pp. 50–53; P. S. Allen, *The Romanesque Lyric* (Chapel Hill, N.C., 1928), Chap. VIII; Tardi, p. 55 ff.

123. See *Miscellaneorum,* 11.6 (*PL,* 88.353), for Fortunatus' recognition of the possibility that his relation with Radegunde was open to misinterpretation. Cf. L. Caron, "Le Poète Fortunat et son temps," in *Académie des Sciences, des Lettres et des Arts d'Amiens, Mémoires,* XXX (1883), esp. pp. 251–58. Modern critics

have had harsh things to say about this "poète épicuréean, l'abbé gastronome": see Samuel Dill, *Roman Society in Gaul in the Merovingian Age* (London, 1926), p. 380; Waddell, p. 298.

124. *Miscellanea,* 8.13 (*PL,* 88.287); Professor Seth Benardete has suggested to me that lines 3–4 might be rendered as follows: "And though color is not the substance of gold or purple, yet it [color] is by itself in flowers—purple in violets, and crocus [is] the form of gold." Frederick Leo gives a rather different version of the text in his edition; MGH, IV[1] (Berlin, 1881), pp. 194–95.

125. E.g., *Miscellanea,* 8.8 (*PL,* 88.284–85), 8.11 (*PL,* 88.286), 11.11 (*PL,* 88.355).

126. E.g., *Miscellanea,* 11.6 (*PL,* 88.353), where Radegunde is both mother and sister; cf. Caron, p. 240 ff; Dronke, pp. 202–205.

127. *PL,* 79.473–74; cf. D. W. Robertson, Jr., *A Preface to Chaucer* (Princeton, N.J., 1962), pp. 57–58. Gregory of Nyssa makes the same contrast, identifying the color of the literal sense with matter and "chaste concepts of the mind" with form: *From Glory to Glory,* ed. Jean Daniélou and Herbert Musurillo (New York, 1961), p. 154. For form and color in medieval aesthetics, Bruyne, *Esthetics,* pp. 9–18.

128. *PL,* 185.571–72 ("dum foris fruor ministerio, non parum latenti delector mysterio"); cf. Curtius, p. 321, on the biblical tradition of the "liber scriptus intus et foris" (the book written within and without).

129. Sörrensen, p. 235; R. Liddesdale Palmer, *English Monasteries in the Middle Ages* (London, 1930), p. 159.

130. Honorius, *PL,* 172.383–84; cf. Gregory the Great, *PL,* 79.495; *Glossa ordinaria, PL,* 113.1136; Bernard of Clairvaux, ed. Eales, I, pp. 295–96 (sermon 48.6).

131. Cited in Domino du Cange, *Glossarium mediae et infimae latinitatis* (Paris, 1842), VI, p. 283.

132. Augustine, *City of God,* 22.24 (*PL,* 41.791–92); trans. Marcus Dodd (New York, 1950), p. 855.

133. Bonaventure, *De reductione artium ad theologian,* II; trans. in Herman Shapiro, ed., *Medieval Philosophy* (New York, 1964), p. 370.

134. Crescenzi, cited in Margurite Charageat, *L'Art des jardins* (Paris, 1962), p. 84; cf. Grimal, *L'Art des jardins,* pp. 59–63.

135. Albertus Magnus, *De vegetabilibus,* 7.1.14; cf. Hautecoeur, p. 95.

136. See Evans, *Pattern,* Chap. II; also *Nature in Design,* esp. p. 85 ff.

137. E.g., in the frequently reproduced illumination from the *Hours* of Anne of Brittany; see Gothein, fig. 135.

138. Ladner, "Vegetation Symbolism," pp. 321–22; cf. Panofsky, *Early Netherlandish Painting,* I, pp. 48, 56; Millard Meiss, *Andrea Mantegna as Illuminator* (New York, 1957), esp. pp. 54–55; also Evans, *Nature in Design,* p. 94.

139. Nicole Dacos, *La Découverte de la Domus Aurea et la formation des grotesques à la renaissance* (London, 1969), p. 121, n. 2; Margaret Phillips, ed., *The Adages of Erasmus* (Cambridge, Eng., 1964), p. 179. Cf. Edgar Wind, *Pagan Mysteries in the Renaissance,* 2nd ed. (New York, 1968), p. 237.

140. Vasari, *Lives,* ed. Gaston de Vere (London, 1912–14), VIII, p. 76. For the loggia: Dacos, pp. 105–109; Oskar Fischel, *Raphael,* trans. B. Rackham (London,

1948), pp. 154–55. Redig de Campos speaks of the "eurhythmic" handling of space and light; cited in Maurizio Calvesi, *Treasures of the Vatican* (New York, 1962), p. 152.

141. André Chastel, *Art et humanisme à Florence au temps de Laurent le Magnifique* (Paris, 1961), pp. 216, 334–35; cf. Chastel, "La Renaissance fantaisiste," *L'Oeil,* XXI (Sept., 1951), pp. 34–41, for a discussion of grotesques as a mannerist attempt to seize upon the "unnameable" vitality of nature.

142. Guarini, *Il Pastor Fido,* Prologue, ll. 29–31; trans. Richard Fanshawe. Cf. Julia Cartwright, *Italian Gardens of the Renaissance* (London, 1914), pp. 90–91, 96.

143. Freedberg, *Painting of the High Renaissance,* I, p. 331.

144. Vitruvius, *On Architecture,* 7.5.3–4; cf. Dacos, pp. 127–28, for Francisco da Hollanda's remarks.

145. G. A. Gilio, *Dialogo* (1564), cited in Dacos, p. 128.

146. Freedberg, I, p. 328.

147. Chastel, *Art et humanisme,* pp. 334–35. Cf. Wolfgang Kayser, *The Grotesque in Art and Literature,* trans. Ulrich Weisstein (Bloomington, Ind., 1963), p. 21; Henri Focillon, *The Life of Forms in Art,* trans. C. Hogan and G. Kubler, 2nd ed. (New York, 1948), p. 19.

148. Gothein, I, pp. 231–34; Charageat, *L'Art des jardins,* pp. 108–110. For a reconstruction of the loggia, William E. Greenwood, *The Villa Madama, Rome* (London, 1928).

149. Dacos, pp. 57–59; E. P. Goldschmidt, *The Printed Book in the Renaissance* (Cambridge, Eng., 1950), pp. 63–70; Charles Mitchel, "Archaeology and Romance in Renaissance Italy," in *Italian Renaissance Studies . . . to Cecilia Ady,* ed. E. F. Jacob (New York, 1960), pp. 455–83. Cf. Gilbert Redgrave, *Erhard Ratdolt* (London, 1894), p. 75; William D. Orcutt, *The Book in Italy* (London, 1928), p. 72; H. W. Davies, *Devices of the Early Printers* (London, 1935), p. 683. Also Roberto Weiss, "A New Francesco Colonna," *Italian Studies,* XVI (1961), pp. 78–83.

150. As do Ligorio and Lomazzo in the late sixteenth century; Dacos, pp. 130–32; cf. Ladner, "Vegetation," p. 321; Gombrich, *Symbolic Images,* p. 20. The author of the illustrations is unknown, but it has been supposed that Colonna himself made preliminary sketches; see George Painter, *The Hypnerotomachia Poliphili of 1499: An Introduction to the Dream, the Dreamer, the Artist, and the Printer* (London, 1963), p. 15.

151. Francesco Colonna, *Poliphili hypnerotomachia* (Venice, 1499; fasc. rpt., London, 1904), Dvii^{r}; the translations in what follows are my own, but I have consulted with profit the French translation by Claudius Popelin (Paris, 1883). For the bucranium: Wind, *Pagan Mysteries,* p. 104; Karl Kerényi, *Eleusis,* trans. Ralph Manheim (New York, 1967), pp. 74–75.

152. Colonna, *Hypnerotomachia,* C1^{r}; cf. Ludwig Volkmann, *Bilderschriften der Renaissance* (Leipzig, 1923), pp. 46, 70, 92.

153. Erasmus cites Gellius (10.11) on the equation of *festinare* and *maturare,* although he emphasizes less strongly than does Gellius the vegetative implications

of *festinare.* He replaces a citation from the *Georgics* with one from the *Aeneid* and thinks of the proverb chiefly (following Suetonius) as a "royal" one. See *The Adages of Erasmus,* ed. Phillips, pp. 171–90; also Wind, *Pagan Mysteries,* pp. 97–112. Cf. Painter, p. 20, on Colonna and Aldus.

154. *The Strife of Love in a Dream,* p. 75. Eleuterilida: *eleutheria,* liberty.

155. Colonna, *Hypnerotomachia,* C1r; cf. Volkmann, pp. 17, 53, 108, 122. Also Guy de Tervarent, *Attributs et symboles dans l'art profane, 1450–1600* (Geneva, 1958), cols. 8–9.

156. E.g., Volkmann, pp. 15, 19, 26, 40, 51. The similarity of Colonna's vase and flowers motif to the emblem of the printer Geofroy Tory has been noted; Tory himself explains that the flowers of his *pot-cassé* (broken jar) signify the life or virtue of the soul (now spilled, since the death of his daughter has broken the vase). See Davies, *Devices,* p. 683. Redgrave, p. 7, attributes to the influence of the *Hypnerotomachia* the popularity in book design of "vases with stems." Cf. Wind, *Pagan Mysteries,* p. 268, n. 1.

157. Colonna, *Hypnerotomachia,* Yviv. For architectural use of the umbilical motif, see Ackerman, *Architecture of Michelangelo,* pp. 169–73.

158. For the cosmic symbolism of Plato's Atlantis and Hadrian's Teatro Marittimo, see Paul Friedländer, *Plato: An Introduction,* trans. Hans Meyerhoff (New York, 1958), pp. 203, 319–22. Like Colonna's Cythera, Campanella's City of the Sun is constituted by seven concentric circles, named for the spheres of the planets; for Bruni's ideal city, see Eugenio Garin, *Science and Civic Life in the Italian Renaissance,* trans. Peter Munz (Garden City, N.Y., 1969), pp. 30–31.

159. For Colonna and Padua: Hautecoeur, p. 115; Charageat, *L'Art des jardins,* p. 117.

160. Anthony Blunt, "The *Hypnerotomachia Poliphili* in Seventeenth-Century France," *JWCI,* I (1937–38), pp. 117–37; also his *Artistic Theory in Italy 1450–1600,* 2nd ed. (Oxford, 1956), pp. 39–43. But for Colonna and Alberti, see M. T. Casella and G. Pozzi, *Francesco Colonna, Biografia e opere* (Padua, 1959), pp. 33–50.

161. Leonardo Bruni, *Dialogi,* I; trans. in David Thompson and Alan Nagel, ed., *The Three Crowns of Florence* (New York, 1972), p. 37.

162. E.g., Paracelsus, *Selected Writings,* trans. J. Jacobi, (New York, 1951), p. 230: "eternal reason cannot exist without natural wisdom because man must find the eternal in the natural." Cf. Henry Pachter, *Paracelsus: Magic into Science* (New York, 1951), pp. 10–12, 213–25. For alchemical ideas in Colonna: Linda Fierz-David, *The Dream of Poliphilo,* trans. M. Hottinger (New York, 1950).

163. Otto Benesch, *The Art of the Renaissance in Northern Europe,* 2nd ed. (London, 1965), Chap. III.

164. Leonard Mascall, *A Booke of the Arte and Maner How to Plante and Graffe All Sorts of Trees* (London, 1575), "Dedication."

165. *Hermetica,* 5.2 (trans. Scott, I, p. 159): "For the Lord manifests himself ungrudgingly through all the universe; and you can hold God's image with your eyes, and lay hold on it with your hands."

166. Blunt, "The *Hypnerotomachia Poliphili,*" for some specific borrowings and

filiations. Also André Chastel, *Marsile Ficin et l'art* (Geneva, 1954), p. 149; Grimal, *L'Art des jardins,* pp. 69–74.

167. The geometrical elaboration of such structures is carried to its most fantastic lengths in the designs of Vredeman de Vries, who also claimed the example of Vitruvius and who like Colonna was less concerned with purely aesthetic harmonies than with the magical appeal of number and emblematic form. See Jan Vredeman de Vries, *Hortorum viridariorumque formae* (Antwerp, 1583); also Gothein, II, pp. 19–20. For Vitruvius and Colonna, see Charles Ephrussi, *Etude sur le Songe de Poliphile* (Paris, 1888), p. 65.

168. Alessandro Perosa, *Giovanni Rucellai ed il suo Zibaldone* (London, 1960), p. 20.

169. Gothein, I, p. 211.

170. Vitruvius, *On Architecture,* 7.5.2 Trimmed foliage joins painting and statuary at a relatively late date; see n. 77 above.

171. Several texts are collected in Don Cameron Allen, *Image and Meaning* (Baltimore, Md., 1960), pp. 125–27.

172. See Axel Boethius, *The Golden House of Nero* (Ann Arbor, Mich., 1960), p. 105, who explains that *domus* refers not just to the palace, but to the entire establishment, which is above all a "fanciful landscape garden"—Martial's "country in the town" (12.57.21).

173. Suetonius, *The Twelve Caesars,* 6.31; Loeb translation of J. C. Rolfe (Cambridge, Mass., 1914).

174. Perosa, *Giovanni Rucellai,* p. 22; cf. Battisti, pp. 15–17, 21.

175. Fritz Baumgart, "La Caprarola di Ameto Orti," *Studj Romanzi,* XXV (1935), p. 104.

176. Ackerman, "The Belvedere as Classical Villa," pp. 81–83.

177. Pontano, *De hortis Hesperidum,* l. 512 ("gratum opus, informemque gregem ad speciosa vocato"). See above, pp. 10–11.

Bibliography

Note: This is not a complete bibliography of subjects touched upon in *The Idea of the Garden in the Renaissance,* but simply a list of studies actually cited. I have included a few editions of primary sources on account of particularly helpful introductions and notes. Other editions employed may be located by use of the index.

Ackerman, James S. *The Architecture of Michelangelo.* 2nd ed. Baltimore, Md., 1971.

———. "*'Ars sine scientia nihil est': *Gothic Theory of Architecture at the Cathedral of Milan," *AB,* XXXI (1949), 84–111.

———. "The Belvedere as a Classical Villa," *JWCI,* XIV (1951), 70–91.

———. *The Cortile del Belvedere.* Vatican City, 1954.

———. *Palladio.* Baltimore, Md., 1967.

———. "Sources of the Renaissance Villa," in *The Renaissance and Mannerism,* Acts of the 20th International Congress of the History of Art, pp. 6–18. Princeton, N.J., 1963.

Allen, B. Sprague. *Tides of English Taste.* Cambridge, Mass., 1937.

Allen, Don Cameron. *Image and Meaning.* Baltimore, Md., 1960.

———. "A Note on Lyly's *Midas,*" *MLN,* LX (1945), 326–27, LXI (1946), 503–504.

Allen, Philip Schuyler, *Mediaeval Latin Lyrics.* Chicago, 1931.

———. *The Romanesque Lyric.* Chapel Hill, N.C., 1928.

Alverny, Marie-Thérèse d'. "La Sagesse et ses sept filles," *Mélanges F. Grat,* I, 245–78. Paris, 1946.

Amherst, Alicia. *A History of Gardening in England.* New York, 1910.

André, Jean-Marie. *L'Otium dans la vie morale et intellectuelle romaine.* Paris, 1966.

Argan, Giulio Carlo. "The Architecture of Brunelleschi and the Origins of Perspective Theory in the Fifteenth Century," *JWCI,* IX (1946), 96–121.

Armstrong, Edward. *Lorenzo de' Medici and Florence in the Fifteenth Century.* New York, 1896.

Armstrong, Elizabeth. *Ronsard and the Age of Gold.* Cambridge, Eng., 1968.
Auerbach, Erich. *Dante: Poet of the Secular World,* translated by Ralph Manheim. Chicago, 1961.
———. *Literary Language and Its Public in Late Latin Antiquity and in the Middle Ages,* translated by Ralph Manheim. New York, 1965.
———. *Mimesis,* translated by Willard Trask. Princeton, N.J., 1953.
———. "Philology and *Weltliteratur,*" translated by Marie and Edward Said, *The Centennial Review,* XIII (1969), 1–17.
Baldwin, Charles Sears. *Medieval Rhetoric and Poetic.* New York, 1928.
Barb, A. A. "Diva Matrix," *JWCI,* XVI (1953), 193–238.
Barfield, Owen. *Saving the Appearances.* London, 1957.
Baron, Hans. "Cicero and the Roman Civic Spirit in the Middle Ages and Early Renaissance," *Bulletin of the John Rylands Library,* XXII (1938), 72–97.
———. *The Crisis of the Early Italian Renaissance.* 2nd ed., Princeton, N.J., 1966.
———. "Franciscan Poverty and Civic Wealth as Factors in the Rise of Humanistic Thought," *Speculum,* XIII (1938), 1–37.
———. *From Petrarch to Leonardo Bruni.* Chicago, 1968.
———. *Humanistic and Political Literature in Florence and Venice at the Beginning of the Quattrocento.* Cambridge, Mass., 1955.
Battisti, Eugenio. "*Natura artificiosa* to *Natura artificialis,*" in *The Italian Garden,* First Dumbarton Oaks Colloquium on the History of Landscape Architecture, ed. David R. Coffin, pp. 1–36. Washington, D.C., 1972.
Baumgart, Fritz. "La Caprarola di Ameto Orti," *Studj Romanzi,* XXV (1935), 77–179.
Baxandall, Michael. *Giotto and the Orators.* Oxford, 1971.
———. *Painting and Experience in Fifteenth Century Italy.* Oxford, 1972.
Benesch, Otto. *The Art of the Renaissance in Northern Europe.* 2nd ed. London, 1965.
Bennett, J. A. W. *The Parliament of Fowls.* Oxford, 1957.
Berenson, Bernard. *Italian Painters of the Renaissance.* New York, 1957.
Bernardo, Aldo. *Petrarch, Scipio, and the Africa.* Baltimore, Md., 1962.
Bezzola, Reto. *Les Origines et la formation de la littérature courtoise en occident.* Paris, 1944–63.
———. *Le Sens d'aventure et de l'amour.* Paris, 1947.
Bidez, Joseph. "La Liturgie des mystères chez les Néoplatoniciens," *Académie Royale de Belgique, Bulletin de la Classe des Lettres* (1919), 415–30.
Billanovich, G. *Petrarca letterato.* Rome, 1947.
Bishop, Morris. *Petrarch and His World.* Bloomington, Ind., 1963.
Bloomfield, Morton. "Authenticating Realism and the Realism of Chaucer," *Thought,* XXXIX (1964), 335–58.
———. "Joachim of Flora," *Traditio,* XIII (1957), 249–311.
———. *Piers Plowman as a Fourteenth-Century Apocalypse.* New Brunswick, N.J., 1962.
———. "Some Reflections on the Medieval Idea of Perfection," *Franciscan Studies,* XVII (1957), 213–37.

Blunt, Anthony. *Artistic Theory in Italy, 1450–1600*. 2nd ed. Oxford, 1956.
———. "The *Hypnerotomachia Poliphili* in Seventeenth-Century France," *JWCI*, I (1937–38), 117–37.
Blunt, Wilfrid. *The Art of Botanical Illustration*. London, 1950.
Bober, Harry. "An Illustrated Medieval Schoolbook," *Journal of the Walters Art Gallery*, XIX–XX (1956–57), 65–97.
Boethius, Axel. *The Golden House of Nero*. Ann Arbor, Mich., 1960.
Bonner, Gerald. *St. Augustine of Hippo*. London, 1963.
Borsook, Eva. "Decor in Florence for the Entry of Charles VIII of France," *Kunsthistorisches Institut in Florenz, Mitteilungen*, Vol. I, Part II (December, 1961), 106–22.
Boyancé, Pierre. *Le Culte des Muses chez les philosophes grecs*. Paris, 1937.
Braunfels, Wolfgang. *Monasteries of Western Europe*, translated by Alastair Laing. Princeton, N.J., 1972.
Bréhier, Emile. *The Philosophy of Plotinus*, translated by Joseph Thomas. Chicago, 1958.
Broadbent, J. B. *Some Graver Subject*. New York, 1960.
Brown, A. C. L. *Ywain, A Study in the Origins of Arthurian Romance*. Boston, 1903.
Brummer, Hans Henrick. *The Statue Court in the Vatican Belvedere*. Stockholm, 1970.
Bruyne, Edgar de. *Esthetics of the Middle Ages*, translated by E. B. Hennessy. New York, 1969.
———. *Etudes d'esthétique médiévale*. Bruges, 1946.
Bukofzer, Manfred. "Speculative Thinking in Medieval Music," *Speculum*, XVII (1942), 165–80.
Burke, Kenneth. *The Rhetoric of Religion*. Boston, 1961.
Burnaby, John. *Amor Dei*. London, 1938.
Buxton, John. *Elizabethan Taste*. London, 1963.
Cabrol, F., and Leclercq, H. *Dictionnaire d'archéologie chrétienne et de liturgie*. Paris, 1907–53.
Callahan, John F. "Greek Philosophy and the Cappadocian Cosmology," *Dumbarton Oaks Papers*, XII (1958), 29–57.
Cameron, Alan. *Claudian: Poetry and Propaganda at the Court of Honorius*. Oxford, 1970.
Carne-Ross, D. S. "The One and the Many," *Arion*, V (1966), 195–234.
Caron, L. "Le Poète Fortunat et son temps," *Académie des Sciences, des Lettres, et des Arts d'Amiens, Memoires*, XXX (1883), 225–303.
Caron, M., and Hutin, S. *The Alchemists*. New York, 1961.
Cartwright, Julia. *Isabella d'Este*. New York, 1923.
———. *Italian Gardens of the Renaissance*. London, 1914.
Casella, M. T., and Pozzi, G. *Francesco Colonna, Biografia e opere*. Padua, 1959.
Cassirer, Ernst. *The Individual and the Cosmos in Renaissance Philosophy*, translated by Mario Domandi. New York, 1964.
———. *Language and Myth*, translated by Susanne Langer. New York, 1946.

———. *The Philosophy of Symbolic Forms,* translated by Ralph Manheim. New Haven, Conn., 1953–57.
———. Kristeller, P. O., and Randall, J. H., Jr., eds. *The Renaissance Philosophy of Man.* Chicago, 1948.
Chambers, A. B. "The Mind Its own Place," *Renaissance News,* XVI (1963), 98–101.
Charageat, Margurite. *L'Art des jardins.* Paris, 1962.
———. "Le Parc d'Hesdin," *Bulletin de la Société de l'Histoire de l'Art Français,* 1950 (Paris, 1951), 94–100.
Chastel, André. *Art et humanisme à Florence au temps de Laurent le Magnifique.* Paris, 1961.
———. "Cortil et théâtre," in *Le Lieu théâtral à la renaissance,* pp. 41–47. Paris, 1964.
———. *Marsile Ficin et l'art.* Geneva, 1954.
———. "La Renaissance fantaisiste," *L'Oeil,* XXI (Sept., 1956), 34–41.
Chavasse, Claude. *The Bride of Christ.* London, 1940.
Chennevières, Philippe de. *Archives de l'art français.* Paris, 1851–52.
Chenu, M. D. *La Théologie au douzième siècle.* Paris, 1957.
Cherniss, Harold. *The Riddle of the Early Academy.* Berkeley, Calif., 1945.
Chew, Samuel. *The Pilgrimage of Life.* New Haven, Conn., 1962.
Clapp, F. M. *Jacopo Carucci da Pontormo.* New Haven, Conn., 1916.
Clark, J. M. *The Abbey of St. Gall as a Centre of Literature and Art.* Cambridge, Eng., 1926.
Clark, Kenneth. *Landscape into Art.* Boston, 1961.
———. *Leon Battista Alberti on Painting.* London, 1945.
Clifford, Derek. *A History of Garden Design.* New York, 1953.
Cobb, Edith. "The Ecology of the Imagination in Childhood," *Daedalus,* LXXXVIII (1959), 537–48.
Cody, Richard. *The Landscape of the Mind.* Oxford, 1969.
Coffin, David. *The Villa d'Este at Tivoli.* Princeton, N.J., 1960.
Colie, Rosalie. *The Resources of Kind.* Berkeley, Calif., 1973.
Commager, Steele. *The Odes of Horace.* New Haven, Conn., 1962.
Conant, Kenneth John. *Benedictine Contributions to Church Architecture.* Latrobe, Pa., 1949.
———. *Carolingian and Romanesque Architecture.* 3rd ed., Baltimore, Md., 1974.
———. "Iconography and Sequence in the Ambulatory Capitals of Cluny," *Speculum,* V (1930), 278–87.
———. "Medieval Academy Excavations of Cluny, IX: Systematic Dimensions in the Buildings," *Speculum,* XXXVIII (1963), 1–45.
Coomaraswamy, Ananda. *Figures of Speech or Figures of Thought.* London, 1946.
———. "Ornament," *AB,* XXI (1939), 375–82.
Corbin, Henry. *Avicenna and the Visionary Recital,* translated by Willard Trask. New York, 1960.
Corcoran, Mary Irma. *Milton's Paradise with Reference to the Hexameral Background.* Washington, D.C., 1945.

Cornford, F. M. *From Religion to Philosophy*. London, 1912 (rpt. New York, 1957).

———. "The Invention of Space," in *Essays in Honor of Gilbert Murray*, pp. 215–35. London, 1936.

———. *Plato's Cosmology*. London, 1937 (rpt. New York, 1957).

———. *Principium sapientiae*, edited by W. K. C. Guthrie. Cambridge, Eng., 1952.

Courcelle, Pierre. *Late Latin Writers and their Greek Sources*, translated by H. E. Wedeck. Cambridge, Mass., 1969.

———. "Tradition néo-platonicienne et traditions chrétiennes de la 'Région de dissemblance,'" *Archives d'Histoire Doctrinale et Littéraire du Moyen Age*, XXXII (1957), 5–33.

Crane, Thomas Frederick. *Italian Social Customs of the Sixteenth Century*. New Haven, Conn., 1920.

Crisp, Frank. *Mediaeval Gardens*. London, 1924.

Crouse, Robert D. "*Honorius Augustodunensis:* The Arts as *Via ad Patriam*," in *Arts libéraux et philosophie au moyen âge*, Actes du Quatrième Congrès International de Philosophie Médiévale, pp. 531–39. Montreal, 1969.

Cumont, Franz. *Recherches sur le symbolisme funéraire des romains*. Paris, 1942.

Curry, Walter Clyde. *Shakespeare's Philosophical Patterns*. Baton Rouge, La., 1937.

Curtius, Ernst Robert. *European Literature and the Latin Middle Ages*, translated by Willard Trask. New York, 1953.

Dacos, Nicole. *La Découverte de la Domus Aurea et la formation des grotesques à la renaissance*. London, 1969.

Dahlberg, Charles. "Macrobius and the Unity of the *Roman de la Rose*," *SP*, LVIII (1961), 573–82.

Daniélou, Jean. *From Shadows to Reality*, translated by Wulstan Hibberd. London, 1960.

———. *Platonisme et théologie mystique*. Paris, 1944.

———. *Primitive Christian Symbols*, translated by D. A. Hunter. Baltimore, Md., 1964.

———. "Terre et paradis chez les pères d'église," *Eranos-Jahrbuch*, XXII (1953), 433–72.

———. *The Theology of Jewish Christianity*, translated by John A. Baker. London, 1964.

D'Arcy, Eric, ed. *The Summa Theologiae*, XIX: *The Emotions*, (St. Thomas Aquinas). New York, 1967.

D'Arcy, M. C. *The Mind and Heart of Love*. 2nd ed. New York, 1956.

Davies, H. W. *Devices of the Early Printers*. London, 1935.

Davies, J. G. *Origin and Development of Early Christian Architecture*. New York, 1953.

Davis, Charles. "Il buon tempo antico," in *Florentine Studies*, edited by Nicolai Rubinstein, pp. 45–69. Evanston, Ill., 1968.

Delaborde, H. François. *L'Expédition de Charles VIII en Italie*. Paris, 1888.

Delorme, Jean. *Gymnasion*. Paris, 1960.

Demus, Otto. *Byzantine Mosaic Decoration*. Boston, 1955.

Denomy, A. J. "An Inquiry into the Origins of Courtly Love," *Mediaeval Studies,* VI (1944), 175–260.
———. "*Jois* among the Early Troubadours," *Mediaeval Studies,* XIII (1951), 177–217.
Diederich, M. D. *Vergil in the Works of St. Ambrose.* Washington, D.C., 1931.
Dill, Samuel. *Roman Society in Gaul in the Merovingian Age.* London, 1926.
Dodds, E. R. *The Greeks and the Irrational.* Berkeley, Calif., 1964.
Dronke, Peter. *Medieval Latin and the Rise of European Love-Lyric.* 2nd ed. Oxford, 1968.
Duhem, Pierre. *Le Système du monde.* Paris, 1913–59.
Dupront, A. "Espace et humanisme," *Bibliothèque d'Humanisme et Renaissance,* VIII (1946), 7–104.
Ecker, Laurence. "Place Concept in Chinese," *Language,* XVI (1940), 17–28.
Economou, George D. *The Goddess Natura in Medieval Literature.* Cambridge, Mass., 1972.
Eliade, Mircea. *Cosmos and History,* translated by Willard Trask. New York, 1959.
———. *Patterns of Comparative Religion,* translated by Rosemary Sheed. New York, 1958.
———. *The Sacred and the Profane,* translated by Willard Trask. New York, 1959.
———. "The Yearning for Paradise in Primitive Tradition," *Diogenes,* III (Summer, 1953), 18–30.
Ellrodt, Robert. *Neoplatonism in the Poetry of Spenser.* Geneva, 1960.
Engelhardt, C. M. *Herrad von Landsperg.* Stuttgart, 1818.
Ephrussi, Charles, *Etude sur le Songe de Poliphile.* Paris, 1888.
Ettlinger, L. D. "Muses and Liberal Arts," in *Essays in the History of Art Presented to Rudolf Wittkower,* edited by D. Fraser, H. Hibbard, and M. Lewine, II, 29–35. London, 1967.
Evans, Joan. *Art in Mediaeval France.* Oxford, 1948.
———. *Clunaic Art of the Romanesque Period.* Cambridge, Eng., 1950.
———. *Life in Medieval France.* 3rd ed. New York, 1969.
———. *Nature in Design.* London, 1933.
———. *Pattern, A Study of Ornament in Western Europe.* Oxford, 1931.
———. *The Romanesque Architecture of the Order of Cluny.* Cambridge, Eng., 1938.
Ewer, Mary. *A Survey of Mystical Symbolism.* London, 1933.
Fabriczy, Cornelius von. *Italian Medals,* translated by G. W. Hamilton. London, 1904.
Faral, Edmund. *Les Arts poétiques du xiie et du xiiie siècle.* Paris, 1924.
———. *Recherches sur les sources latines des contes et romans courtois du moyen âge.* Paris, 1913.
Festugière, André. *Personal Religion among the Greeks.* Berkeley, Calif., 1954.
———. *La Révélation d'Hermès Trismégiste.* Paris, 1949–54.
Fierz-David, Linda. *The Dream of Poliphilo,* translated by M. Hottinger. New York, 1950.

Fischel, Oskar. *Raphael,* translated by Bernard Rackham. London, 1948.
Fleming, John W. *The Roman de la Rose.* Princeton, N.J., 1969.
Fletcher, Angus. *Allegory.* Ithaca, N.Y., 1964.
Focillon, Henri. *The Life of Forms in Art,* translated by C. Hogan and G. Kubler. 2nd ed. New York, 1948.
Fraenkel, Eduard. *Horace.* Oxford, 1957.
Frankfort, Henri; Frankfort, Mrs. H. A.; Wilson, John A.; and Jacobsen, Thorkild. *Before Philosophy.* Baltimore, Md., 1964.
Frankl, Paul. *The Gothic.* Princeton, N.J., 1960.
———. "The Secret of the Medieval Masons," *AB,* XXVII (1945), 46–60.
Freedberg, S. J. *Painting of the High Renaissance in Rome and Florence.* 2nd ed. New York, 1972.
Friedländer, Paul. *Plato: An Introduction,* translated by Hans Meyerhoff. New York, 1958.
Frommel, Christoph. *Die Farnesina und Peruzzis architektonisches Frühwerk.* Berlin, 1961.
Gadol, Joan. *Leon Battista Alberti, Universal Man of the Early Renaissance.* Chicago, 1969.
Garin, Eugenio. *Italian Humanism,* translated by Peter Munz. Oxford, 1965.
———. *Portraits from the Quattrocento,* translated by Victor and Elizabeth Velen. New York, 1972.
———. *Science and Civic Life in the Italian Renaissance,* translated by Peter Munz. Garden City, N.Y., 1969.
Giamatti, A. Bartlett. *The Earthly Paradise and the Renaissance Epic.* Princeton, N.J., 1966.
Giet, Stanislas, ed. *Homélies sur l'hexaéméron,* (St. Basil). Paris, 1950.
Gilbert, Felix. "Bernardo Rucellai and the Orti Oricellari," *JWCI,* XII (1949), 101–31.
Gilman, Stephen. *The Art of La Celestina.* Madison, Wis., 1956.
Gilson, Etienne. *The Christian Philosophy of Saint Augustine,* translated by L. E. M. Lynch. New York, 1960.
———. "La Cosmogonie de Bernardus Silvestris," *Archives d'Histoire Doctrinale et Littéraire du Moyen Age,* III (1928), 5–24.
———. *The Mystical Theology of Saint Bernard,* translated by A. H. C. Downes. London, 1940.
———. *The Philosophy of St. Bonaventure,* translated by Dom Illtyd Trethowan. London, 1938.
———. " 'Sub umbris arborum,' " *Mediaeval Studies,* XIV (1952), 149–51.
———. "Sur deux textes de Petrarch," in *Studi petrarcheschi,* VII, edited by U. Bosco, pp. 35–50. Bologna, 1961.
Girouard, Marc. *Robert Smythson and the Architecture of the Elizabethan Era.* London, 1966.
Goldin, Frederick. *The Mirror of Narcissus in the Courtly Love Lyric.* Ithaca, N.Y., 1967.

Goldschmidt, E. P. *The Printed Book in the Renaissance*. Cambridge, Eng., 1950.
Gombrich, E. H. "Alberto Avogadro's Description of the Badia of Fiesole and of the Villa of Careggi," *Italia medioevale e umanistica,* V (1962), 217–29.
———. *Norm and Form*. London, 1966.
———. *Symbolic Images*. London, 1972.
Gothein, Marie Luise. *A History of Garden Art,* translated by Mrs. Archer-Hind. New York, 1928.
Graf, Arturo. *Miti, leggende e superstizioni del Medio Evo*. Turin, 1892.
Greenhill, E. S. "The Child in the Tree," *Traditio,* X (1954), 323–71.
Greenwood, William E. *The Villa Madama, Rome*. London, 1928.
Grimal, Pierre. *L'Art des jardins*. Paris, 1954.
———. "De Lucilius à Cicéron: caractères généraux du dialogue romain," *L'Information Littéraire,* VII (1955), 192–98.
———. *Les Jardins romains*. Paris, 1943.
Gruyer, Gustave. *L'Art ferrarais à l'époque des princes d'Este*. Paris, 1897.
Gundersheimer, Werner. *Ferrara: The Style of a Renaissance Despotism*. Princeton, N.J., 1973.
Gunn, Alan M. F. *The Mirror of Love*. Lubbock, Tex., 1952.
Gutkind, Kurt S. *Cosimo de' Medici*. Oxford, 1938.
Hackforth, Reginald. *Plato's Phaedrus*. Cambridge, Eng., 1952.
Hadfield, Miles. *Gardening in Britain*. London, 1960.
Haller, R. S. "The *Altercatio Phyllidis et Florae* as an Ovidian Satire," *Mediaeval Studies,* XXX (1968), 119–33.
Halliburton, R. J. "The Inclination to Retirement—The Retreat at Cassiciacum and the 'Monastery' of Tagaste," *Studia Patristica V, Texte und Untersuchungen,* LXXX (Berlin, 1962), 329–40.
Hamberg, Per Gustaf. "The Villa of Lorenzo il Magnifico at Poggio a Caiano," *Figura* (n.s.), I (Stockholm, 1959), 76–87.
Hathaway, Baxter. *The Age of Criticism*. Ithaca, N.Y., 1962.
Hautecoeur, Louis. *Les Jardins des dieux et des hommes*. Paris, 1959.
Held, Julius S. "Flora, Goddess and Courtesan," in *De artibus opuscula xl: Essays in Honor of Erwin Panofsky,* edited by Millard Meiss, pp. 201–218. New York, 1961.
Heninger, S. K., Jr. "Some Renaissance Versions of the Pythagorean Tetrad," *Studies in the Renaissance,* VIII (1961), 7–35.
Hersey, George L. *Alfonso II and the Artistic Renewal of Naples 1485–1495*. New Haven, Conn., 1969.
———. *The Aragonese Arch at Naples, 1443–1475*. New Haven, Conn., 1973.
Hertz, Robert. "La Prééminence de la main droite," *Mélanges de sociologie religieuse et folklore,* pp. 99–129. Paris, 1928.
Hexter, J. H. *Reappraisals in History,* Evanston, Ill., 1961.
Hinks, Roger. *Carolingian Art*. Ann Arbor, Mich., 1962.
Hirschfeld, Peter. *Mäzene: Die Rolle des Auftraggebers in der Kunst*. Munich, 1968.
Hollander, John. *The Untuning of the Sky*. Princeton, N.J., 1961.
Holt, Elizabeth. *A Documentary History of Art*. Garden City, N. Y., 1957–58.

Holton, Gerald. "Johannes Kepler's Universe," in *Toward Modern Science,* 2nd ed., edited by Robert Palter, pp. 460–84. New York, 1969.

Hopper, Vincent F. *Medieval Number Symbolism.* New York, 1938.

Horn, Walter. "On the Author of the Plan of St. Gall and the Relation of the Plan to the Monastic Reform Movement," in *Studien zur St. Galler Klosterplan,* edited by J. Duft, pp. 103–27. St. Gallen, Switz., 1962.

———. "The Plan of St. Gall—Original or Copy?" in *Studien zur St. Galler Klosterplan,* edited by J. Duft, pp. 79–102. St. Gallen, Switz., 1962.

———. and Born, E. "The 'Dimensional Inconsistencies' of the Plan of St. Gall," *AB,* XLVIII (1966), 285–308.

Hovingh, P. F., ed. and trans. *Alethia* [Claudius Marius Victor], *La Prière et les vers 1–170 du livre I avec introduction, traduction, et commentaire.* Groningen, Neth., 1955.

Howard, Donald. *The Three Temptations.* Princeton, N. J., 1966.

Huizinga, Johan. *Erasmus and the Age of Reformation,* translated by F. Hopman. New York, 1957.

Hulubei, Alice. "Naldo Naldi," *Humanisme et Renaissance,* III (1936), 169–86, 309–29.

Hussey, Christopher. "Burghley House," *Country Life,* CXIII (1953), 1828–32, 1962–65, 2038–41, 2104–2107, 2164–67.

Hutton, Edward. *Country Walks about Florence.* New York, 1908.

Ivins, William M., Jr. *Prints and Visual Communication.* Cambridge, Mass., 1953.

Jackson, B. D. "Life of William Turner," in William Turner, *Libellus re herbaria.* Facsimile reproduction, Ray Society, London, 1965.

Jaeger, Werner. *Paideia,* translated by Gilbert Highet. 2nd ed. New York, 1945.

———. *The Theology of the Early Greek Philosophers.* Oxford, 1936.

Johnstone, Paul H. "In Praise of Husbandry," *Agricultural History,* XI (1937), 80–95.

———. "The Rural Socrates," *JHI,* V (1944), 151–75.

Jonas, Hans. *The Gnostic Religion.* Boston, 1958.

Jung, C. G. *Psychology and Alchemy,* translated by R. F. C. Hull. London, 1953.

Jung, Marc-René. *Hercule dans la littérature française du xvi*e *siècle.* Geneva, 1966.

Kahn, Charles H. *Anaximander and the Origins of Greek Cosmology.* New York, 1960.

Kantorowicz, Ernst. *Frederick the Second,* translated by E. O. Lorimer. London, 1931.

Kaske, R. E. "Langland and the *Paradisus Claustralis,*" *MLN,* LXXII (1957), 481–83.

Katzenellenbogen, Adolf. *Allegories of the Virtues and Vices in Medieval Art.* London, 1939.

———. *The Sculptural Programs of Chartres Cathedral.* Baltimore, Md., 1959.

Kayser, Wolfgang. *The Grotesque in Art and Literature,* translated by Ulrich Weisstein. Bloomington, Ind., 1963.

Kerényi, Karl. *Eleusis,* translated by Ralph Manheim. New York, 1967.

Kermode, Frank. "Adam Unparadised," in *The Living Milton,* edited by Frank Kermode, pp. 85–123. London, 1960.

———. *Shakespeare, Spenser, Donne.* New York, 1971.

Kern, Edith. "Gardens in the *Decameron Cornice,*" *PMLA,* LXVI (1951), 505–523.

Kernolde, George R. *From Art to Theater.* Chicago, 1944.

Kirk, Kenneth E. *The Vision of God.* 2nd ed. London, 1932.

Kirkconnel, Watson. *The Celestial Cycle.* Toronto, 1952.

Kitao, Timothy. "Prejudice in Perspective: A Study of Vignola's Perspective Treatise," *AB,* XLIV (1962), 173–94.

Klein, Robert. "The Figurative Thought of the Renaissance," *Diogenes,* XXXII (Winter, 1960), 107–23.

———. *La Forme et l'intelligible.* Paris, 1970.

———. "Pomponius Gauricus on Perspective," *AB,* XLIII (1961), 211–30.

Klibansky, Raymond; Panofsky, Erwin; and Saxl, Fritz. *Saturn and Melancholy.* London, 1964.

Köhler, Erich. "Narcisse, la fontaine d'Amour, et Guillaume de Lorris," *Journal des Savants* (April–June, 1963), pp. 86–103.

Koyré, Alexandre. *From the Closed World to the Infinite Universe.* Baltimore, Md., 1957.

Krautheimer, Richard. *Early Christian and Byzantine Architecture.* Baltimore, Md., 1965.

———. *Studies in Early Christian, Medieval, and Renaissance Art.* New York, 1969.

———. and Krautheimer-Hess, Trude. *Lorenzo Ghiberti.* 2nd ed. Princeton, N. J., 1970.

Kristeller, Paul. *Andrea Mantegna,* translated by S. A. Strong. London, 1901.

Kristeller, Paul Oskar. *Eight Philosophers of the Italian Renaissance.* Stanford, Calif., 1964.

———. *The Philosophy of Marsilio Ficino,* translated by Virginia Conant. New York, 1943.

———. *Studies in Renaissance Thought and Letters.* Rome, 1956.

Kuhn, Thomas S. *The Copernican Revolution.* 2nd ed. New York, 1959.

Kurz, Otto. "Huius nympha loci," *JWCI,* XVI (1953), 171–77.

Labaude, L.-H. "La Cathédrale de Vaison," *Bulletin Monumental,* LXIX (1905), 253–321.

Ladner, Gerhart. *The Idea of Reform.* Cambridge, Mass., 1959.

———. "*Homo viator:* Medieval Ideas on Alienation and Order," *Speculum,* XLII (1967), 237–59.

———. "The Philosophical Anthropology of St. Gregory of Nyssa," *Dumbarton Oaks Papers,* XII (1958), 59–94.

———. "Vegetation Symbolism and the Concept of Renaissance," in *De artibus opuscula xl: Essays in Honor of Erwin Panofsky,* edited by Millard Meiss, pp. 303–322. New York, 1961.

Laistner, M. L. W. *Thought and Letters in Western Europe.* 2nd ed. Ithaca, N. Y., 1957.

Langlois, Ernest. *Origines et sources du Roman de la Rose.* Paris, 1891.

Lavisse, Ernest, ed. *Histoire de France,* V[1]: *Les Guerres d'Italie,* by Henry Lemonnier. Paris, 1903.

Lazzari, Alfonso. *Ugolino e Michele Verino.* Turin, 1897.

Leavis, F. R. *The Common Pursuit.* London, 1952.

Leclercq, Jean. "Le Cloître, est-il un paradis?" in *Le Message des moines à notre temps.* Paris, 1958.

———. "Les Deux compilations de Thomas de Perseigne," *Mediaeval Studies,* X (1948), 204–209.

———. *The Love of Learning and the Desire for God,* translated by C. Misrahi. New York, 1962 (Mentor edition).

———. *Pierre le Vénérable.* Abbaye S. Wandrille, France, 1946.

———. *La Spiritualité de Pierre de Celle.* Paris, 1946.

———. *La Vie parfaite.* Paris, 1948.

Levey, Michael. *Painting at Court.* New York, 1971.

Levin, Harry. *The Myth of the Golden Age in the Renaissance.* Bloomington, Ind., 1969.

———. "Semantics of Culture," *Daedalus,* XCIV (1965), 1–13.

Lévy-Bruhl, Lucien. *How Natives Think,* translated by L. Clare. New York, 1966.

Lewis, C. S. *The Allegory of Love.* Oxford, Eng., 1936.

Litman, Alexander. *Cicero's Doctrine of Man and Nature.* New York, 1930.

Lovejoy, A. O. *The Great Chain of Being.* Cambridge, Mass., 1936.

Löwith, Karl. *Meaning in History.* Chicago, 1949.

Lowrie, Walter. *Action in the Liturgy.* New York, 1953.

———. *Art in the Early Church.* 2nd ed., rev. New York, 1965.

Lubac, Henri de. *Exégèse médièvale.* Paris, 1959–64.

MacDougall, Elisabeth. "*Ars Hortulorum:* Sixteenth-Century Garden Iconography and Literary Theory in Italy," in *The Italian Garden,* First Dumbarton Oaks Colloquium on the History of Landscape Architecture, edited by David R. Coffin, pp. 35–39. Washington, D.C., 1972.

Mack, Maynard. "Introduction," *English Masterpieces IV: Milton.* 2nd ed. Englewood Cliffs, N. J., 1961.

McLaughlin, E. T. *Studies in Medieval Life and Literature.* New York, 1894.

Marcel, Raymond. *Marsile Ficin.* Paris, 1958.

Marrou, Henri Irénée. *A History of Education in Antiquity,* translated by George Lamb. New York, 1964 (Mentor edition).

———. *Saint Augustin et la fin de la culture antique.* Paris, 1938.

Martin, John Rupert. *The Illustration of the Heavenly Ladder of John Climacus.* Princeton, N. J., 1954.

Martz, Louis. *The Paradise Within.* New Haven, Conn., 1964.

Masson, Georgina. *Italian Gardens.* New York, n. d.

Mazzeo, Joseph A. *Medieval Cultural Tradition in Dante's Comedy.* Ithaca, N. Y., 1960.

———. *Structure and Thought in the Paradiso.* Ithaca, N. Y., 1958.

Meiss, Millard. *Andrea Mantegna as Illuminator.* New York, 1957.

———. *Painting in Florence and Siena after the Black Death.* Princeton, N. J., 1951.

Mitchel, Charles. "Archaeology and Romance in Renaissance Italy," in *Italian Renaissance Studies . . . to Cecilia Ady,* edited by E. F. Jacob, pp. 455–83. New York, 1960.

Mommsen, Theodore. "Petrarch and the Story of the Choice of Hercules," *JWCI,* XVI (1953), 178–92.

Murley, Clyde. "Plato's *Phaedrus* and Theocritean Pastoral," *Transactions of the American Philological Association,* LXXI (1940), 281–95.

Muscatine, Charles. *Chaucer and the French Tradition.* Berkeley, Calif., 1957.

———. "The Emergence of Psychological Allegory in Old French Romance," *PMLA,* LXVIII (1953), 1160–82.

Neilson, William A. *The Origins and Sources of the Court of Love.* Boston, 1899.

Nelli, René. *L'Erotique des troubadours.* Toulouse, 1963.

Nelson, John Charles. *The Renaissance Theory of Love.* New York, 1958.

Nelson, William. *The Poetry of Edmund Spenser.* New York, 1963.

Nichols, John. *The Progress and Public Processions of Queen Elizabeth.* London, 1823.

Nicolson, Marjorie. "Milton and the Telescope," *ELH,* II (1935), 1–32.

———. *Mountain Gloom and Mountain Glory.* Ithaca, N. Y., 1959.

Nolhoc, Pierre de. *Pétrarque et l'humanisme.* 2nd ed. Paris, 1907.

Nordström, Johan. *Moyen âge et renaissance.* Paris, 1933.

Norris, R. A. *God and the World in Early Christian Theology.* New York, 1965.

Nuchelmans, G. "Philologia et son mariage avec Mercure jusqu' à la fin du xiie siècle," *Latomus,* XVI (1957), 84–107.

Nygren, Anders. *Agape and Eros,* translated by P. S. Watson. Philadelphia, 1953.

Ong, Walter J. *Ramus, Method, and the Decay of Dialogue.* Cambridge, Mass., 1958.

Orcutt, William D. *The Book in Italy.* London, 1928.

O'Toole, C. J. *The Philosophy of Creation in the Writings of St. Augustine.* Washington, D.C., 1944.

Otto, Rudolf. *The Idea of the Holy,* translated by J. W. Harvey. 2nd ed. New York, 1950.

Pächt, Otto. "Early Italian Nature Studies and the Early Calendar Landscape," *JWCI,* XIII (1950), 13–47.

Pachter, Henry. *Paracelsus: Magic into Science.* New York, 1951.

Painter, George. *The Hypnerotomachia Poliphili of 1499: An Introduction to the Dream, the Dreamer, the Artist, and the Printer.* London, 1963.

Palmer, R. Liddesdale. *English Monasteries in the Middle Ages.* London, 1930.

Pane, Roberto. *Architettura del Rinascimento in Napoli.* Naples, 1937.

Panofsky, Erwin. *Abbot Suger on the Abbey Church of St. Denis and Its Art Treasures.* Princeton, N.J., 1946.

———. "Artist, Scientist, Genius," in *The Renaissance: Six Essays,* pp. 121–82. 2nd ed. New York, 1962.

———. *The Codex Huygens and Leonardo da Vinci's Art Theory.* London, 1940.
———. *Early Netherlandish Painting.* Cambridge, Mass., 1953.
———. *Hercules am Schiedewege.* Berlin, 1930.
———. *The Iconography of Correggio's Camera di San Paolo.* London, 1961.
———. *Meaning in the Visual Arts.* Garden City, N. Y., 1957.
———. *Renaissance and Renascences in Western Art.* 2nd ed. New York, 1969.
———. *Studies in Iconology.* New York, 1939.
Paré, Gérard Marie. *Les Idées et les lettres au xiii*e *siècle: le Roman de la Rose.* Montreal, 1947.
———. *Le Roman de la Rose et la scholastique courtoise.* Ottawa, 1941.
Parent, J. M. *La Doctrine de la création dans l'école de Chartres.* Paris, 1938.
Parry, Adam. "Landscape in Greek Poetry," *Yale Classical Studies,* XV (1957), 3–29.
Patch, Howard Rollin. *The Other World.* Cambridge, Mass., 1950.
———. *The Tradition of Boethius.* New York, 1935.
Pauli, W. "The Influence of Archetypal Ideas on the Scientific Theories of Kepler," translated by Priscilla Silz, in C. G. Jung and W. Pauli, *The Interpretation of Nature and the Psyche,* pp. 147–240. New York, 1955.
Peebles, Rose J., "The Dry Tree: Symbol of Death," in *Vassar Medieval Studies,* edited by C. F. Fiske, pp. 59–79. New Haven, Conn., 1923.
Pèrcopo, Erasmo. "Per l'entrata solenne di Carlo VIII in Napoli," in *Studi di storia napoletana in onere di Michelangelo Schipa,* pp. 347–51. Naples, 1926.
Perella, N. J. *The Kiss, Sacred and Profane.* Berkeley, Calif., 1969.
Pézard, André. "Nymphes platoniciennes au paradis terrestre," in *Medioevo e Rinascimento, Studi in onore di Bruno Nardi,* II, 543–94. Florence, 1955.
Piaget, Jean. *The Child's Conception of the World,* translated by J. and A. Tomlinson. London, 1929.
Picard, Charles. "Dans les jardins du héros Academos," *Institut de France, Séance Publique Annuelle des Cinq Académies du Jeudi 25 Octobre 1934, Discours* (Paris, 1934), 45–70.
Piehler, Paul. *The Visionary Landscape.* London, 1971.
Plumpe, J. C. *Mater Ecclesia.* Washington, D.C., 1943.
Pollman, Leo. *Das Epos in den romanischen Literaturen.* Stuttgart, 1966.
Popelin, Claudius, ed. *Le Songe de Poliphile de Francesco Colonna.* Paris, 1883.
Porter, A. Kingsley. *Medieval Architecture.* New York, 1909.
Poulet, George. *Studies in Human Time,* translated by Elliott Coleman. Baltimore, Md., 1956.
Praz, Mario. *Studies in Seventeenth Century Imagery.* 2nd ed. Rome, 1964.
Puppi, Lionello. "The Villa Garden of the Veneto from the Fifteenth to the Eighteenth Century," in *The Italian Garden,* First Dumbarton Oaks Colloquium on the History of Landscape Architecture, edited by David R. Coffin, pp. 83–114. Washington, D.C., 1972.
Quaestan, J. "A Pythagorean Idea in Jerome," *AJP,* LXIII (1942), 207–215.
Rahner, Hugo. "The Christian Mystery and Pagan Mysteries," in *Pagan and*

Christian Mysteries, edited by Joseph Campbell, pp. 146–210. New York, 1963 (Harper Torchbook edition).

———. *Greek Myth and Christian Mystery,* translated by B. Battershaw. New York, 1963.

Rambaud, Michel. "Le Quatrain mystique de Vaison-la-Romaine," *Bulletin Monumental,* CIX (1951), 157–74.

Rand, E. K. *Founders of the Middle Ages.* Cambridge, Mass., 1928.

Ranke, Leopold. *The History of the Popes,* translated by E. Foster. London, 1847.

Read, Conyers. *Lord Burghley and Queen Elizabeth.* New York, 1960.

Réau, Louis. *Iconographie de l'art chrétien.* Paris, 1955–59.

Redgrave, Gilbert. *Erhard Ratdolt.* London, 1894.

Reinhardt. H. "Der St. Galler Klosterplan," *Historischer Verein des Kantons St. Gallen, Neujahrsblatt,* XCII (1952), 1–34.

Remy, E. " 'Dignitas cum otio,' " *Le Musée Belge,* XXXII (1928), 113–27.

Reumont, Alfred von. *Lorenzo de' Medici,* translated by R. Harrison. London, 1876.

Richmond, Hugh. *Renaissance Landscapes.* The Hague, Neth., 1973.

Rist, J. M. *Plotinus, the Road to Reality.* Cambridge, Eng., 1967.

Robb, Nesca. *Neoplatonism of the Italian Renaissance.* London, 1935.

Robbins, Frank E. *The Hexaemeral Literature.* Chicago, 1912.

Robertson, D. W. "The Doctrine of Charity in Medieval Literary Gardens," *Speculum,* XXVI (1951), 24–49.

———. *A Preface to Chaucer.* Princeton, N. J., 1962.

———. "The Subject of the *De Amore* of Andreas Capellanus," *MP,* L (1953), 145–61.

Roche, W. J. "Measure, Number, and Weight in St. Augustine," *New Scholasticism,* XV (1941), 350–76.

Roques, René. *L'Univers dionysien.* Paris, 1954.

Roscoe, William. *The Life and Pontificate of Leo the Tenth,* revised by Thomas Roscoe. London, 1846.

———. *The Life of Lorenzo de' Medici.* Philadelphia, 1803.

Rosen, Edward, ed. *Three Copernican Treatises.* 2nd ed. New York, 1959.

Rosenmeyer, Thomas G. *The Green Cabinet.* Berkeley, Calif., 1969.

Røstvig, Maren-Sofie. *The Happy Man.* Oslo, 1954.

Rousselot, Pierre. *Pour l'histoire du problème de l'amour au moyen âge.* Münster, 1908.

Ruch, Michel. *Le Préambule dans les oeuvres philosophiques de Cicéron.* Paris, 1958.

Saxl, Fritz. *Lectures.* London, 1957.

———. "Pagan Sacrifice in the Italian Renaissance," *JWCI,* II (1939–40), 346–67.

———. "A Spiritual Encyclopedia of the Later Middle Ages," *JWCI,* V (1942), 82–134.

Scaglione, Aldo. *Nature and Love in the Late Middle Ages.* Berkeley, Calif., 1963.

Schlee, Ernst. *Die Ikonographie der Paradiesesflusse.* Leipzig, 1937.

Schoek, R. T. "Andreas Capellanus and St. Bernard of Clairvaux," *MLN,* LXVI (1951), 295–300.

Schramm, Percy Ernst. *Sphaira-Globus-Reichsapfel.* Stuttgart, 1958.
Schulz, J. "Pinturicchio and the Revival of Antiquity," *JWCI*, XXV (1962), 35–55.
Scoular, Kitty. *Natural Magic.* Oxford, 1965.
Segal, Charles. "Nature and the World of Man in Greek Literature," *Arion,* II (1963), 19–53.
Shaw, James Eustace. *Guido Cavalcanti's Theory of Love.* Toronto, 1949.
Silverstein, Theodore. "The Fabulous Cosmogony of Bernardus Silvestris," *MP,* XLVI (1948–49), 92–116.
Simon, Marcel. *Hercule et le Christianisme.* Paris, 1955.
Simone, Franco. *The French Renaissance,* translated by H. Gaston Hall. London, 1969.
Simson, Otto von. *The Gothic Cathedral.* 2nd ed. New York, 1962.
Sinaiko, Herman L. *Love, Knowledge, and Discourse in Plato.* Chicago, 1965.
Singer, Charles. "The Herbal in Antiquity," *Journal of Hellenic Studies,* XLVII (1927), 1–52.
Singer, Dorothea. *Giordano Bruno, His Life and Thought.* New York, 1950.
Singleton, Charles. *Journey to Beatrice, Dante Studies II.* Cambridge, Mass., 1954.
———. "On Meaning in the Decameron," *Italica,* XXI (1944), 117–24.
———. *Purgatorio, Commentary.* Princeton, N. J., 1973.
Smalley, Beryl. *The Study of the Bible in the Middle Ages.* 2nd ed. Oxford, 1952.
Smith, E. Baldwin. *Architectural Symbolism of Imperial Rome and the Middle Ages.* Princeton, N. J., 1956.
Solmsen, Friedrich. *Aristotle's System of the Physical World.* Ithaca, N. Y., 1960.
Sörrensen, Wolfgang. "Garten und Pfanzen im Klosterplan," in *Studien zur St. Galler Klosterplan,* edited by J. Duft, pp. 193–277. St. Gallen, Switz., 1962.
Spargo, J. W. *Virgil the Necromancer.* Cambridge, Mass., 1934.
Spitzer, Leo. *Classical and Christian Ideas of World Harmony.* Baltimore, Md., 1963.
———. *Essays on English and American Literature.* Princeton, N. J., 1962.
———. *Studies in Historical Semantics.* New York, 1948.
Starnes, D. T., and Talbot, E. W. *Classical Myth and Legend in Renaissance Dictionaries.* Chapel Hill, N. C., 1955.
Stein, Harold. *Studies in Spenser's Complaints.* New York, 1934.
Steinberg, Ronald Martin. "The Iconography of the Teatro dell' Acqua at the Villa Aldobrandini," *AB,* XLVII (1965), 453–63.
Stewart, Stanley. *The Enclosed Garden.* Madison, Wis., 1966.
Stock, Brian. *Myth and Science in the Twelfth Century.* Princeton, N. J., 1972.
Stolz, Anselm. *The Doctrine of Spiritual Perfection,* translated by A. Williams. St. Louis, Mo., 1938.
Stone, Donald, Jr. "Old and New Thoughts on Guillaume de Lorris," *Australian Journal of French Studies,* II (1965), 157–70.
Stone, Lawrence. *The Crisis of the Aristocracy 1558–1641.* Oxford, 1965.
Struever, Nancy. *The Language of History in the Renaissance.* Princeton, N. J., 1970.

Summerson, John. *Architecture in Britain 1530–1830.* 5th ed. Baltimore, Md., 1970.
———. "The Building of Theobalds," *Archaeologia,* XCVII (1959), 107–26.
———. "Theobalds: A Lost Elizabethan Palace," *The Listener,* LIII (1955), 567–68.
Tardi, D. *Fortunat.* Paris, 1927.
Tatham, Edward Henry Ralph. *Francesco Petrarca, the First Modern Man of Letters.* London, 1925–26.
Tayler, Edward. *Nature and Art in Renaissance Literature.* New York, 1964.
Taylor, Gladys. *Old London Gardens.* London, 1953.
Taylor, Jerome, ed. *The Didascalicon of Hugh of St. Victor.* New York, 1961.
Tervarent, Guy de. *Attributs et symboles dans l'art profane, 1450–1600.* Geneva, 1958.
Tietze-Conrat, E. *Mantegna.* New York, 1955.
Tobin, Mildred Dolores, ed. *Orientii Commonitorium.* Washington, D.C., 1945.
Tolkowksy, S. *Hesperides.* London, 1938.
Tolnay, Charles de. "Music of the Universe," *Journal of the Walters Art Gallery,* VI (1943), 83–104.
Toulmin, Stephen, and Goodfield, June. *The Fabric of the Heavens.* New York, 1961.
Trinkaus, Charles. *In Our Image and Likeness.* Chicago, 1970.
Turner, A. Richard. *The Vision of Landscape in Renaissance Italy.* Princeton, N. J., 1966.
Tuve, Rosemond. *Allegorical Imagery.* Princeton, N. J., 1966.
———. *Seasons and Months.* Paris, 1933.
Ullman, B. L. *The Humanism of Coluccio Salutati.* Padua, 1963.
Underhill, Evelyn. *Mysticism.* New York, 1940.
Underwood, D. A. "The Fountain of Life in Manuscripts of the Gospels," *Dumbarton Oaks Papers,* V (1950), 41–138.
Valency, Maurice. *In Praise of Love.* New York, 1958.
Van der Leeuw, G. *Religion in Essence and Manifestation,* translated by J. E. Turner. 2nd ed. New York, 1963.
Van der Meer, F. *Augustine the Bishop,* translated by B. Battershaw and G. R. Lamb. London, 1961.
Van Winden, J. C. M. *Calcidius on Matter, His Doctrine and Sources.* Leiden, 1959.
Verheyen, Egon. *The Paintings in the Studiolo of Isabella d'Este at Mantua.* New York, 1971.
Vinge, Louise. *The Narcissus Theme in Western European Literature,* translated by R. Dewsnap and N. Reeves. Lund, Sweden, 1967.
Volkmann, Ludwig. *Bilderschriften der Renaissance.* Leipzig, 1923.
Waddell, Helen. *Mediaeval Latin Lyrics.* 5th ed. London, 1948.
Walker, D. P. *Spiritual and Demonic Magic from Ficino to Campanella.* London, 1958.
Wallerstein, Ruth. *Studies in Seventeenth-Century Poetic.* Madison, Wis., 1950.

Watson, Arthur. "The Speculum Virginum with Special Reference to the Tree of Jesse," *Speculum,* III (1928), 445–69.
Weinstein, Donald. "The Myth of Florence," in *Florentine Studies,* edited by Nicolai Rubinstein, pp. 15–44. Evanston, Ill., 1968.
Weiss, Roberto. "A New Francesco Colonna," *Italian Studies,* XVI (1961), 78–83.
Wetherbee, Winthrop. *Platonism and Poetry in the Twelfth Century.* Princeton, N. J., 1972.
White, John. *The Birth and Rebirth of Pictorial Space.* 2nd ed. London, 1967.
Whitfield, J. H. *Petrarch and the Renascence.* Oxford, 1943.
Wiles, Bertha. *The Fountains of Florentine Sculptors.* Cambridge, Mass., 1933.
Wilhelm, James. *The Cruelest Month.* New Haven, Conn., 1965.
Wilkins, Ernest Hatch. *The Life of Petrarch.* Chicago, 1961.
———. *Petrarch at Vaucluse.* Chicago, 1958.
———. *Studies in the Life and Works of Petrarch.* Cambridge, Mass., 1955.
Will, R. "Le Climat religieux de *l'Hortus deliciarum* d'Herrade de Landsberg," *Revue d'Histoire et de Philosophie Religieuses,* XVII (1937), 522–66.
Williams, Arnold. *The Common Expositor.* Chapel Hill, N. C., 1948.
Williams, Charles. *The Figure of Beatrice.* London, 1943.
Williams, George H. *Wilderness and Paradise in Christian Thought.* New York, 1962.
Willis, Robert. "Description of the Ancient Plan of the Monastery of St. Gall, in the Ninth Century," *Archaeological Journal,* V (1848), 85–117.
Wilson, E. Faye. "Pastoral and Epithalamium in Latin Literature," *Speculum,* XXIII (1948), 35–57.
Wind, Edgar. *Bellini's Feast of the Gods.* Cambridge, Mass., 1948.
———. *Pagan Mysteries in the Renaissance.* 2nd ed. New York, 1968.
Wirszubski, C. "Cicero's *Cum dignitate otium:* A Reconsideration," *Journal of Roman Studies,* XLIV (1954), 6–13.
Wittkower, Rudolf. *Architectural Principles in the Age of Humanism.* 2nd ed. New York, 1965.
———. "Brunelleschi and 'Proportion in Perspective'," *JWCI,* XVI (1953), 275–91.
———. "Chance, Time, and Virtue," *JWCI,* I (1937–38), 313–21.
———. "Transformations of Minerva in Renaissance Imagery," *JWCI,* II (1938–39), 194–205.
Wölfflin, Heinrich. *Renaissance and Baroque,* translated by Kathrin Simon. Ithaca, N. Y., 1966.
Wolfson, H. A. *Philo.* Cambridge, Mass., 1947.
Wulf, Maurice de. *History of Medieval Philosophy,* translated by E. C. Messenger. London, 1925.
Yates, Frances. *The Art of Memory.* Chicago, 1966.
———. "The Art of Ramon Lull," *JWCI,* XVII (1954), 115–73.
———. "The Ciceronian Art of Memory," in *Medioevo e Rinascimento, Studi in onore di Bruno Nardi,* II, 871–903. Florence, 1955.
———. *Giordano Bruno and the Hermetic Tradition.* Chicago, 1964.

———. "Queen Elizabeth as Astraea," *JWCI,* X (1947), 27–82. Reprinted in *Astraea, The Imperial Theme in the Sixteenth Century.* London, 1975.

———. *The Rosicrucian Enlightenment.* London, 1972.

———. *Theatre of the World.* Chicago, 1969.

Zeller, Eduard. *Plato and the Older Academy,* translated by S. F. Alleyne and A. Goodwin. London, 1888.

Zilsel, Edgar. "Copernicus and Mechanics," *JHI,* I (1940), 113–18.

Index

C

D

H

I

J

K

P

Q

R

S

T

U

V

W

X

Y